Franciscan Frontiersmen

FRANCISCAN FRONTIERSMEN
How Three Adventurers Charted the West

Robert A. Kittle

University of Oklahoma Press : Norman

For Luanne

This book is published with the generous assistance of the Academy of American Franciscan History, Oceanside, California.

Library of Congress Cataloging-in-Publication Data

Names: Kittle, Robert A., 1953– author.
Title: Franciscan frontiersmen : how three adventurers charted the West / Robert A. Kittle.
Description: Norman : University of Oklahoma Press, 2017. | Includes bibliographical references and index.
Identifiers: LCCN 2016046267 | ISBN 978-0-8061-5698-9 (cloth) | ISBN 978-0-8061-6097-9 (paper)
Subjects: LCSH: Font, Pedro, 1737–1781—Travel—West (U.S.) | Crespí, Juan, 1721–1782—Travel—West (U.S.) | Garcés, Francisco Tomás Hermenegildo, 1738–1781—Travel—West (U.S.) | West (U.S.)—Discovery and exploration—Spanish. | California—Discovery and exploration—Spanish. | West (U.S.)—History—To 1848. | Franciscans—West (U.S.)—Biography. | Franciscans—Spain—Biography. | Pioneers—West (U.S.)—Biography. | Explorers—West (U.S.)—Biography. | BISAC: HISTORY / United States / State & Local / West (AK, CA, CO, HI, ID, MT, NV, UT, WY). | HISTORY / United States / State & Local / Southwest (AZ, NM, OK, TX).
Classification: LCC F592 .K58 2017 | DDC 978.1/01—dc23
LC record available at https://lccn.loc.gov/2016046267

The paper in this book meets the guidelines for permanence and durability of the Committee on Production Guidelines for Book Longevity of the Council on Library Resources, Inc. ∞

Copyright © 2017 by the University of Oklahoma Press, Norman, Publishing Division of the University. Paperback published 2018. Manufactured in the U.S.A.

All rights reserved. No part of this publication may be reproduced, stored in a retrieval system, or transmitted, in any form or by any means, electronic, mechanical, photocopying, recording, or otherwise—except as permitted under Section 107 or 108 of the United States Copyright Act—without the prior written permission of the University of Oklahoma Press. To request permission to reproduce selections from this book, write to Permissions, University of Oklahoma Press, 2800 Venture Drive, Norman, OK 73069, or email rights.oupress@ou.edu.

2 3 4 5 6 7 8 9 10

Contents

List of Illustrations / vii

Prologue: Soldiers of the Crown, Soldiers of the Cross / 3

ONE The Conquest Begins / 22

TWO Search for an Elusive Eden / 41

THREE Eureka! / 62

FOUR Beyond the Río Colorado / 69

FIVE Overland to California / 76

SIX Start Mounting Up / 96

SEVEN Desert Nativity Scene / 107

EIGHT Uprising at Mission San Diego / 125

NINE A Forgotten Soldier of the Cross / 140

TEN Apostolic Pilgrimage / 152

ELEVEN Solitary Sojourn in the High Desert / 162

TWELVE Unfinished Quest / 178

THIRTEEN Steering through Unexplored Waters / 192

FOURTEEN Fatalistic Venture / 211

FIFTEEN Slaughter on the Colorado River / 225

SIXTEEN Retribution on the Colorado / 232

SEVENTEEN Final Journey / 239

Epilogue: An Imperfect Legacy / 243

Notes / 255

Index / 277

Illustrations

FIGURES

1. Ruins of San Fernando de Velicatá / 33
2. Painting of first Mass at Monterey by Léon Trousset, 1877 / 67
3. San Xavier del Bac, 1902 / 71
4. Yuha Well / 90
5. Painting of the Anza expedition / 101
6. Drawing of the uprising at Mission San Diego / 137
7. Hopi Pueblo of Oraibi / 175
8. Mission San Carlos Borromeo / 190
9. Schematic of frigate *Santiago* / 197
10. Antonio María de Bucareli y Ursúa / 216
11. Painting of Francisco Garcés and Juan Barreneche / 230
12. Portrait of Pedro Fages / 234
13. El Templo de San Diego del Pitiquito, Sonora / 240
14. Drawing of reception of La Pérouse, Mission Carmel, 1786 / 252

MAPS

1. Iberian Peninsula / 11
2. Portolá expedition / 45
3. Anza's colonizing expedition / 109
4. New Spain settlements in northern Sonora and southern Arizona / 143
5. Route of Garcés's wanderings / 157

Franciscan Frontiersmen

Prologue

Soldiers of the Crown, Soldiers of the Cross

> We Americans have yet to really learn our own antecedents. Thus far, impress'd by New England writers and schoolmasters, we tacitly abandon ourselves to the notion that our United States have been fashion'd from the British Islands only, and essentially form a second England only—which is a very great mistake....
> To that composite American identity of the future, Spanish character will supply some of the most needed parts. No stock shows a grander historic retrospect—grander in religiousness and loyalty, or for patriotism, courage, decorum, gravity and honor.
> —Walt Whitman

Foreboding blankets the air in the remote settlement of Santa María Magdalena, a lonely outpost on the edge of Spanish Christendom in the saguaro-strewn Sonoran Desert just south of the present-day U.S.–Mexican border. It is 16 November 1776, a Saturday morning, but hardly an ordinary one. In recent weeks uprisings by hostile Apaches and their Native confederates have grown in ferocity in the exposed Franciscan mission fields of the northern frontier.

Menacing signs of an impending assault on tiny Santa María Magdalena's fifteen families, including Spanish settlers and Indian converts to Christianity, have left the homesteaders uneasy, fearful for their lives. Only the day before, urgent word reached Santa María Magdalena that Indians were attacking Ímuris, a Spanish pueblo a few miles to the north in the arid Sonoran tableland. This prompted the dispatch of six friendly Natives to aid in the defense of Ímuris, leaving Santa María Magdalena even more at the mercy of a dreaded Indian onslaught. The station is now so vulnerable that its defenses consist of not a single Spanish soldier or firearm but only four converted Indians with a few bows and arrows.[1]

Pedro Font, a thirty-eight-year-old Franciscan from Catalonia, in northeastern Spain, has just finished saying Mass in Santa María Magdalena's church, a morning ritual carried out despite his gnawing apprehensions. Short and broad-shouldered, with a round face, sparse beard, and balding black hair, Font stands out for his fair

European complexion, the gray woolen robes of his religious order, and his hemp huaraches (sandals). His excitability, temperamental nature, and acerbic manner are well known to his fellow friars and Indian wards alike. Font's fears are not eased by the reality that he himself volunteered for this dangerous assignment encircled by bellicose tribes in the northwestern reaches of New Spain.

As he is returning to his Spartan room in a linear-shaped adobe at eight o'clock in the morning, the mission's quiet is shattered by the shrieks of twenty to thirty Apaches and their allies, the Seris and Piatos, descending from every direction.[2] Some mounted on horseback, others on foot, the war party is armed with heavy wooden clubs, lances, and bows and arrows. The Seris are known to poison the tips of their arrows with a lethal venom extracted from vipers.[3] Brandishing small oval shields, the warriors are covered for protection in thick leather smocks like those worn by the Spanish soldiers.

As the combatants howled in unison and began to pillage the pueblo, Font sought refuge in his house. The Native inhabitants and their small children came running to join him. For the next two hours, in three successive raids, the Apaches and their allies carried off whatever valuables they could find. First to go were the few horses, cattle, and oxen kept in a corral beside the house, where Font and the huddled residents of Santa María Magdalena looked on, helpless to stop the plunder. Then, in a confused mob, the marauders began to sack the dwellings of the friendly Indians and set fire to them. Some of the attackers were cimarrones—Indians who were runaways from the mission and therefore knew its layout well.

A renegade known to Font by his Spanish name, Juan Cozinero, charged into the elongated structure where the residents were holed up. He almost certainly was a fugitive from Santa María Magdalena, because the surname given to him by the Spanish meant "the cook." Lighting a firebrand from the hot coals in the kitchen hearth, the assailant quickly scaled a ladder and torched the roof, which was made of dried grass and earth.

With flames starting to consume the dwelling, the arsonist and other heathens, as the Spaniards called them, broke down the door of the church and made off with the richly colored silk vestments worn by Font when he said Mass. They stole the holy chalice and spilled onto the ground the sacred oils used during Mass. They defiled the baptismal font and candlesticks, then ripped from its niche a tall statue of San Francisco Xavier, a revered sixteenth-century Jesuit missionary from the Pyrenees

Mountains of Spain. They threw the wooden carving to the floor, breaking off an arm. Before retreating momentarily into the chaparral with their booty, the Indians removed from the altar and tore up the large bound missal containing the Gospels read aloud during Mass. Pages of paper were prized by the Natives for rolling cigarettes from tobacco handed out to them by the Franciscans as gestures of friendship.

By this time Font and the Indian women and children faced a treacherous predicament. They were trapped in a burning building with flames engulfing one room after another, all lined up in a row. Of the seven rooms, only the large parlor and two smaller rooms beyond it had thus far escaped the blaze. Stored in the two smaller rooms were heaps of dried wheat, as incendiary as gunpowder.

As smoke choked the survivors' lungs and stung their eyes, it was plainly just a matter of minutes before the fire would reach them. Font barricaded the group in the parlor to await their fate. Then the rebels mounted their final assault, this one with the intent to finish off the lives of the Spanish intruders, because there was nothing left of the mission to steal or destroy. Inside the blazing dwelling, the few remaining settlers of Santa María Magdalena confronted the choice of dying in the smoke and flames or fleeing outside and being killed by the warriors' lances.

"Here we were," recounted Font, "with the fire near, without arms, and with the enemy at the door. . . . I cried out to God as best I could, and resigning myself to die, I waited for them to come in and deliver the final blow and end my life."[4]

The Indians hurled a large rock three times against the wooden door of the house, splintering a hole in it. From inside, three Native archers accompanying Font shot their last arrows through the opening in an attempt to stave off the inevitable. At this the Indians withdrew into the courtyard but remained ominously in sight.

A few moments later, just as abruptly as the raid had erupted, the war party retreated hastily into the desert landscape. A band of armed Spaniards on horseback from nearby San Ignacio had arrived on the scene. Barely in time to avert a wholesale massacre, a friendly Indian who had fled at the outbreak of violence had alerted the residents of San Ignacio, who were close enough, anyway, to see the smoke rising above Santa María Magdalena.

Thanking God for having narrowly spared his life, Font emerged from the parlor just as the flames were reaching it. With the help of others he extinguished the blaze, managing to save his diary, some books, and the storerooms of grain. But the scene around him bristled with devastation. Every house and other structure had been burned to the ground, and everywhere baptized Indian women were weeping.

Entering the patio of his dwelling, Font encountered a gruesome display. A pregnant Spanish settler who had been caught by the enemy was dispatched where she stood, impaled on the dirt floor with the attackers' lances. Her name was Josefa María. Beside her on the ground lay her child, a young girl, mortally wounded, her intestines hanging out. Font knelt down, heard the mother's confession, and administered the last rites of the Catholic Church. The following night she died. A married Indian woman of the pueblo was more fortunate. She was taken into captivity as a slave, along with her two young sons and two infants.

Amid the smoldering ruins, Font was bitter that his own repeated warnings to his Franciscan superiors about the mounting Indian unrest and what he foresaw as "our final extermination" had been ignored in the Spanish viceroy's headstrong campaign to subjugate the tribes of northwest New Spain.[5] The peril posed by the Apaches was especially combustible. "They are savagely cruel," recorded the Jesuit missionary Juan Nentvig, "and when left to themselves they will kill one another."[6] Within a couple of hours, the priest in charge of the San Ignacio mission, Father Francisco Sánchez Zúñiga, arrived in the belief that Font had been slain.[7] Finding him roaming about the carnage, Zúñiga gave him a horse and the two rode together back to San Ignacio, arriving at three o'clock in the afternoon.

In the days ahead Font returned to Santa María Magdalena several times to bury the dead, a somber task that fell regularly on the shoulders of the Franciscan padres. Escaping the pueblo offered scant relief from the tribesmen of the Spanish borderlands. "If the Piatos do not kill us, it may be that the Apaches will do so," Font wrote in a letter two days after the atrocities at Santa María Magdalena.[8] "They are so insolent and strong that even now there are hardly enough forces to resist them. They are ruining this country with their hostile acts, robbing cattle and killing people."

In the tumult of Spain's conquest of California in the last half of the eighteenth century, three figures stand out for their exploits. Pedro Font, Francisco Garcés, and Juan Crespí endured terrifying storms at sea, Indian depredations, starvation, thirst, scurvy, dysentery, malaria, earthquakes, marauding bears, and crushing loneliness as they carved trails through desolate lands. Hardship was their steady companion.

These pious, scholarly men led surprisingly daring lives. After forsaking the cloisters of Spain for the rigors of the Seraphic Foreign Legion of Franciscan padres in the New World, they labored as soldiers of the crown and soldiers of the cross. History offers few other examples of such improbable heroes. Their journals and field notes, recorded by firelight after an arduous day in the saddle, illuminate a striking tale, but one that has been lost on the zephyrs of history. Together, these unheralded Franciscans opened a swath of North American continent surpassing in size and importance that explored by Lewis and Clark a generation later. But their feats were eclipsed by the American Revolution, which was erupting at the same moment along the Eastern Seaboard.

Of the three explorers, Font is the least celebrated, perhaps because of his mercurial makeup. But historians are grateful for his overarching achievement—recording in lively detail the day-to-day events of the crucial Anza colonizing expedition of 1775–76, to which he was assigned as chaplain and diarist. This was one of the Spanish crown's most audacious undertakings—transporting a sprawling caravan of 240 travelers, mostly families with small children, across twelve hundred miles of drought-hardened desert, mountains, and dangerous Indian territory from Sonora in present-day Mexico to the new mission and town of San Francisco in northern California. Three women were pregnant when they set out and gave birth on the trail, including one who delivered a healthy boy but died herself a few hours later. Five other women suffered miscarriages. Many more nursed their infant children from the backs of mules.

Font had a prickly personality. He was a chronic complainer and often supercilious. He could be haughty and sarcastic, frequently denigrating the Indians for what he saw as their primitive ways. Always quick to spot the weeds in someone else's garden, Font clashed frequently with his superiors, most notably with Lieutenant Colonel Juan Bautista de Anza himself. From Font's journals, composed in a neat, decipherable hand, leap vivid accounts of the trials of daily life on the frontier. He was a keen observer of not just what was happening around him but also human nature—that of the Spaniards and Indians alike. Most important, he spoke his mind unflinchingly, a trait that offended not only his contemporaries but even some politically correct scholars today.

Among Font's other attributes were a resonant singing voice, an artistic flair for drawing illustrated choir books, and musical talent in playing the *psalterio*, a three-sided stringed instrument held on the lap like a zither and strummed with the fingers. The *psalterio* was especially useful for appealing to the Indians during religious services. Far more worthwhile, from a historical standpoint, was Font's skill as a cartographer. On the trail he was never without a compass—an object of fascination to the Indians, who believed it possessed magical powers—and he was proficient at using a quadrant, a forerunner of the sextant, to gauge latitude through celestial observations. This critical bit of information identified one's location on a north–south axis only. The ability to measure longitude, which gave one's position on an east–west axis, had not yet been mastered. All the same, Font's legacy includes some of the earliest accurate maps of California, from San Diego Bay to San Francisco Bay. On his charts he was the first to name California's principal mountain chain the Sierra Nevada—the snowy range.⁹

Font was born in 1738 in Girona, an ancient walled city in the shadow of the snow-topped Pyrenees. A hundred years before the birth of Christ, Romans occupied the area and built a forum and citadel. In the centuries that followed, the Visigoths conquered Girona and were ultimately displaced by the Moors. In 785 A.D., Charlemagne reclaimed Girona at the start of the Reconquista, the seven-hundred-year-long campaign to wrest the Iberian Peninsula from the hand of Islam. Today multitudes of church bells echo throughout Girona's cobblestone streets, just as they did in Font's day. The main cathedral, with its impressive Baroque façade, still dominates a hilltop in the old quarter of the city, surrounded by the remnants of Roman fortifications, including stone walls and lookout towers.

As a new priest at the age of twenty-four, Font encountered in Girona two traveling Franciscans from the College of Santa Cruz in Querétaro, Mexico. They were visiting Spanish friaries in search of recruits to expand the Franciscans' outreach to the indigenous tribes in the Sonoran Desert. Signing up for missionary work generally meant a hazardous one-way trip to the other side of the world, with little prospect of ever returning to Spain or ever seeing one's family again. Indeed, it was not uncommon for young friars to gaze out at the boundless Atlantic for the first time at the port of Cádiz and decide on the spot to forgo the journey to the New World. According to Fray Francisco Palóu, out of thirty-five would-be missionaries who were to set sail to New Spain on one 1749 voyage, five backed out "on account of their fear of the sea, which they had never seen."¹⁰ The desertions created an opening on board ship for Junípero Serra, who was to become the headstrong founder of the California missions.

Despite the glaring hazards of eighteenth-century sea travel, Font renounced his comfortable life in Girona and sailed from Cádiz, the "Gateway to the Indies," into the open Atlantic on 1 August 1763 to a rough-hewn future of unknowns. The crossing to Veracruz, Mexico, took one hundred harrowing days.¹¹ Aboard the small frigate *Júpiter* were a crew of one hundred and a bevy of twelve naïve, fresh-faced Franciscans bound for the missionary fields of New Spain. To promote King Carlos III's colonizing objectives, the priests' travel and meager living expenses were paid by the royal exchequer. Among the Franciscans on board was the newly ordained Francisco Garcés, marking the beginning of a lifelong friendship with Font.

Because Spain had recently been engaged in hostilities with England, whose warships roamed the Atlantic, and because of the threat of preying pirate ships, the

Júpiter was armed with twenty-two guns and escorted as far as the Canary Islands by the seventy-four-gun man-of-war *Guerrero*. The *Júpiter*, launched a decade earlier from the Cádiz shipyard, was only 110 feet long, one of the smaller hulls in the royal armada. Below deck were cramped wooden berths where the greenhorn padres slept when they weren't retching their stomachs' contents over the rail.

As a storm in the mid-Atlantic engulfed the *Júpiter*, the pumps could not keep up with the deluge of seawater filling the bilge and cargo holds. The Basque captain, José Calvo, fearing the vessel was about to sink, risked his naval career by ordering that eight of His Majesty's cannons be dumped overboard to create more buoyancy. The command was obeyed without hesitation, saving the ship—no doubt to the profound relief of Font and Garcés.

Two contemporary friars, Andrés Antonio Martínez and Juan José de Castro, who traveled the Atlantic in a similar ship, described the moments when the sea rose to Olympian heights during rough weather:

> The ship, as if it were momentarily on the highest part of Mount Lapido [a summit in Galicia, northwest Spain], would plunge suddenly to the deepest part of the river, and then as quickly rise to the same height. Each wave, or mountain of water, that broke against the side of the ship made every joint creak, so that with each blow we expected the end. Other waves, reaching as high as the main yards, washed over the ship, soaking it from stem to stern. As a result, such a quantity of water flooded the decks and hold that we had to operate the pumps without letup. Bunks swam. When one huge blow broke over us only a miracle saved the captain, three of our friars, and two Jesuits from being swept into the sea. All around there were gasps, sighs, and acts of contrition.[12]

From the time of their first meeting on the voyage of the *Júpiter*, Font and Garcés were linked by destiny. Both men were born in the same year, and both died in 1781 within several weeks of each other at the age of forty-three in the New World, never having seen their homeland again. In the intervening years, their paths would cross many times in the Spanish borderlands.

Garcés sprang from the arid steppes and rocky soil of Zaragoza province in the medieval Kingdom of Aragón. The stark, almost treeless landscape of his birthplace bore a strong resemblance to the dry central valley of California, which he would later explore. Garcés's peasant parents were tenants on land owned by the count of Morata in the farming village of Morata del Conde, known today as

Morata de Jalón (see Map 1). His paternal uncle, also named Francisco, was the personal chaplain to the counts.[13] On the day after he was born, 13 April 1738, Garcés was baptized in the parish church of Santa Ana, an imposing structure with an eight-sided, blue-domed bell tower dominating the village alongside the Plaza Mayor. The church had been built more than a century earlier to serve the counts of Morata, who had been the royal overlords of the region since 1538. Next door to the church was the counts' Baroque palace.

Garcés's original baptismal record can still be found today in a bookcase of the parish rectory across the street from the church, resting in a three-centuries-old bound volume held together with red ribbons. The entry begins with Garcés's full name scrawled in the margin by the village's Franciscan priest, Pedro Gerónimo Villalva Reton, 279 years ago: "Francisco Thomas Hermenegildo Garces."[14] Thus at his baptism the infant was given the names of three saints. The cumbersome appellation Hermenegildo, after an obscure sixth-century Spanish martyr, still adorns the narrow Calle Hermenegildo Garcés in Morata de Jalón. The town library bears the same name.

At the age of fifteen Garcés received his first formal Franciscan instruction at the Convento de San Cristóbal, an isolated mountaintop friary built in 1550 above the village of Alpartir, about ten miles from his birthplace. The Franciscans there practiced a harsh discipline based on the abstemious life of Saint Francis of Assisi.[15] Garcés studied the classics and philosophy.

Today all that is left of the Convento de San Cristóbal are evocative stone ruins overlooking the broad Río Grío Valley and its patchwork of terraced orchards and olive groves irrigated with river water. Wind whistles through the remaining red adobe walls, and grass sprouts from the cracks. The stillness is unbroken by human voices. Just above the friary, higher up the mountain, are the remains of two *ermitas*—stone hermitages where for centuries the Franciscan brothers spent time in contemplative solitude. Today the Convento de San Cristóbal is a lonesome spot where one can vividly imagine the life of righteous study and ascetic discipline embraced by the teenaged Garcés. This placid scene stands in jarring contrast to the violent existence he would soon endure as a volunteer missionary in New Spain.

When Garcés sailed from Cádiz he was twenty-five years old. His embarkation papers described him as "of average build, sparse beard, not overly swarthy, with black eyes and black hair."[16] In a painting by an unknown artist in the late eighteenth century, he is portrayed as a typical barefoot friar, wearing a gray habit of undyed sheep's wool, a crucifix around his neck, with a round, boyish face. A sketch drawn later depicts Garcés as clean shaven and wearing the broad-brimmed

Map 1. The Iberian Peninsula, including the birthplaces of Pedro Font, Francisco Garcés, and Juan Crespí. After crossing the Atlantic as young friars, Font, Garcés, and Crespí never saw their homeland again.
Cartography by Bill Nelson. Copyright © 2017 by the University of Oklahoma Press.
Inset: Baptismal record of Garcés in Santa Ana parish church, Morata de Jalón, 1738. *Author's collection.*

leather sombrero that the padres favored to protect themselves from the southwest sun. But on the trail Garcés usually went unshaven for weeks at a time, prompting some Indians to identify him simply as el Barbudo (the Bearded One).

More than any other Franciscan, Garcés developed close relationships with the Indians. He respected the indigenous people in ways most Europeans never did. He did not hold himself apart from them. He learned their languages and preached to them in their languages. He lived and traveled among them, usually alone as the only white man, eating mice and lizards as they did when there was nothing else to eat, and sleeping with them on a sheepskin blanket on the ground under the stars. Many Indians affectionately called him el Viejo (the Old One), even though he had not yet reached middle age.

Garcés's writing style was straightforward and unsophisticated, his penmanship atrocious, his spelling not much better. The lines of his diaries tend to undulate like waves as they make their way up and down across the page. He very likely was hampered by dyslexia. Whenever he could, he employed a scribe to copy his official reports in a clearer hand, observing that "because of my bad handwriting" those written by himself "have not met with the greatest appreciation" in Mexico City.[17] Garcés's learned superior at the missionary College of Santa Cruz, Fray Romualdo Cartegena, complained to the viceroy that "the simplicity and artlessness of that father is great."[18]

All the same, Garcés's reports from the trail were valued for their geographic detail and insight into the desires and intentions of rival tribes. Even King Carlos III in Madrid extended his royal appreciation to Garcés for his discoveries and the productive ties he developed with the Indians. From the quill pen and tiny, almost illegible scribbles of Garcés we learn such intimate details of Indian life as the fact that some aborigines, seeing horses and mules for the first time, mistook them to be the wives of the Spaniards, greeting the steeds as humans and offering them human food. In his flowing Franciscan robes, Garcés was asked by some Natives whether he was a man or a woman. Font wrote in his diary:

> Father Garcés is so well fitted to get along with the Indians and go among them that he appears to be but an Indian himself. Like the Indians he is phlegmatic in everything. He sits with them in the circle, or at night around the fire, with his legs crossed, and there he will sit musing two or three hours or more, oblivious to everything else, talking with much serenity and deliberation. And although the foods of the Indians are as nasty and dirty as those outlandish people themselves,

the father eats them with great gusto, and says that they are good for the stomach, and very fine. In short, God has created him, as I see it, solely for the purpose of seeking out these unhappy, ignorant and rustic people.

Garcés fulfilled his greatest legacy by brokering peace terms among divergent, warring Indian bands stretching from Sonora to California. Wherever he traveled and preached, he stressed in forceful terms that God and the king of Spain wanted all of the tribes to live in harmony. Curtailing bloodshed among the Natives was crucial to Spain's efforts to colonize the West. Surprisingly, given the long-running enmities among Indian groups, Garcés succeeded in establishing a general peace on dozens of occasions, often involving multiple tribes. His best work was carried out among the opposing factions living along the strategically important Colorado River. Because of his intercessions, many Indian lives were saved from the endemic violence that characterized Native life in northwest New Spain. It is a cruel irony of history, then, that Garcés met a merciless death at the hands of Native Americans he had come to trust. Garcés was also unique among the Franciscans for his solitary odysseys, which stretched for months at a time. Ever restless, he would set out alone on the back of mule, or perhaps with a couple of Indian guides. He carried in his leather saddle bags very little food, relying instead on Indian villagers to feed him. When his escorts refused to venture into lands controlled by their Native enemies, Garcés pressed on alone despite the danger. When his thirsting guides insisted on turning back to the last watering hole, Garcés forged ahead without them. At one point in the barren desert even his saddled mount abandoned him to return to a source of water. Garcés continued on foot.

Because of his errant wanderings in unsafe territory, sometimes riding through the starlit night to avert the daytime heat, he was given up for dead on multiple occasions. He was the trailblazer whose epic journeys led the way from Sonora across the sand dunes of the terrible desert later known as el Camino del Diablo (the Devil's Road), to the Pacific coast of California—and from the Colorado River to the mountains of New Mexico, and up into the broad valley that dominated the center of California. Yet, despite his prolonged travels in unknown terrain, Garcés never learned to swim and seemed to have a fearful aversion to water. Whenever he came to a body of water too deep to wade across, such as the Colorado River, he cajoled the Indians into building him a raft. Or, as occurred a number of times, three or four Indians who were good swimmers would ferry him across the water by grasping hold of his hands and feet, the padre floating supinely on his back like a plank. "Altogether," concluded the historian Herbert E. Bolton, "his pathfinding, accomplished without the aid of a single white man, covered more than a thousand miles of untrod trails, and furnished an example of physical endurance and human courage that have rarely been excelled."[19]

Crespí was seventeen years older than Font and Garcés. But he too died within a few months of the other two, in the first hours of 1782, at the age of sixty, after having endured hunger and cold and deteriorating health and many other deprivations, both on the trail and at sea. Like Serra, who launched the string of twenty-one missions ultimately established by the Franciscans in California, Crespí was born on the island of Mallorca. His parents attended the parish church of Sant Jaume, a fourteenth-century Gothic edifice on a narrow lane in the heart of the old city of Palma de Mallorca. Catalán and its dialect Mallorquín were the languages of Mallorca, which meant Crespí was baptized Joan; only later in life did he assume the Spanish equivalent, Juan.

After receiving the Franciscan habit on 4 January 1738, at the age of sixteen, he studied philosophy under Serra at the Convento de San Francisco in Palma, forging an enduring collaboration that continued on both sides of the Atlantic until his death.[20] The remains of both men are entombed alongside each other on the left, or Gospel, side of the main altar at the rustic Basilica of Mission San Carlos Borromeo at Carmel, California. Serra, who died two years after Crespí, asked to be buried next to his soul mate. The marble marker on the stone floor atop Crespí's vault identifies him simply as "Compañero de Serra." For several decades in the mid-nineteenth century, the graves of both men lay under tons of rubble after the mission fell into ruin and the roof of the church collapsed. Restoration did not begin until 1884, after the mission had survived under three flags—those of Spain, Mexico, and the United States.

On 24 September 1749, at the age of twenty-eight, Crespí sailed from Cádiz aboard a 919-ton, 60-gun merchant ship named *Nuestra Señora de Begoña*, joining other Franciscans bound for missionary training at the College of San Fernando in Mexico City. The passenger list described him as short, with fair skin, blue eyes, and black hair.[21] Before departing for distant shores, he penned a poignant farewell letter to a family who had befriended him in Palma, ending with a plaintive "Adiós. Adiós. Adiós."[22] Throughout the crossing, Crespí suffered horribly from sea sickness, an infirmity that afflicted him every time he boarded a ship, despite many thousands of miles of travel in the open ocean.

Two years later he was assigned to work among the Indians in the remote highlands of the Sierra Gorda in central Mexico. He journeyed to Mission San Francisco del Valle de Tilaco, the easternmost of the five Sierra Gorda outposts, where he labored for fifteen years with one other padre in isolation from the outside world. Even getting to the mission from the nearest point of civilization, the Franciscan College of Santa Cruz in Querétaro, meant a mule trek of 175 miles. It began through a dry desertscape of cactus, ocotillo, mesquite, and scrub until ascending the western escarpment of the Sierra Gorda into forests of pine and oak. The final leg scaled the pass called la Puerta del Cielo (the Door of Heaven), at 8,200 feet above sea level, before descending into verdant woodlands nourished by warm, plentiful rains from the Gulf of Mexico.

Beautifully restored today, the ornate, multihued Mission Tilaco sits at 3,540 feet above sea level in a picturesque valley. Its original furnishings—paintings and sculptures brought from Mexico City—were paid for in part from Crespí's own meager stipend.[23] The elaborate façade, termed "mestizo Baroque," is adorned with red and green and yellow stone carvings of oversized flowers, grape clusters, ears of corn, tropical leaves, a rabbit, a two-headed eagle, and other motifs familiar to the Pame Indian artisans who created them in the mid-eighteenth century. Also displayed on the exterior are statues of Saint Francis of Assisi, the Apostles Peter and Paul, and depictions of other tenets of the Catholic faith.

In Crespí's time the Natives, accustomed to living outdoors and unfamiliar with large buildings, were at first fearful of entering the church they had built with their own hands. Consequently, Crespí sometimes said Mass in the courtyard in front of the soaring façade, using the religious figures behind him as a "sermon in stone." (Lamentably, some of the statues are headless, having been used for target practice by anti-clerical Mexican soldiers billeted at the mission during the Mexican Revolution of the early twentieth century.)

Some things have not changed in Tilaco since Crespí's day. The mostly Indian campesinos are still summoned to Mass by the hand ringing of the mission bell, using a fifty-foot-long rope that stretches down the exterior wall of the church from the top of the belfry to the ground. In springtime, the rhythmic chirrup of multitudinous *cicharras*, a variety of cicada, still punctuates the surrounding farmland. And Tilaco remains a secluded enclave in the Sierra Gorda. Until the 1960s its only link to the outside world was the same crude footpath trod by Crespí upon his arrival in 1752. A paved road did not reach the mission until 1997. Today, the parishioners have forgotten the name Juan Crespí, the man who brought Christianity to Tilaco over two and a half centuries ago.

Crespí's bucolic life at Mission Tilaco changed dramatically when King Carlos III abruptly expelled the Jesuit missionaries from New Spain in 1767 and ordered the Franciscans to take their place. The sovereign and his suspicious advisers feared that the assertive, independent-minded Jesuits reserved their true loyalties for Pope Clement XIII in Rome rather than for the Spanish crown. Also of concern were the private armies of mercenaries funded by the Jesuits on the frontier, a potential source of conflict with the king's regular troops. Carlos III may even have believed the Jesuits were scheming to murder him.[24]

The next spring Crespí and his friend Serra were sent to occupy the Jesuit missions on the Mexican peninsula of Baja California. Thus when José de Gálvez, the king's inspector-general in Mexico, decided to establish Franciscan missions in upper California, Crespí was assigned by Serra to serve as chaplain and diarist on the first overland expedition up the coast, led by the pioneer Gaspar de Portolá, described by his biographer as the "founder of California." Crespí carried out this assignment on the back of an old reddish mule that he affectionately called la Sonoreña.[25] (The beast's name likely stemmed from the fact that she was from Sonora.) Crespí traveled over a thousand miles on the back of la Sonoreña from Loreto in Baja California to San Francisco in northern California, keeping her as his companion on the trail for fifteen months. He was crestfallen when later he learned that his favorite mount had been consigned, due to her advancing years, to the pack-mule corral.

At age forty-eight, Crespí found that his adventures in the New World were only just beginning. In addition to many marches up and down the length of California, he kept meticulous journals of an expedition under California governor Pedro Fages to reconnoiter the San Francisco Bay area and identify the Sacramento and San Joaquin Rivers and the northern reaches of California's central valley. His last great exploration was a strenuous and perilous maritime voyage aboard the frigate *Santiago* to claim for Spain the coast of the Pacific Northwest as far north as the Queen Charlotte Islands near present-day Alaska.

In contrast to the diaries of Font and Garcés, Crespí's writing tends to stick to the facts at hand. His style is more prosaic, less lively. But he never fails to capture the fleeting moment with his exquisite descriptions of, for example, the exotic body tattoos of the Indians or the beautiful red Castilian roses he found on the trail, evoking wistful memories of home. He was a humble, gentle soul, a faithful missionary who always pressed ahead without complaining, regardless of the setbacks he encountered. Not least of these was a lifelong aversion to cold weather and fog, which seemed to inflict greater suffering on him than on others. "It turned overcast this afternoon with very thick fog and a northwest wind," Crespí recorded in his diary on 1 April 1769 while on a trek up the Baja California peninsula, "so that we could not bear the chill." Three days later he wrote: "A very heavy frost fell last night, so that we were near perishing of the chill."[26]

After Crespí's death, his close Franciscan friend from their childhood days in Palma de Mallorca, Francisco Palóu, who also labored in the California mission fields, wrote that Crespí persevered through life "with a dovelike simplicity," and that he "had a poor memory and could not learn by heart or recite from memory the doctrinal sermons at Mass on Sunday."[27] Font described his friend as possessing "a great deal of simplicity, with no self-conceit."[28] These remarks can be seen as describing Crespí's intellectual limitations. Nonetheless, he was widely admired in his day, by both Spaniards and Native Americans, for his unassuming manner and dogged pursuit of saving souls.

Bolton aptly noted that Crespí "participated in all of the major path-breaking expeditions . . . [covering] nearly 2,000 miles of land travel and a sea voyage of twice that distance. . . . Missionary, globe trotter, and diarist he was; breviary, pack mule, caravel, and quill might decorate his coat of arms. . . . In his precious diaries the human toils, the adventures, the thrills, the hopes, the fears of three historic journeys on the Pacific coast are embalmed."[29]

As the vanguard of Spain's final northward thrust into California in the twilight of empire, Font, Garcés, and Crespí were imbued with the zeal of conquest—a spiritual conquest, to be sure, but a conquest nonetheless. Adding a new realm to the already overextended Spanish Empire by staking claim to the West Coast and halting encroachments by English voyagers and, potentially, Russian fur traders was the principal aim of King Carlos III, the Bourbon reformer whose ambitions always surpassed the resources of his royal treasury, depleted as it was by endless European wars and his own extravagant lifestyle. (Despite the crown's pecuniary condition, Carlos III never scrimped on his own lavish royal barges and other excesses, rotating his court and its hundreds of courtiers from one sumptuous palace to the next with the changing of the seasons, even as his loyal subjects on the California frontier pleaded for a fresh consignment of underwear.) For Font, Garcés, and Crespí, the prime purpose of planting the cross was to save from eternal damnation the souls of an entire race of Native Americans—whether they wanted to be saved or not. The Franciscans measured their success simply, by how many Indians they baptized.

It was in their role as apostolic agents of the Roman Catholic Church that these friars rose to the demands of history, entangled as those demands were with the secular vision of a Spanish kingdom stretching from Tierra del Fuego at the tip of South America all the way to Alaska. Religious zealotry was an indispensable component of King Carlos III's expansionist policies, resting in part on Spain's historical experience in driving out the Moors and other perceived heretics from the Iberian Peninsula. As historian Mark Williams has noted, "Spaniards conquered the Americas with memories of the Reconquest still fresh."[30]

Yet another fundamental motivation, shared fervently by both clergy and lay leaders, was an overweening sense of Spanish cultural superiority. Americans who relish their superpower status today should well understand this trait, which was deeply imbedded in the Spanish national character of the eighteenth century. The Indians of the New World were seen as crude, pagan souls who were ignorant of the redeeming light of the Catholic Church, the one true church. The sole path to salvation for the unwashed Natives was conversion to Christianity, the same choice Spaniards offered to Jews and Moors in the days of the Inquisition. This paternalistic feeling extended to every sphere of daily life. The Indians, after all, were universally illiterate, their men walked around naked even in winter, and most had not learned the rudimentary practices of agriculture, surviving instead as hunter-gatherers, a prehistoric state as far as the Spaniards were concerned.

"The Franciscan missionaries, falling easy victims to racial bias, tended to regard the Indians as simple and childlike and take a patronizing attitude toward them," wrote the twentieth-century historian Francis F. Guest, himself a Franciscan scholar.[31] Guest calls this strong spirit of chauvinism *españolismo*, a complacent self-satisfaction with everything Spanish and a disdain for everything foreign.[32] So it is not surprising that Spaniards referred to themselves as *gente de razón* (people of reason). By definition this term excluded unbaptized Indians, who were labeled infidels or heathens. The presumption was that Indians lacked the simple reasoning power of white Europeans. On the contrary, the Natives were looked upon as unfortunate wretches in desperate need of the civilizing influence of Spanish culture—its Catholic religion, above all, but also its social organization, its ways of economic advancement, its habits of daily dress and diet and personal cleanliness, its music and art, its rigid custom of monogamy, and its sedentary life in fixed towns rather than the nomadic existence of hunter-gatherers.

Spanish culture was driven by the idea of men engaged in steady progress toward material wealth and comfort, all carried out under the all-encompassing concept of a single God and eternal life for those who believed in Him. Native American culture, on the other hand, rested on the concept of a circle of life and the harmonious rhythms of nature, in which human existence changed little throughout the ages. Under such circumstances, a titanic clash of cultures was inescapable.

Influential Native men quite naturally resisted giving up all but one of their wives in order to become baptized Christians. Most indigenous people in California, accustomed to moving their villages from the coast to inland hunting grounds at different times of the year, were reluctant to settle down in permanent Spanish missions or pueblos. Nor did those who actually lived at the missions show great enthusiasm for the hard work of building unfamiliar—and, to the Indians, unnecessary—adobe structures, a trait that caused the Spaniards to perceive them as lazy. (The Indians were, of course, unpaid laborers.) Planting crops and tending herds of cattle and sheep were alien concepts for most Natives, as was the ownership of land.

For that matter, the notion of private property was not understood by Indians, who were used to communal ownership of nearly everything. So, when a Native walked off with a cow or even a comb of his liking, the Spaniards saw this as the immoral act of a thief. Whenever an Indian child became deathly sick, as many commonly did upon contact with European illnesses for which they had no natural immunity, the friars rushed to baptize him and thereby save his soul for entry into heaven. But all that the Indians noticed was that when a priest prayed over an ill child, the usual result was the death of the child—a clear-cut cause and effect.

Because Spaniards tended to take their cultural ascendancy for granted, they grossly underestimated the task of assimilating Indians into the transplanted Spanish society of the New World. This myopic approach to subjugating a vast array of linguistically and culturally diverse tribes, many of whom were at war with each other, was most pronounced in Mexico City, where a series of powerful viceroys made decisions without benefit of firsthand experience in the borderlands. The friars who risked their lives at exposed stations strung along the hinterland were far more knowledgeable about the real outlook, attitudes, sensibilities, and temperament of the Indians. Time and again they accurately predicted when an Indian assault was imminent.

But their warnings about impending attacks or the shortsighted tactics of the king's zealous administrators in Mexico City were generally ignored in the determined rush to colonize California on the cheap. One of the most blatant examples of Spanish cultural insensitivity occurred in 1781, when soldiers allowed their livestock to devour the planted crops of the Yuma, or Quechan, Indians along the Colorado River at the Yuma crossing, thereby destroying the Natives' winter food supply. The protests of Father Garcés and the Indians themselves were brushed aside, helping set the stage for the slaughter of scores of Spanish colonists by Indians who formerly were allies. Garcés himself perished in the three-day rampage.

Contrary to the popularized view that mission life afforded an amicable existence to both the friars and the Native Americans under their guardianship, the harsh truth is that King Carlos's bid to extend his dominion over California and the

Southwest came at a steep price in recurrent bloodshed. The upheaval at Santa María Magdalena endured by Font was not at all out of the ordinary. Within just a few days of that attack, the same Apaches, Seris, and Piatos—only this time a larger war party numbering about forty—destroyed the nearby settlement of Sáric. The seasoned Franciscan in charge of the mission, Father Antonio Ramos, reported burying ten bodies the next day and warned his superiors that a raid on the pueblo of Ímuris was expected soon.[33]

Founded in 1687 by the pioneering Jesuit explorer Eusebio Francisco Kino, Santa María Magdalena had been attacked before. A rebellion by Pima Indians in 1695 left both Santa María Magdalena and San Ignacio in ruins. Today, Father Kino's remains are interred in a place of honor at Santa María Magdalena, but in Font's day the settlement was a neglected, tumbledown outstation, a mere auxiliary to the larger San Ignacio mission. "The church is large but dilapidated and only a chapel to San Francisco Xavier has any decent furnishings," stated a contemporary report on Santa María Magdalena.[34]

At many missions, but especially those along the rim of heathendom (as the Spaniards called the northern borderlands), daily life was filled with uncertainty and misfortune. For the Natives, the greatest calamities of all were the periodic epidemics of lethal diseases introduced unwittingly by the European intruders. So great was the death count that the Indians were often buried in mass unmarked graves rather than individual plots.

In 1820 the *padre-presidente* of the California missions, Mariano Payeras, decried the "rapid depopulation of *rancherías* [Indian villages] which with profound horror fills the cemeteries."[35] In 1802 an outbreak at Mission Soledad near California's central coast claimed the lives of five or six Indians a day.[36] Without any previous exposure, which would have provided a degree of natural immunity, Indians succumbed readily to measles, tuberculosis, smallpox, pneumonia, diphtheria, cholera, syphilis, and other sexually transmitted diseases. Native children were especially susceptible to death from foreign illnesses. Venereal afflictions left many Indian women sterile, further depressing the aboriginal population. Confining unmarried Indian women in cramped adobe dormitories at night and gathering all of the Indians together in church as a daily ritual spurred, unknowingly, the spread of contagious diseases.

Through it all, the padres bemoaned the mounting Indian casualties. Yet no one had any understanding of the causes or ways to stem the pestilence. Anthropologists estimate that, when the Spaniards arrived in California in 1769, the Native population was as much as 310,000.[37] By 1834, when the Mexican government disbanded the missions, the Indian population had been reduced to 150,000, with nearly all of the decimation caused by European diseases. By way of contrast, the 2010 U.S. Census recorded an Indian population in California of 578,623.

On their initial forays through terra incognita, the Spanish adventurers often were aided by the Indians, who guided them along their way, provided valuable local knowledge, and gave them food in exchange for colorful glass beads and other trinkets manufactured in Italy and elsewhere in Europe. Trunk loads of gewgaws accompanied the Spaniards on every expedition. The practice of distributing glass beads to gain favor with indigenous peoples was started by Christopher Columbus and introduced in California fifty years later by the Spanish navigator Juan Rodríguez Cabrillo.[38] When the Spanish interlopers began to build permanent settlements in Native lands, however, Indian hostility often mounted, ending in regular spasms of violence. The simple reality was that most Native Americans never acquiesced to Spain's colonizing ventures.

Today a contentious debate endures over the Franciscans' role on the frontier. Naïve observers are appalled to discover that the padres viewed the aborigines as childlike creatures in mortal need of Spanish religion and culture. A fresh generation of Indian academicians has arisen to defend their Native lifeways of the eighteenth century as a culture deserving of equal respect. Some overwrought revisionists vilify the missionaries as perpetrators of genocide. Traditionalists argue that, to understand the Franciscans, they must be examined not simply through the optic of contemporary standards but also within the complex historical context in which they lived. What is plain is that the padres, because of their close day-to-day relationships with the Indians, determined in large measure whether the Natives accepted or resisted Spain's intrusion. (A fuller discussion can be found in the Epilogue.)

In the mid-nineteenth century Pablo Tac, a Luiseño Indian educated by the padres, reflected the Native perspective: "It was of great mercy that the Indians did not kill the Spanish when they arrived, and very admirable, because they have never wanted another people to live with them."[39] Ironically, Tac himself died around the age of twenty of smallpox contracted after he was taken to Rome by the Franciscans. As California historian Kevin Starr has pointed out, "Throughout the Spanish colonial era, a state of war existed between the Spanish settlers and the majority of native Americans in the region. . . . [E]ven a sympathetic observer, acknowledging the benevolent intent of the mission system, must see it by the standards of the twenty-first century, as a violent intrusion into the culture and human rights of indigenous peoples."[40] Pedro Font, Francisco Garcés, and Juan Crespí catapulted into this violent intrusion with only the noblest of aims. Little did they know what scrapes providence had in store.

CHAPTER ONE

The Conquest Begins

> He went forth conquering, and to conquer.
> —King James Bible, Revelation 6:2

A clutch of primeval pepper trees, planted more than two centuries ago by Franciscan padres, stands sentinel over a twenty-foot-tall cross on Presidio Hill overlooking San Diego Bay. In the shade of this leafy bower, the cross is almost unseen amid the bustling urban landscape that surrounds it. Erected a hundred years ago, the monument is made of red brick roof tiles salvaged from the old presidio, where Spanish troops were first garrisoned to guard against Indian attacks in 1769. On 16 July of that year Fray Junípero Serra put up a crude wooden cross, hung a mission bell from a sturdy tree limb, and rang it briskly to attract the attention of Indians living in the riverbed below. Resplendent in his colorful silk vestments, he said a High Mass amid solemn hymns and musket salutes and then unfurled the royal standard to celebrate the founding of Spain's first settlement in present-day California. The serenity of this green, parklike setting today belies the rude calamities that nearly thwarted this opening thrust in Spain's conquest of California.

In the summer of 1769 Juan Crespí, age forty-eight, was all too mindful of the misfortunes to be confronted on the uncharted Pacific coast. The Portolá expedition's just-completed, fifty-two-day march of more than three hundred punishing miles up the Baja Peninsula to establish a mission at San Diego had exposed the daily struggles of the hinterland. Crespí survived days when no water could be found, starvation rations were imposed as the food supply ran out, and five Christian Indian attendants died from illness, hunger, and thirst.[1] With each death it fell to Crespí, the official chaplain and diarist of the caravan, to bury the Natives along the trail and plant crosses on their graves. One of the dead was his own interpreter.

But the most frightening moments occurred when Kumeyaay warriors whose ancestors had occupied the land for ten thousand years boldly accosted the vulnerable

Spanish intruders. On 7 May 1769, as the explorers descended from the California cordillera along the rugged spine of the Baja Peninsula, riding northward on muleback through dense shrub about fifty miles south of San Diego Bay, they encountered the first signs of trouble. A party of twenty-nine naked Indians heavily armed with war clubs, lances, and bows and arrows, with overflowing quivers slung over their backs, appeared on the tops of nearby hills to the east. It was evident to all that the Natives were outfitted for battle.

With hand gestures and war whoops, the warriors told the Spaniards to venture no farther, to return to where they came from. Some Indians held up their bows and arrows and imitated firing on the convoy. The confrontation, punctuated by the Indians' unrelenting shouts, continued throughout the day's march, but the Natives stayed just out of range of the muskets of the Spanish soldiers. When his train encamped for the night, Commander Fernando Rivera y Moncada ordered that the watch be doubled and that everyone remain on guard against an attack.

The next day the Indians appeared again. This time, amid steady howling, they pressed in closer to the travelers as they continued their trek. When the Spaniards drew near a low pass between two knolls, they found that the Native warriors were almost on top of them, within arrowshot, still clamoring for the interlopers to go back where they came from.

Fearing an ambush in the pass, Commander Rivera ordered the trailing pack train to be brought forward and arranged in a defensive position. Then he told his twenty-seven soldiers to don their battle gear: loaded and primed firearms with affixed bayonets, rawhide shields carried in the left hand to deflect arrows, and heavy sleeveless leatherjackets that were impenetrable to arrows unless shot from point-blank range.[2] When mounted, the troops also wielded lances and broadswords. Rivera arrayed his men in a line of battle facing the Natives, who withdrew a bit to higher ground but kept their bows and arrows poised in their hands, ready to shoot.

Brandishing a short musket, Rivera gathered up six of his lancers and advanced on horseback toward the hill occupied by the Indians, who continued their angry shrieks. At Rivera's approach, three warriors fired their arrows into the air. Each projectile landed a few feet from Rivera. This prompted the commander to discharge his musket at the most aggressive warrior. One of his soldiers also fired on the Native war party. "Neither of them hit a single Indian," reported José de Cañizares, Rivera's young second-in-command, "but the sound of the shot was medicine enough to drive [the Indians] from the top of the hill."[3] In his official account, Crespí put it more colorfully: "Once the heathens heard the two shots, their legs could not take them fast enough up the crest of the hill."[4]

The Kumeyaay combatants retired some distance away but continued to harass the expedition with jeers and gestures. After a couple of hours, the war party let out a collective howl and disappeared behind the hills. The frontiersmen resumed their march to San Diego.

Crespí had remained behind the protective line of soldiers and had watched the flare-up with dismay. The top man in charge of the Spanish crown's northward campaign into California, Inspector-General José de Gálvez, had given strict orders that the Indians were to be approached in peace and were not to be molested except in self-defense. Indeed, Gálvez's written commands stipulated that the "expedition's chief object is that of spreading religion among the heathens . . . through the peaceful means of founding missions to achieve the spiritual conquest." He further instructed that the explorers' "principal concern [must be] not to exasperate or antagonize the [N]atives, but to do everything possible to attract them and gain their good will by treating them well and making small shows and gifts of trinkets or of food."[5] The Natives in this instance posed a threat. But were Rivera's actions needlessly provocative? The commander's objective was to subdue the indigenous people of California. In contrast, Crespí's aim was to turn them into good Christians, loyal to church and king. This would not be the last time that strained relations would emerge between the Franciscans and the hawkish Rivera over his treatment of the Indians.

Aspiring plans for Spain's northward expansion into California had been laid as early as 1606, when King Philip III proposed establishing a seat of government on Monterey Bay, south of modern-day San Francisco.[6] Four years earlier, the Spanish conquistador Sebastián Vizcaíno had explored the California coastline in search of suitable harbors for the Manila galleons returning to Acapulco laden with silks, spices, beeswax, porcelains, rugs, and other riches from the Orient.

The ships' crews suffered devastation from scurvy during their seven-month-long return passages across the Pacific. In fact, it was not unheard of for so-called ghost ships to drift along the California coast with their entire crews dead from scurvy. At least one galleon laden with treasures sailed right past Acapulco. Its crew was composed entirely of cadavers.

The sooner the ships could make landfall on the coastline of northern California en route to Mexico, the sooner the sailors could escape the gruesome grip of scurvy, which promised a slow, tormenting death. Seafarers of the eighteenth century did not know what caused scurvy, but they observed that returning to land usually alleviated the affliction. Some unfortunate seamen, already debilitated by their months at sea, were buried up to their necks in sand on the beach in a futile bid to cure them.[7] Others thought the disease was carried by the northwest winds that dominated the California coast. The real cause of this lethal malady was an acute deficiency of vitamin C, found most abundantly in citrus and other fresh fruits—nourishment that was absent from the typical shipboard diet of hard biscuits and dried meats.

Driven by the prevailing westerlies, eastbound galleons crossed the Pacific at about 40 degrees north latitude, which meant they reached the California coast in the vicinity of Cape Mendocino, three hundred miles north of San Francisco Bay, before swinging south for Acapulco. Monterey Bay, then, would make a suitable way station for the Manila trade. But it was hardly the most desirable harbor on the California coast, as Vizcaíno claimed in grandiloquent reports upon his return to Madrid. "'Tis all that could be wished for as a refuge for ships bound from the Philippines," he wrote in his navigation journal. "'Tis a harbor sheltered from all wind points and surrounded by peaceful, tractable heathens." In truth, a manifestly better port was San Diego Bay, which Vizcaíno named in honor of his flagship and a fifteenth-century Spanish saint when he dropped anchor there on 10 November 1602. All the same, the crown's fixation with Monterey Bay as the ideal future capital of California persisted for two centuries.[8]

In the meantime, though, the crown's zeal for colonizing California at the beginning of the seventeenth century had dissipated. Spain was engaged in one European conflict after another, depleting the royal treasury and making costly far-flung conquests less enticing. Consequently, after Vizcaíno's 1602–1603 eventful voyage of discovery, Madrid closed its eyes to California for the next 160 years.

The imperial court's neglect of California began to change after Carlos III acceded to the throne in 1759. Although the empire was already suffering internal decay, Carlos saw himself as a champion who could unite his Iberian domain and restore Spain's greatness abroad. With a tall, lanky frame and a prominent nose shaped like an eagle's beak, he spent lavishly on himself and his many opulent palaces—heedless of the royal exchequer's impecunious condition. He was undeterred, therefore, by the expenses associated with overseas adventures.

By 1768 alarming rumors were circulating in Madrid that Russian fur traders were encroaching on the west coast of North America, jeopardizing Spain's long-standing claim to the territory. In truth, Russian hunters of sea otters had ventured no farther than the Aleutian Islands. They were still far from the Alaskan mainland and thousands of miles from Monterey Bay. With the signing of the

1763 Treaty of Paris ending the Seven Years' War, Spain and France had suffered defeat at the hands of the British, the world's leading sea power. So, in addition to his inflated fears about the Russians, Carlos III worried that English voyagers would trespass on his North American realm. The English, after all, were known to be searching for the mythical Northwest Passage—called the Strait of Anian by the Spaniards—which supposedly connected the Atlantic and Pacific oceans, providing a shortcut across the top of North America from Europe to the Far East.

With these perceived threats on his mind in the spring of 1768, Carlos III authorized a royal expedition to establish missions and presidios at San Diego and Monterey in order to safeguard his virgin California empire from foreign intrusion. The official put in charge was the king's trusted inspector-general in New Spain, José de Gálvez, who was given both sweeping authority and (at least on paper) the resources necessary to carry out this redoubtable undertaking.

At this particular moment, Father Crespí was ensconced at the primitive outpost of Mission La Purísima de Cadegomó on the Baja Peninsula, where he had recently been assigned after Carlos III removed the Jesuits from their missions throughout the realm and directed the Franciscans to replace them. Although Crespí was nearing the end of his fifth decade and was past middle age, as it was then perceived, he was about to embark on a decade of arduous explorations stretching from Mexico to Alaska. His fate changed precipitately when Father Serra, the fifty-five-year-old *padre-presidente* of the Baja missions, assigned his longtime friend and fellow Mallorcan to join the first overland contingent to occupy San Diego and Monterey. Crespí's role would be to minister to the spiritual needs of the Spanish pathfinders—including saying Mass each morning on the trail—and, far more important from the standpoint of history, to record a daily account of their discoveries in an alien land.

To organize the colonizing venture, Gálvez immediately assembled his own *junta de guerra*, or war council, at his lodgings in the Royal House at the shipbuilding port of San Blas on Mexico's Pacific coast. He decreed that four separate delegations—two by land and two by sea—would set out independently from Mexico and rendezvous at San Diego. After they established a fledgling presence there, the combined forces would continue as soon as possible on a march of nearly five hundred miles to Monterey Bay. A third ship loaded with supplies would follow closely on the footsteps of the initial companies to keep them replenished with food and other essentials.

The first overland section would be led by Commander Rivera, the forty-four-year-old military officer with extensive experience on the northwestern frontier.

Born in Compostela, Mexico, Rivera had already conducted a reconnaissance mission over part of the route up the Baja Peninsula to San Diego Bay with the noted Jesuit explorer and missionary Wenceslaus Linck. When Spain sent the Jesuits into exile, Linck returned to his native Bohemia, leaving Rivera as the Spaniards' most knowledgeable expert on Baja. Crespí, astride his old, reddish-brown mule, joined Rivera's detachment.

The second overland contingent, about one-third the size of the first, would be led by Captain of Dragoons Gaspar de Portolá, a mustachioed, never-married, fifty-three-year-old Catalonian nobleman. He bore the new title of military governor of the Californias—that is, of Lower (*Baja*) California, part of present-day Mexico, and Upper (*Alta*) California, part of the present-day United States. Earlier in his career with a light cavalry regiment, Portolá had fought for the Spanish crown in Italy and Portugal. He still carried a scar from a wound received in the Battle of Modena on the Olmo during the War of the Austrian Succession.

An obedient, dutiful military officer through and through, Portolá also had made good on the banishment of the Jesuits at gunpoint from the Baja Peninsula. Because of his high rank, the foray to San Diego and Monterey would be known to history as the Portolá expedition. Serra, the senior religious figure in the group, would travel with Portolá's detachment, which would follow Rivera's section by about nine weeks. At the time, the *padre-presidente* referred to this historic undertaking as the Sacred Mission.

Accompanying Portolá was his Genoa-born manservant and cook, Ignacio, a short-tempered man who on the trail killed a female burro with his sword because the animal blocked his path. Serving the short, balding Serra on the journey was his sixteen-year-old servant, a converted Indian named Juan Evangelista Benno. The youth, given the name Benno after a Jesuit priest, learned to speak and read Spanish and acted as Serra's altar boy at Mass. Unlike other Indians of the expedition, Benno was outfitted in full Spanish attire and given his own mule and riding boots.

Months before the land parties embarked, the two maritime elements were to sail up the one-thousand-mile-long Baja coast for San Diego—an exhausting, hazardous, and scurvy-prone journey against the prevailing winds and currents. The square-rigged vessels of the day had great difficulty sailing upwind. All along the California coast, the steady breezes came out of the northwest. This meant that on a voyage directly up the coast, which ran to the northwest, mariners fought stiff headwinds and contrary currents, making slow progress. To overcome these adversities, experienced captains steered directly westward from the Mexican coast for up to four hundred miles into the open ocean, where they could catch favorable winds, called northies, to sail northward. Then, only after reaching a point north of their objectives on the California coast would captains turn eastward, return to the mainland, and run downwind to their destinations. This added about a thousand miles to the trip but saved many strenuous weeks at sea.

Captain Juan Pérez, a Mallorcan by birth and veteran of the Manila-to-Acapulco trade route, followed this well-established tactic when he sailed from Cabo San Lucas at the tip of the Baja Peninsula to the harbor at San Diego.[9] Under his command was the *San Antonio*, a 193-ton armed *paquebote* (supply ship) newly built at San Blas along the lines of a British brigantine.[10] Thirty-two men comprised the ship's complement. Laden with provisions to sustain the Portolá expedition, the two-masted *San Antonio* weighed anchor on 15 February 1769 and reached San Diego on 11 April—an uneventful trip of fifty-six days.

The *San Antonio*'s sister ship—the two-masted, armed paquebote *San Carlos*—was less fortunate. Under the command of Don Vicente Vila, a seasoned naval officer from Andalusía, the *San Carlos* left the port of La Paz on the southeastern coast of the Baja Peninsula on 10 January—more than a month ahead of the *San Antonio*'s departure—and yet did not arrive in San Diego until 29 April. This protracted passage of 110 days, nearly double that of the *San Antonio*, was due largely to Vila's decision to follow the coastline rather than sail far out into the Pacific before turning northward. (By contrast, the *San Carlos*'s return passage downwind to San Blas the next year took only 24 days.)

To be fair, Captain Vila at the start of his journey encountered rough seas and light winds, a combination that caused the *San Carlos* to roll and yaw violently in the swells. At four o'clock in the morning on Sunday, 22 January, seaman Augustín Medina had his leg broken by the powerful brunt of the shifting tiller. Six days later the tiller itself broke off at the socket, and a spare one had to be rigged.

Water then began to accumulate below decks, but the ship's caulker could find no leaks. In his logbook, Captain Vila revealed the problem: "It was found to be fresh [drinking] water from the casks, as the staves were spreading with the violence of the constant pitching."[11] For days the *San Carlos*'s vital water supply dribbled away as the brittle wooden barrels continued to leak. The captain may have felt he had no choice but to remain near the coast in order to find a suitable spot to take on fresh water.

On Saturday, 4 March, with his water supply nearly exhausted, Captain Vila tacked inshore to look for a harbor where he could make repairs and acquire water. At two o'clock in the afternoon, as he tried to anchor at a protected cove close to the shore in about thirty-five feet of water, with a bottom of black sand and red pebbles, the wind shifted with great force, driving the *San Carlos* toward the beach.

The multiple anchors that Vila had deployed dragged across the bottom. To escape an almost certain shipwreck in the breakers, Vila ordered the anchor cables cut and then immediately stood away to seaward, leaving his anchors behind on the bottom.

Although he had extricated himself from a dangerous situation, the captain now found that the winds and currents were forcing him to sail southward, the opposite direction from his intended port of call at San Diego. Five days later, the *San Carlos* was still heading on a mostly southerly course in sight of land when Vila found a sheltered spot to anchor at what he identified as Isla Cerros, known today as Cedros Island, about half-way up the Baja coastline. At nine o'clock in the morning he sent a contingent ashore in the launch to look for water: Lieutenant Pedro Fages and several armed soldiers, part of an onboard cadre of twenty-five infantry volunteers from Catalonia. Fages returned in the afternoon with a vial of brackish water procured from a stream a full two miles from the beach. After consulting about the poor quality of the water with the ship's surgeon, a Frenchman with the Spanish name of Pedro Prat, and after considering his rapidly diminishing supply onboard, Vila decided to dispatch Fages ashore again with a launch full of empty barrels to be filled. The lieutenant and his subordinates spent the night on the island.

Aboard the *San Carlos* at anchor, Vila braved an apprehensive night because the swells and the current were forcing him toward the beach. The next morning he gave the order to get under way immediately in order to avoid running aground. But the contrary winds continued to push the *San Carlos* toward the surf line. Just when it appeared catastrophe was inevitable, from the south-southwest a light breeze known to sailors as a catspaw caught the *San Carlos*. "Instantly, all our sails filled away, and we were able to escape the imminent danger in which we had found ourselves," Vila recorded in his log. He attributed his deliverance to "Divine Providence."[12]

By the time the *San Carlos* recovered the launch and Fages, he had obtained a paltry six casks of water. The stream was accessible only by a steep path, and the heavy filled barrels had to be carried by hand the two miles back to the beach and then heaved into the launch bobbing in the surf. For the next five days, Vila executed a series of laborious short tacks back and forth to remain near shore while additional casks of water were brought on board. But the progress was achingly slow, with only twenty-nine barrels accumulated.

On Tuesday, 14 March, Miguel Costansó, an engineer assigned to the expedition, discovered a much better watering spot very close to the beach, where up to forty casks a day could be filled. Fages and his soldiers immediately went to work at the new spring. For the next week, the *San Carlos* continued to haul aboard water until about two hundred casks were filled and stowed below deck.

Vila now resumed his journey to San Diego. But the contrary winds and currents continued to force the *San Carlos* southward. For the next month, Vila tried to make northerly headway but actually remained south of the watering spot on Cedros Island. At one o'clock in the afternoon on Wednesday, 19 April, boatswain's second mate Fernando Álvarez, the coxswain of the launch, died. Scurvy now stalked the *San Carlos*, and not a single member of the ship's company, not even Captain Vila, could escape it. The persistent inability to make northerly progress can only have added to the crew's sense of impending death. Sailors aboard the *San Carlos* called their vessel by the nickname El Toisón de Oro (The Golden Fleece). At this gloomy juncture, those familiar with the nautical quest in Greek mythology must have considered the alias a curse that brought only hard luck to the *San Carlos*.

The very next day, however, favorable winds arrived from the south and south-southwest. Vila ordered every inch of canvas unfurled, and the *San Carlos* ran north throughout the day. This marked the fulcrum upon which fate finally began to favor the maritime wayfarers. On 1 March the *San Carlos* had been north of 30 degrees of latitude before being driven south by the wind, the currents, and the search for water. Not until 20 April did the ship advance north of 30 degrees once again. For fifty-one consecutive days, the *San Carlos* had lingered south of its previous high point on the chart.

From now on, the ship made good northerly progress, riding sporadic catspaws with the topsails set. But the lost time, more than seven weeks, had turned the *San Carlos* into a fertile incubator for scurvy. At six o'clock in the evening on 23 April, the pilot, Manuel Reyes, succumbed. His body was cast overboard at eight o'clock the next morning. After more than fourteen weeks before the mast, nearly every member of the sixty-two-man ship's complement was suffering the hideous effects of the disease. Many said their confessions to the naval chaplain, Fray Fernando Parrón, and received the last rites of the church in preparation for dying. Parrón, an experienced, forty-one-year-old Spanish missionary with a heavy black beard and swarthy complexion, was himself very sick from scurvy. He would battle the affliction even months after reaching land.

The dreadful progressive nature of scurvy had been apparent aboard ship for days. It began with sailors feeling weak, with pain in their legs, and dark purple spots appearing on their thighs and elsewhere. Then came diarrhea, swelling skin, hemorrhaging from the nose, spongy gums, and the loss of teeth. The final stages, when the victim lacked the energy to walk or even to stand, were usually characterized by grotesquely swollen limbs, jaundice, and fever. Then came death.

The scurvy outbreak only worsened when Captain Vila inadvertently sailed almost two hundred miles north of San Diego before discovering an error on the part of earlier Spanish navigators who, due to their crude instruments, placed the harbor farther north than it actually was.[13] When the *San Carlos* finally reached San Diego on 30 April, after her keel was trapped briefly in the kelp forests at the entrance to the harbor, Captain Vila was unable to walk. Only two crew members were in good health. The rest were felled by scurvy complicated by malnutrition. Due to the longer-than-expected journey, the food stores had run out. The ship's surgeon, Doctor Prat, was too weakened by scurvy to tend to the sick. Captain Vila's young cabin boy, Manuel Sánchez, was beginning to show symptoms.

Aboard the *San Antonio*, anchored in the bay for the last two weeks, half the seamen were down with scurvy and two had died. Only seven sailors were still fit for work. Captain Pérez also was in poor health. Those still strong enough to exert themselves spent their time burying the dead, whose numbers mounted daily, and ferrying the sick to hospital shelters set up on the shore.

Captain Vila hoped the fresh air in San Diego, as opposed to the fetid air below decks where the sick and dying were berthed, would bring them relief. That was not the case. Over the days ahead, crew members of both the *San Carlos* and the *San Antonio* continued to perish. On 10 May, the cabin boy died, along with a Philippine sailor named Matheo Francisco. With the two maritime expeditions now perilously short of food and other provisions, the survivors staked their future on the arrival of the *San José*, the third armed paquebote dispatched from Mexico with supplies and equipment—including three mission bells—to bolster Spain's toehold in California.

Vila believed the *San José* was already on its way up the coast. In fact, the supply ship had left port more than once. But each time, its Italian commander, Domenico Antonio Callegari, returned to San Blas with tales of difficulties that prevented the *San José* from continuing on to San Diego.[14] He eventually was replaced by a more competent officer, Jorge Estorace, who succeeded in putting the *San José* to sea later in the summer.

To join the first overland division under Commander Rivera, Father Crespí set out from Mission La Purísima de Cadegomó with a soldier named Miguel Islas, two Indian boys, and a small pack train on Sunday, 26 February 1769. In Crespí's baggage were valuable religious articles he had lifted from the Jesuit missions: silk priest's robes of red, white, and gold, imported from Canton, along with precious silver and gold altar items such as chalices and incense boats.[15] His gear included a magnetic compass and a quadrant used to gauge latitude from the angle of the sun during the expedition's northward journey. His one personal luxury was a snuff box filled with tobacco, which he readily shared with the Natives along the way.

Crespí's immediate destination was San Fernando de Velicatá, about four hundred miles to the north on the Baja Peninsula, where Rivera was assembling his expedition after rounding up horses, mules, saddles, equipment, food, and other supplies from the already impoverished Baja missions. After a forced trek with little respite, Crespí reached Rivera's encampment—a cluster of huts made of tree branches and bulrushes—at one o'clock in the afternoon on Wednesday, 22 March. For the Spanish, this was the edge of the known world.

Crespí spent the next day on his back, recuperating from his travels. But this was the only day of rest he would get. The very next day, Good Friday, Rivera set out for San Diego at four o'clock in the afternoon, following the same trail used by Father Linck three years earlier. The detachment included 189 mules, a dozen or so horses, a few burros, three muleteers, the twenty-seven leatherjacket soldiers for protection against Indian attacks, and forty-two converted Natives from the Baja missions. The Christian Indians would perform menial chores for the Spaniards throughout the march and also serve as interpreters with other tribesmen.

Ten of the soldiers were designated as scouts. Their job was to guide the way by finding Indian trails and suitable natural features such as level valleys to facilitate the movement of such a large procession over rough, rocky, unmapped terrain.[16] When necessary, the scouts used machetes, steel pry bars, shovels, and pickaxes to carve a path through almost impenetrable thickets. Above all else, the scouts were responsible for finding watering holes big enough to provide not only for the men but, equally critical, for the thirsty mounts and pack animals. This often required the soldiers to dig wells in the desert sand.

On departure from Velicatá, Rivera hauled with him on the backs of mules two barrels of water, along with other filled containers, because he knew there was no water to be found on the first day's march. Most of the Spaniards rode black mules. The horses were generally held in reserve for hunting. The Indians of the expedition were expected to keep up on foot, which was not difficult because the long pack train advanced at a relatively feeble pace. Most of the Spaniards slept in tents or other portable covering, while the Indians slept in the open air.

The Native attendants also were expected to feed themselves as much as possible by foraging off their surroundings, which were desert-like and barren of much sustenance. In this unforgiving landscape, even essential pasturage for the animals was scarce. The main source of natural food was mescal, the large starchy bud of the agave plant,

FIGURE 1. Abandoned ruins of San Fernando de Velicatá on the Baja Peninsula, staging point for Captain Fernando Rivera y Moncada's overland march to San Diego in the summer of 1769, with Juan Crespí as chaplain and diarist.
Photo by David Kier.

which the Indians roasted in a makeshift oven like a loaf of bread. They first dug a pit, built a fire in it, and covered the flames with stones.[17] When the stones were glowing hot, the mescal was placed on top and covered with wet straw and earth. After several hours, the baked mescal turned into a sweet, juicy, nutritious starch.

Because the Indians were required to scrounge for their own grub, their rations from the expedition's supplies were very meager, usually consisting of a thin cornmeal gruel—which Crespí complained was watered down. It was the Indians who suffered most when the provisions for the entire party began to run low a few weeks later. Crespí noted as well that the Indians at times were deprived of adequate drinking water.

Even before departing, a number of Natives were sick and malnourished from their strenuous treks to Velicatá. In a letter written shortly after his arrival in San Diego, Father Serra acknowledged that some Indians died of "sheer starvation." Writing to the superior of the Franciscan College of San Fernando in Mexico City, Father Juan Andres, Serra observed that "Father Crespí and his companions . . . experienced dire hunger on the road. They arrived at this port emaciated."[18]

As soon as the caravan set up camp on the second night out of Velicatá, Crespí heard the confession of an Indian who was gravely ill. The next morning he said Easter Mass, with every member of the expedition in attendance. On this day a married Indian who had been given the Spanish name of Rafael died. He had come from Mission Santa Gertrudis on the Baja Peninsula. Crespí heard the man's confession on his deathbed and administered the last rites of the church. After the burial, the padre planted a cross on the grave.

Two days later, with the procession camped along a small stream, seven more Indians fell sick. One of them "lay totally senseless, with very little hope of his living until the morning," Crespí wrote in his journal.[19] At dawn the next day the Indian died. His name was Luís. He had been baptized at Mission San Ignacio on the Baja Peninsula and was married to a Native named Monica. Crespí buried him and left a cross on the grave. Another Indian was so weak that he had to be carried on a litter—by other Indians, of course. When one of the soldiers became ill, he too was transported on a litter by the Indians. Rivera ordered that five other ailing Natives return to their missions. During this day's march, five Indians from Mission San Borja and four from Mission Santa Gertrudis ran away. "We shall feel their absence sorely," Crespí recorded. Not surprisingly, given the harsh conditions endured by the Indians, deserters were a constant problem. "This is not to be wondered at," Crespí wrote, "since they did not give them food where there was mescal, which was lacking most of the way." Of the nearly four dozen Natives who set out with Rivera, only thirteen reached San Diego. Among those who stuck it out were the two Indian boys who left La Purísima de Cadegomó with Crespí in February.[20]

Serra, too, lamented the number of Indian auxiliaries who abandoned the second overland division. "Thus, little by little, we go losing our companions, who are more necessary than some think, as only he who sees it from near could form a worthy conception of how they work, ill fed and without salary," Serra wrote in his journal. When one of the mares on the expedition gave birth to a mule colt, which obviously could not keep up on the trail, the hungry Indian attendants skinned it, cut it into pieces, roasted the meat on the fire, and devoured it. "Much good may it do them," Serra offered.[21]

After Rivera's train stopped for the night, the five sick Indians who had been sent away in the morning suddenly reappeared in camp. They had been confronted on the trail by ten heavily armed Natives who had threatened them, prompting them to return to the expedition for their own protection. In these early days on the march, the Spaniards encountered few Natives, although some were occasionally spotted in the hills, keeping their distance. Others abandoned their villages as the train approached, leaving only fresh footprints. What a sight the foreign caravan must have been to the elusive tribesmen of the peninsula. To begin with, the Native men went about without clothes. How strange the Spaniards must have appeared, clad as they were from neck to knee in everything from breeches and waistcoats to leatherjackets and Crespí's gray woolen robes. Many of the Indians coveted the foreigners' garments, and they went to extraordinary lengths to acquire them. Serra complained that every time he offered food to the Natives, they tugged at his sleeve and begged him for his habit instead. In his journal, Portolá expressed disgust when Native men offered their women for sex with the Spaniards in exchange for articles of clothing, including those worn by the commander himself. Such propositions can only have made it more difficult for Portolá to maintain discipline among his troops.

Then there were the large herds of horses and mules, exotic beasts that the Indians had never seen before. Crespí recorded that the Indians often showed fear when the mules came near. They soon learned to repeat the Spanish word—*Mula! Mula!*—to warn each other of the approaching steeds. And, for those Natives who heard it for the first time, the crack of musket fire must have been alarming.

On 16 April, Crespí got an up-close look at the indigenous population when an Indian man, a boy, and two women were brought into camp. The males were nude but the women covered their genitals with bunched reeds and their backsides with deer hides or sea lion skins. "How the adult [male] heathen might be distinguished from the ugliest demon ever depicted, I cannot say," was Crespí's first impression. "For a single glance at his face, with its bands of white, yellow, and red paint, was enough to horrify one."[22] In his journal, Cañizares described the man as an extremely arrogant witch doctor who yanked out bits of his hair in a fit of anger at having been detained by the Spaniards. Rivera distributed ribbons and glass beads to the four Natives and sent them on their way.

Giving gifts was a key tactic in the Spaniards' bid to show their goodwill and gain the cooperation of the Indians. Colorful ornaments of all kinds appealed to most aborigines. Tobacco was especially favored by the men. An inventory signed by Gálvez detailing items for the Portolá expedition included 396 yards of assorted ribbons, 165 strings of glass beads, 80 packages of loose beads made of coral, enamel, and ivory, 50 pairs of metal earrings set with stones, 144 strings of rosary beads, 7 metal finger rings set with stones, 4 bales of tobacco leaf weighing 500 pounds total, and a box of 2,212 cigars.[23]

When Crespí's Indian interpreter, Manuel Valladares, died on the trail, his remains were buried in a grave that was too shallow. Several weeks later, as the second overland convoy advanced along the same road, the bones of the Indian were found scattered about the ground, apparently unearthed by a hungry animal. The culprit may have been a mountain lion, one of which shadowed the second contingent for four days, roaring chillingly at night. Serra recovered the interpreter's half-eaten remains and respectfully reburied them.

By the first week of May, the explorers' food stocks were almost depleted, and they were still many miles from their destination. Ten days before reaching San Diego, all of the dried beef, the main source of protein, had been consumed. Only a small amount of chocolate was left, so that the strong, bitter breakfast cup savored by every Spaniard was watery. The ground meal was running out. On 5 May, Rivera imposed severe rationing.[24] Each man, with the exception of the padre, was allotted daily only eight ounces of flour made into two thin tortillas—barely enough food "to prevent fainting," in Cañizares's words.[25]

Crespí glossed over this crisis in his journal, but he poured out his true sentiments in a letter to his friend Fray Francisco Palóu after arriving in San Diego. He began: "I do not know how to tell your Reverence what we suffered from hunger on this journey."[26] Crespí placed the blame on Rivera, who misjudged how many days it would take to reach San Diego. The commander left behind at Velicatá as much flour as he took, along with extra stores of jerked beef, cornmeal, chocolate, wine, and brandy. What was more, Crespí asserted, the trip could have been made in a month rather than fifty-two days if Rivera had not dallied for more than a day at many spots. (The second section under Portolá made the trip in thirty-nine days.)[27] "Words fail me in which to tell your Reverence of the danger that this man put us in because of his whim," declared Crespí.[28] On 13 May, as the starving party crawled northward, Crespí spotted in the far distance San Diego Bay and the mainmasts of the *San Antonio* and *San Carlos* riding at anchor. At this day's campsite there was no firewood to cook the thin tortillas. Commander Rivera thus decided to burn the poles of his campaign tent. During the night a heavy rain fell, drenching the already cold and miserable party. It is unclear from the historical record whether or how Rivera put up his tent on this sodden night.

As the expedition approached the harbor the next day after a six-and-a-half-hour march, Rivera ordered his soldiers to fire off a salvo in salute. The two ships responded with their brass cannons, and soldiers on shore discharged their muskets. At five o'clock in the afternoon, members of the overland detachment and the surviving seafarers finally embraced on the rocky shore of San Diego Bay.

Crespí called this "a day of great merriment and rejoicing for everyone."[29] But in truth the bivouac at San Diego was a scene of funereal grimness. Along the shoreline were thatch-covered huts set up as a sick bay to care for men dying of scurvy. One large hospital shelter built of spare sails from the *San Carlos* housed ten sick sailors from the *San Antonio*. Nearby was a cemetery that grew larger each day. Twenty-three sailors and soldiers from both ships had perished. Those still on their feet were growing weaker.

When Portolá reached San Diego at the end of June, the death total was even higher. "I found the sea expedition . . . as good as immobilized and in so unhappy and deplorable a state as moved my deepest pity," Portolá recorded. "All of them without exception, soldiers, sailors and officers, are tainted with the scurvy, some of them brought low completely, others half crippled, others upon their feet but without strength; and this terrible malady has now taken off thirty-one men."[30]

Crespí spent a few weeks, while awaiting the arrival of Governor Portolá and Father Serra, surveying his alien surroundings—the "distant roads" described in the official title of his journal. On his wanderings, Crespí often was in the company of the scurvy-stricken Lieutenant Fages and engineer Costansó, a half dozen Catalonian volunteer soldiers, and Fray Juan Vizcaíno, the chaplain from the *San Antonio*. He found many large Indian villages ringing the bay, including one of thirty or forty Kumeyaay families alongside the San Diego River, which flowed into the harbor and was the source of freshwater for the Spaniards. The settlement, called Cosoy by the Natives, consisted of low, pyramid-shaped huts made of branches covered with mud.

When the Spaniards first disembarked from their ships, the Indians were not entirely impressed with the soldiers' muskets, viewing them as "simple sticks," according to Costansó's account.[31] To show the Natives the superiority of Spanish arms, Lieutenant Fages had a piece of leather suspended as a target and invited the Indians to shoot their flint-tipped arrows at it. Then he ordered his soldiers to fire at the same target with their muskets. The demonstration caused some of the Kumeyaay to run away in surprise and fear. Other Native men showed such respect for Fages, a veteran military officer from Catalonia, that they offered him the hospitality of their wives.

The Indian men went naked but heavily armed with war clubs, wooden sabers, and bows and arrows. They painted their bodies all over and wore seashells dangling from their pierced ears.[32] In a later report to the viceroy, Fages described the Natives as "of a light brown color with homely features and ungainly figures. They are dirty, very slovenly, and withal evil-looking, suspicious, treacherous, and have scant friendship for the Spaniards."[33]

Using nets woven from plant fibers, they were great fishermen, hauling in sardines, rays, and large quantities of mussels from one-man rafts built of bulrushes. They used the same nets on land to capture birds and rabbits. They also were shrewd traders, exchanging their catch for glass beads, cloth, and other articles brought by the Spaniards, who had been long deprived of fresh food.

Perhaps not surprisingly, the Kumeyaay refused all offers of food from the Spaniards, believing the scourge of scurvy was caused by the foreigners' strange diet. Even the Native children treated the food offered to them as though it were poison. "They are, all of them, very sharp, smart, greedy Indians, and very great thieves," wrote Crespí, referring to the disappearance of such items as clothing, blankets, spurs—even Father Serra's spectacles—in the sticky hands of the Natives.[34] The padre spotted plentiful grape vines and many sweet-scented rose of Castile bushes, whose red flowers he held in his hand and smelled, bringing to mind tender memories of Spain. The Spanish explorer Vizcaíno, 167 years earlier, had observed the same proliferation of roses when he reconnoitered Point Loma, the headland that formed the western shore of San Diego Bay.[35] Serra in his journal also marveled at what he called the "Queen" of flowers along the trail. "When I write this I have before me a branch of rose bush with three roses opened, others in bud, and more than six unpetaled. Blessed be He who created them!"[36]

Crespí used his spare time to write a letter to Fray Juan Andres, superior of the Franciscan College of San Fernando in Mexico City, asking that he allow Fray Antonio Cruzado to be transferred to California. Crespí and Cruzado had labored together for fifteen years among the Pame Indians at Mission Tilaco in the highlands of Mexico. Thrown together as the only Spaniards in that isolated station, Crespí and Cruzado became fast friends. Cruzado had been passed over when the first contingent of Franciscans was chosen for the spiritual conquest of California. A tall, thin man with a fair complexion, a light beard, blue eyes, and reddish hair, Cruzado made it to California two years later. He spent the rest of his days administering to the California Natives and died at the advanced age of eighty at Mission San Gabriel. In the same letter to his superior, Crespí made a polite plea for a new woolen habit with a hood, a tunic, and a waist cord, along with four to six thick handkerchiefs to combat dust on the trail. His old habit had been worn out on his exhaustive travels up the Baja Peninsula.[37]

At eleven o'clock in the morning on the first day of July, Serra at last reached San Diego, accompanied by the last members of the second overland detachment. With the whole expedition united for the first time, Portolá took stock of its plight. Nearly all of the crew of the *San Carlos* were dead or incapacitated. The sailors of the *San Antonio* were not much better off. Most of the equipment aboard the ships had not been unloaded, because most crew members were too weak to work. Food and other provisions were in critically short supply, and it was uncertain when the replenishment ship *San José* might appear.[38]

It would have been entirely reasonable under the circumstances to call off the expedition at this point. But Portolá was a determined, iron-willed leader. The appalling losses suffered by the two maritime contingents would not deter him from carrying out his orders to reach Monterey. "I shall stop at no hindrance, obstacle, or risk," he declared later in a letter to the viceroy. "My resolve has been either to die or to fulfill my mission."[39]

In short order Portolá decided to dispatch the *San Antonio*, with an undermanned crew composed of the few remaining healthy mariners from both vessels, to go to San Blas with an urgent plea for fresh supplies. Even some very sick sailors joined the crew of the *San Antonio* in hopes of being cured in San Blas. Nine seamen died of scurvy on the passage back to Mexico and were buried at sea; most of the others were close to death when they reached port.[40] The *San Carlos*, meantime, remained at anchor in San Diego indefinitely, lacking the necessary crew to put to sea.

The two overland contingents would join forces and continue on as planned to Monterey Bay, claiming it in the name of King Carlos III. To achieve this, Portolá and Rivera were counting on the *San José* to overtake the land expedition or, at the least, rendezvous with it at Monterey. Considering the shortages of nearly all essential provisions, there was no time to squander. The *San Antonio* departed San Diego on 9 July, 1769, accompanied by a packet of letters—and fervent prayers—from the desperate men left on shore. The overland expedition set off five days later, leaving behind Serra, the ailing Franciscan chaplains Juan Vizcaíno and Fernando Parrón, a guard of eight leatherjacket troops, Captain Vila, surgeon Prat, the sick sailors and soldiers, two muleteers, a carpenter, a blacksmith, and nine of the Indian allies who were part of the second overland section. For added protection against Indian attack, two artillery pieces were hauled ashore, and the guns of the *San Carlos* anchored in the bay were trained to provide covering fire for the encampment.

Two days after Portolá left for Monterey, the equally determined, iron-willed Serra founded Mission San Diego de Alcalá on presidio hill above the harbor.

According to his lifelong friend Francisco Palóu, Serra's ambitious objective was nothing less than to "bring under subjection to the gentle yoke of our Holy Faith all the savage tribes of pagans who inhabited this New California."[41] In a report sent from San Diego, Portolá acknowledged that pressing on to Monterey with the scanty food supply available to him was "a rather bold decision. . . . I shall take all the amount I can of provisions, letting God's Providence care for our relief by sea, with the arrival of the packet *San José*."[42] At stake now in Portolá's decision were the lives of Crespí and the rest of the truncated party bound for Monterey. If the *San José* failed to show, they would face starvation.

The Kumeyaay left no written record of their reaction to this now-permanent intrusion into their homeland. The scene in the harbor of the two tall ships and their booming cannons must have aroused awe. The oral history of the Indians at San Diego held that the arrival of the Spanish was a spiritually auspicious event because it was marked by both an eclipse of the sun and an earthquake. A total eclipse of the sun did occur on 4 June 1769, shortly after the arrival of the *San Antonio*, the *San Carlos*, and the overland procession led by Rivera. It could be seen in San Diego as a partial eclipse, although none of the Spanish diarists made mention of it. And, indeed, soon after departing San Diego the combined Portolá expedition was about to experience a series of earthquakes—and a raft of much worse troubles.[43]

CHAPTER TWO

Search for an Elusive Eden

> Exploration is really the essence of the human spirit.
> —Frank Borman

On the sprawling Camp Pendleton marine base in southern California, an inconspicuous shrine juts out from a remote, windswept bluff with a commanding view of the Pacific. A few miles away marines in high-tech hovercraft are storming the beach in an exercise simulating warfare on some distant shore. But the bluff top is a hushed, solitary place meant for contemplation. A wooden bench facing the ocean sits alongside a ten-foot-high white cross surrounded by a patch of green lawn. To the left, a gravel trail descends into Los Cristianitos Canyon. At the bottom, shaded by a dense stand of sycamores and live oaks, water ushers from a spring. Beside the gurgling flow, hidden from the world, is a historical plaque commemorating the first Christian baptisms in present-day California, performed during the Portolá expedition on 22 July 1769. The spot is so dark and secluded that brawny young marines stay away, claiming it is haunted.

For Father Crespí and his Franciscan companion, Fray Francisco Gómez, that July afternoon 248 years ago afforded a chance to do what they had come to New Spain to do—save Native souls from eternal damnation. Like Crespí, Father Gómez had dedicated his life to missionary work, heedless of the privations of the frontier. Chosen by *padre-presidente* Junípero Serra to be Crespí's compañero on the trail, Gómez was forty years old and wore a light black beard. His dark hair and dark eyes matched his swarthy skin.[1] Born near Burgos, the historic capital of Castile in northern Spain, he had labored in the New World for nearly a decade.

Only eight days earlier the Portolá expedition had departed San Diego on a hazardous, six-month-long march in search of Monterey Bay. On halting for the day, Crespí and Gómez learned from the soldier scouts that an infant girl at a nearby Indian village was dying in her mother's arms. Commander Portolá directed three soldiers to escort the two padres to the village, at their request, so they could baptize the girl, thus allowing her soul to enter heaven. Franciscan practice was to baptize adults only after they had received voluntary instruction in the Catholic faith, but children could be baptized at any time if they were in danger of dying. The ancient church doctrine of original sin held that no soul could enter heaven without benefit of baptism.

The padres found the child held tightly in her mother's embrace, too sick to nurse. Quite naturally, the mother did not want to hand over her daughter to two foreigners clad strangely in broad-brimmed leather sombreros and ankle-length robes of undyed gray wool. With the use of signs, Crespí tried to reassure the mother that they would not harm her child, that they wanted only to pour a little water over her forehead, say some prayers, and thereby open the doors of heaven to her when she died. The Indian woman, perhaps desperate to do anything she could to save her baby, grudgingly allowed the brief baptismal rite, but only while clutching the infant rigidly to her breasts. Father Gómez conducted the ceremony and gave the girl the Christian name of María Magdalena. Crespí was certain María Magdalena would die soon, but he rejoiced that "we have won this soul's passage to heaven."[2]

Later, as Crespí was writing his field notes for that day's march, he learned of another Indian girl, about two years old, who also was dying. When he and Gómez reached the child, they discovered she had been burned all over her body, but the circumstances of her misfortune were not clear. This time Crespí christened the youngster, naming her Margarita. With these first baptisms in California, Crespí in his journal offered the hope that the two little girls would reach heaven and pray for the conversion "of all these poor wretches here."[3] (Centuries later, the names Magdalena and Margarita still adorn places near present-day Camp Pendleton.)

The two padres had set out from San Diego with a poorly provisioned pack train of three hundred beasts and a party of sixty-seven men under Portolá's command.[4] They hoped to recognize Monterey Bay from the accounts of early Spanish seafarers, including those of Sebastián Vizcaíno in 1602 and José González Cabrera Bueno, a sailing master who in 1734 printed at a Franciscan friary in Manila a navigation guide to the California coast. Portolá's men carried with them copies of these old descriptions of untouched Monterey Bay, primarily as it was seen from passing ships, along with various charts compiled over the years by Spanish mariners. The early accounts also included the approximate latitude of the harbor, even though the primitive cross-staff and other navigational instruments used at the time made those observations unreliable.

For protection against hostile Natives, the expedition included twenty-seven mounted leatherjacket soldiers. They were augmented by Lieutenant Pedro Fages and six of his Catalonian volunteers, the only reasonably healthy survivors of the original twenty-five who sailed on the *San Carlos*. The lead scout was thirty-five-year-old Sergeant José Francisco Ortega, an experienced officer and former warehouse clerk and miner. Born in Mexico, Ortega had been assigned earlier to the Loreto presidio.

Portolá's file was rounded out by Captain Fernando Rivera y Moncada, engineer Miguel Costansó who, like Crespí, kept a daily journal, and seven muleteers. In addition, four converted Indians were along as personal servants. They were accompanied on foot by a larger contingent of fifteen baptized Natives from the Franciscan missions of Baja California who would provide much of the manual labor needed to keep the procession moving.

It is highly likely that among the Christian Indians was an enigmatic, twenty-four-year-old figure named Sebastián Tarabal, a Cochimí tribesman.[5] Among California Natives, Sebastián's lasting relationship with the Spanish explorers was without equal. He would go on to serve church and crown loyally through many adversities on the trail, chiefly as a scout and interpreter, for the next six years. He ranged widely across the northern borderlands, from San Diego to San Francisco, from Sonora to the Four Corners region of the American Southwest. He joined both Crespí and Pedro Font on separate expeditions and for a crucial time became the constant traveling companion and intimate friend of the restless Francisco Garcés. Because of Sebastián's wanderings, the Spaniards called him El Peregrino (The Pilgrim). His name has vanished from the pages of history, yet his contributions rivaled those of the celebrated Sacagawea, the Lemhi Shoshone woman who thirty-five years later guided Lewis and Clark in the Pacific Northwest.

Sebastián came from the middle reaches of the Baja Peninsula. He was born around 1745, probably at Mission San Ignacio, run by Jesuits at the time. Records show he married María Dolores Kinajan at nearby Mission Santa Gertrudis in 1764. They had a daughter, Juana María, who was born at Santa Gertrudis on 27 May 1769 as Portolá was carrying out his march from San Fernando de Velicatá to San Diego. Thus, the father was not present at the birth.

Although the Spaniards were fastidious record keepers, they did not think it necessary to list the names of the Natives who assisted the Portolá expedition. This underscored the simple truth that Europeans tended to view the Indians as childlike rather than as equal human beings. Nevertheless, ample evidence compiled by the historian Harry W. Crosby suggests that Sebastián joined the second overland detachment with Portolá and Serra when they set out from Velicatá to San Diego. On 26 April 1769, Serra marched northward from Mission Santa Gertrudis to Velicatá with an unspecified number of unnamed Indian volunteers in tow, Sebastián presumably among them. The Native left his heavily pregnant wife behind. As further evidence of Sebastián's participation in the Portolá undertaking, a baptismal record dated 17 December 1769 at Mission Santa Gertrudis lists the godmother as "María Dolores, wife of Sebastián Tarabal who is in Monterey."[6] On that precise day, the Portolá party was on its return journey from Monterey to San Diego.

Before embarking for Monterey, Portolá ordered a corporal and six soldiers to scout the way for the first two days of the march. They set out from San Diego Bay early on the morning of 12 July 1769 and returned late the next afternoon with a report that the first watering place was more than fifteen miles away. This was too great a distance for the slow-moving pack train to reach in a day. So, before the travelers left San Diego harbor on a north-northwest course at four o'clock in the afternoon of 14 July, all of the mounts and pack animals were given their fill of water. They would have to carry their loads without another drink for twenty-four hours, covering the fifteen miles over two days.

After riding through flat grasslands populated with a great many rabbits and hares—and a galloping herd of seven antelopes—the expedition set up camp on the first night near a village of friendly Indians who traded their big sardines for Spanish beads. Father Crespí and Father Gómez shared a small tent. Nobody got stung by the large numbers of scorpions skittering about the encampment. It must have seemed an auspicious start. No one imagined the torments that lay ahead.

Portolá's advance upcountry marked the beginnings of what later would be known as El Camino Real (The King's Road)—not much more than a cleared footpath that eventually stretched seven hundred miles along the coast from San Diego to Sonoma. Although El Camino Real evolved gradually during the years of Spanish rule in California, its ultimate function was to connect the twenty-one missions founded by Franciscans. Many still claim the Franciscans sowed bright yellow mustard along the primitive route to mark the way for travelers. Each spring, mustard plants still erupt in riotous bloom along much of U.S. Route 101, which traces the old Camino Real. The Spaniards did indeed introduce mustard as a seasoning to the New World. But the weed was naturally aggressive and propagated quickly out of control.[7] The romantic tale of the friars dropping mustard seeds along the trail is almost certainly apocryphal.

For the next two weeks, the expedition stuck to a northwest trajectory through easy-going flatlands studded with antelopes, wolf packs, coyotes, grapevines, and sweet-smelling rose of Castile bushes. Watering holes for the animals were sometimes scarce. Along the way Indians told of fearsome bears in the mountains to the east, arousing curiosity among the Spaniards. When the scouts hunting on

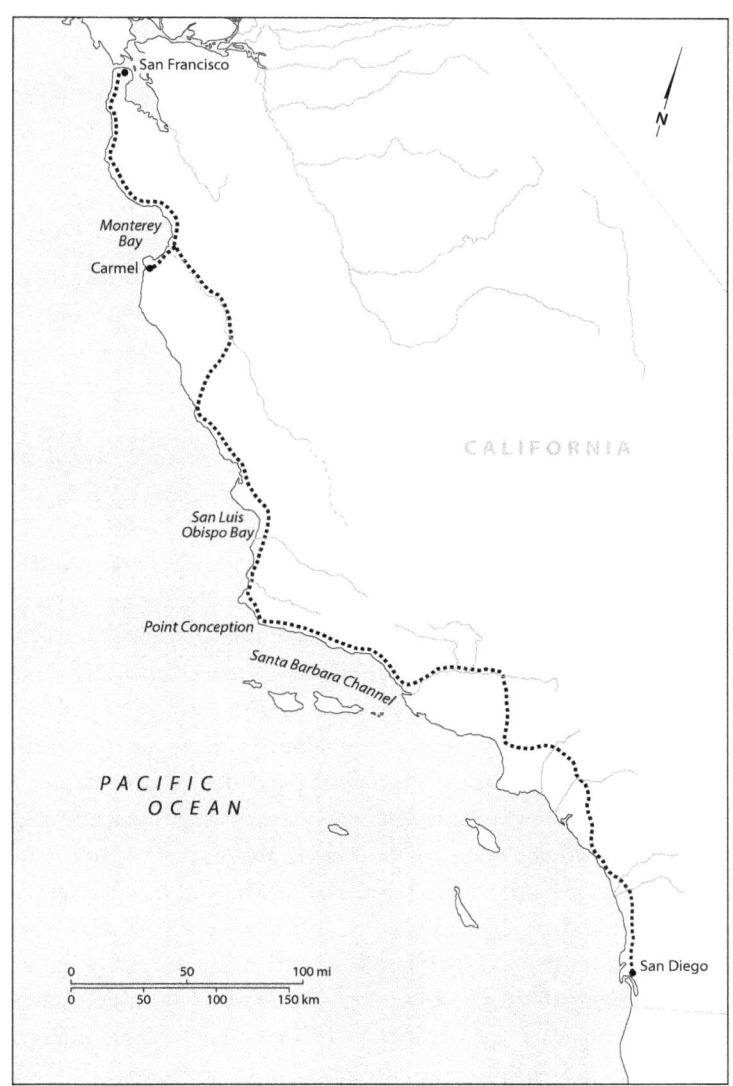

MAP 2. Spain's first overland expedition under Gaspar de Portolá along the California coast in 1769–1770 failed to recognize Monterey Bay as the ideal harbor described by Sebastián Vizcaíno in 1602.

Cartography by Bill Nelson. Copyright © 2017 by the University of Oklahoma Press.

horseback succeeded in shooting an antelope, everyone relished the taste of the fresh meat roasted over the fire.

The pathfinders encountered Native villages, some as large as two hundred inhabitants, consisting of round huts covered with bulrushes. Many of the dwellings were topped with bonitos, needlefish, and large sardines laid out to dry in the sun. The Natives kept short-eared dogs, and the men smoked handsome clay pipes. They were welcoming and eager to trade their fish, rabbits, sage gruel, and baskets of edible grass seeds for trinkets and tobacco. The warriors painted their naked bodies in hideous, multicolored hues and were armed with war clubs and bows and arrows. In a sign of peace, they often approached the Spaniards with their strings detached from their bows. Other Natives wore bear claws around their necks. There was no hint of violence.

At one settlement, where some of the children were fair skinned and had reddish hair, Crespí and Gómez taught them the traditional Spanish greeting of "Amar a Dios" (Love God). "Whenever we would retire to our little tent," Crespí recorded in his journal, "the moment we came out to get anything they would see us and all together would break out with 'Amar a Dios! Amar a Dios!'" The Natives also eagerly kissed the crucifixes and rosaries carried by the padres. "I have had the little ones repeating the Acts of Faith, Hope, and Charity over and over. These heathens have so entirely won my heart that I very gladly would have stayed with them," Crespí declared.[8]

At midday on 28 July the expedition was camped alongside a river southeast of what is now Los Angeles when a forceful earthquake struck. Commander Portolá seemed especially unnerved by the violent movement of the ground, acknowledging in his journal that he uttered prayers of supplication to the Virgin Mary. The shaking lasted about half as long as it took to say a "Hail Mary" and was followed by three aftershocks.[9] One Indian shaman was "no less thunderstruck than ourselves," Costansó wrote in his diary. "With horrid cries and great expressions of fear he commenced imploring the heavens, turning himself about toward all quarters and acting as though conjuring the weathers."[10] This was only the first of more than a dozen earthquakes the expedition would endure in coming days.

The soldiers called the river, which was full of catfish, El Río de los Temblores (Earthquakes River), in keeping with their habit of naming places for identifiable natural features. The Franciscans, on the other hand, preferred to name places for saints and other religious figures. Accordingly, Crespí gave the spot a more lavish name—El Dulcísimo Nombre de Jesús, del río de los Temblores (The Sweetest Name of Jesus, of the Earthquakes River).[11] On modern maps it is known as the Santa Ana River. As the train continued on a northwesterly track, Father

Crespí and Father Gómez started each day by saying Mass separately, with some of Portolá's men and the Indian converts in attendance. From outdoor makeshift altars, the padres offered frequent prayers to Saint Joseph, the designated patron of the Sacred Mission.

Wednesday, 2 August 1769, marked a historic day, even though members of the expedition did not realize it. After a three-hour westward trek they set up camp in a wide valley alongside a full-flowing river about fifty feet wide. The spot was lush with green foliage, rose bushes, tall cottonwoods, and sycamores. In his journal Crespí described it as "a most beautiful garden," and the best site he had yet seen for a mission. Not far away, Rivera and his scouts discovered, according to Crespí, "about forty springs of pitch or tar, boiling in great surges up out of the ground, and [they] saw very large swamps of this tar, enough to have caulked many ships with."[12] These burning subterranean springs became known as the La Brea Tar Pits, the word *brea* meaning tar in Spanish.

On the Catholic Church calendar, 2 August celebrated Saint Francis's restoration of a small chapel at Assisi, Italy, in 1211 A.D. Known in Spanish as La Porciúncula, the chapel became the first church of the Franciscan order. Crespí therefore named this propitious California bivouac Nuestra Señora de los Ángeles de la Porciúncula (Our Lady of the Angels of the Porciúncula). Thus was born the name Los Angeles for America's second-largest city. This was the most prominent of many surviving names conferred on places in California by Crespí.

On Sunday, 6 August, the wayfarers rested for a day near a village where they were entertained by Indians playing handsomely carved wooden flutes. Most of the Native men had only one wife, but their chiefs had two wives each. Although the men went about naked, the women were clad in fine deerskins from their waists to their ankles.

Here, for the second time since leaving San Diego, Commander Portolá was told by the Indians that farther north there lived other bearded men who rode mules, were armed with guns and swords, and were accompanied by padres dressed in long habits. On 28 July, an earlier gathering of Indians had told the very same story. In the weeks ahead, as the Spaniards made their way up the coast, they would hear the identical report at different times from different groups of Natives. On some occasions the Indians mimicked firing muskets and riding horseback. Others claimed that men on horses had passed through the area but had never returned. Adding to the conundrum, Crespí recorded in his field notes on 20 July that the caravan encountered Native women wearing around their necks glass beads from Castile. He wondered, somewhat implausibly, whether the beads might have survived from Vizcaíno's voyage 167 years earlier, or whether they were from Spaniards dwelling farther up the coast.

Who were these unknown people to the north? Crespí speculated in his journal that perhaps the Spaniards from New Mexico had made a foray across the deserts and mountains to the California coast. There is no historical record of any such campaign. Historians from the eighteenth century to the present have asserted with confidence that the Portolá expedition was the first overland journey by Europeans in modern California.

Were the Indian reports of 1769, documented by both Crespí and Costansó, the result of simple miscommunication between the Natives and the Spaniards, who after all relied heavily on sign language? If so, how did the miscommunication happen on several separate occasions? Or had the robust Indian telegraph relayed reports of the Spaniards in New Mexico to the California coast, with the inaccurate information that they lived to the north rather than to the east? To this day, the matter remains a mystery.

By mid-August the explorers were hugging the shoreline along the Santa Barbara Channel south of present-day Ventura. This was the land of the Chumash, who hauled prolific loads of fish into their nets and traps from oceangoing canoes built of pine planks lashed together and coated with tar. Some of the boats were twenty-five feet long but still lightweight and accommodated four men, who rowed with remarkable speed using long, kayak-style paddles with blades on both ends. Unlike traditional canoes made for shallow inland waters, the Chumash vessels had wooden keels, making them maneuverable and seaworthy in the coastal swells. As an engineer, Costansó marveled in his journal that the Indians could construct such fine craft with no other tool than flint to work the wood. Some villages had fishing fleets of fifteen or more canoes.

The Chumash also fished with three-pronged spears skillfully fashioned from bones. Their fishhooks were made from carved seashells. For catching sardines, the Indians used large baskets baited with ground-up cactus leaves, landing large quantities of fish. A few days later, when the Spaniards came across an Indian shipyard near bubbling tar pits where a canoe was being built, the soldiers dubbed the place La Carpentería (The Carpentry Shop). The name is still attached to a picturesque seaside town in Santa Barbara County.

The Chumash buried their dead in elaborate, neatly tended cemeteries, which they proudly showed off to Crespí. Men were laid to rest in one cemetery and women in another. Tall poles painted in various bright colors marked many of the graves, with the hair or articles of clothing of the departed dangling from the poles. In the case of women, their baskets or other handiwork were suspended above their graves. The cemeteries were also decorated with many large whale bones and delicately worked stone fonts.

In a later report, Lieutenant Fages described a Chumash funeral in which an Indian leader smoking a large stone pipe led a procession of Natives in circling three times the laid-out remains of the deceased. With each pass, the rabbit skins covering the body were lifted and three mouthfuls of smoke were blown on the dead person's head. Amid singing and "a dolorous cry and lament from all of the mourners," the body then was carried to the cemetery and interred, according to Fages's account.[13]

The Indians along the Santa Barbara Channel, both men and women, dressed in elaborate attire. The men covered the top halves of their bodies with cloaks made from the skins of hares, foxes, or sea otters. They went nude from the waist down, with the exception of the chief, who wore an ankle-length cloak as a sign of rank. The women wore antelope hides that extended to their knees. They decorated these hides with seashells and stones colored red or black, and they sported necklaces and bracelets made of snail shells. Fages observed that men who wanted the clean-shaven look plucked their whiskers, one by one, with a pair of clam or oyster shells used like tweezers, a painful procedure. Similarly, they shortened their hair by burning it over the fire, a precarious operation.

In other Chumash villages Crespí was bewildered to find two or three men wearing red deerskin skirts, identical to those of the women, and bedecked in earrings, beads, shell necklaces, and other female jewelry. These cross-dressers stayed with the women throughout the day, performing women's work, while the other men (wearing no clothes at all) went out fishing. Fages noted that these peculiar Natives were "sodomites by profession" and held "for common use" by other men. This was not the last time Spanish sensibilities would be ruffled by the sight of effeminate Native men, who were held in high esteem by their Indian peers. In his journal Crespí concluded: "Who is wise enough to tell what mischief this may be?"[14]

When the column camped for the night on 15 August, the Natives presented the Spaniards with more fish than they could eat. To make music, the Indians carved beautiful wooden flutes and bone pipes, which they wore around their necks. After darkness fell, the tribesmen began to serenade the expedition from a distance, with the music continuing late into the night. Portolá worried that perhaps the Indians were summoning others in preparation for an attack. His fears were unwarranted. The Natives wanted only to entertain their visitors. The nocturnal concert did not inspire Costansó, who grumbled in his diary that the music was "highly discordant . . . [and] did nothing save to annoy us and keep us awake."[15]

Five days later another band of Indians, heavily painted and covered with feathers, sought to amuse the expedition with dancing and music after nightfall. They carried split canes, which they rattled to make a percussive beat keeping time with their songs. They too played pipes "whose tones grated upon our ears," according to Costansó. Fages described the incident more diplomatically, pointing out that the music was "very displeasing for us, who are not accustomed to distressing the ear with this kind of composition." Portolá feared the cacophony would scare the mounts and pack animals, so he distributed beads to the entertainers and sent them on their way.[16]

On the morning of Monday, 21 August, south of present-day San Luis Obispo, the scouts killed their first bear, one of about twenty spotted in a troop. Crespí was awed by the size of the creature, which he compared to a young bull. He described the slain animal as "a fierce sort of beast in every way, and God deliver any living thing from its claws, which are horrid to behold!" Fages, too, was impressed by the bears, describing them as "ferocious brutes, hard to hunt. They attack the hunter with incredible quickness and courage."[17]

At key moments the bears along the Central Coast provided a bountiful source of meat for the underfed expedition. Fages became such a skilled bear hunter that the other soldiers called him L'Os, short for El Oso (The Bear). But Crespí shuddered in fear whenever he encountered the beasts. A bear killed by the scouts on 2 September was "monstrously big," Crespí recorded, with hind feet more than twelve inches long and six inches wide. "The head, and all of the creature, are a fearful thing to see, with two fangs a good finger thick on both sides of the mouth. . . . These huge ones have more meat on them than a large beef has."[18]

On 7 September in a valley north of San Luis Obispo, the scouts sighted bears again, prompting Portolá and six of his men to take to their horses and mount a big-game hunt. A she-bear with two cubs was finally brought down, but only after taking seven shots from the scouts' muskets. It took a musket ball to the head to kill her as she tried to protect her bawling cubs by pulling them beneath her with her forepaws. The now-motherless cubs scampered away.

On another occasion a mule-mounted soldier accompanying the pack train wounded a bear, prompting it to charge. The bear caught the mule by the tail and twice pulled it to the ground as the mount struggled desperately to get free. The rider escaped unharmed, but the mule was badly mauled, with a large claw wound on its shoulder. Costansó wrote in his diary that the instant bears were wounded "they charge full tilt upon the hunter, who can only escape by spurring his horse, for their first rush is swifter than could possibly be supposed from the outer appearance and awkwardness of such brutes."[19]

Crespí noticed there were no Indian villages where bears were plentiful. The troopers called this spot La Cañada de los Osos (Bear Hollow). Nearby today is the unincorporated coastal town of Los Osos in San Luis Obispo County.

Four days after the bear hunt, at a campsite north of present-day Morro Bay, the Spaniards were visited by Indians who had with them a small bear cub, about the size of a large dog, which they had found in a cave. Whenever the Indians could steal a cub from its mother, they fattened it like a hog for eventual eating. Unlike the black and brown bears seen to date, this cub was a distinct gray color, marking it in all likelihood as a fearsome grizzly.[20] It was still so young that its fur bristled whenever anyone approached it. The surrounding area was well worn by beaten trails and tamped-down resting spots left by a great many large bears. The Indians offered the cub as a gift to the Spaniards, who prudently declined it. The soldiers called this site El Paraje del Osito (the Bear Cub Place).

Indian women along the central coast gave birth entirely alone, often in straw-coated pits that they themselves dug in open fields as soon as labor began, according to Fages's firsthand account. After delivering the baby, the woman cleaned away the afterbirth and flattened the soft cartilage of its nose, before bathing herself without ceremony in cold water. From birth, the baby was swaddled to a small, coffin-shaped cradle board, which the mother carried suspended by cords from her shoulders, freeing her hands to do work.

On 12 September 1769, while sticking close to the shoreline in frigid fog, the expedition began to confront very difficult, broken terrain, with ravines and flowing streams hampering its progress. The scouts were kept busy clearing a path with their machetes, pickaxes, and crowbars. The next day the explorers reached the foot of the towering Santa Lucía Mountains, recognizable from the early accounts by Vizcaíno, Cabrera Bueno, and other navigators. The Santa Lucía Range is better known today as the Big Sur Coast, an exceptionally rugged stretch of seashore acclaimed for its thousand-foot-high peaks plunging steeply down to the surf. Here Portolá ordered a two-day halt while he dispatched Captain Rivera and eight scouts to search for a pass through the formidable ocean cliffs ahead. Crespí, who always suffered more than others from the chill, complained that because of the fog he had not seen the face of the sun for days, and the nights were already intolerably cold.

Portolá struck out to the northeast early in the morning on Saturday, 16 September, following the route reconnoitered by the scouts. The sheer escarpment blocking their path rose so abruptly that Costansó declared it was "insurmountable for goats and deer, let alone for men." Crespí concurred, writing in his field notes: "On merely viewing from below the way by which we must climb, it becomes almost impossible to believe that it can be done." This day's strenuous march covered only three miles. The next day, the vertiginous ascent was so dizzying that Crespí was afraid to look down. He feared the mules would lose their footing and tumble backward over the precipice. And, as he ruefully noted, the tallest summits still lay ahead.[21]

The next several days were the most arduous ever as the expedition made its way up and down very steep grades, surrounded by cypress trees and tall pines. All hands, regardless of rank, worked together in hacking a trail through thick brambles. The weather turned colder, with heavy frosts at night, and the mountain Indians warned of looming snowfall. The food stocks were running short. Morale sagged when the explorers reached the crest of a high mountain only to find that more and even higher peaks stretched away beyond the horizon. As he looked northward from the height, Crespí declared the country to be "untravelable." Portolá, never one to complain about the travails he confronted, recorded tersely in his diary that the mountains were "impassable."[22] Even worse, several of the soldiers were now showing symptoms of scurvy, with purple patches appearing on their skin and pain in their legs. Some were so fatigued as to be unfit for duty, putting a heavier workload on the others.

It was the end of September before the wayworn travelers finally put the Santa Lucía Range behind them. They emerged onto a coastal plain where the grass had been burned off by the Indians to increase its yield of edible seeds. Following a river downstream on Sunday, 1 October, the party spotted the Pacific and, jutting out into it, a point covered with pine trees. Curving northward along the shore was a broad beach forming a bight stretching for many miles.

With his quadrant, Crespí shot the angle of the sun and declared the latitude to be 36 degrees, 53 minutes north. (The observation was actually 12 minutes too high.)[23] The latitude was roughly in keeping with where Monterey Bay should be, based on Vizcaíno's journal, which placed it at 37 degrees. The Spanish seafarers' histories also stipulated that the bay was bounded on the south by a point of pines, and on the north by Punta Año Nuevo, a projection of land named by Vizcaíno when he visited it on New Year's Day in 1603. The pine trees were so prominent that the explorer Juan Rodríguez Cabrillo named it La Bahía de los Pinos on 17 November 1542, when he became the first European to spot the bay. Vizcaíno, who relished renaming the places discovered by Cabrillo, rechristened it Monte Rey after his patron, the viceroy of New Spain, Gaspar Zúñiga de Acevedo, Conde de Monte Rey.

Filled with relief and high spirits at the prospect of reaching Monterey Bay at last, Crespí, Rivera, Costansó, and five soldiers climbed to the top of a hill and gazed northward in search of Punta Año Nuevo. In the far distance they could see clearly a prominent headland protruding into the Pacific. To the south, they could see clearly the point of pines. At that moment, the eight men atop the hill were sure they were viewing the scene described by Vizcaíno and others as Monterey Bay.

But there was a problem. There was no sign of the well-protected port that Vizcaíno described as the best anchorage on the California coast. Looking at the broad, exposed bight, Portolá and his men could not visualize a roadstead where ships could anchor shielded from the wind and waves of the open ocean. Vizcaíno had stated flatly in 1602 that "the harbor is secure against all winds." Beyond that, he had described the southern end of the bay as "a great pine forest from which to obtain masts and yards, even though the vessel be of a thousand tons burthen, [with] live oaks and white oaks for shipbuilding, and this close to the seaside in great number."[24] To Portolá's explorers, the trees on the point of pines appeared too small and spindly to fit Vizcaíno's grandiose description. Crespí penned in his journal: "We were, however, greatly confounded by the sight of high sea with no shelter or harbor in view anywhere—instead only embayment and high sea."[25]

The next morning Rivera set out with ten scouts to explore the entire area and locate the great sheltered bay depicted by Vizcaíno. The captain and his men returned the next afternoon with crushing news. There was no protected harbor, either north or south of the point of pines. Nor was there any indication that there once had been a port that had silted up over the years—a desperate theory being advanced by some in Portolá's party.

In a later letter written to Inspector General José de Gálvez, Crespí explained the disappointment felt by every member of the expedition: When Rivera "returned to report that never a trace had been seen of any harbor, large or small, after all the surroundings had been scouted . . . [the] news was the most distressful possible for everyone."[26] Portolá responded to Rivera's bleak findings by calling an urgent meeting for the next day to decide a course of action. Soon after daybreak on 4 October, eighty-three days after departing San Diego, Crespí and Gómez said a special Mass dedicated to Saint Francis, whose feast day it was. They implored God to guide the expedition safely on its Sacred Mission. On this dire day, nearly every member of the party was on his knees in attendance. Afterward, Portolá convened his small junta de guerra, or war council. The group consisted of six men—the commander, the two padres, Rivera, Costansó, and Fages.

To begin, the commander detailed the severe challenges facing them. Eleven men were stricken with scurvy, and eight of those were sick enough to be declared disabled and unable to work, according to Portolá's count.[27] (Costansó claimed that fully seventeen men were "half crippled" with scurvy; Crespí pegged the number at twenty.) What was more, the scourge was almost certain to claim more victims in the days to come. Virtually every member of the expedition was exhausted by the excessive toils of the trail. Vital provisions were in short supply, down to fifty sacks of flour, twelve sacks of dried beef, and four sacks of vegetables.

The whereabouts of the packet *San José* and its relief supplies were still unknown. Colder weather was in store with the approach of winter. Should the battered expedition continue its northward exploration, or should it return to San Diego having failed its mandate to locate Monterey Bay?

Not a single member of the junta wanted to abandon the campaign. It was possible that Monterey lay farther north than the latitude stated by Vizcaíno. The great navigator was wrong, after all, about the latitude of San Diego, which actually was about two degrees (138 miles) farther south than he reckoned. Perhaps Monterey Bay was just over the northern horizon. Rivera proposed that the party rest for six days to give the sick men and the worn-out mounts a chance to recover. Then they should resume the journey north. Portolá and the rest of the junta endorsed Rivera's plan unanimously, but the period of rest was shortened to just two days. In his diary entry for the day, Costansó wrote an uncharacteristically emotional account of the meeting, concluding: "Should God allow us all to perish while searching for Monterey, we should have fulfilled our duty to God and to man, by striving till death to complete the undertaking upon which they had sent us."[28]

As the expedition prepared to resume its trek upcountry on 7 October, scurvy became a major encumbrance. Some of the men could barely move without help. It took two or three soldiers to lift them into the saddle, and their ability to ride was questionable. Carrying them by litter would have consumed precious Indian manpower and slowed the caravan to a tortoise's pace. Instead, eleven of the men were attached to wooden frames and lifted onto the backs of mules.[29] To a few of the sickest soldiers the padres administered the last rites of the church, using the holy oils brought along for this purpose, in preparation for dying. "With these poor souls, who knows how we shall get on henceforward," Crespí wrote. "God be with us and aid us in our troubles."[30]

Led by Sergeant Ortega, the scouts went out immediately to chart a path northward. They found footprints of large animals with cloven hooves, which they thought were buffalo. In fact, they probably were elk tracks; buffalo from the high plains never migrated as far as the California coast. When the scouts happened upon a large encampment of five hundred Indians in round, grass-covered huts, the unsuspecting Natives were filled with terror. At the sight of armed, bearded men atop mules, some of the Indians fled in horror. Amid much shouting, others ran to their weapons. Women burst into tears and shielded their children. Ortega defused the situation by dismounting, making signs of peace, and offering beads as gifts. In turn, the Native men all at once seized their arrows and darts and drove them into the ground, point downward, as a gesture of friendship.

In his field notes, Lieutenant Fages recorded that many of the tribes surrounding Monterey Bay were at constant war with each other. They were lighter-skinned than the Indians to the south, and some of the men cultivated long black mustaches. They worshipped the sun and held predawn ceremonies in its honor. Like the Chumash along the Santa Barbara Channel, they buried their dead in cemeteries, "with the exception of those who die in war, for [they] are eaten by the relatives of the slayer," according to Fages.[31]

Only a few days into the northward march, the animals became weary from exertion and lack of pasturage. One soldier simply left his lame, half-starved mule behind. The days now were overcast with fog and the nights were frigid, causing Crespí great discomfort. Southeast of modern-day Santa Cruz, the explorers encountered trees larger than any they had ever seen before. Half a dozen men with their arms outstretched could not join hands around the giant trunks. They called them *palos colorados* (red trees)—the great redwoods of northern California.

By the middle of the month more men, too weak to ride, began falling to the ground from their mules, forcing the entire train to halt while they were braced in the saddle with back rests like those used by women on horseback in Andalusía in southern Spain. Many soldiers had lost the use of their swollen legs. The train progressed at a crawling pace in order not to unsettle the infirm. Both Crespí and Gómez said special Masses, imploring Saint Joseph to provide relief to those dying of scurvy.

On 20 October rain began to fall, at times heavily, soaking the explorers and making for sleepless nights, especially for the Indian attendants, who had no tents. There was much concern that the dampness and chill would be fatal to the sickest men. But the opposite occurred. Even those closest to death began to recover. Both Crespí and Costansó attributed their improved health to the rain showers. The real credit goes to the discovery of evergreen madrono trees beside a stream still laden with edible, ripe red berries the size of rosary beads. The fruits no doubt contained ample concentrations of vitamin C. The soldiers named the stream La Salud (Healing Creek).

By 25 October the bedraggled expedition was south of what is now San Jose. The supply of vegetables and dried meats had run out, leaving only flour tortillas and bran cakes for the men to eat, along with whatever seed gruel or other food they could barter from the Indians. Most of those afflicted with scurvy were making swift recoveries. Both Portolá and Rivera were hit with a bad bout of diarrhea, prompting a two-day rest for the expedition. Before long, most of men were suffering from loose bowels. The soldiers wryly called this spot El Valle de los Cursos (Diarrhea Valley). When some of the men inspected a nearby settlement of abandoned Indian huts, they came back covered with fleas. So, naturally, the place was called Ranchería de Las Pulgas (Flea Village).

With the provisions dwindling rapidly, Portolá reached the reluctant decision on Saturday, 28 October, that pack mules should be slaughtered at intervals to boost the soldiers' rations. In truth, the soldiers were not yet hungry enough that mule meat appealed to them, especially since they had just succeeded in killing a few ducks. Repulsed by the thought of eating such tough carcasses, the men refused to go along with mule butchering—at least, at first. Sheer want would change their minds soon enough.

On 31 October the pathfinders sighted to the northwest the distinctive Farallon Islands, which rose like seven white pillars in the Pacific, given their name by Vizcaíno in 1603. More than a century later Cabrera Bueno also made note of the islands, thirty miles west of the coast. This now was powerful evidence that the expedition had overshot Monterey Bay, that it actually lay more than a hundred miles to the south. The next day Portolá decided to rest his train and send Sergeant Ortega and eight scouts on a three-day reconnaissance mission. In the meantime, several soldiers were given permission to go out hunting deer on horseback in order to bring in some sorely needed meat.

After dark on Friday, 3 November, Ortega and the returning scouts fired off a salute as they approached Portolá's camp. They brought news of having found an extraordinarily expansive harbor connected to the Pacific by a wide inlet. What they were describing was San Francisco Bay and the Golden Gate, a discovery that for centuries had eluded the Spanish seafarers who traversed the coast. Yet, the scouts were even more excited about having learned from the Indians through sign language that a ship was anchored in the big bay. Some of Ortega's men had already come to the conclusion that this must be the supply packet *San José* at anchor in Monterey Bay, awaiting Portolá's arrival.

The result of Sergeant Ortega's report, then, was to sow even more confusion about the elusive Monterey. Portolá decided to continue northward on an urgent basis to find the great harbor and the vessel described by the Indians. That night a powerful north wind tore through the camp, flattening the tents and everything else standing. The next afternoon, the expedition set out at one o'clock. After a five-mile march into the mountains southeast of San Francisco Bay, the full party stopped at the top of a hill and looked down on the huge harbor and, in the distance, the Golden Gate. Crespí described the scene as "a vastly big, vastly splendid harbor in which all of the navies not only of our Catholic monarch might lie, but those of all of Europe."[32] San Francisco Bay indeed could accommodate many ships, but there was no sign whatsoever of the vessel reported by the Indians. Once again, the *San José* was a phantom ship, nowhere to be found.

The next day Portolá continued his northward advance up the western side of San Francisco Bay, still praying to find the *San José*. Each time the explorers encountered Indians, they used signs to ask a thousand questions about the possible whereabouts of the supply ship. Some of the more gullible members of the expedition were pleased and encouraged at the vague gestures and pointings of the Natives, which seemed to confirm what the Spaniards wanted to hear—namely, that the ship had been spotted somewhere in the bay.

With no meat left, and their rations cut to a griddle cake a day, the explorers devoured whatever food was offered to them by the bay-area Natives, who carried staffs painted in many colors and decorated with large bunches of feathers. The Native food included the usual sage gruel but also parched seeds made into dough and bowls of mush and white porridge. On 9 November the starving men hit upon eating acorns from white oaks. Acorns were a staple of the Indians' diet, but they processed them first by leaching out the heavy tannins with hot water, a step the Spaniards skipped. Consequently, the men became horribly ill with stomach distress, indigestion, and fever.

Once again Portolá rested his column and sent Ortega and his scouts out on a four-day mission to see if they could make contact with the *San José*. When they returned after dark on Friday, 10 November, they were downcast, having found no hint of the ship and admitting they did not really understand the Indians' sign language. Mindful that the expedition was in danger of perishing from hunger, the commander called a meeting of his junta de guerra for nine o'clock the next morning.

To open the deliberations, Portolá reminded his officers and the two friars that "our honor, and even our lives" were at stake.[33] The members were unanimous now in believing that Monterey Bay must be behind them. The well-known Farallon Islands and the physical features of San Francisco Bay ruled out this spot as the place described by earlier mariners as the "bahía famosa," the famous bay of Monterey. On this day, Saturday, 11 November 1769, Portolá decided with the full backing of his men to turn back for San Diego. They would redouble their search for Monterey on the way. The expedition broke camp and marched south for five hours that afternoon.

The lack of food now reached crisis proportions, with the meager rations not enough to sustain the party for long. On 15 November Portolá ordered a day-long pause so that the soldiers and Indian helpers could collect as many mussels as possible from the rocks along the shore. The soldiers named the spot Punta de Almejas (Mussels Point). The next day the men went out hunting for geese and returned with a bounty of twenty-two birds. Costansó in his journal credited "Divine Providence" for their success.[34] Over the next twelve days, more geese were shot regularly from the huge flocks of thousands encountered by the explorers. On 27 November, this much-needed food source ceased, with the geese abruptly disappearing. The soldiers then resorted to shooting pelicans and sea gulls, which the famished explorers ate without complaint. A few days later a mule was slaughtered, but even now many of the men could not bring themselves to eat it. The baptized Indians had no such qualms.

On 27 November the expedition returned to the Point of Pines, making much better time on the southward jaunt because everyone had recovered from scurvy. Rivera and his scouts, along with six Indian attendants, were sent out for four days to search a second time in vain for the fabled bay detailed in the histories. While he was away, three of the Christian Indians asked to go out hunting and then deserted. When Rivera returned, he related that two of the Indians in his party also had absconded. Costansó poured out his frustrations in his journal: "In view of what had been happening to us, we were at a loss. How can we claim that so famous a harbor as Monterey, one so much praised and cried up in its day by men of repute . . . has not been found despite the most exquisite, earnest efforts practiced at the expense of a great deal of sweat and toil?"[35]

On 7 December Portolá convened his third war council. The fifty sacks of flour that existed at the first war council in October had dwindled to sixteen, and the sacks of dried meat and vegetables had been eaten up long ago. Mule on the hoof was now the main provision of the expedition. Fresh snow covered the higher elevations to the east and south, and the commander worried that the return route to San Diego would be blocked by a heavy snowpack in the weeks to come. In that event, he argued, the entire party would perish. As if to underscore his concerns, a fierce south wind arose that afternoon, churning up a storm at sea and battering the expedition. Some members of the war council still wanted to hang on at Point of Pines, but Portolá made the executive decision that there was no option left but to go back to San Diego. The prospect of returning in failure, his honor compromised, must have weighed heavily on him.

On Sunday, 10 December, before riding south, the explorers put up a tall timber cross on the shoreline so that it could be seen from far out at sea. Carved into the timber were these words: "Dig at the foot you will find a writing." Inserted in a flask buried at the bottom of the cross was a long message, most likely composed by Costansó. It detailed the expedition's futile search for Monterey, from San Diego Bay to San Francisco Bay, and back to the Point of Pines. "At last, having lost all belief or hope of finding it after all this endeavor, effort and toil," the note declared, the expedition "is setting out today for San Diego, without any more provisions than fourteen sacks of flour. It prays for God Almighty to guide its way, and for His Providence to bring thee, sailor, to thine own safe harbor." Then came a plaintive, almost despondent, plea for relief supplies. Any passing ship's captains "are implored, should they touch shore here within a few days from the date of this writing, after informing themselves of its content and of the expedition's sad state, to endeavor to sail close along the coast toward San Diego, so as to aid the expedition with provisions if at all possible, if it should be so fortunate as to sight one of the vessels and be able to signal its own position to them by flags or by musket fire. Praise be to God."[36]

Defeated and dejected, the members of Portolá's campaign had convinced themselves that they had failed their solemn duty to locate Monterey Bay. In truth, it was right in front of them, even if it did not resemble the protected maritime haven embellished by Vizcaíno in his reports 166 years earlier. They also overlooked an important clue. On the day before their departure from the Point of Pines, the Indian helpers found on the beach a heavy, rusted iron hoop used to shore up the mainmast of a ship. The discovery should have made it plain to Portolá that the unsheltered bay had been visited earlier by Spanish adventurers.

As the explorers resumed their trek to San Diego, they still held out hope that the replenishment ship *San José* might appear on the horizon and alleviate their suffering. Whenever they were in sight of the ocean they kept a keen eye out for his majesty's paquebote. They believed the ship had left the Mexican port of San Blas seven months earlier, which left more than enough time for it to reach the coast of northern California. Where could it be?

For the next few days, the expedition was sustained by the return of large flocks of geese. The weather continued to get colder, bringing strong winds and, at night, heavy frosts. While saying Sunday Mass early in the morning on 17 December, Crespí nearly collapsed from the cold. His extremities, especially his hands, became cramped and turned numb, and he became sick to his stomach. After nearly wailing aloud in his pain, he interrupted the Mass to warm his hands over hot coals. Only then was he able to finish the morning ritual.

As the party hacked its way through the Santa Lucía Range once again, an aged mule was killed every third day to provide meat. By now, no one was passing up the tough mule flesh. By one count, no fewer than fourteen mules were eaten on the return trip to San Diego.

On Wednesday, 20 December, Portolá rested his men because the pack mules were worn out. Here he discovered that a number of hungry soldiers had stolen flour from the diminishing supplies. In response, he distributed all of the remaining flour to each member of the expedition, making everyone responsible for his own share. Each Spaniard received eight small jars of flour. The Indians got only four jars each. He also passed out additional rations of biscuits, chocolate, and cheese to the officers and the two padres. In his diary, Crespí recorded the acute situation in which the Spaniards and their Indian allies now found themselves: "This is all of the provision there is for getting between here in the Santa Lucía Mountains and San Diego harbor."[37] At this point, San Diego was still more than a month's march away.

Starvation was averted in the days ahead by trading with the Natives—glass beads for gruel, mush, dried fish, fresh deer meat. On New Year's Day 1770, south of present-day San Luis Obispo, the soldiers spotted a large mother bear with two or three cubs trailing after her. They immediately saddled their horses and went out to hunt her. They returned after killing the mother and one of her fat cubs, providing "a fine feast-time for the camp," Costansó recounted in his journal. Bear meat was notoriously strong flavored. But on this occasion, wrote Costansó, "we thought it better than the richest veal."[38]

As the expedition at last approached San Diego toward the end of January, many worried there would be nothing left of the fledgling frontier outpost they had left more than six months earlier. "Truth to tell," recorded Costansó, "everyone had a dread that if the grip of disease and death had continued among the men, nothing might be left of the settlement but a waste." At mid-day on 24 January, the scouts sighted the pole stockade and other low structures of Mission San Diego. The soldiers fired off a salvo in salute, alerting the mission's survivors. After many joyous embraces among these hardy adventurers, everyone sat down to a meal. "We ourselves having no lack of appetite," Crespí wrote in his journal, "and what with getting ahold of a griddle cake such as we had not had for many a day, and the excitement, all of our troubles were forgotten."[39] All the same, the explorers were downcast that, in their minds, they had failed to find Monterey. Crespí reflected their letdown in a somewhat defensive report from San Diego to Inspector General Gálvez in Mexico City: "I hope that your Lordship will not take offense because the port of Monterey has not been found; for, believe me, your Lordship, this expedition has done its full duty before God and the whole world, as faithful and obedient vassals of our Catholic monarch."[40]

Equally discouraging, there was still no trace of the *San José*, the supply packet that could have fulfilled their prayers. It was not until 6 July 1770 that the *San José* finally embarked from San Blas laden with provisions for the California missions.[41] This time she was under the command of Jorge Estorace, a respected pilot trained at San Blas, who had served under Captain Vicente Vila aboard the *San Carlos* on its troubled passage to San Diego the previous year.

After sailing into the broad Pacific, the *San José* and its urgently sought-after cargo simply vanished, never to be heard from again. One potential clue to its fate washed up on the beach at Mission Carmel near Monterey three years later: A fifteen-foot-long section of broken mast from a large sailing ship.[42] The spar, made of pine, was studded with iron nails, some of which were standard boltheads and others consisting of one head and two points. Very little rust was found on the nails, suggesting the mast had not been in the water very long.

Juan Bautista de Anza, who arrived at Mission Carmel a few months after the timber washed ashore, directed that it be sent to the San Blas shipyard to determine whether it came from the *San José*. To punctuate Anza's instructions, Viceroy Antonio María de Bucareli y Ursúa ordered that the mast be examined by the naval experts at San Blas and that they declare, under oath, whether it was from the *San José*. This apparently was never done, because Father Pedro Font inspected the artifact when he visited Mission Carmel a full two and a half years later. Some maritime officials, including veteran sailing Captain Juan Pérez, declared that the timber was not from a ship at all. To this day, the *San José*'s disappearance remains a mystery.

Despite their many setbacks and misfortunes, every member of the Portolá party survived the thousand-mile march to San Francisco and back. The contingent left behind in San Diego was not so fortunate. Eight of the fourteen sick Catalonian volunteers died of scurvy. Four more sailors and six Indian attendants also were buried. The cemetery grew to fifty graves.[43] Even now, padre-presidente Serra was suffering symptoms of scurvy, as was Fray Fernando Parrón.

A Kumeyaay raid on the encampment on 15 August 1769 had cost the life of a young Spaniard who had volunteered to be Serra's page. A number of other Spaniards had been wounded. Most of the supplies brought to San Diego by ship and pack train had been used up. It was only a matter of time before the mission would have to be abandoned for lack of food. An inventory signed by Portolá four days after his return concluded that, even if the Indian helpers were given only half rations, "the whole amount of existing supplies will last no longer than twelve and a half weeks."[44] So, even in the midst of the grateful reunion at San Diego, a new crisis was fermenting.

CHAPTER THREE

Eureka!

> Some are born great, some achieve greatness, and some have greatness thrust upon them.
>
> —William Shakespeare

On a typical afternoon Monterey Harbor is a thriving mix of tourist bustle, commercial maritime ventures, and industrial enterprises operating side by side. Anglers cast their lines from the municipal wharf and members of the Monterey Peninsula Yacht Club tend to their boats in the marina. Wholesale fish companies, seafood markets, restaurants, and pubs vie for the attention of visitors. Another, older pier nearby has been transformed from a working fishermen's hub where sardines were once the economic mainstay into a swank venue of fine eateries, art galleries, tackle and bait shops, whale-watching cruises, and party-boat concessions. Everywhere there are pelicans, gulls, cormorants, and sea lions—countless sea lions.

The sea lions are about the only thing Juan Crespí would recognize about the place. When he visited this spot along the shore, about a hundred yards southeast of the modern municipal pier, on 25 May 1770, he saw thousands of sea lions, which he called *lobos marinos* (sea wolves).[1] They were so densely packed together for warmth that, to Crespí, they looked like "a cobblestone pavement."[2] The occasion marked the Portolá expedition's return to Monterey Bay after having failed to recognize it the year before. Joining Crespí in surveying the shoreline for the second time were Commander Gaspar de Portolá and Lieutenant Pedro Fages.

What a difference six months had made in their formerly skeptical outlook! "We saw the closing-in made by the mainland with the Point of Pines," Crespí recorded, "and with a single voice, all three of us broke out, 'This is Monte-Rey Harbor!,' without our having the slightest doubt left as to the fact. . . . I know not how to describe the joy and happiness we felt at seeing the end of all of the steps we had spent upon finding it."[3]

Long before reaching this Eureka! moment, Portolá had to deal with the urgent shortages of food and other supplies he encountered upon his return to San Diego.

Without relief provisions very soon, the entire California campaign would collapse in failure—no doubt a horrifying prospect for the honor-minded Portolá. The commander decided immediately to dispatch Captain Rivera with twenty soldiers back to Velicatá, more than three hundred miles south on the Baja Peninsula, where he could obtain cattle, flour, corn, chocolate, and other basics to sustain Mission San Diego. A portion of the scarce rations in San Diego was doled out to Rivera and his men, including six precious sacks of flour, the bare amount needed for them to survive on their forty-day trek.[4] The party departed San Diego on 11 February 1770. Portolá, Junípero Serra, and Crespí stayed behind, vainly staking their hopes on the arrival of the doomed supply ship *San José*. Even if the *San José* failed to appear, the return of the *San Antonio*, which had been sent back to San Blas for aid seven months earlier, was anticipated any day.

Portolá was not one to yield to adversity. But he now was responsible for the lives of the fifty-four Spaniards and fourteen converted Indians who were hanging on at San Diego. Over the strenuous objections of Serra, the commander set a deadline by which the mission would be abandoned unless a supply ship arrived beforehand. Francisco Palóu, an intimate confidant of both Serra and Crespí from their school days in Palma de Mallorca, called the deadline "the sharp arrow which wounded the zealous heart of our Venerable Father Fr. Junípero."[5] Carefully calculating the remaining rations and the time it would take for the failed expedition to reach the succor of Velicatá, Portolá set 19 March as the absolute date for deserting Mission San Diego—and forsaking His Majesty's Sacred Mission to California.

With unintended irony, the date imposed by Portolá coincided with the feast day of Saint Joseph, designated by Inspector General José de Gálvez as the patron of the expedition. Serra immediately gained Portolá's approval to begin a novena to Saint Joseph, nine successive days of Masses, special prayers, and recitation of the rosary beseeching the campaign's guardian for assistance. At the same time, Serra and Crespí vowed in secret to remain behind among the Indians at San Diego if Portolá and the rest of his party returned to Baja California. Such defiance of authority was not out of character for Serra, but it was almost inconceivable for Crespí, a humble man for whom obedience was a cardinal virtue. In a letter to Palóu, Serra vowed to stay in San Diego even after "the provisions are exhausted and also our hope . . . to endure up to the very last."[6]

The novena was begun on 11 March, 1770, with every Spaniard and Indian joining in the prayers. More than a week passed without any sign of a packet boat. On the final day, 19 March, a High Mass was sung, Serra preached a sermon, and many of the soldiers received communion. The expedition was already loaded for departure the next morning. At three o'clock that very afternoon, the seeming miracle sought by Serra's novena occurred. The topmasts of the *San Antonio* were sighted, clearly and unmistakably, in the Pacific off San Diego. In joyous thanksgiving, Serra led the men in singing the *Te Deum*, an exultant anthem dating to the early Christian church. Its opening line in Latin translates: "Thee, O God, we praise!" For the rest of his life, Serra faithfully celebrated a solemn High Mass on the nineteenth of each month to honor Saint Joseph and offer gratitude for his intercession.

Contrary winds and currents prevented the *San Antonio* from actually entering San Diego Bay for four more days. Captain Juan Pérez tacked back and forth near the Coronado Islands south of the harbor entrance before finally being able to drop anchor in the roadstead, marking the end of a difficult passage. After setting out from San Blas on 20 December 1769, the *San Antonio* was blown by heavy weather more than a thousand miles out to sea.[7] By the time Pérez returned to the mainland along the Santa Barbara Channel, he was low on water and forced to go ashore at a Chumash village where he could fill his casks.

The Natives told him of the Portolá expedition's having passed through the area traveling northward and then returning southward short of food. To imitate the Spaniards riding mules, the Indians straddled the *San Antonio*'s water barrels. This valuable intelligence, coupled with Pérez's desire to obtain a replacement anchor from the idled *San Carlos*, prompted him to abandon his original destination, Monterey, and to sail instead down the coast to San Diego. With this providential turn of fate, the *San Antonio* now sat in the harbor "laden to her masthead with all sorts of provisions," in Crespí's words.[8]

The *San Antonio*'s bounty changed everything. Prodded by Captain Pérez and Serra, Portolá decided to renew the search for Monterey. He would lead another overland contingent up the coast, with Crespí as the diarist, and Captain Pérez would go by sea, with Serra as his maritime chaplain. The padre-presidente assigned Fray Francisco Gómez and Fray Fernando Parrón to stay behind as the first permanent missionaries at San Diego. Serra himself was determined to found a mission at Monterey and remain there with Crespí as his assistant.

The *San Antonio* sailed from the port of San Diego on 16 April after Serra said a morning Mass on board. Maneuvering the vessel into the open ocean was a time-consuming challenge in itself, due to the adverse sea conditions. Lacking a desk, Serra seated himself uncomfortably on the bare deck and wrote a letter to Palóu in Loreto, asking that he send wax and incense for the new mission at Monterey. For delivery, the letter was handed by Serra to sailors in a launch that returned to shore just as the *San Antonio* finally sailed away.

It had been more than a year since Serra had received word of any kind from his Franciscan superiors or the civil authorities in Mexico City. The solitude and isolation of frontier life were beginning to wear on him. Crespí, too, bemoaned their desolation, describing it as being "exiled here in another world." Serra closed his letter to his friend with a characteristically fatalistic view of his future in this forsaken corner of the empire: "Finally, farewell, my dear friend, and may the Divine Majesty unite us in Heaven."[9]

The overland party was composed of thirty men, including seven leatherjacket troops, twelve Catalonian volunteer soldiers, two muleteers, and five unmarried Indians. Portolá also had the able assistance of Lieutenant Fages and engineer Costansó. The commander set out from San Diego the day after the *San Antonio* sailed. With quickened marches, the caravan made good time over the same route traveled twice previously.

During the night of 23 April 1770, while the procession was camped along a river near present-day Los Angeles, the mounts stampeded in unison, running five miles away before they could be halted and rounded up. Many large wolves had been spotted in the area, and Crespí speculated that the scent of the predators spooked the mules. Plentiful bear droppings also were found, another potential contributor to the mounts' skittishness. Before breaking camp the next morning, the men were rattled by a strong earthquake. By now, the perils of the trail were becoming familiar.

South of present-day San Luis Obispo on 12 May, the explorers came upon a large troop of bears, numbering forty to fifty. Five soldiers were sent out on horseback to hunt the brutes as they reared up from behind tall clumps of pampas grass. The troops returned after killing three bears—enough to feed the men for two weeks. The local Natives were awed by the lethality of Spanish muskets against the fearsome animals. The Indians "can do them no more harm with their arrows than as if they were to shoot candy at them," Crespí recorded.[10] The Indians helped skin the bears and were given a good share of the meat.

A week later, while crossing the rugged Santa Lucía Range, Portolá learned that two of the three runaway Christian Indians who had deserted the first expedition were living in a village nearby. He sent two soldiers, accompanied by Native guides, to the village. They returned with Raimundo, a married Indian from Mission San Ignacio in Baja California, and Benito, a single Indian from the same mission. The two reported that the third runaway, Feliciano, had died of natural causes and that they had buried his body on the beach. Portolá's men welcomed the runaways without reprisals, and the two Indians rejoined the expedition. At this same spot, the starving mule that had been abandoned on the earlier foray northward was returned by the locals. The mount was fattened and healthy, having received tender care from the mountain Natives.

On 24 May, thirty-eight days after departing San Diego, the expedition returned to Monterey after fording the Carmel River, where the spring runoff came up to the mules' bellies. There was no sign of the *San Antonio* in the harbor, even though the sea journey should have been completed in less time than the overland march. While the pack train was being unloaded, and even before dismounting, Portolá, Fages, and Crespí went to find the cross that had been erected on the beach during the first expedition. To their surprise, at the base of the cross was a heap of fresh mussels, which appeared to be a peace offering left by the Indians. The marker was surrounded by arrows driven into the ground—interpreted by the Spaniards as a sign of obeisance—along with darts decorated with feathers. Dangling from one dart was a string of fresh sardines, and from another a piece of meat. The sight of these offerings "melted our hearts," Crespí observed in his journal, "seeing that the heathens were in some fashion paying some kind of worship to the sacred wood."[11]

It was here that the trio became absolutely convinced this was indeed the Monterey Bay described by the early seafarers. Everywhere they looked, they saw signs of confirmation. For instance, Vizcaíno described the Point of Pines as having tall trees fit for making masts and spars for large ships. On the previous trip, Crespí had declared the pines to be too spindly for this purpose. Now, viewing the very same trees with a radically different mind-set, he and Portolá and Fages all agreed they were ideal for ships' masts. Whereas on the previous trip the bay's exposure to the open ocean was emphasized, engineer Costansó now declared it to be shielded "upon all sides, save the north-northwest, the only place where it is unprotected."[12]

Eight days later on Thursday, 31 May 1770, the *San Antonio* was spotted off the Point of Pines. The soldiers fired their muskets to signal the ship, and Captain Pérez responded with a salvo from his deck guns. That evening he brought the ship into the harbor and dropped anchor near the cross in six fathoms with a sandy bottom, in the approximate anchorage described by Vizcaíno, Cabrera Bueno, and others. Some of the crew were experiencing early symptoms of scurvy, and one seaman was near death.

The forty-six-day passage had been hard sailing, with bad weather and adverse winds driving the *San Antonio* 150 miles southward from San Diego before she could catch favorable gusts and make northerly headway. The day after the *San Antonio*'s arrival, Portolá, his officers, and Crespí went aboard and were served lunch. Serra announced that on the following Sunday he would celebrate a High Mass on the

FIGURE 2. Junípero Serra says Mass at Monterey to celebrate Spain's proclaiming possession of California. Oil painting by Léon Trousset (1877).
Courtesy of the Diocese of Monterey, Carmel Mission Basilica Museum.

shore as part of a solemn ceremony to take formal possession of Monterey Bay and its surrounding lands in the name of King Carlos III.

The sailors on the morning of 3 June built a chapel-like shelter of branches on the beach, with an altar set up inside. Placed on the altar was a stirring image of the Virgin Mary, given to Serra by Inspector General Gálvez for this specific purpose. The shelter was under the shade of a towering oak tree. In 1602 Vizcaíno's chaplain had said Mass on the beach under an oak tree, and Crespí was now sure that this was the very same tree. Nearby, bells were hung from tree branches. (The inventory of goods sent by land to California, signed by Gálvez the previous year, listed three copper bells.)[13] A wooden cross, blessed by Serra, was driven into the sand in front of the altar. Next to it fluttered the monarch's dark blue royal standard.

With the entire body of Spaniards and converted Indians in attendance, Serra in his finest silk vestments sang a High Mass, with Crespí and Costansó as his feeble choir (see figure 2). He began by chanting the *Veni Creator Spiritus* (Come Creator Spirit), an ancient Gregorian hymn to the Holy Spirit. To highlight the liturgy, the bells were rung, the soldiers' muskets were fired, and the cannons of the *San Antonio* thundered. Serra, celebrated as a gifted orator with a magnificent singing voice, preached a sermon. The High Mass was concluded with the singing of the *Te Deum*. Then Commander Portolá and his officers conducted a ceremony to take official possession of Monterey and the rest of California for Spain.

Ten days after concluding the ceremonies on the shore, Serra drafted another plaintive letter to his friend Palóu. Again he poured out his agony at being so secluded from the world. "It is just a year last month since I received my last letter from Christian people," he wrote, "so your Reverence can well imagine how hungry we are for news." In particular, Serra wanted to know how his old friends were faring. He pleaded with Palóu to send any word "as might bring comfort to us poor hermits so far separated from human society." Noting that he intended to send his only companion, Crespí, as the missionary to the planned third mission at present-day Ventura, he acknowledged that "it would be the greatest of all hardships for me to be located in a place from which the nearest friar is eighty leagues [208 miles] distant. I therefore beg your reverence to do what you can to shorten this period of cruel solitude" by dispatching more Franciscans to California.[14]

Word of the successful occupation of Monterey reached Mexico City on 10 August 1770. On 15 June, a courier on horseback had been dispatched from the newly founded Mission San Carlos Borromeo de Monterey, carrying a pouch with the formal documents of possession signed by Commander Portolá.[15] With a four-day rest stop in San Diego, the post rider made remarkable time on a solitary journey of over two thousand miles. This was a dangerous mission, because couriers traveling solo were vulnerable to Indian attack. The couriers were an especially rugged, independent breed, risking their lives as they rode alone for weeks at a time, often over unmapped trails in alien territory. Yet their role was essential to maintaining communications across the remote reaches of Spain's sprawling dominion.

Upon learning the news from California, Viceroy Marquis de Croix and Inspector General Gálvez ordered that the bells of the grand Metropolitan Cathedral of the Assumption of Mary be rung in celebration. The peals from the cathedral tower were answered by every other church bell in the city. Amid general jubilation, the viceroy and Gálvez received the grandees of the capital at the viceregal palace. After much toil and suffering, including the loss of scores of men, a new realm had been added to His Majesty's empire. Now the question was, could Spain's grasp on California be maintained in the face of pressing adversity?

CHAPTER FOUR

Beyond the Río Colorado

> At the same time that we are earnest to explore and learn all things, we require that all things be mysterious and unexplorable, that land and sea be indefinitely wild, unsurveyed and unfathomed by us because unfathomable.
>
> —Henry David Thoreau

Glimpsed at a distance from Interstate 19, Mission San Xavier del Bac rises like an ivory Taj Mahal on a limitless plateau of the Sonoran Desert, just south of present-day Tucson, Arizona. So striking is the sight that the mostly Tohono O'odham Indian parishioners call their church La Paloma Blanca del Desierto (the White Dove of the Desert). Founded on the middle Santa Cruz River by the pioneering Jesuit explorer Eusebio Francisco Kino in 1692, San Xavier del Bac has survived a tempestuous past as Native peoples and Spaniards clashed in fierce showdowns, filling the abandoned graveyards that today surround its grounds.

On 20 January 1768 Francisco Garcés, along with thirteen other Franciscan friars and a contingent of Spanish dragoons, set sail aboard the packet boat *San Carlos* from San Blas, Mexico's principal naval port on the Pacific coast. The ship's destination was Guaymas, more than five hundred miles to the north on the eastern shore of the Sea of Cortez. From Guaymas, Garcés was to journey by mule another three hundred miles northward to his new assignment, San Xavier del Bac, the northernmost outpost in New Spain. Sent to replace the Jesuit missionaries expelled by King Carlos III eleven months earlier, Garcés volunteered for San Xavier del Bac even though the station had been ransacked and burned repeatedly by Apache tribesmen, with the livestock stolen, Spanish soldiers slaughtered, and women and children taken into captivity. Remote San Xavier del Bac was one of the most hazardous posts in the Spanish realm.

As soon as the *San Carlos* put to sea, she encountered strong northwest headwinds that forced the captain to return to San Blas. He resumed the voyage after the winds shifted temporarily from the east, but the seas remained rough and many onboard became terribly seasick. To provide some relief, the *San Carlos* put in at the port of Mazatlán, about a third of the way to Guaymas. Six of Garcés's fellow friars, overcome by nausea and vomiting, abandoned the ship at the dock and made their way overland to Sonora. With Garcés back on board, the *San Carlos* finally reached its destination in May "after inexpressible hardships," in the words of the contemporary Franciscan chronicler Juan Domingo Arricivita.[1] The protracted passage lasted a grueling 104 days, mainly because the *San Carlos* was struggling against adverse winds and currents.

Garcés reached San Xavier del Bac on 30 June 1768 (see figure 3). At age thirty, he was ready to fulfill the missionary commitment he had made before sailing from Spain five years earlier. He found the northern reaches of Sonora inhospitable, but there is no sign in the historical record that he voiced any complaint. Because "of the dangers to which those expose themselves who go there," wrote Arricivita, "owing to the frequent invasions of the infidels, who, like savage and cruel enemies, wreak bloody havoc on whomsoever their mad rage encounters, the land remains desolate and uninhabited."[2]

Only two months after his arrival at San Xavier del Bac, Garcés set off on his first austere journey of discovery, letting it be known he did not intend to work alongside the Pápago Indians in the fields, as his Jesuit predecessors had done.[3] On 29 August 1768, accompanied by four Indians furnished by the Pápagos and a Native interpreter from the mission who wanted to become a Christian, Garcés departed in search of the Gila River, about 185 miles to the northwest. In his saddle bags were meager provisions—jerked beef, pinole (a drinkable mixture of cornmeal, water, and sugar), and a jar of ground sugar to distribute as treats to children. On the back of his mule he carried a trunk bearing the silk vestments and ornamental chalice and glass cruets used to say Mass. The Indians he encountered received him generously around their campfires at night, showing intense curiosity in his robes and hemp sandals. More important, they were impressed that he rode in such threatening territory without an escort of Spanish soldiers.

After returning to San Xavier del Bac the next month, Garcés was afflicted with a debilitating illness. For more than a day he lay in a coma-like state, unaware of his surroundings and shivering with chills. The isolated pueblo was virtually without medicines to help him. Fearing the padre was near death, the Franciscan in charge of Mission Guevavi, several miles to the south, moved Garcés there for better care. While he was recuperating, the Apaches struck San Xavier del Bac again. This time they murdered a Pápago chieftain and captured two Spanish soldiers, later torturing them to death. Leaving the town in ruins, the Apaches made off with the horses and cattle. Had Garcés not been moved to Guevavi, he almost certainly would have been slain in the Apache raid. This would not be his last rendezvous with his own mortality.

FIGURE 3. Founded in 1692, Mission San Xavier del Bac, south of present-day Tucson, was the most dangerous assignment on the northern frontier because of repeated Apache raids.
Photo dated 1902, courtesy of Library of Congress.

In the autumn of 1770 a smallpox epidemic spread throughout the Indian villages of northern Sonora. On 18 October Garcés set out again from San Xavier del Bac to administer to the sick and baptize as many as possible before they died. Riding at night under a bare sliver of moon to dodge the daytime heat, he was welcomed in the Native communities he had visited two years earlier. Many of the Indians were suffering from chills and fever, appearing to Garcés as mere skeletons. In one village on the Gila River he baptized twenty-two dying Natives, and in another he went to the aid of a sick boy whose groans beckoned the padre. By this time he was able to preach in the local language. Most of the Indian men went about naked, prompting some to examine Garcés's robes and ask whether he was a man or a woman, and whether he was married.

The following year, 1771, Garcés received permission from his religious superiors to undertake a much more ambitious expedition, this one to the Colorado River and beyond in order to reconnoiter potential sites for new missions that would link Sonora to the Pacific coast. The three fledgling missions recently established in California by Junípero Serra were struggling to survive on the paltry provisions delivered by sea. A more robust supply route by land was urgently needed. But no one was sure exactly just how far it was to the ocean, because the Spaniards did not yet have an accurate way to measure longitude—distances on the earth's surface from east to west. Even worse, they knew that reaching California meant crossing a waterless desert, something no European had ever done. Then there was the matter of fording the mighty Colorado, which many believed would require a fleet of boats. Some thought the river crossing was simply impossible to achieve with a mule train.

In keeping with his modus operandi, Garcés resolved to make the trip essentially alone, without an armed escort or the company of any other white men. "By going alone and relying only on the support of divine providence," he recorded in his diary, "one is guided without fear, and the people one meets are more inclined to give information about *rancherías* [Indian settlements], springs, and roads. It is true that in this way the minister does not carry so much authority, but thus he will be less conceited, more charitable and humble."[4]

He struck out on horseback directly west on 8 August 1771, at the height of the summer heat, accompanied by a single Pápago, a respected tribal elder. At that moment the padre's health was not good. His legs were swollen and he had considered leaving San Xavier del Bac to seek a cure closer to civilization. Instead, he embarked into unknown lands where measles and smallpox were rampant, equipped with scant food and only his outfit for saying Mass. (He later praised the "fish, mice, and lizards" that he ate with the Indians.)[5] Juan Bautista de Anza, captain of the nearby Tubac presidio, strongly opposed this foray into dangerous Indian territory. He, too, was contemplating an expedition across the Colorado but did not yet have approval from the viceroy in Mexico City. Arricivita asserted that Anza "resented" Garcés's wanderings. In spite of this, the two explorers later become great comrades.[6]

As he pushed on toward the Colorado, Garcés stopped at Indian villages to preach around the campfire and baptize those on the verge of death. Given the inflated daytime temperatures, the Natives often sat up most of the night talking in a circle around the fire. They warned Garcés not to go near the river because the Yuma Indians who lived on the east side scalped strangers, and the Quiquima Indians on the west side were just as hostile. The friendly tribesmen gave him a jug, likely a hollowed out gourd, to carry water in as he rode from one watering spot in search of the next. Eight days after leaving San Xavier del Bac, his reluctant Indian guide deliberately smashed the water container and declared they could go no farther. Garcés insisted on continuing, telling the Indian that the river could not be far away. While the padre was taking a siesta, the guide stole a horse and returned to his village.

This left Garcés to travel on alone. For two days and nights he wandered, unsure of where he was. Watering holes were scarce. There was nothing to forage from the sterile land. After riding for hours under the stars, he stopped at daybreak to rest. Unexpectedly, his dehydrated mount ran away, the saddle still on its back. Now Garcés had no choice but to continue on foot. He followed his compass to the west until he found himself tramping through marshy quagmires that at some places were impassable. At sunset the next day he spotted his horse. "Doubtless my weak frame was not equal to this labor," he wrote in his diary, "and I found my horse, which came through a different path than mine through the marshes."[7]

The next day Garcés stumbled upon a melon patch cultivated by the Yumas, who planted their crops in the muddy Colorado flood plain after the river receded from the spring snowmelt. As he gorged himself on the melons, fourteen armed Yuma men appeared. Rather than scalp him, they offered to build two suitable rafts to ferry him across the river. This was a stroke of good fortune because Garcés could not swim. At that moment he was still not certain he had reached the Colorado, because the expansive marshlands along its banks were thick with forests of ten-foot-tall tule reeds and broad lagoons that looked more like lakes than a river.

Perhaps to his surprise, the Yumas shared with Garcés their maize, watermelons, edible greens, mesquite pods, and bread made mostly of seeds. In addition to improving his digestion, the food helped restore his health, he believed. The Yumas staged for him dances marked by a violent gait and merry singing, keeping time with a hollow gourd filled with pebbles.

More than once Yuma women were presented to him for sex. When he declined, the women "inquired of me through ugly motions whether I did not have relations with women as their men did," he recorded. "Fixing my glance upon the crucifix, which I carried on my breast, and raising it to heaven, I indicated to them that in this respect I did not live like them. This resulted in their showing greater affection for me and greater respect for a type of man that was unfamiliar to them."[8]

After the Indians ferried him across the river, Garcés rode on alone to the south and then to the north and northwest, still not sure whether he had crossed the Colorado. After a few days of solitary rambling, he reached the foot of a mountain range, prompting him to turn back to the east and return to the river. At some point during his time among the Yumas, who lived mostly on the east side of the river at the strategic spot where the Gila flowed into the Colorado, Garcés encountered a petty chieftain whose Indian name was Olleyquotequiebe. This Native term meant "one who wheezes." The Yuma leader warmed to the padre and acted as an accommodating host. He later would be given the Spanish name Salvador Palma. Neither man knew it at the time, but their incipient relationship held great portent for Spain's gathering conquest of California.

At the river Garcés gained the encouraging intelligence that the Yumas maintained regular contact with the Kumeyaay, their linguistic cousins on the Pacific coast. This meant that traversing the desert was not an impossibility after all. In fact, the ocean was a march of only seven days away, Garcés learned.

Some of the Yumas wore earrings made of seashells acquired in trade with the coast. What was more, they had some familiarity with the Franciscan mission at San Diego, founded two years earlier. Pointing to the west, the Natives talked about items the Spaniards on the coast possessed—the garments and boots of the fathers, the mysterious compass needle, the magnifying lenses used to start fires. This tempted Garcés to press on to the Pacific, but he demurred because he did not want to prolong his absence from San Xavier del Bac. Already there were rumors circulating back in Sonora that Garcés had been slain by the Yumas, a very plausible scenario. Captain Anza in particular voiced his concerns, perhaps to reinforce his previous warnings that the padre's expedition was ill advised.

On 15 October 1771, Garcés left the river on a 250-mile ride to present himself at Caborca, a principal Spanish settlement in northern Sonora, where he could report his findings. The trip required him to cross an especially arduous stretch of the Sonoran Desert, where watering holes were almost entirely lacking. The place was later branded El Camino del Diablo (The Devil's Highway). On 27 October he reached his destination and made a final entry in his diary: "Little by little, eating very delicious organ cactus fruit, I arrived at Caborca, girded (about the waist) with my handkerchief, for having run short of rope I had used my (habit) cord, an old one, which was soon used up."[9] He also gave thanks to God that the inflammation in his legs had disappeared. Upon his return to his post at San Xavier del Bac, two hundred miles north of Caborca, Garcés had been away for two months and twenty days. "[A]lthough he had met with perplexing troubles and difficulties," concluded Arricivita, "either because of harsh treatment by the Indians, going astray on barren roads, the fording of rivers, the sterility of the land, the anguish from thirst and hunger, the unwholesomeness of the food, or many other desperate dangers, nevertheless his upright purpose brought him out unscathed."[10]

Garcés had now flung open the door to California, a reality that was not lost on Anza, who sought out the padre to learn every detail of his foray across the Colorado. By fording the river on a raft built for him by friendly Indians, Garcés had shown that the river was not an insurmountable barrier to supply trains or even settlers traveling overland from Sonora to the missions on the Pacific. The friendships he had just begun with the Yumas held the promise of establishing a permanent Spanish crossing at the confluence of the Gila and Colorado Rivers. Indeed, the Yumas under Salvador Palma seemed to plead for Spanish settlements in their land, if for no other reason than to provide some protection from the bloodlust of their enemies, the Apaches.

In his official report, Garcés stated his belief that the route he discovered west of the Colorado would ultimately have led him to the presidio of Monterey, the newly established capital of California. From his desk in Mexico City, Viceroy Antonio María Bucareli y Ursúa called Garcés's discoveries "creditable" and "important." He added: "The spiritual zeal and apostolic labors of Father Garcés not only are worthy of praise, but promise the rich fruit of an abundant harvest of souls willing to submit themselves to the pale of our sacred religion."[11] At that moment neither Garcés nor Bucareli could foresee that forging an overland route to unite Sonora and the California coast would prove far more difficult—and bloody—than simply surveying the path and befriending the Indians.

CHAPTER FIVE

Overland to California

> This is the greatest factor: the way in which the expedition is equipped, the way in which every difficulty is foreseen, and precautions taken for meeting or avoiding it. Victory awaits him who has everything in order—luck, people call it.
>
> —Roald Amundsen

Deep in the reclusive badlands of the Yuha Desert, just north of the U.S.-Mexican border, are the remnants of a long-abandoned watering spot. The old well occupies a desolate site in the bottom of a dusty desert wash, miles from the nearest paved road, surrounded by a barren landscape of sand and slabs of black rock. On this range there is almost no vegetation, only a smattering of spindly ocotillo and stunted mesquite trees, not a speck of shade. The ground is marked with a residue of white salt, a symptom of the lifeless terrain. Footprints of desert kangaroo rats are visible in the sand, but larger, less hearty fauna find too little to survive on here. A broken-down wooden marker, weathered by the sun and unceasing desert breeze, tells the significance of this place, which bears the incongruously poetic name of Santa Rosa de las Lajas (Saint Rose of the Flat Rocks). It was here on Tuesday, 8 March 1774, that Captain Juan Bautista de Anza and Francisco Garcés reached a turning point in their campaign to open an overland route from Mexico to the fledgling Spanish missions in California.

Their story begins in an outburst of violence on 2 December 1773, when Apache warriors fell upon the horse corral at the Tubac presidio, on the Santa Cruz River south of modern Tucson, Arizona. By the time the Apaches' war whoops had faded away, they had stolen 130 mounts and pack animals.[1] As commander of the garrison, Anza had stockpiled the steeds to equip his imminent expedition across the desert from Sonora in present-day Mexico to the Pacific coast of California, a venture into sterile territory that no other European had ever attempted. Now, his planned thrust was upended.

For more than a century, the Apaches had been fierce opponents of Spanish settlement all along the incendiary northern frontier of New Spain. Raiding livestock—horses, mules, cattle, oxen—belonging to either Europeans or other

Indians was a traditional part of the Apache way of life, a mainstay of their economy. As a consequence, the Apaches were on hostile terms with most other tribes of the region. In fact, the persistent strife across the borderlands was attributable almost entirely to the Apaches' warlike ways.

Generally nomadic, the Apaches had migrated in previous centuries from what is now Alaska into the heartland of North America. Apaches of the Southern Plains lived primarily by hunting buffalo until they were forced westward and southward by the Comanches. They were among the first Native Americans in the Southwest to become skilled horsemen after the arrival of the Spaniards.

Time and again they bedeviled the Spanish soldiers with lucrative lightning strikes against economic targets. Anza himself had spent most of his military career fighting the Apaches, as had his father, who was slaughtered in an Apache ambush when Anza was only three years old. Born in a frontier town in Sonora, Anza was a thirty-eight-year-old, third-generation military officer, having begun his career as a soldier at the age of fifteen. Descended from Basque pioneers, he already had a reputation as a tenacious Indian fighter. A few years earlier, in an engagement to suppress the marauding Seris in the high country of Sonora, he was struck in the face with a glancing blow from a poison-tipped arrow.[2] Although his cheek bled heavily, he recovered without difficulty. In his campaigns against the Indians to date, Anza had been wounded no fewer than four times.[3]

Because of the Apache assault at Tubac, the commander now was forced to delay his departure and also to redraw his planned route to California toward a more southerly course. This would enable him to bypass Apache strongholds to the north and rebuild his *cavallada*, or horse herd, by collecting fresh mounts from Spanish settlements along the way. With a new date of 8 January 1774 set for the expedition's embarkation, the Apaches struck Tubac again with lethality on 2 January, making off with many of the best remaining mounts and killing a Spanish sergeant and some muleteers.[4] Undeterred, Anza began his march across the desert on schedule this time, determined to make up his livestock losses at other Spanish missions and presidios, and to reach California before the heat of summer made the trail impassable.

The need for a supply route by land to the isolated Pacific coast was glaring. The five missions founded thus far in California were barely sustainable by sea. Most were in sorry shape due to a lack of basic provisions and equipment; at some missions food was being rationed and hunger was an ever-present threat to survival. In Mexico City many officials worried that the inchoate California establishments were on the brink of collapse. From San Diego to Monterey, the only means of supply from the core of New Spain was a small flotilla of His Majesty's sailing ships—a very tenuous lifeline. A supply packet normally reached the missions only once a year.

As underscored three years earlier by the unexplained disappearance of the supply ship *San José*, sea travel along the California coast was a dangerous undertaking. Sailing against the prevailing winds and currents on the northbound passage presented a particular challenge. It was not uncommon for supply packets to spend three or four months at sea just to get from the port of San Blas on Mexico's western coast to the capital of California at Monterey. This was longer than a typical Atlantic crossing. During such protracted passages scurvy was yet another deadly hazard. Beyond that, ships could transport only a fraction of what a mule train could carry. And there was no room on the vessels for the livestock and large numbers of settlers, including women and children, needed to populate California and strengthen Spain's hold on its new realm in the face of rumored Russian incursions.

Thus a great deal was at stake in Anza's impending expedition. For decades many Spaniards had believed the vast Sonoran Desert was an insurmountable barrier to overland travel to California. Very little was known about what lay west of the Colorado River, except for a broad field of three-hundred-foot-high sand dunes barring the way. Even east of the river the route was so arid and inhospitable that in the years ahead numerous travelers perished of thirst. Apart from the scarcity of water, oppressive temperatures, formidable mountain ranges, and rebellious tribes, there was great uncertainty about just how far it was to the Pacific coast. Many putative experts overestimated the distance by a considerable amount. Anza's plunge across this unforgiving terrain would confront all of these unknowns squarely.

As early as 2 May 1772, Anza wrote to the viceroy in Mexico City seeking permission for an exploratory foray from Sonora to Monterey, in actuality a trek of about a thousand miles. In 1737 Anza's father had proposed a similar mission but failed to gain support. First Anza the son consulted closely with Father Garcés. In 1771 the restless Franciscan had crossed the Colorado alone, on a poor horse and provisioned with only a bit of chocolate, cornmeal mush, and jerked beef in his saddle bags, and scouted part of the route to the coast. Although of vastly disparate backgrounds—one a soldier's soldier, the other a humble man of the cross—the two men formed a powerful team in advocating for the venture. Both were convinced that the perceived obstacles to reaching California were inflated. To buttress his case, Anza assured Viceroy Antonio María de Bucareli y Ursúa: "I will not spare any labor to succeed, and if it should be necessary I will sacrifice myself in the enterprise."[5]

As always, Anza's request had to go up an elaborate chain of command. In time, it was approved by the viceroy and his council of advisers in Mexico City, then forwarded to Don Julián de Arriaga, minister of the Indies in Madrid. Arriaga briefed King Carlos III and shared with him the many reports sent from Mexico City by the viceroy endorsing the expedition. On 12 May 1773, from his sumptuous palace at Aranjuez on the Tagus River south of Madrid, the king approved Anza's preliminary plan to open a road to California. Such were the limitations of frontier communications that, by the time the king gave his final approval, handed down at his royal hunting lodge at El Pardo, Anza was already replenishing his train at the well of Santa Rosa de las Lajas, having embarked from Tubac a full two months earlier.[6]

Just a few days before his departure, Anza received unexpected news from Salvador Palma, chief of the Yuma tribe, known today as Quechans. The Indian leader's original name, Olleyquotequiebe, was translated roughly as "wheezy," perhaps because he had respiratory problems. Upon his baptism as a Christian, he was given the name of Salvador Carlos Antonio Palma. The Yumas' homeland was located at the confluence of the Gila and Colorado Rivers, the strategic ford on the desert route from Sonora to California, at present-day Yuma, Arizona. For some time, Anza had been cultivating good relations with Chief Palma and his people. Without their support, the incipient overland trail would be blocked. For his part, Palma was beguiled by the Spaniards, using his close ties with them to enhance his standing among his own tribal members.

Palma had recently arrived at the Altar presidio southwest of Tubac, accompanied by another Native, Sebastián Tarabal, who was no stranger to the Spanish outposts in California. A Cochimí Indian born on the Baja Peninsula south of San Diego, Sebastián had been living with his pregnant wife, María Dolores, at Mission Santa Gertrudis in 1769 when Junípero Serra passed through collecting Native volunteers for the Portolá expedition. In the summer of 1773, Sebastián and María Dolores were living at Mission San Gabriel near present-day Los Angeles.

As a baptized Christian, Sebastián was obligated under the padres' stringent rules to remain at the mission. Leaving without permission to visit family members in the wild was punishable by flogging if a runaway was captured by Spanish soldiers and brought back. All the same, Sebastián decided to flee mission life. Like so many other indigenous people, Sebastián, then about age twenty-eight, may simply have become disenchanted with the drudgery and regimented, sedentary ways imposed by the Franciscans. In October 1773 he struck out from Mission San Gabriel with his wife and an unmarried male relative, likely his brother-in-law. Their destination was the Yuma tribal lands along the Colorado, where Sebastián may have had acquaintances.

The three fugitives traveled southeast into the scorched desert, unsure of the route to the river or of the locations of watering spots along the way. When they reached the trackless sand dunes near what is now the U.S–Mexican border in Imperial County, California, they roamed lost for three days without water. Sebastián's wife and their companion died of dehydration. Sebastián alone made it to the Colorado River, where he came to the attention of Chief Palma, and ultimately emerged at the Altar presidio. Perhaps eager to ingratiate himself with Anza, Palma delivered the rugged runaway from Mission San Gabriel back into Spanish hands.

Anza recognized immediately what a stroke of good fortune this was. Here was a plucky deserter who had just found his way across the unmapped wasteland that Anza proposed to traverse in the opposite direction. Rather than punish Sebastián, as mission regulations provided, Anza enlisted him as a guide to help lead the expedition to Mission San Gabriel. Not entirely trusting Father Garcés's knowledge as a guide, the commander decided on the spot, according to Serra, "to follow wherever the Indian Sebastián might wish to lead them."[7] This meant that the route proposed by Garcés would be abandoned in favor of the course recommended by Sebastián. The enigmatic Native now had a new nickname among the Spaniards—El Peregrino (The Pilgrim).

On Saturday, 8 January 1774, Anza was ready to launch his caravan. In the morning, amid colorful pageantry so characteristic of the Spanish crown, a solemn High Mass was chanted in the chapel of the Tubac presidio to invoke divine assistance for the expedition. Musket volleys were fired, and there were many shouts of "Viva!" to celebrate an auspicious start to the journey.[8] At one o'clock in the afternoon, the march began.

Along with the commander and Sebastián, the company consisted of thirty-four men, including twenty volunteer soldiers and a corporal from the Tubac garrison; five muleteers; a special courier named Juan Bautista Valdés, sent by the viceroy to bring back to Mexico City prompt news of the expedition; an Indian trained as a carpenter; a Native interpreter; two personal servants for Anza; and two chaplain/diarists. The viceroy stipulated that Father Garcés was to accompany the expedition because he was familiar with part of the country. Dispatched as Garcés's traveling companion was Fray Juan Díaz, a thirty-six-year-old Franciscan born in Seville, Spain. Díaz was known for his strict adherence to Franciscan rules and his skill as a preacher.[9] Garcés and Díaz did not know it at the time, but within a few years their fate would be inextricably bound in martyrdom.

The convoy was provisioned with thirty-five packloads of supplies, including food, munitions, tobacco, shovels and picks for digging wells, cooking implements, tents, and other equipment. Sixty-five cattle on the hoof were to be driven behind the mule train as food along the way. Anza also logged 140 saddle animals, but this figure included an unspecified number that he hoped to obtain early in the march at the mission and pueblo of Caborca, a settlement of ninety families in the Altar River Valley of Sonora.

On 20 January, after weathering two days of rain and steady snowfall in the high desert, the plodding train reached Caborca, about 160 miles southwest of Tubac, where Anza halted for two days, hoping to round up additional horses and mules and leave behind some mounts that already were worn out. The commander's expectations were dashed as soon as he saw what saddle animals were available. "Two small droves of mules were shown to me," he recorded in his journal, "but whereas I had flattered myself that I should leave this pueblo amply supplied with the mules which I needed, I saw only stacks of bones. . . . Although this was to me a matter of great sorrow, because of the lack which I might experience on a long journey, I yielded to the situation since there was no other recourse and no means of remedy."[10] Anza collected only three more mounts. As a small consolation, a muleteer dispatched to the nearby silver mining camp of Cieneguilla returned with badly needed shoes for the animals.

The next leg of the march to the northwest toward the Colorado River was through exceedingly dry, treeless terrain inhabited by the impoverished Pápago Indians. Twenty-three years earlier, they had risen in bloody rebellion against the Jesuit missionaries here. In his journal Díaz described the nomadic Pápagos as "extremely independent and liberty-loving. They care nothing for the conveniences of life which civilized men so much love, although they are extremely fond of repose. They lack almost completely a sense of honor and shame, which is so fundamental to civilized life. They are ignorant of eternal truths." Garcés, always more charitable to the Natives, praised the intelligence and industriousness of the Pápagos, while noting that in their harsh environment they often had too little to eat. To supplement their meager diets, they ate crawling, yellowish-green worms and dried them for later consumption.[11]

Anza followed old Indian footpaths along El Camino del Diablo, sometimes marching under the stars to close the long gaps between watering holes. At one point, the animals had to travel for forty-six hours, over fifty-four miles of trail, without a drop to drink and only some mesquite sprouts for forage. Periodic stretches of sand dunes exhausted the mounts and the cattle. Garcés grumbled in his diary that Anza was blindly following a very onerous path sought by the Indian guide Sebastián. The friar wanted to pursue a more northerly course. "Although when seen at a distance," wrote Garcés, "it looks like a beautiful and vast plain that these sand wastes occupy, certain it is that it would be difficult to find a worse piece of country."[12]

On Saturday 5 February, the expedition stopped at a poor watering spot that Anza called El Agua Escondida (the Secluded Water). The train was now in present-day Arizona, east of the Colorado River and south of the Gila River. The flow from the well dug by the soldiers was so spotty that only the mounts and pack animals could be watered by nightfall. The thirsty cattle had to wait until the next day.

While camped at El Agua Escondida Anza was approached by a Christianized Pápago named Luís, who had just returned on foot from the Colorado River with a disturbing warning from Chief Palma of the Yumas. A renegade faction of the tribe upstream was hatching a scheme to ambush the expedition, kill Anza and the two padres, and steal the livestock and other valuables. Palma stressed that he remained loyal to the Spaniards, but he was unable to dissuade the Yuma dissenters from their planned attack. The ringleader was a rival tribal leader called Pablo by the Spaniards.

In a later declaration, Palma explained that rumors of the advancing expedition, with men under arms, "greatly disturbed [my] people, and, fearful of some attack, they resolved to receive [Anza] with weapons in their hands, and to risk their lives rather than permit themselves to be trodden under foot. . . . When I found them intractable I saw myself under the necessity of declaring that in spite of them I should defend the Spaniards with only those who might remain obedient to me; and though not a soul should follow me I alone would place myself at their side, even if it cost me my life."[13] Garcés, lacking as usual any sense of fear for his own safety, offered to go ahead alone and meet with the conspirators in a bid to pacify them. The commander sensibly rejected this as too dangerous.

The last thing Anza wanted was to engage in hostilities with the Yumas, even though he had confidence in his musket-trained troops to prevail in an armed clash. After conferring with Garcés and Díaz, Anza decided to send for Palma by dispatching his messenger back to the river on horseback, with the promise of the horse and other presents if he returned with the Yuma chief for a rendezvous in the desert. Meanwhile, the scarcity of water and pasturage at El Agua Escondida meant that Anza had to push on toward the Colorado.

On the trail two days later, in the middle of more difficult dunes, Anza encountered the returning Pápago messenger and a delegation of nine Yuma tribesmen mounted bareback on good mares. The Natives were barefoot, naked, armed with bows and a few arrows, and carrying firebrands to keep their exposed bodies warm in the winter chill. Yuma men considered it unmanly to cover their genitals, as their women did with willow-bark skirts and rabbit furs. Palma was not among the group, because he was temporarily away hunting. The headman of the group assured Anza that the unrest among the Yumas had been quelled and that he could proceed safely.

By the time the explorers reached their campsite at the junction of the Colorado and the Gila, they were surrounded by hundreds of welcoming Natives—men, women, children—who threw fistfuls of dirt into the air to show their friendship. "[E]very minute [there] assembled more people of both sexes, who the longer they looked at our persons, our clothes, and other things used by us, the more they marveled," Anza wrote in his journal. Even the usually tolerant Garcés complained that the curious Yumas, especially the women, had much too keen a desire to touch the Spanish men. "One of the laughable things," he added in his diary, "is to see their skill and slyness in stealing and taking things with their feet, which they use as well as we manage our hands."[14]

Late in the afternoon, Chief Palma reached Anza's camp and the two embraced in fellowship. To reward Palma's loyalty and underscore his allegiance to Spain, Anza with great ceremony before the assembled tribe hung around the chief's neck a red ribbon bearing a coin with the image of King Carlos III. (Several denominations of Spanish reales bore the sovereign's likeness.) The medal was a symbol of the authority conferred upon Palma by the king, Anza declared. It also was aimed at establishing the Yumas as loyal vassals of the crown. Rising to the occasion, Palma asked Anza for his cane, another conspicuous symbol of authority, and brandished it in his hands as he harangued his people about the importance of living in peace with the Spaniards.

On the morning of 8 February Palma led the expedition to a crossing point on the Gila River, in anticipation of fording the larger Colorado the next day. The ford on the Gila was a short distance upstream from where the two bodies of water converged. At this spot the river was about 125 yards wide and 4 feet deep. This was the height of the dry season, about two months before the start of the annual snowmelt.

Anza ordered the pack train unloaded so that the cargo could be carried across by the soldiers. But, by this time, descending upon the scene were about two hundred naked Yuma men, their faces painted a ferocious red and black. Palma proposed that the strongest and tallest of his tribesmen wade across the stream with the cargo on their heads—something they obviously were experienced at doing. The Yumas were noticeably taller people than other desert tribes. Díaz recorded in his diary that he measured the height of one man at six foot three inches, a relative giant among indigenous men of North America.[15]

Not entirely sure he could trust the Indians not to make off with his supplies, Anza first rode across the river on his horse, accompanied by half of his armed soldiers; the other half were left to guard the provisions and equipment on the first bank. Then the horse herd, pack mules, and cattle were driven across, followed by the eager Yumas balancing heavy loads on their heads. The Native men had voluminous heads of hair, which they piled up on top and dusted with a mud powder the color of lustrous silver. To protect their coiffures, they slept sitting up all night.

Not for the first time, Garcés's inability to swim and his dread of flowing water became apparent. While every other member of the company forded the Gila on horseback, Garcés cajoled three or four Yuma men into ferrying him across in their arms as he floated on his back. In his journal, he remarked how large the river was, neglecting to report that it was shallow enough to wade across.[16]

Once the fording operation was completed at three o'clock in the afternoon, Anza lined up the Natives and passed out gifts of glass beads and tobacco. While in the process, he was accosted by an Indian from downriver who groaned and wailed pitifully, beseeching the Spaniards to come and witness the cremation of his recently deceased father. For Anza, there simply was no time for that.

The next morning the same procedures were followed to ford the Colorado River, only this time the Spaniards were aided by what Anza estimated to be a throng of six hundred Yuma men and many additional women and children. The Colorado was much broader than the Gila. The commander measured it to be nearly six hundred feet across, but about the same depth as the Gila. A short distance downstream, where the Gila entered, the Colorado was much wider still, and this was the driest period of the year. Due to the intrusion of seawater from the nearby Sea of Cortez, the river was a little salty.

"We all succeeded in crossing on horseback without wetting anything of importance," the commander recorded. He overlooked soaking-wet Garcés, who commented matter-of-factly in his diary: "I crossed the Colorado River in the arms of Indians, because I did not trust the horse."[17] This marked the first time the king's armed forces had crossed the river. In typical Castilian celebration, Anza ordered a salute of musket volleys. The Indians were impressed by this spectacle, which they had never seen before. But the sudden roar of firearms frightened some so badly that they threw themselves to the ground.

At eight o'clock in the morning on Thursday, 10 February 1774, Anza raised his train and began a southward march down the west side of the Colorado, intent on getting around the towering sand dunes that lay directly to the west. This impenetrable erg, or dune field, was forty-five miles long and six miles wide. It lay along a northwest–southeast axis and was formed by windblown sands from an ancient, dried-up lake. Once again, Anza's company had more help than it wanted from the Yuma tribesmen, who followed along by the hundreds, with five or six men volunteering to drive each animal, and others clearing brush ahead of the train. In camp that night Anza passed out more glass beads, tobacco, and a beef steer that was too worn out to continue on the trail. After dark one of the many hangers-on stole a lance and an ax. When Anza reported the theft to Palma, who also was traveling with the party, the chief promised to punish the offender, recover the items, and give them back on the expedition's return trip.

On Saturday, 12 February 1774, the expedition camped on the shore of a lake formed by the overflow of the Colorado during summer floods. Anza named it La Laguna de Santa Olaya. It was situated a few miles south of the current U.S.–Mexican border. There was plenty of freshwater and pasturage for the livestock. Neither Sebastián nor Garcés was familiar with this stretch of unexplored trail, which stirred some unease. A Yuma offered his assistance as guide until Sebastián, whom Anza was counting on, could get his bearings.

After both friars said Mass early the next morning, Palma rained tears as he said goodbye. This was the southern limit of his territory, and the Yumas were on bad terms with the Cajuenches downstream. In an emotional farewell to Anza, Palma promised to have waiting for him on his return a raft made of strong timbers to ferry him across the Colorado, which by then would be many miles wide at flood stage.

Throughout the day's march the expedition found only two pools of dirty brackish water unfit to drink, and no pasturage. The loaded mules began to weaken and struggle. Anza drove the train until sunset, when a free-flowing stream of bad water was found. Sebastián and Garcés disagreed which direction to follow in order to reach an adequate watering spot. Early the next morning the Yuma guide turned back, not wanting to enter the land of his enemies. This day's trek was truncated because of the dearth of good water and forage. Ominously, despite the short march, the pack mules "arrived in a most disastrous condition," Anza noted in his diary.[18]

Departing at seven o'clock the next morning without any local guides, the caravan bogged down after only a few miles when the trail disappeared into dense, shifting dunes. The already exhausted mules, heavily burdened with cargo, could barely continue. Making matters worse, as Anza forthrightly acknowledged, "we became lost entirely, because the wind moves the dunes about and carries the sand in various directions."[19] Amid this dicey predicament, Sebastián was just as lost as the commander.

Recognizing the deteriorating state of his pack train, Anza proposed that half the supplies be left behind at Santa Olaya with a contingent of soldiers and one of the padres. The commander would press ahead with a scaled-down train and meet up with the rear company on his return to the Colorado. Garcés raised strong objections to this division of forces. He was confident that not far ahead was a Cajuenche village he had visited in 1771. There was an abundance of water and pasturage there. In his earlier wanderings Garcés had named the place San Jacome.

Despite his own misgivings, Anza went along with Garcés—for the moment. The march was resumed over an expanse of deep sand, with steep dunes wearing out the pack animals. Some of the soldiers now had to proceed on foot because their mounts were too tired to carry them. This meant that the men, too, were fighting fatigue. At sunset Anza called a halt. The oasis of San Jacome was nowhere in sight.

With Anza's blessing, Garcés set out on his own in the darkness to find the Indian village. He took with him Father Díaz and two soldiers. The absence of moonlight on this date hampered their nighttime search. The party returned hours later without success. Still convinced that San Jacome was close by, Garcés struck out yet again under the stars, accompanied by the only five soldiers whose horses were in good enough shape to withstand the trip. It was after midnight when they came back. The sought-after watering spot had not been found. A lesser commander might have rebuked Garcés for his shortcomings as a scout. But Anza stated generously in his diary that "in lands little traveled and without prominent landmarks, like this, it is not strange that one should make a mistake." The company passed the night without water or pasturage.[20]

Assessing his situation, Anza concluded that if ample water and forage were not found the next day, which he thought doubtful, the entire party might perish. It was time to reverse course. At first light the next morning, 16 February, he began to retrace his steps to the previous bivouac of Santa Olaya, where the animals and men could be replenished. More and more of his soldiers were now marching on foot because their mounts were exhausted. Although the train moved at a very slow pace on this day, three riding animals and two cattle died. Many other animals had become sick from feeding on a foul plant that was plentiful in places where there was no grass. The noxious weed caused the animals to give off a bad odor and slobber heavily with a dark drool. Camp was made that afternoon at a poor well, which the men aptly called Pozo de las Angustías (Well of Tribulations).

On the next day's trek, four more horses perished. Most of the company was advancing wearily on foot. The train now was staggered out all along the trail instead of staying in tight formation. The leading elements finally reached Santa Olaya on Saturday, 19 February. The last of the pack animals did not arrive until 24 February. Others had died along the way. It was 2 March before the expedition had recuperated enough to resume its journey. Anza had squandered a full seventeen days roaming lost in the dunes, retracing his path, and reviving his caravan.

As soon as he reached Santa Olaya, Anza in near desperation sent a Native messenger to Chief Palma, asking that he come and meet with the commander. Because Palma was once again away from his tribe, another Yuma leader arrived in Anza's camp. The Spaniards were not aware of it at the time, but this was none other than Pablo, the dissident tribesman who had plotted to attack the expedition. Because Pablo was homely, the Spaniards called him El Capitán Feo (The Ugly Chief). Pablo returned to Anza one of two mules that had wandered off or been stolen from the convoy. The Indian declared that a Native from another tribe, the Quiquimas, had butchered the second mule for food. Pablo had taken revenge on the thief, he claimed, by killing his wife with an arrow. He offered the very arrow to the commander. This horrified Anza, who remarked in his diary that it showed "the little weight and scruple attached by these unhappy people to killing one another."[21] Garcés, who intuitively understood the Natives better than other Spaniards did, scoffed at the whole tale as a hoax by Pablo. He noted that the Indian was wearing around his neck the shoes of the slain mule, suggesting that he, rather than the Quiquima, was the real culprit.

While the Spanish pathfinders rested for more than a week and the animals grazed in green pastures, the expedition was surrounded night and day by inquisitive Yuma tribesmen, including eventually Chief Palma. To pass the time, a soldier played a violin, much to the delight of the Indians. Before long the Yuma women were dancing *seguidillas*, Castilian folk dances in triple time, which the soldiers taught them.

For a reward of a few glass beads and tobacco, the Natives learned to greet the Spaniards by parroting: "Ave María, Viva Dios y El Rey!" (Hail Mary, Long Live God and the King!). Father Díaz used these days to preach to the Natives and instruct them in the teachings of the church. He taught them to pronounce the names María and Jesús, and how to cross themselves as good Catholics did. "Some of them learned how to make the sign of the cross, although very imperfectly," he wrote in his diary.[22] His proselytizing took with some of the Indians, who voluntarily delivered their aboriginal religious idols to be smashed to pieces by the padre.

In the meantime Garcés received permission from Anza go on his own six-day reconnaissance mission lower down the Colorado River. Garcés had visited these same tribes three years earlier and he hoped to learn from them vital information about watering holes on the planned route to the coast. He set out with three Indians and a small store of glass beads and tobacco as gifts. As was his practice, he carried almost no food, trusting instead on the tribes downstream to feed him.

On his trip he was recognized by many of the Natives he had met on his earlier travels. On 26 February the Indians persuaded him to cross over to the east side of the river, and some old men built a raft for him. As he floated along, with the raft guided by strong Native swimmers, Garcés looked approvingly at the fields of wheat that lined the fertile banks. The next day he recrossed the Colorado and headed back to Santa Olaya. By the time he arrived at the encampment, after traveling all through the night under a waxing moon, he was on foot because his horse had given out.

Upon his return, Garcés learned that Anza had decided to leave most of his supplies, including the cattle and many pack animals, along with four muleteers and three soldiers, under the care of Chief Palma at his village near the confluence of the Colorado and the Gila. This was necessary in part because only about a dozen pack mules were fit to continue the march. The loss of so many animals to the Apache raids at Tubac and Anza's inability to replenish his stock were now being felt keenly. The commander would press on with a less wieldy train.

Chief Palma was so accommodating that he even offered to have his own men carry the supplies to the river on their backs in order to spare the feeble mules. Anza insisted this was not necessary. Father Díaz acknowledged the plan was risky, but he judged it to be "the only one by which it was possible to absolve the obligation to fulfill our orders." The soldiers showed their support by pledging to finish the slog on foot, if necessary, considering the weakened condition of the mounts. The sole dissenter was Garcés, who still harbored ambitious hopes of finding a more northerly shortcut to Monterey that bypassed Mission San Gabriel. Leaving the provisions behind would make this more difficult. But Garcés did not belabor his opposition. When he learned of Anza's plan, he wrote, "I bowed my head."[23]

At two o'clock in the afternoon on Wednesday, 2 March, Anza set out with his remaining troops, the strongest horses, and ten mules carrying enough food for a month, barely enough to reach Mission San Gabriel. There he would seek replenishment before marching on to Monterey along the now well-trod Camino Real. Instead of retracing the disastrous route of the previous month, he would head farther south to get around the sand dunes. Accompanying the expedition in the lead was a local Indian guide.

For the next four days, water and pasturage remained spotty. The wells contained barely enough to sustain even the much smaller contingent under Anza's command. Two days after starting out, the expedition found the elusive San Jacome, the Indian village and watering hole that Garcés had tried to find in the dark. The site had been abandoned because the well had dried up. Garcés remarked in his diary "how close we had been to it on the night when we sought the place."[24] The next day, as they plodded to the northwest, having at last rounded the worst of the dunes, the explorers passed the shores of an expansive dried-up lake with large numbers of dead fish stranded on its beaches. This was Laguna Salada, just south of the current U.S–Mexican boundary.

On Sunday, 6 March, Anza learned that the Native guide had absconded during the night, leaving behind his bow and arrows on the ground where he had slept. The entire company was now suffering from lack of water. And Sebastián still did not recognize his surroundings.

Without a local guide, Anza dispatched a corporal and six soldiers ahead of the expedition into the mountains to the north to search for water. The advance squad, mounted on horseback and armed with muskets, lances, and swords, encountered an Indian boy and seized him in an attempt to learn where water might be found. The frightened youth led them to a place where sweet, clear water flowed. Soon the boy's father appeared and, with great timidity, pleaded with the Spaniards to let his son go. The corporal obliged, after giving the Natives glass beads and tobacco. Although the soldiers urged the two to remain, they quite naturally took off. Anza already had instructed his men to avoid the use of force and to treat the Indians well so that "we may not acquire a bad name at first sight."[25]

A similar incident occurred the next day, when the advance soldiers surprised six Natives and took them captive. The Indians, members of the Kumeyaay tribe whose territory stretched all the way to the Pacific, shared their own drinking water with the Spaniards. They also directed the soldiers to a spot not far away where water could be found in abundance by digging wells. Then the terrified Kumeyaay begged to be set free. The soldiers complied after giving them gifts.

The precise place to dig, the Indians had said, was among mesquite hummocks at the bottom of a wash. With their detailed knowledge of their environment, the tribesmen knew that mesquite shrubs put down deep roots, extending nearly two hundred feet. Clumps of mesquite acted as markers in the desert for underground water. When the soldiers began to dig, clear, freshwater flowed from the sand in abundance. This was Santa Rosa de las Lajas, the first adequate watering spot since Santa Olaya (see figure 4). Anza allowed his men and the animals to rest for a day and revive themselves.

Far more encouraging, Sebastián knew where he was now. From here, he was certain he could lead the expedition onward to Mission San Gabriel. Garcés, too, recognized the stretch of desert ahead of them. "We celebrated our arrival at this place," Anza wrote in his journal, "and therefore we now promise ourselves that our expedition will not fail."[26] This was the turning point that assured success.

Everyone's spirits soared when Sebastián successfully led the company to a good watering spot on 10 March, 1774. He had passed through the area the previous

FIGURE 4. Yuha Well, in the desert wasteland of southeastern California, saved the 1774 Anza exploratory party, including Francisco Garcés, from dying of thirst. Kumeyaay Natives guided Anza's scouts to the watering spot, named Santa Rosa de las Lajas (Saint Rose of the Black Rocks) by the Spaniards. *Photo by Thomas E. Teske, MD.*

year on his way to the Colorado River, and many of the local Indians recognized him. Some also remembered Garcés from his 1771 travels. In the Native guide's honor, Anza named the place San Sebastián.

For the next twelve days, Anza led his party on a northwest route through the low desert, where the land was below sea level, and up into the sterile mountains where rain and snow delayed their progress. Many of the soldiers were marching on foot after their horses gave out. The expedition left the high desert through a gap that Anza named El Puerto Real de San Carlos (The Royal Pass of Saint Charles), in honor of the king. Then the party descended into a broad verdant plain known today as the Cahuilla Valley and on northward past great flocks of white geese and many bears to the swollen Santa Ana River. To get the cargo across this narrow but deep waterway, the soldiers felled cottonwood trees and built a makeshift bridge. At sunset on Tuesday, 22 March, after fording the San Gabriel River, Anza rode up to the entrance of Mission San Gabriel and formally announced himself to the very surprised corporal of the guard.

The four unsuspecting Franciscans assigned to Mission San Gabriel and the small escort of young soldiers could hardly believe that Anza had crossed the unexplored desert from Sonora. With great jubilation the friars rang the mission bells and chanted the *Te Deum*, a hymn of thanksgiving to the Lord. There were many musket rounds and shouts of "Victoria!" The next day the priests sang a High Mass to honor Carlos III—"our invincible and most amiable monarch," Díaz called him—and to give praise for Anza's breakthrough.[27]

The man in charge of Mission San Gabriel was Fermín Lasuén, a thirty-seven-year-old padre from Cantabria, Spain. A gentle, gracious man with dark, curly hair, Father Lasuén had brought Sebastián and his wife to Mission San Gabriel the previous year. One can only imagine his amazement when he unexpectedly came face-to-face with the Native runaway. Although no record of their reunion has survived, it is clear that no disciplinary action was taken against Sebastián. He would remain in faithful service to Spain across the borderlands for years to come. On the day before Anza had arrived at San Gabriel, his food supply had run out. "On the last day," Serra reported to Mexico City, "they had eaten absolutely nothing, and in the preceding days very little, the captain and the fathers asserting that they did not have even a little cake of chocolate."[28]

The commander was eager to restock his troops and continue his march over the well-established road to Monterey. So, he was shocked to find that the settlement itself was almost out of provisions. "We found the mission in extreme poverty, as is true of all the rest," Garcés recorded in his diary. Anza added: "The missionaries and the soldiers of the guard have no other daily ration than three tortillas of maize and the herbs of the fields, which each one seeks for himself."[29] The padres of the mission were barely holding on until fresh supplies could be delivered from San Diego, where the frigate *Santiago* had recently set anchor. It was distressingly plain to Anza, Garcés, and Díaz that there was neither enough food nor enough mounts at Mission San Gabriel to resupply the expedition.

After consulting with his two chaplains, Anza decided to seek the essential relief stocks in San Diego. He sent four soldiers and seven mules on a 240-mile roundtrip trek to the port, along with a letter addressed to Captain Juan Pérez of the *Santiago* asking for food. From the commander of the San Diego presidio he requested the mounts he needed to sustain his march.

On Tuesday, 5 April 1774, the mule train returned from San Diego. Captain Pérez could spare very little from his ship's supplies because he was bound on a long maritime expedition of his own to waters as far north as present-day Alaska. The rations he sent consisted of only six bushels of corn, half of which was spoiled; one cask of jerked meat unfit to eat; a barrel of flour; and two bushels of dried beans, which would be of no use on the trail because Anza's men did not have pots in which to boil them. In all, the provisions would last the expedition only sixteen days. What was more, the San Diego garrison could not spare a single saddle animal.

It was now clear that Anza lacked the food and mounts required to get his whole body to Monterey. So, he decided to make the trek on his own with a light party of six soldiers, four from his party and two from Mission San Gabriel who knew the way. Anza was recognized as a tireless rider who could cover sixty-five miles a day when not encumbered by a pack train. The rest of the company, including the two friars, were to be sent back to the Colorado River to await Anza's return from Monterey. Most of the expedition's provisions were already at the river under the care of Chief Palma.

In the meantime, Anza dispatched the viceroy's personal courier, Juan Bautista Valdés, on an eighteen-hundred-mile ride back to Mexico City with news that the expedition had conquered the desert and reached Mission San Gabriel. In Valdés's bulging pouch, among other documents, were the diaries kept to date by Anza, Garcés, and Díaz, and a lengthy letter from Anza explaining his success to Viceroy Bucareli. The normal route for a post rider bound for the capital of New Spain was 850 miles down the Baja Peninsula to the port of Loreto, where he boarded a ship to San Blas, the naval base on the west coast of Mexico. From there he traveled five hundred miles in the saddle to Mexico City. Many letters experienced long delays at Loreto because ships were not immediately available to make the crossing to San Blas.

With this problem in mind, Anza decided to send Valdés overland to Mexico City along the road just forged by the explorers. This had the added benefit of underlining the utility of the new route, which clearly would speed communications between the California missions and the viceroy. Two soldiers were ordered to accompany the courier as far as the presidio at Altar, Sonora. The rider made good time on this dangerous, mostly solitary journey. Leaving Mission San Gabriel on 18 April, he was in Mexico City by 14 June, when he gave an oral declaration detailing the expedition's accomplishments.[30] Apparently unable to read or write beyond signing his name, accompanied by a simple rubric, Valdés dictated his testimony to Don Melchor de Peramás, the viceroy's secretary, who committed it to paper.

At nine o'clock in the morning on Sunday, 10 April 1774, Anza set out from Mission San Gabriel. Ahead of him the road to Monterey stretched for more than three hundred miles. On Monday, 18 April, after a very long day's ride, his small delegation reached the Monterey presidio. The commander calculated he had ridden 1,063 miles from his starting point at Tubac.

The military detachment at Monterey and the padres at nearby Mission Carmel, the most distant outposts of the Spanish realm in North America, were even more destitute than those at Mission San Gabriel. Anza blamed their misery on the chronic drawbacks of trying to supply the missions by sea. In time, he was sure, the newly opened road would relieve their misfortunes and bring stability to the establishments in California. For the present, Anza penned in his journal, "I cannot find the words adequate to praise the merit of the friars, the commander, and the troops for remaining in these places."[31]

On Friday of the same week as his arrival, Anza was back in the saddle en route back to Tubac, which he still served as commander. Journeying south along El Camino Real on Wednesday, 27 April, the commander was surprised at two o'clock in the afternoon to encounter northbound on the trail Padre-Presidente Serra, who was returning to Monterey after a visit to Mission San Gabriel. Their chance meeting along the Santa Barbara Channel gave Serra the opportunity to learn all about the expedition from Sonora. Anza wanted to keep up his march, but Serra in his indomitable way persuaded the commander to stop for the night and brief him fully on the undertaking. By happenstance Serra had been in Mexico City when Anza's petition to carry out the expedition had arrived the previous year. Serra had enthusiastically endorsed the venture to the viceroy.

On Friday, 6 May, after recrossing El Puerto Real de San Carlos, the trailing pack animals in Anza's train were ambushed by a fusillade of arrows from Indians hiding in the brush. Three mules were injured, but only slightly. The soldiers captured four of the culprits, and the man judged to be the ringleader was given a beating and threatened with death if he repeated the offense. A short distance away, Anza found a message carved in Spanish in the trunk of a willow tree, advising travelers to be on guard against Indian attack. It had been left by Father Garcés, who had experienced a similar assault at the same spot on his return to the Colorado River a few weeks earlier. In that incident, the Natives targeted the fattest horse belonging to the Spaniards. After wounding the mount with their arrows during the day, the Indians crept stealthily into camp after dark, killed the animal, and dragged it off without the sentries on horseback detecting them. "It seems that [the attack] was committed through a hankering for meat," Garcés concluded in his diary.[32]

Four days later Anza and his men reached the confluence of the Colorado River and the Gila River, where Chief Palma kept his headquarters. The Colorado was now growing wider each day with runoff from the melting snowpack in the mountains to the north. As he had promised, Palma had a raft waiting for Anza to ferry him across both rivers.

With the spring flood the water took on a reddish hue and the current was stronger than usual, but the raft carrying Anza, Father Díaz, and Anza's servant was guided by a small army of Yuma swimmers. The chief himself picked up Anza and carried him to the raft. "I had such confidence," Anza wrote in his journal, "that in all my life I have never crossed a river with greater assurance, since even though the craft had been wrecked, I had close at hand more than five hundred persons ready to rescue me."[33]

Also as promised, Palma returned the ax that one of his tribesmen had stolen from the expedition earlier. To show his appreciation, and to strengthen the chief's ties to the crown, Anza presented him with his own *bastón*, or walking stick, a symbol of Spanish authority. He also gave him four cattle to slaughter for food, and some articles of clothing. The Yuma leader, who usually went about naked, was especially pleased with the fancy apparel, which he donned on important occasions.

As Anza pressed on up the Gila toward his final destination of Tubac, Garcés set out alone on a small expedition up the Colorado to the land of the Jalchedún tribe. In earlier instructions, Viceroy Bucareli had asked that Garcés dispatch a letter by Indian courier to the Franciscan missionaries in northern New Mexico. If Garcés received a reply from New Mexico, he was to inquire of the Indian courier how many days it took him to travel from New Mexico to the Colorado River. This would establish a rough estimate of how far Santa Fe was from California.

Nearly everyone recognized this was, at best, an unlikely gambit. From his previous wanderings, Garcés knew that Jalchedún men wore dark blue blankets, which they acquired in trade with the Moqui—now known as Hopi—of northern New Mexico. So, he sought to find a courier among the Jalchedunes who would deliver his letter. The Jalchedunes advised him that the Moqui lived a journey of five days away, and that the missionaries were seven days away.[34] They offered to convey the letter after their mesquite bean pods ripened in the summer. Garcés knew the Natives well enough to surmise that the delivery likely never would be made, and he was right. Yet in his own mind he was determined to make the trip to the Moqui himself one day. It was 10 July before the wandering Franciscan made his way back to his home at Mission San Javier del Bac south of Tucson.

On Thursday, 26 May 1774, Anza was in the saddle at sunrise with the goal of reaching the Tubac presidio before dark—a ride of more than fifty miles. Arriving home just as the sun was setting over the Sierrita Mountains, Anza penned a final entry in his journal: "Herewith the expedition has come completely to an end, and with the successes and the advantages which are set forth in the foregoing document, wherefore may the Lord of Hosts be blessed and praised."[35] From Mexico City to Monterey, Anza's breakthrough appeared to clear the way for the colonization of California, thus solidifying Spain's grasp on a huge slice of the North American continent. Yet, as events were to play out, achieving the next step was anything but easy.

CHAPTER SIX

Start Mounting Up

> I am not belittling the brave pioneer men, but the sunbonnet as well as the sombrero has helped to settle this glorious land of ours.
>
> —Edna Ferber

The secluded station known as La Canoa sits in a broad desert plain overseen by the black silhouette of the Santa Rita Mountains to the east. This corner of the Sonoran Desert in southeastern Arizona is a dusty place where tumbleweeds propelled by the warm breeze pile up against stands of prickly pear cactus. More than half a mile above sea level, the packed, rocky soil is welcoming to scorpions and venomous vipers. Nearby, the Santa Cruz River vanishes into the sand for much of the year. This is a lonely, forlorn spot, made even more so by its place in history.

It was here on 23 October 1775 that a caravan of Spanish sojourners under the command of Juan Bautista de Anza set up their tents for the night. The aim of their expedition was to deliver settlers to the new mission and pueblo of San Francisco in northern California, more than a thousand miles away. The campsite was chosen because of a spring that flowed from the ground into the fallen trunk of a dead cottonwood tree, creating a watering trough shaped like a canoe.

After the sun set, thirty-year-old Manuela Piñuelas Felíz went into heavy labor. With her were her thirty-four-year-old soldier husband, José Vicente Felíz, and their six children, three boys and three girls ranging in age from twelve to two. The delivery by candlelight at nine o'clock at night in a field tent was protracted and difficult, with the baby turned crossways and eventually delivered feet first. All the same, it was a healthy boy who let out a lusty cry. He was sure to survive.

In the primitive conditions of the outback, the afterbirth could not be extracted from the mother. The meager medicines at hand on the trail were not effective. At three o'clock in the morning Manuela's life began to dim. The priests were awakened and she was given the last rites of the Catholic Church. A few hours later, just before dawn glimmered faintly over the high desert, the gravely weakened mother could hang on no longer. When she died, José Vicente was left a widower with seven children, including the newborn, christened José Antonio Capistrano. The infant would be nursed by another lactating mother. During each day's march, at least ten women were nursing young children from the backs of mules.

In the afternoon of Tuesday, 24 October, after a dousing rain ended, Manuela Piñuelas's body was wrapped in a blanket and tied to the back of a pack animal. Father Francisco Garcés and four soldiers escorted it to the nearest mission, San Xavier del Bac, twenty-three miles to the north. The next morning Garcés said a funeral Mass in the chapel and afterward buried Manuela's remains in the cemetery next to the church. José Vicente and his children—José Francisco, José Doroteo, José de Jesús, María de Loreto, María Antonia, María Manuela, plus the suckling baby—remained behind and were not present at the humble funeral.

As the main body of homesteaders, 240 strong, later approached San Xavier del Bac on horseback, Father Pedro Font led them in reciting the rosary for Manuela's soul and singing a hymn of praise to the Virgin Mary. Upon reaching the mission in the evening, Father Thomas Eixarch baptized the newborn. The hardy boy survived the rigors of the trail and made it to California. He died there eleven months later, another victim of the high infant mortality of the day. His body was buried at Mission San Gabriel.

Manuela's unexpected death, however sorrowful, did not disrupt the expedition, which was only just beginning to get under way. While at San Xavier del Bac, a distant outpost where Apache attacks were common, Font performed no fewer than three weddings of young people who had met only recently. The padre, always a stickler in ecclesiastical matters, refused a fourth couple who asked to be married. His reason was that the woman had been engaged to another man and did not have his consent to break off the relationship. Here, then, the robust cycle of human life played out on the trail—birth, death, and marriage, all within the span of three days.

The historical arena for the colonizing band had been set the previous year when Anza and Garcés opened an overland trail from Sonora to California. Viceroy Antonio María de Bucareli y Ursúa was eager to establish two new missions and a garrison at San Francisco Bay in order to bolster Spain's claim to the territory and ward off Russian or English interlopers. Anza proposed to recruit the settlers, mostly poor families with large broods, from the frontier pueblos of Sonora, Sinaloa, Fuerte, and Culiacán in northwest New Spain.

In recent times the region had been devastated by floods, epidemics, and recurrent Apache depredations. "Most of their inhabitants I have just seen submerged in the direst poverty and misery," Anza wrote to the viceroy, "and so I have no doubt that they would most willingly and gladly embrace" the chance to start a new life in

California. But he advised that the impoverished settlers "will have to be equipped from shoes to hair ribbons" at the crown's expense.[1]

To accomplish this, an itemized inventory of the necessary clothing and its projected cost, down to the last real, was prepared by Juan José de Echeveste, the viceroy's purchasing agent in Mexico City. Planning for thirty families with six children each, Echeveste decreed that each woman would be furnished with three blouses, three white cotton petticoats, two skirts, two jackets, two pairs of stockings, two pairs of hose, two pairs of shoes, one hat, six yards of ribbon, and two rebozos.[2] The rebozo was a multipurpose shawl made of wool or cotton in various colors, about three feet wide and seven feet long, draped around a woman's neck and shoulders. A baby swaddled in the rebozo could breast-feed while the mother rode along the trail. Or the child could be carried in the rebozo on his mother's back, freeing her hands for work. The wrap kept both mother and child warm. It was useful for many other things, too, such as gathering kindling for a fire.

Oddly, Echeveste provided three pairs of cotton underdrawers for each man, but none for the women. The paucity of underwear, for women, men, and children, was to become just one of many discomforts endured by the settlers during long days in the saddle. Another was a shortage of soap. The purchasing agent supplied only twelve pesos' worth of suds for the whole party. It was used up in the early days of the trek. In place of the rebozo, each man received a cloth cape lined with baize. Unmarried soldiers often draped their cloaks over branches at night to form a shelter in which to sleep. To clothe the 180 children, mothers were given several yards of linen, cotton, and ribbon from which to sew garments.

For the families, ten field tents made of bleached canvas with wooden poles were provided. This meant that roughly three families, with an average of six children each, slept in a single tent. The official chaplain and diarist on the expedition, Father Font, merited his own tent. As commander, Anza already had a large circular tent, which he used not only for sleeping but for writing his own journal on a portable desk and for holding meetings with his officers.

The commander and the chaplain also were provisioned with a much better mess, even though Anza declared it was contrary to his wishes. Their rations included hams, sausages, biscuits, chocolate, cheese, a barrel of wine, olive oil, vinegar, and such spices as saffron, pepper, cloves, and cinnamon. The standard fare for the rest of party consisted of fresh beef, with one bovine from a traveling herd slaughtered each day, flour tortillas, beans, corn mush sweetened with white sugar, and chocolate pressed into thick tablets. In addition, there was a shipment of three barrels of brandy, to be distributed to the men at Anza's discretion.

For the twenty recruits being trained as soldiers for the two new missions, there were twenty carbines, twenty swords, twenty lances, twenty cartridge boxes with fourteen charges, forty leather powder flasks with primers, thirty shoulder belts, and twenty-two leatherjackets made of seven thicknesses of deerskin. The heavy, sleeveless leatherjacket, which stretched from the shoulders to the knees, provided protection against Indian arrows. By the time Echeveste completed his inventory, detailing everything from copper camp kettles and horseshoe nails to coarse blankets and buckskin boots, the total cost came to 21,927 pesos and 2 reales. Viceroy Bucareli promptly approved the expenditures and ordered that they be covered by 12,000 pesos taken from the Pious Fund of the Californias, a large account raised from wealthy contributors by the Jesuits before their expulsion, with the remainder to be paid by the royal exchequer.

For his second foray across the desert, Anza was elevated from the rank of captain to lieutenant-colonel of the cavalry. Bucareli assigned Font, who was then minister at Mission San José de los Pimas, as the company diarist because he knew how to use a quadrant and mathematical tables to make solar observations and calculate latitudes along the way. Since Garcés had made the trek the previous year, he was ordered to accompany Anza as far as the Colorado River and wait for him there until his return from California. During the interim Garcés was directed by the viceroy to scout out sites for new missions along the river and to "ascertain the spirit and disposition of the Natives toward the catechism and toward vassalage to our sovereign."[3] As his companion on the trail, Garcés selected Father Eixarch, an acquaintance from Mission Tumacácori, near Garcés's home mission of San Xavier del Bac.

Anza assembled the leading elements of his train at the presidio of San Miguel de Horcasitas in Sonora. The full procession would be put together at Tubac, nearly two hundred miles to the north in present-day Arizona. With Font in tow, the commander and a partial pool of settlers set out from Horcasitas in the afternoon on Friday, 29 September 1775. The commander and the padre came to mutual agreement that the patron saint of the expedition would be the Virgin of Guadalupe, a revered figure in New Spain. The initial leg of the ride was through dangerous Apache country. Font grumbled in his first diary entry that he lacked a compass, which he needed to record the course followed by the caravan each day. When one was later lent to him, he grumbled that it was a "very small, poor compass that could barely point."[4]

On the fourth day of the march, Font was stricken with diarrhea, an ailment that plagued him intermittently for much of his life. He felt too weak to put up his tent and tried in vain to find someone to help him. He renewed his request to Anza for a personal servant to tend to such chores, but Anza was in no rush to comply. A week later, as the expedition drew nearer to Tubac, Font once again asked Anza for a servant. "Although he promised to give me one, he still did not do so," Font wrote peevishly in his diary.[5] After the train reached Tubac and paused for several days to gather up the full contingent, Font's diarrhea worsened and he spent four straight days in bed. Once he was back on his feet, the commander sent him a servant named José Miguel de Silva, a young married man from Sinaloa.

On Sunday, 22 October, Font and Garcés sang a High Mass in the Tubac chapel, enlisting the aid of the Virgin of Guadalupe for a successful journey. Then Font preached a stern sermon, exhorting the fully assembled colonists to persevere in the face of expected hardships on the road. He compared the planned crossing of the Colorado River to the Israelites crossing the Red Sea to reach the biblical Promised Land, warning that God would punish anyone who abused the Indians along the way, just as he punished the people of Israel for not heeding the words of Moses.

At eleven o'clock the next morning, Anza gave the command: "Vayan subiendo!" (Start mounting up!) This set in motion a rambling convoy that stretched far across the arid tablelands of the Sonoran Desert (see figure 5). Leading the train were four soldiers scouting the path ahead. Next came Anza, riding as the vanguard of his charges. He was followed by Father Font. Then came the long train of settlers, with each soldier shepherding his wife and children, sometimes with more than one youngster sharing a mule. Mothers with little ones in their arms rode astride their mounts. The line of hardy volunteers included no fewer than ninety-two children under the age of twelve, six under the age of two, and ten under one year.[6] Several women were pregnant when they set out from Tubac and gave birth during the thousand-mile march.

This roving mélange of frontier society was susceptible to Indian assault, as Font noted in his diary: "If the Apaches had attacked, doubtless we would have suffered losses, as our few soldiers were raw and inexperienced, and rode so constantly engaged with their little children that at times there would be one or another soldier carrying two or three young ones with him, and most of them rode with a child."[7] Trailing the settlers was a lieutenant who formed a rear guard. Next in file were three pack trains, consisting of 140 mules laden with provisions. Twenty muleteers herded them. They were followed by extra mounts without riders.

With mares, burros, and a few colts thrown in, there were 695 mounts. Given the rough terrain and major rivers to be crossed, there were no wagons or carts. Everything to sustain the colonists for the next five months was carried on four legs.

FIGURE 5. Juan Bautista de Anza and Pedro Font set out from Tubac in the vanguard of 240 colonizers, mostly women and children, on 23 October 1775. Three babies were born on the trail. From a painting at Tubac Presidio State Historic Park.
Courtesy of the National Park Service.

At the rear, driven along by three mounted cowhands, were 325 head of cattle, the staple of the expedition's food supply. Surplus cattle not slaughtered en route were to become breeding stock at the new settlements on San Francisco Bay.

Among the auxiliary personnel were seven servants for Anza and the padres, and three Indian interpreters. The commander also brought along Sebastián Tarabal, the onetime Native runaway who had helped guide the exploratory expedition across the desert to Mission San Gabriel the previous year. He was assigned variously on the payroll as a muleteer, a cook, and an interpreter.

Under Padre Font's orchestration, each day's march was imbued with religious ardor. It began in the morning when Font, attired in his colorful vestments, said the daily Mass, either in the open air or in his tent, which functioned as a portable church. As soon as the assembled company began to move, he intoned in the saddle the *Alabado*, a hymn of praise to God, and the settlers sang the responses. After dismounting for the day, families in separate groups prayed the rosary out loud at vespers and sang the *Alabado* again. "With the variety of sound, it was a pleasant thing to hear," Font recorded.[8]

On Friday, 27 October, with the expedition bivouacked near present-day Tucson, two of the Native muleteers deserted on foot. Anza asked the friendly Pima Indians of the area to help round them up. At eight o'clock that evening, six Pimas rode into camp with one of the captured fugitives. The commander, no doubt determined to make an example of the deserter, ordered him to be given twelve lashes and confined in the guard post to keep him from running away again. Font called the flogging a mere "down payment" on the punishment the Native could have received.[9] The soldiers aptly called the spot Llano del Azotado (Plain of the Lashed). Two days later, the second muleteer was brought in and dealt twenty-five lashes. Anza gave a reward to his captors and deducted the sum from the runaway's pay.

The assemblage continued on through flat desert terrain where there was little water and even less pasturage for the animals. The treeless landscape was heavily pocked with gopher holes, which meant that the hundreds of mounts and pack mules kicked up thick, clinging dust clouds that tormented the travelers. Despite it all, Anza wrote, "no dissatisfaction whatever has been shown by the people who have made the march, and this is a thing to marvel at, especially in the women and children, and their patience under the hardships is an indication of the contentment with which they are accepting their lot."[10]

At one o'clock in the afternoon on Monday, 30 October 1775, Anza was met by a delegation of ten mounted Pima chieftains whose villages lined the Gila River. They reported that while a large number of Pimas were out hunting the day before, they came upon a smaller band of armed Apaches, their bitter enemies. In the ensuing battle, two Apaches were killed and the rest fled. The Pimas presented the soldiers with the trophy scalps of the slain Apaches.

Anza ordered that the next day be spent at rest, while he and the three friars went to visit the crumbling pueblo ruins of Casa Grande, near present-day Coolidge, Arizona. The Spaniards called the impressive five-hundred-year-old complex Moctezuma's Palace, in the mistaken belief that the Aztecs built it.

After reaching the southern bank of the Gila River, now only knee deep at the end of the dry season, the settlers celebrated the feast day of San Carlos in honor of their sovereign on Saturday, 4 November 1775. Because the wife of a soldier fell ill, Anza canceled that day's march. Font and Eixarch said separate Masses in the morning, followed by a special High Mass sung by Garcés. He was accompanied by Font playing his psalterio, the stringed instrument he had brought along at Anza's request. To add to the festive mood, the commander passed out a generous pint of *aguardiente*, strong fruit brandy, to each of the men. This infuriated Father Font. "There was more than a middling amount of drunkenness among the troops," he declared in his journal, "to the extent that more than one of them stayed drunk until the next day."[11]

Over the next forty-eight hours, two more women became seriously sick, with strong pains in their lower sides. Some of the saddle animals also became sick. The cause of their distress was the brackish water in the lakes near the campsite. The entire area was marked by briny soil that looked as though flour had been spread over the ground. Font, meantime, was overcome with shivering after dinner on Monday, 6 November. An hour later he was hit with a high fever, followed by more chills. This was a familiar pattern for him. It was tertian fever, likely caused by earlier exposure to malaria, another ailment that would plague him on and off for the rest of his life. On some days his tertian fever and diarrhea both flared up, making it difficult for him to finish the march. This campsite earned the name of Las Lagunas del Hospital (Hospital Lakes).

The next day Anza ordered the train to pull out, even though two of the women were still very sick. His priority was to get to a healthier source of water. Before the march began, an Indian stealthily made off with a small china pot belonging to Anza. The thief was quickly caught and made to return the item. The commander did not bother to mention the incident in his journal, but Font observed acidly: "This matter of thievery is a trait common to every Indian."[12]

Once the caravan got on the move at one o'clock in the afternoon, the dust was so thick that it hampered breathing and made it impossible to see more than a short distance. The huddled families were beginning to get a taste of the omnipresent hazards of the trail. During this day's trek, two saddle animals died, most likely because of the salty water at Las Lagunas del Hospital.

The Opa Indians of the area were receptive to the Spaniards. Font noted that, unlike the Pimas along the Gila River, the Opas did not stink or have rotten teeth. They dressed in cloaks, which they wove from their cotton crop, but they also wore dark woolen capes with white streaks, which they acquired in trade with the Hopis of New Mexico. Their hair was tied up with a woolen cord and wrapped into a wreath on top of their heads. Feathers and other decorations adorned their hairdos. Using soot or red clay, the Opas painted rays on their faces and bodies. They made necklaces and earrings from beads and dangled ornaments from their pierced noses. Unsurprisingly, they were very fond of the red, yellow, and green beads passed out by Anza as gifts. The commander came supplied with six hundred skeins of beads. Knowing the Natives well, he had asked that there be no black beads but an abundance of red ones.

On Friday, 10 November, Anza granted another day of rest because several members of his party were in no shape to ride. The wife of a soldier delivered a stillborn child and had to remain in her tent, her whole body swollen. Another soldier who had not been feeling well for a few days suffered what appeared to be a stroke. Font, too, was down with chills, fever, and vomiting. Father Eixarch was battling a recurring fever. In all, five patients were "dangerously ill," Anza recorded.[13] On top of this, the cattle were showing signs of exhaustion due to the skimpy forage, and one died on the road.

Font's malarial fever usually was at its worst in the afternoon. In the morning on Thursday, 16 November, he already was having a bad day. To make it easier on him, Anza directed that two soldiers escort him right away to the place where the expedition would camp for the night, a spot called San Bernardino. This would give him a chance to recuperate in his tent while the rest of the band traveled the ten miles to catch up. Eixarch was feeling feverish as well, so he went along. José Miguel de Silva, Font's attendant, followed with the padre's two pack mules.

Striking out at 8:30 in the morning, the travelers should have reached their destination by noon. But the soldier who acted as guide unintentionally passed the campsite by, then pressed ahead at a good pace in an effort to find his way. The servant and the pack mules could not keep up, lagging farther and farther behind the soldiers and friars. Font, by now suffering mightily from alternating fever and chattering teeth, reproached the trooper repeatedly for getting lost, a tactic that did nothing to improve the situation. After 2 o'clock in the afternoon, Font could bear no more. "Suffering as I was with fever . . . I at last took myself in hand," he wrote in his journal, "and said that I was not going any further. . . . And so I started off toward the [Gila] river and as soon as I reached the cottonwoods, got down and said that I was not going away from there, back or forward."[14]

Silva and the pack mules did not find their way to Font until sunset. In the meantime, the escort soldiers headed back to the main convoy, no doubt happy to rid themselves of the mercurial padre. When word reached Anza that the friars had been left alone, he dispatched Sergeant Juan Pablo Grijalva to find them. Once Grijalva reported back, the commander sent two soldiers with some chocolate tablets, dried fruit, and cake to spend the night with them. It was a raw evening as the first chill of late autumn set in. By morning the water in the water bags was frozen.

In the hours before dawn on Sunday, 19 November, with the settlers billeted on the banks of the Gila, twenty-five-year-old Ana María de Osuna gave birth to a boy. Mother and child were doing well, but Anza suspended that day's trek. María was the wife of Ignacio Gutiérrez, age thirty, a soldier recruited from the silver mining camp of Los Álamos in Sonora. They had with them two older daughters, María de los Santos, age eight, and María Petrónia, age seven. After saying Mass in the morning, Font baptized the infant, naming him Diego Pascual. His birth came six days after the feast day of San Diego de Alcalá. The place of his birth was known as San Pascual. This marked the second live birth since the expedition departed Tubac.

At dawn the next day Font awoke in his tent with uncontrollable shivers. The night had been the coldest yet felt by the settlers, with more subfreezing temperatures, but the cause of Font's problem was the onset of another malarial episode. At noon the chills were replaced by a high fever. To add to his misery, his diarrhea returned in the worst way. Unable to eat and lacking an appetite, Font was extraordinarily weak. He recovered a bit after Francisca Ruelas, a soldier's wife, gave him a potion of water boiled with cilantro and oregano. Fortunately, Anza ordered another day of rest because María de Osuna was not yet strong enough to climb into the saddle with her newborn. Six horses perished because of the cold.

During the night of Thursday, 23 November, María Gertrudis Rivas went into premature labor. She was the wife of Ignacio Linares, an experienced soldier from the Tubac presidio. Anza directed that she be given medicine to stop the contractions, according to his account. Font wrote in his journal that Anza gave her a plate of special food. After another day's rest, the woman's pains subsided and she was able to travel.

On Tuesday, 28 November, the Spaniards reached the junction of the Gila and the Colorado rivers, where Yuma Chief Salvador Palma and his tribesmen were ready to assist them in getting across both waterways. Anza ordered his troops to fire off a musket volley in salute, prompting the Natives to shout and cheer. The shallow Gila was forded easily by the entire party on horseback at 1:30 in the afternoon. Camp was established that night on the east bank of the Colorado. To show their hospitality, the Yumas fed the settlers beans, squashes, corn, wheat, and a surfeit of three thousand watermelons. Font's ambiguous relations with the Indians were clear in his diary entry for the day: "After nightfall, Yumas and Opas stayed around the fire until late, lying stretched out upon the ground and half buried in the sand and heaped together like swine, as is their habit, singing in their mournful fashion and using a basket to strike a drum. I spent some time with them myself."[15]

Anza was dismayed to find that the crossing spot on the Colorado that he used the previous year was no longer available because the river had risen. He mounted his horse at seven o'clock the next morning in search of another ford. When he could discover no suitable place to cross, he directed the soldiers to begin rounding up logs to build rafts. This plan fell apart when the Indians said the river was now too cold for them to swim across towing rafts, as they had done for Anza in 1774 on his return from California. This forced the commander to settle for an unsatisfactory crossing point where the river split into three branches. All three together were four hundred yards across, by Garcés's estimate.[16] Each flow was around four feet deep, which meant that many of the pack animals, loaded down with provisions, would have to swim across all three branches.

This delicate operation began soon after Font said Mass at sunrise the next day. First the baggage was distributed equally among all of the surplus animals, which resulted in a half load on each back. As a precaution, Anza stationed ten men along the bank downstream to intercept anybody or anything that fell into the river. The tallest and strongest horses forded first. Then soldiers waded across leading the bridles of mules and horses carrying women and children. The water reached up to the backs of even the tallest horses, so everyone got wet. In midstream a man on horseback with a child in his arms lost his balance and tumbled into the frigid water. The man almost lost his grip on the child, but they were rescued immediately. A blanket and some baskets were all that floated away.

Font, feeling ill and light-headed, rode across the river with the aid of three naked Yuma men, one in front leading the horse and one on each side holding him up in the saddle. Father Garcés, unable to swim and afraid to ride across, was carried to the other side by three Indians, two at his head and one at his feet, as he stretched out face upward on the water—with his eyes closed. Font wryly noted in his journal that when Garcés was ferried across he looked like a corpse. In his diary, Garcés omitted any mention of the drama.

Once all of the people reached the west bank and began to dry out, the pack trains were led across, followed by the livestock. The fording was completed successfully in three hours. The only load that got thoroughly soaked belonged to Font. It contained his holy oils and vestments for saying Mass. A careful reading of his diary suggests the mishap may have been intentional, due to Font's incessant nagging: "Since so little attention was being paid to me and to whatever I said, despite my charging the muleteers to be careful not to let it get wet and my begging the same thing of my commander, it may have been for that very reason that this was the load with which they used the least care."[17]

Anza had now succeeded in overcoming a tremendous obstacle on the road to San Francisco, and he had done so without the loss of lives or equipment. By any account, this was a singular achievement. At this moment the commander did not realize it, but the most treacherous days of the journey still lay ahead.

CHAPTER SEVEN

Desert Nativity Scene

> For unto us a child is born, unto us a son is given.
> —King James Bible, Isaiah 9:6

Two very different plots of land—one near the desert badlands west of the lower Colorado River and the other an abandoned cemetery five hundred miles away beneath a vegetable patch at the corner of Benton and Sherman Streets in Santa Clara, California—serve as bookends for the life of Salvador Ignacio Linares. His birth marks a jubilant hour in the Anza expedition. His unexpected death at age thirty-one, just days after his wife gave birth to twin boys, dramatizes the tribulations of an otherwise ordinary life on the Spanish frontier in the waning days of the eighteenth century.

The desert site denotes where the Anza party camped for two nights in the horrible month of December 1775. This scraggy wilderness stands nearly 2,400 feet above sea level, high enough to get an occasional snowstorm. The only way to reach it is on foot or horseback. The nearest paved road is about a three-hour hike away. A modern map helpfully advises that this area is closed entirely to humans in summer to protect the endangered bighorn sheep that inhabit the steep cliffs nearby, in company with mountain lions and black-tailed mule deer. Trekking across this inhospitable terrain is not easy. Spiny, thirty-foot-tall ocotillos dot the landscape. Underfoot, barrel cactus and chollas cactus, each one sprouting sharp needles, create a wall-to-wall hazard for man or steed. Rocks the size of footlockers protrude from the sandy soil. Unbroken footprints of slithering desert iguanas color this otherworldly setting. The only sound is the desert wind.

Five million years ago, this high desert actually lay at the bottom of the Pacific Ocean, as evidenced by marine fossils dug up in the surrounding elevations. The grinding of tectonic plates for eons along the San Andreas Fault gradually upheaved the land and built mountains topping six thousand feet, forming a barrier to coastal rains and creating an astringent environment where triple-digit temperatures hover for weeks at a time. Only a scorpion could love this raw, shadeless place, and very many of them do.

In the midst of all of this, at a place known today as the Upper Willows of Coyote Canyon, rests a stone historical marker which, due to its extreme isolation, few humans will ever see. Overshadowed by the high ridgeline of the Santa Rosa Mountains, Coyote Canyon becomes a raging desert wash when late-summer thunderstorms strike with astonishing ferocity. Runoff from the deluge is channeled into a debris-filled torrent that sweeps along everything in its path, sculpting the landscape. A muddy high-water mark taller than a man's head on a boulder near the historical marker attests to the flood of the previous year. To escape these monsoonal ravages, the marker with a bronze plaque bearing the name of Salvador Ignacio Linares was erected eight feet above the ground, atop two megalithic rocks.

After fording the Colorado River on Thursday, 30 November 1775, Anza detoured his train to the south. This was necessary to bypass soaring alluvial dunes built up over centuries by windblown sands from a dried-up lakebed. Due to silt deposits and frequent earthquakes, the course of the river shifted radically over time as it meandered over a flat plain. Ahead lay the most dreaded stretch of the journey—the trial that would determine the fulfillment or failure of the expedition.

Before setting out across this expanse (see map 3), Anza rested at an encampment on the west bank of the Colorado. Two members of the party were so ill he feared they would die before the day was out.[1] After being given medicine on Anza's orders, both made their last confessions to the priests.

Meanwhile, Father Garcés and Father Eixarch prepared to remain behind to work among the Yuma Indians until Anza's return from Monterey, confident in Chief Palma's declarations that the Spaniards were welcome to live among his people. Palma even announced he had identified a tract of high ground on the west bank where a future mission could be built well above the river's broad flood tide. The muleteers spent the better part of three days building a *jacal*—a thatched hut made of thick, reedy marsh grasses—for Garcés and Eixarch to occupy in Palma's village.

The two friars were not to be abandoned without provisions, although Font noted in his diary that they both complained to him in private about the meager supplies. Anza left them, according to his own meticulous accounting, two boxes of colorful glass beads to distribute among the Indians, a large cask of tobacco (a product the Indian men very much favored), a packload of ground flour, a packload of pinole (coarsely ground, toasted maize kernels mixed with water and herbs to make mush), a packload of beans, three large casks of jerked beef, a large box of biscuits, a box of chocolate, a box of sugar, twelve wax candles, twelve cakes of soap, three

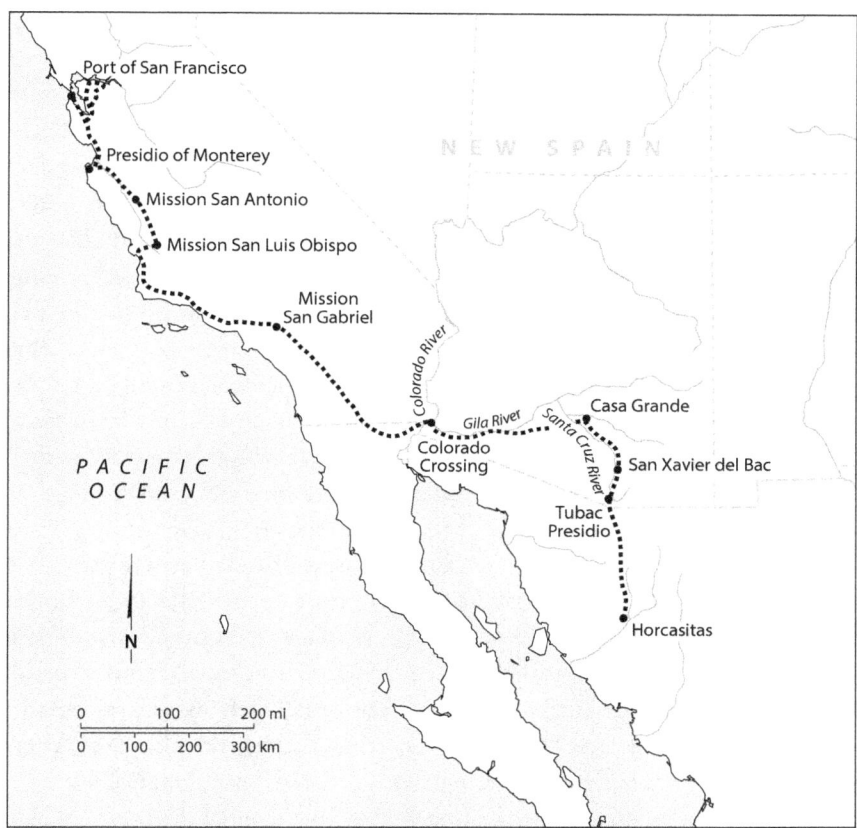

MAP 3. Starting in Sonora, Mexico, the impoverished families of the 1775–1776 Anza colonizing expedition traversed twelve hundred miles of wilderness to reach San Francisco. *Cartography by Bill Nelson. Copyright © 2017 by the University of Oklahoma Press.*

hams, one bottle of wine, one bottle of brandy, twenty-five pounds of lard, and six medium-sized cheeses.[2] The food supply was rounded out with five adult beef cattle on the hoof. Among the implements were one ax and one earthenware griddle.

Also left at the disposal of Garcés and Eixarch were three Indian interpreters, two servants, and two muleteers, along with thirteen riding animals. In Font's caustic estimation, the Native interpreters were of no use because their grasp of Castilian was very poor. One of the servants was a young boy who had volunteered as an unpaid attendant to Padre Eixarch. One of the muleteers was the veteran Indian guide, Sebastián Tarabal.

Font could not refrain from observing in his diary that the food stocks "were something, but not much," considering they would have to feed nine mouths for six months through the coming winter until Anza returned to the river. As it turned out, the Yuma women provided ample additional beans, maize, gourds, and wheat. What was more, Font grumbled, the wine "could not be used for saying Mass since it was so bad that it did not even resemble wine in color or flavor and they had to send to Caborca for some."[3] At best, the wine had passed its prime. Eixarch was not one to complain gratuitously, but he noted in his diary that even after taking only a small sip during Mass the wine had "the vilest taste" and "makes me vomit."[4] The bottle was only half full when he received it, and the contents looked like water mixed with mud. He strained it through a clean cloth but still it came out just the same. It certainly appeared that someone had drunk the wine surreptitiously and replaced it with muddy water. Father Eixarch refrained from saying Mass for a time and dispatched two Yuma messengers for more wine and candles, since the dozen left by Anza would not be nearly enough to last until his return.

The small Spanish party and their provisions were placed under the protection of Yuma Chief Palma, whom Anza had come to trust completely, viewing him as the key to peaceful relations with this tribe controlling the vital Colorado River crossing. As they prepared to part ways, Anza at nightfall presented Palma on behalf of the viceroy a splendid outfit of royal attire. The Yuma chieftain, who customarily wandered about naked or clad in nothing more than a tattered blanket, used Anza's personal tent as a dressing room. He emerged, preposterously, brandishing a gift bestowed on him by the crown—a silver-topped cane of office denoting his high standing among the Spaniards. He was bedecked in a Spanish-style shirt and breeches, a yellow suede jacket with decorations, a blue cape with gold braid, and a black velvet cap decorated with imitation jewels. Barbara Levy, a modern-day storyteller of the Yuma, or Quechan, tribe describes Palma as "tall, graceful, powerful, magnetic"—adjectives that do not appear in the Spaniards' accounts of him.[5] The unfolding events of the next few years would demonstrate, tragically, that Anza's confidence in the sartorial Indian leader was not always warranted.

With winter approaching, the weather turned foul on the first day of December. As dawn broke, a strong wind from the northwest howled so hard that the settlers had to struggle to keep their tents from blowing away, and it was impossible to keep cook fires burning. "Wherever we walked, a cloud of dust blew into the air," Font recorded. "And since it was very fine, dirty, and sticky sand, from the fine powder of dry silt which the river leaves, it made it impossible for us to breathe or to see, our clothing and everything becoming soiled with it."[6]

In the evening, a delegation of three Native women and a man, members of the Jalchedún nation who lived upstream from the Yumas, arrived unannounced at the Spanish post to express their desire to make peace.[7] Garcés, ever attentive to the ways of foreign tribes, quizzed the man about the affairs of the Jalchedunes. The Indian declared that in the land of the Jalchedunes there was a Native sorcerer who had escaped from the Franciscan missions along the California coast. As he made his way inland toward the Colorado River, he was killed and his remains cremated by hostile tribesmen. But somehow he managed to come to life again. His death and resurrection were repeated numerous times as he traveled through unfriendly territory. The great wizard now carried a viper and roamed about killing the Jalchedunes, leaving them terrorized. According to Font's account, Anza was "somewhat mortified" by this ludicrous tale. Even Garcés, who showed more respect for Native Americans than other Spaniards did, dismissed the Jalchedún's story as "a great joke."[8] On Sunday, 3 December, running well behind his planned schedule for reaching the safety of Mission San Gabriel, Anza resumed his advance down the right bank of the Colorado, even though the two sick members of the party were still near death. Under his orders from Viceroy Antonio María de Bucareli y Ursúa in Mexico City, Anza was to complete the journey from Tubac to Monterey in no more than seventy days—an entirely unrealistic timetable, considering the large number of women and children traveling with him. He had been given enough provisions to last only that long.

The night turned bitter cold and two saddle animals died of exposure, a portent of what lay ahead as frigid temperatures took hold in the high desert. The number of colonists needing medical attention now grew to eleven. Font's malarial fever returned briefly. All the same, Anza pressed his party back on the trail at 9:30 in the morning, through what he described as "impenetrable thickets" and marshes that retarded his progress.[9] At one point the cattle had to follow a different route because the brush was too thick for them to pass through. In the evening, Anza summoned the Indians to dance in front of his tent by the light of the campfire, which greatly annoyed Font, who at that very moment was lecturing them in his own tent about their duty to protect Garcés and Eixarch from harm.

As troubles began to mount, morale among the sojourners must have suffered. The periodic conflict between Font and Anza flared. The Franciscan's haughty air was inflicted, not for the last time, on the patient leader of the expedition. In more than one instance Font interjected himself into matters that were the sole purview of the commander, questioning his leadership in a veiled way. In a later report Font poured out a shrill lament that Anza had presented the fancy clothes to

Chief Palma all by himself, excluding the padres. Anza "is so fond of appropriating all of his accomplishments to himself and of winning respect that he refuses to let anyone else have a part in them, nor does he let anyone into his fellowship who might in any way attract people's appreciation, which he desires all for himself," Font wrote. "Nor did he ever, during the whole way, give me so much as a string of beads in case I should take a notion to give any Indian a present. . . . I note all of this down so that what usually occurs with commanders during such expeditions should not pass unknown."[10] After lodging several more petty complaints, including that Anza had never asked him to play his psalterio to appeal to the Indians, Font concluded with the Latin exclamation, *A militibus libera nos, Domine* (Deliver us from soldiers, Lord.).[11]

As the leaden skies of late fall began to darken, the only encouraging news was that the two ill settlers recovered, and Anza could take comfort that the sole death among his charges to date was the mother who perished in childbirth on the first night out of Tubac. In contrast to the Sonoran Desert, which covers much of northwest Mexico, the topography of the Colorado Desert of southeastern California was exceptionally varied, rocky, and treacherous. The path ahead ranged through barren, bleached-dry sinks 275 feet below sea level to mountain passes almost 4,000 feet above sea level. Water was hard to find at any elevation, and the rare water lurking just beneath the surface was often salty and contaminated, unfit for consumption by man or mule. Essential pasturage for the cattle, pack mules, and saddle mounts was scanty or nonexistent, forcing the animals at one point to go two days without food or water.[12] Even firewood for cooking and warmth was scarce at critical moments.

The relatively solid, compact ground of recent days' marches was about to turn into deep drifting sands in which the pack mules became mired. In winter, temperatures in the desert fell sharply at night, often accompanied by penetrating fog and snow. This posed the danger that both humans and animals might freeze to death. Making the situation more difficult, weather conditions could change for the worse without warning, leaving the vulnerable women and children little time to seek shelter.

On the sixty-seventh day out of Tubac—Monday, 4 December 1775—the weather turned even colder. The next morning, the water bags left outside overnight had turned to ice. When Font arose at dawn, he found that even the urine in the pot inside his tent had frozen. Another mule and a horse were found dead from the cold.

After halting for the day near a lake in the bottomlands west of the Colorado River, the expedition was greeted by a large number of El Cojat Indians bearing gourds, beans, and other foods to barter for glass beads with Anza's soldiers. A steer was butchered outside Anza's tent, as was done most days to feed the settlers. Font was sitting nearby with Anza, drinking his daily chocolate, when the Indians gathered around and pressed in close to witness the slaughtering.

The pungent body odors of the naked Natives reinforced by the putrid smell of their flatulence were more than Font could stand. He leapt to his feet and asked an Indian for his seven-foot-long staff, used in the Natives' hoop-rolling game. Holding the rod horizontally, Font gently moved the crowd backward. One Indian man took offense and angrily pushed his way past Font's staff. The others did the same, regrouping at close quarters as before. Then the owner of the staff snatched it from Font's hands.

Confronted with the glares of the Indians encircling him, Font retreated to his tent. The Cojats' initial friendliness toward the Spaniards, Font huffed, "might turn to arrogance when it becomes a matter of subduing them into catechism and subordination." He accused them of being "greater thieves than others," because during the night they made off with a sword, a griddle, and some clothing. But he observed that being a thief was "a characteristic of every Indian."[13]

The personal habits of the indigenous people along the Colorado River were especially offensive to Font. Men generally went about naked, leaving their genitals exposed from the belief that their women did not want them to cover up.[14] Font took the time to put in writing that the men frequently stroked their penises in front of others and that if scolded—as they certainly were by Father Font—they merely laughed and did it some more. He also was disgusted by Indian men urinating while walking merrily along. "At least the animals stopped to piss," he declared.[15]

With beans a staple of their diet, the Indians were prone to flatulence. Nor did they consider it impolite to pass gas in the company of others. When Chief Palma was told it was improper to release his flatulence around others, he responded that he could not do otherwise because if he held it in he would explode. On one occasion, Anza asked an Indian to bring him a light for his cigar. Standing close to Anza while holding the burning match stick, the Indian let loose with what Font called "a formidable fart." When the commander objected to such behavior, the Indian merely smiled. "If they are sitting upon the ground all that they do is to lift their haunch a little on one side," Font recorded, "and since the farts they emit are such long, strong, full-formed ones, they raise dust off the ground with the gust."[16]

The Yuma women did not cover their breasts, but they clothed their genitals and buttocks with short skirts made of thin strips of willow and cottonwood bark woven together and tied around the waist. When they walked, the pieces of bark rubbing together made a rustling sound. One curiosity for Font was the spectacle of effeminate Native men wearing the same bark skirts and going about with the women, never joining the men. The Indians seemed to take a very tolerant view of this, but Font denounced the cross-dressers as "sodomites dedicated to the unspeakable deed."[17]

In sexual matters, generally, the clash between European and Indian mores could not have been starker. Font was distressed by the promiscuity of Indian women who were shared among the men, and also by the custom of offering a wife to sleep with an honored guest. Polygamy was practiced freely, posing an obstacle to Christian conversion because the padres insisted that a man renounce all of his wives save one before he could be baptized. The practical effect of this rule, Garcés pointed out in a later letter, was that there were few Indian converts between the ages of twenty and sixty. Throughout the Franciscan missions in California at this time, the vast majority of baptisms were of children and the elderly.[18] The Yumas painted their bodies all over with different rays and patterns. The men colored themselves red with ochre, black with charcoal, and white with clay, which Font thought made them look "like something hellish, especially at night."[19]

The women painted themselves with red only. Unlike in Spain, it was not the women but the men who adorned themselves with baubles and dyed their hair. The men wore necklaces made of dried heads of small insects that looked like scarabs. They pierced their ears in three or four places and dangled pendants from them as earrings. For nose rings, they punctured their septa and decorated them with a bluish stone or a piece of bone or stick. The glass beads brought by the Spaniards for trading and gifts were so popular among the Yumas that one day the expedition was inundated with more than two thousand watermelons for trade—so many that most of them had to be left behind because there was no way to transport them.

Font's contempt for the Indians' primeval ways contrasted sharply with Garcés's solicitousness, his eagerness to sit cross-legged with them around the fire for hours at night, his readiness to learn their languages and eat the same food they ate, and even to spit constantly on the ground as they did. While the expedition was camped for two nights at the site called La Laguna de Santa Olaya west of the Colorado River, Garcés appeared with a pack mule, a young boy, and two interpreters, including Sebastián Tarabal. He had left Padre Eixarch alone among the Yumas and was making his way downriver to meet new tribes and explore where the Colorado entered the Sea of Cortez. Finding that a large number of Indians had come to trade, Garcés passed out glass beads and tobacco as gifts, then gathered the Natives together to preach to them. The scene was vintage Garcés, the zealous evangelist whose overriding ambition in life was to plant the cross and save souls.

With the Indians seated around him, Garcés unfurled a large linen banner bearing on one side the peaceful image of the Virgin Mary cradling the Christ Child in her arms. On the opposite side was the disturbing picture of a condemned man being consumed by the fires of hell. Responding to Garcés's sermon, the Indians expressed great delight at the loving vision of the mother and child, and many professed their eagerness to become Christians and go to heaven where the mother and child were. Then Garcés dramatically exhibited the alternative to Christian conversion—eternal damnation in the devil's flames. These Indians already believed that beneath the earth there was a Hadean place populated with vicious dogs and other frightful creatures, so they were receptive to Garcés's pitch. "The sight of the lost soul so horrified them that they would not look at it and wanted the picture reversed," Garcés wrote in his diary. Font praised the performance. For him it was an illustration that God had created Garcés "wholly suited to seek out these unfortunate, ignorant, and rustic people."[20]

While resting at La Laguna de Santa Olaya, Anza penned seven dispatches to Viceroy Bucareli, bringing him up to date on the campaign. In one dispatch, dated 8 December 1775, he assured Bucareli that Palma, captain of the Yumas, deserved the credit for the tribe's eagerness to have the Spaniards establish permanent residence among them. "All his tribe desire to submit entirely to our religion and our sovereign," Anza wrote. "For this purpose he has notified all his people, and they are agreed to obey the precepts of the law and likewise those of his Majesty."[21] This judgment of the Yumas' everlasting devotion to the Spaniards and their God and king was appallingly flawed, as future events would demonstrate with bloody consequences.

In a separate letter written on the same day to Bucareli, Anza acknowledged he should have reached Mission San Gabriel by now. To speed his advance, Anza customarily had a quick breakfast of nourishing chocolate and then put off the one real meal of the day, typically chili and beans, until after the party had encamped for the night, thus making for a demanding day on the trail. He blamed his tardy progress on the pregnancies, with two women having delivered babies and two others having suffered miscarriages after departing Tubac. "It is these events that have caused the greatest delay, because it has not been possible to mount the women on horses until after four or five days," he claimed. This was an exaggeration; Anza had never paused for more than three days on account of the pregnancies. The commander's messages, composed in his florid hand and signed with his distinctive rubric resembling a swirling tornado, were put in a courier's pouch for the post rider's punishing run back to Mexico City.[22]

At 9:30 in the morning on Saturday, 9 December, Anza's caravan set out to the northwest. Garcés offered his farewells and headed downriver to the southwest, accompanied by several Indians and his interpreters. From his previous journey through this area a year earlier, Anza was well aware of the twin dangers on the path ahead—the acute shortage of water and of grazing land for the animals. What he did not anticipate was a dreadful cold snap accompanied by a driving snowstorm.

To cope with the lack of water, Anza divided the expedition into three sections, with each one departing a day after the other. This way, the few watering holes and wells along the way would not be overtaxed, or so Anza hoped. A single horse in the desert needed thirty gallons of water a day, and some of the paltry springs on this part of the trek produced only a few gallons of water an hour. The mules, heartier than the horses, could survive on less water and less forage.

The cattle, which were the most in jeopardy without adequate water, would be driven separately by a slightly shorter route. Unlike the horses and mules, the unruly cattle could not be watered by hand from woven baskets in places where there was only a trickle from a spring. In addition, each mount was assigned half a mule load of maize and bundled grass as feed when the desert was bare of vegetation. The first section to depart included Anza, Font, twelve soldiers with their families, and pack mules laden with equipment and supplies. Adding to Font's discomfort, his recurring fever had returned, this time along with diarrhea.

As the vanguard moved out, leaving behind the riparian habitat of recent days, the terrain turned bleak and infertile. The ground was so salty that it was white in places. Shifting sands, oyster and mussel shells, and other marine traces showed that the landscape had once been beneath the sea. Many of the inland lagoons and other water sources were too saline for consumption. Even some of the deeper wells dug by the party were briny. But on the first night a small well of relatively good freshwater was opened. The mules and horses had to be watered from baskets and fed the forage carried by every member of the party, including Anza and Font.

Font's keen eye spotted the dried droppings of the mounts and cattle of the previous year's expedition—an indication of how little rain, if any, had fallen in the interim. On 11 December the weather turned "cruelly cold," Anza noted, and there was no firewood to be found.[23] Spidery clouds overhead began to thicken.

After an arduous eleven-hour march, with no stop for a midday meal, the exhausted party reached the site called Santa Rosa de las Lajas (Saint Rose of the Flat Stones). The men sent ahead to dig wells had had very little success in producing water. When Anza arrived on the scene he urgently threw himself personally into the task, realizing that lives hung in the balance. Yet Font afforded the commander no credit. "With hard work the wells were deepened a bit and our patroness, the Most Holy Virgin of Guadalupe, willed that water should flow," Font declared. "Had this not happened, the expedition was at risk of perishing for lack of water on her feast day, which was tomorrow."[24]

At two o'clock the next morning, Anza was already at work with a shovel reopening the wells. The saddle animals were watered by the light of a waning moon. At half past noon, with a strong, cold wind blowing, the expedition set out again. Anza ordered a halt after a four-hour march at a spot where there was some pasturage and firewood. "Fuel was extremely necessary as a protection from the severe cold," he recorded.[25] The blackening sky threatened rain from every direction. By morning, there were snowflakes in the air.

A few underfed, stunted Indians with rotten teeth appeared during this day's march, and Font marveled at how they went about totally naked despite the cold and even bathed each morning in a spring, unbothered by the frigid weather. These tribesmen hunted hares with finely spun nets and a curved stick, called a *kapu*, thrown like a boomerang. To catch rabbits, several Indian men would drive them through the underbrush with sticks and into the carefully positioned purse nets.[26] At times the brush was set on fire to drive the rabbits out. But these particular Indians were subsisting mostly on roots and grass seeds. They were so undernourished that they hungrily scooped from the ground a few grains of corn, dirt and all, which had been dropped when the mules were fed.

At daybreak on 14 December it began to snow hard. A fierce wind battered the tents. The gusts of the previous day's march had been especially brutal on the women and children. With the snow piling up, it was impossible to continue onward. The entire party shivered and hunkered down by whatever fires they could keep burning. Font spent the day in Anza's larger, circus-like tent because it provided better shelter and had a fire for warmth. Rain and snow continued to fall throughout the day and evening. When it finally stopped snowing around eleven o'clock at night, the desert was buried under a white cloak that reflected the moonlight and made the night seem as bright as day. But, with the disappearance of cloud cover, the temperature dropped quickly. The commander wrote simply, "This was a night of extreme hardship."[27] Because of the snowstorm, Anza decided to rest for a few days and allow the two other sections of the expedition and the cattle to catch up. The first to arrive were the cattle, with ten head having succumbed in the storm. The herds had been driven without food or water and were in very poor shape. Overnight, six more cattle and a mule froze to death.

At midday on 15 December the second group of settlers straggled into camp, having been caught in the open by the storm. Some were suffering from hypothermia.

One man was near death and had to be bundled up between four fires for two hours to save his life. The group also had lost five saddle animals. The next morning four more cattle were found dead because of the freezing weather.

At eleven o'clock in the morning Anza learned that during the night four Indians had stolen three of the rapidly dwindling mounts. He immediately dispatched a sergeant and four soldiers to recover the precious saddle animals and let the Indians know that a repeat offense would be met with force of arms. By evening, the soldiers had returned with all of the steeds, which they found in two Indian villages.

By Sunday, 17 December, the third division still had not appeared. Anza sent two soldiers and twenty fresh mounts to rescue them. When the missing party finally reached camp at three o'clock in the afternoon, many were suffering from hypothermia and were in danger of dying. Six mounts had been left by the wayside when they could go no farther, and four others died along the way. The ensign in charge of the group had severe pain in his possibly frostbitten ears and could not hear. Two more cattle died of the cold in camp. The next day, two more perished. In an effort to salvage the meat, the carcasses were turned into well-salted jerked beef, but its taste and smell made it unpalatable.

Once the expedition was united again in one camp, there was a fandango lasting late into the night. María Feliciana Arballo, a widow aged twenty-four traveling with her two small daughters, entertained the boisterous celebration with some bawdy songs, known as *glosas*.[28] This required the singer to tell a story through extemporaneous, rhyming lyrics. Arballo's performance angered an unmarried man who had become close to her. Anza was forced to intervene when the man began to punish the woman, quite likely with physical abuse. Font, though, scolded Anza: "Let it be, sir, he is doing the right thing," to which Anza replied: "No, Father, I must not allow these excesses in my presence."[29]

At Mass the next morning, Font condemned the revelry, declaring that the settlers seemed to be thanking not God but the devil for their being safely reunited. His scoldings must have grated on the men, especially. The padre's sullen disposition was not helped by the return of his diarrhea, which kept him up at night and forced him to lie down whenever possible.

Records of María Feliciana Arballo's earlier marriage in Culiacán, Mexico, show she was a *mulata libre*, that is, a free woman of mixed African and Latino forebears.[30] After the unexpected death of her husband, who had been one of Anza's recruits, she had pleaded with Anza to allow her to join his expedition and start a new life in California. Although Anza may have had reservations about taking a vulnerable widow and her two children on such a rigorous journey, he placed her in the care of Augustín Valenzuela, a soldier who was traveling with his wife and young daughter.[31] Arballo departed from the Anza party when it reached Mission San Gabriel. In a ceremony conducted by Francisco Garcés in April 1776, she wed forty-year-old Juan Francisco López, a soldier at the mission. One of the witnesses was Anza's stalwart Indian guide, Sebastián Tarabal, who was about to follow Garcés on a marathon trek across the borderlands. Arballo's descendants played prominent roles in California's early development under Spanish, Mexican, and American rule.

When Anza broke camp with the familiar cry of "Vayan subiendo!" and resumed the march at midday, the shortage of mounts caused by the steady attrition of recent days was conspicuous. The expedition left Tubac with 695 saddle animals, including the packtrain.[32] But because of the losses, children now had to double up on horses. In some cases a soldier and two children rode a single horse. This sorely taxed the animals, which were already exhausted and suffering from the cold. Nearly all of the remaining steeds were scrawny, their ribs protruding from their hides. To alleviate the shortage of mounts, twenty pack mules were jettisoned of their loads and given to the settlers to ride. Even so, there no longer were enough mounts to go around and some members of the expedition had to proceed on foot.

On the night of 20 December about fifty cattle suffering from dehydration stampeded and returned to the previous day's watering spot, a marsh that the Spaniards called San Sebastián in honor of the Indian guide, Sebastián Tarabal. By the time the cowhands caught up with them, every single animal had become mired in the swampy terrain and had died. The cattle had failed to follow a solid trail through the marsh over which they had been led to water previously. Anza was distressed and somewhat defensive over this huge loss of His Majesty's cattle. Font, characteristically, blamed the commander, and the two spent the day in their own tents without speaking to each other except at mealtime.

Naked, malnourished Indians continued to be spotted in the high sierra above the expedition. Upon reaching one campsite, the soldiers startled five Indians. They fled in panic, leaving their belongings behind. Anza ordered that their possessions—baskets for gathering seeds, rabbit-skin blankets, and a bow—be left in a prominent spot where they could find them later. Occasionally, some of the braver tribesmen entered camp in search of food. Font described them as "so savage, wild, dirty, unkempt, ugly, small and stunted that it is only because they have a human form that one must believe that they are men." Anza reported they were "so lean and emaciated that they looked more like skeletons from the grave than living beings."³³ A light rain greeted dawn on Christmas Eve—*Noche Buena*, or Good Night, to the travelers. Anza pressed his charges onward. During that day's five-hour trek, the party found the abandoned antlers of bighorn sheep that had been hunted by the Indians. As they ascended a broad canyon, the ground turned stony, making it rough going for the mounts and those on foot. There was no water here, in fact nothing green in sight.

The creosote bushes littering the terrain gave off a foul odor as they always did when it rained. Font called this smelly plant *hediondilla*, the Spanish word for "stinky," and he pronounced it an ill omen because it grew only in harsh country. By the time the expedition stopped to set up camp for the night, drizzle and an eerie fog had descended on the huddled settlers. Visibility was reduced to about a dozen yards. Nearby was an Indian village, which the Spaniards called Los Danzantes (The Dancers), because when the Natives there talked they gesticulated wildly, leapt in the air, swirled about, and bumped their haunches together, reminding Font of frolicking goats.

Anza ordered the party to rest for the night sooner than he had wanted, because twenty-two-year-old María Gertrudis Rivas Linares had gone into labor on the back of a mule. Accompanying her were her thirty-year-old husband, Ignacio, who had been recruited as a soldier from the Tubac presidio, and their three children, María Gertrudis, age seven, Joseph Ramón, age four, and María Juliana, age three.³⁴ The Linares family was not out of the ordinary among the sturdy pioneers who abided the hardships of the trail. Like 27 percent of the colonists recruited by Anza, the Lineareses were of mixed Spanish and Native blood.³⁴ Census records listed Ignacio as an *indio* and María as an *española*.³⁵

In the evening, as the other settlers noisily celebrated the birth of the Christ Child, Font was summoned to María's tent. Remembering the awful death in childbirth at the start of the expedition of Manuela Piñuelas, María Linares was fearful of dying herself. Given the high mortality rate of women in childbirth under the best of circumstances, not to mention the primitive conditions of the trail, María's alarm was not surprising. She had asked for Font to come and hear her last confession, in the event she did not survive the labor. He heard the woman's admissions, comforted her as best he could, and returned to his tent. Playing out now in this frigid, fog-shrouded encampment was a uniquely poignant nativity scene.

To mark Noche Buena, Anza ordered that beef be served for dinner and that afterward half a liter of *aguardiente*—literally "fiery water," a strong brandy—be passed out to each soldier. As soon as the ever-meddlesome Font learned of the plan to distribute alcohol, he confronted Anza. In his journal, Font detailed a verbatim version of what ensued:

> To see whether I might stop this drunkenness, after dinner I said to our commander, "Sir, even though my bringing up the matter is useless and I have no role to play here, I have learned that there is to be drinking today." He replied, "There is." "But sir," I continued, "I say that I do not think it good for us to celebrate the birth of the child Jesus with drunkenness." "Father," he said to me, "I am not giving it out for them to get drunk on." "Surely that must be so," I said, "since if you did, the evil would be all the greater; but if you know they will get drunk, don't give it to them." He said to me in reply, "It is provided to me by the king, and they give it to me so that I can give it to the troops." I responded, "Fine, but that must have meant in case of need." "But Father," he said, "better they should get drunk than commit something else." I answered, "But sir, getting drunk is a sin, and he who cooperates with sin also sins, and thus if you are aware that someone gets drunk upon thus-and-so much, give him less or don't give him any." He did not utter another word. I went off to my tent without having been able to hinder this disorder, since he had already decided to issue it."[36]

Much to Font's regret, dancing and loud singing continued into the night. He disdainfully declared that the revelers were "untroubled by our being in the midst of such hard mountains, in rains, and so set back by worn-out and dead animals and cattle. Such is the rule, there, of these absolute gentry [Anza]. I have narrated this event to prove it!"[37]

As the celebrations continued through the evening, María Linares's labor progressed in her tent. Part of the traditional Christmas Eve celebration in New Spain, dating back to the 1500s, was the singing of "La Posada" (The Inn), commemorating the story of the birth of Christ, when there was no room at the inn for Mary and Joseph. The first verse was sung by "*los peregrinos*," the pilgrims or wanderers, a designation that surely was not lost on the vagabond Anza party. In English translation, the pilgrims' refrain is, "In the name of heaven / I ask you for shelter / For my wife is tired / She can go no farther." Not long before the stroke of midnight, as the cattle were lowing and the campfires dying, María Linares came through the delivery without harm. In her arms she cradled a boy.

This was the third live birth to occur since the expedition left Tubac. Two other women had miscarriages along the same route. In addition, three women miscarried before the departure from Tubac. The commander expressed relief in his journal that of the eight women, only one had died—another indication of just how hazardous childbirth was at the time.

The heavy fog persisted on Christmas morning. Anza decided to rest his train for the day. Font, having recovered somewhat from his diarrhea, said Mass three times. Always a man of rectitude, he used his sermons to needle Anza by sternly condemning the drinking of the night before. Afterward he baptized the newborn. In recognition of the holy day of his birth, the boy was solemnly christened Salvador (Savior) Ignacio Linares. Font took full credit for calling the baby Salvador, although his parents surely must have had some say in the matter.[38]

Determined not to dally the next day, Tuesday, 26 December, Anza broke camp at a quarter to nine in the morning under a welcome bright sun, commenting that the new mother "was better and had the pluck to march."[39] Thus it was that, just thirty-six hours after giving birth, María Linares was back in the saddle, nursing her infant and shepherding along the trail her three older children with the help of her husband.

In a low spot during the day's march the expedition came upon a deserted Native village. The inhabitants had abandoned their huts and gopher holes as soon as they spotted the cattle being driven ahead of the settlers. Judging from their fresh tracks, the Indians had climbed like deer to the safety of higher ground, and not a single Native was to be seen.

In this isolated spot today, shallow mortar holes carved by Natives in low boulders mark the site of the village. The cup-shaped mortars were used with a heavy rock to grind acorns into flour, a staple of the Indians' diet. Native rock art nearby depicts a horse with rider—an astonishing sight, no doubt, to the Indians of Font's day.[40] Elder Katherine Siva Saubel, a modern descendant of the Cahuilla Indians who inhabited these mountains, recounted the tribe's oral history of the Anza party: "What did our people do when [the Spaniards] came across here? My dad was born in 1872, so he knew about it; old people had told him all about it. . . . I asked him what they thought about the [Spanish] people and he said they thought they were ghosts coming through because they were so white. The Cahuilla were all scared; they hid and wouldn't show themselves."[41]

The sunshine was replaced by sleet by the time Anza ordered a halt around two o'clock in the afternoon near a crucial milestone 3,912 feet above sea level. They had attained El Puerto Real de San Carlos (The Royal Pass of Saint Charles), the gateway out of the unforgiving desert and into coastal California. Anza had named the pass the previous year in honor of his sovereign, Carlos III.

What a welcome sight the green mountains ahead must have been to the weary travelers. The topography suddenly turned lush and fertile, with running streams and oak trees with acorns and shrubs. The next day Font spotted patches of fragrant red roses with five petals like those he remembered from Castile. The padre also found three abandoned Indian huts surrounded by discarded acorn shells and human excrement—another bothersome indication to him of how "filthy" the mountain Indians were.[42]

Just as it was getting dark on the day after Christmas, about five o'clock in the afternoon, the ground began to shake and a strong rumble like thunder filled the air. As if the trail had one last surprise, a powerful earthquake rattled the expedition, followed a few minutes later by a strong aftershock. Anza was so taken aback by the temblor that he declared it lasted a full four minutes.

While encamped at the pass two days later, Anza took stock of his ragged followers. The previous day some of the women had begun to weep when they spotted deep snow in the mountains ahead, fearing they would have to cross them. They likely were spying the high peaks of the San Bernardino range to the northwest. Coming from what Anza called *tierra caliente* (a hot land), the women were terrified of the snow-covered summits. In reality, the expedition would bypass those high peaks by traveling to the west of them. Anza sought to reassure the anxious women by telling them that once they reached coastal California in a few days' time, the weather would turn benign like the winter climate of their homeland in Sonora.

María Linares was now stricken with hard post-partum spasms and could not march, forcing another one-day delay. There were pressing shortages of saddle animals and cattle. Provisions of all kinds, especially soap and shoes, were scarce. The settlers had endured the perils of the desert without complaint and without loss of life, but they had been battered by one of the coldest winters in years. To address their deteriorating plight, Anza dispatched by courier to Mission San Gabriel an urgent appeal to Fernando Rivera y Moncada, the military governor of California, for relief provisions.

The commander's prime request was for the settlers themselves. "Since they have been in the service eight months, the clothing they have been given was destroyed and worn out," Anza wrote. "Because of that, and because the season is so raw, they are in need of reparation. Therefore, I have taken this opportunity to give your Honor this notice that, if you do not feel it is inconvenient, you might find someone to send a provision of underclothing. That is truly what is needed by all the men, women, and children. Of course, they will be able to make do with their exterior clothing and the use of some blankets until they have such" replenishment. The commander closed his letter with a plea for more cattle and saddle animals and whatever other supplies Rivera deemed appropriate.[43]

The viceroy's seventy-day deadline for reaching Monterey had passed a full three weeks earlier, and the party was still four hundred miles from its destination. Anza had only about a week and a half worth of supplies left.[44] Without a huge infusion of aid very soon, the expedition was doomed to collapse.

CHAPTER EIGHT

Uprising at Mission San Diego

> What anguish and sorrow were mine, my pen cannot describe.
> —Fray Vicente Fuster, 28 November 1775

On a scenic spot overlooking the San Diego River today, a whitewashed concrete cross rises ten feet above the ground. Flanked by the gnarled trunks of ancient pepper trees and surrounded by flowering shrubs, the monument stands alone, off by itself, under blue skies on a sunlit promontory just outside the walls of Mission San Diego, the first of the Franciscan outposts in California. Tourists visiting the site pay little notice to the marker. In the distance they can hear the roar of freeway traffic and other rumblings of a bustling urban scene. A tarnished bronze plaque at the base of the memorial bears the name of Fray Luís Jayme, the first Franciscan martyr in California.

Erected almost a century ago, the cross commemorates the night of 4–5 November 1775, when six hundred Kumeyaay warriors pillaged the unprotected Mission San Diego, burned it to the ground, and killed three Spaniards, including Father Jayme, a thirty-five-year-old friar from Mallorca.[1] This was one of the largest and most coordinated Indian assaults ever mounted against the California missions. The sickening episode in the mission's early history is overlooked by modern visitors as they amble about the manicured grounds and purchase religious-themed souvenirs in the gift shop. Yet for Pedro Font more than two centuries earlier, the upheaval was an unforgettable occurrence.

Word of the Kumeyaay uprising reached Font after he had finished saying Mass around ten o'clock in the morning on New Year's Day 1776. Having descended from the San Carlos Pass a few days earlier into the comparatively lush, verdant valleys of coastal California, the Anza expedition was camped on the south bank of the swift-flowing Santa Ana River. Preparations were being made to ford the river when a corporal from Mission San Gabriel arrived on horseback with a reply to Anza's dispatch of 27 December requesting relief supplies from Commander

Fernando Rivera y Moncada, the military governor of California. The soldier, Guillermo Carrillo, was accompanied by the three couriers who had earlier relayed Anza's appeal to San Gabriel. He brought seventeen mounts as aid for the caravan, along with urgent news of the bloodshed at San Diego.

Anza's immediate impulse was to gather up his troops, advance directly to the coastal settlement, and quell the Native unrest at once through force of arms.[2] He was, after all, a veteran Indian fighter above all else, having engaged in numerous campaigns throughout northwestern New Spain. But the corporal relayed two other important developments. One was that the Indians around Mission San Gabriel were believed to be plotting an imminent attack there, too. The other was that Commander Rivera himself was expected to arrive soon at San Gabriel from his headquarters at the Monterey presidio. Consequently, Anza decided to continue on to San Gabriel and confer with Rivera, his superior, before taking further action.

Revelation of the massacre at San Diego came at a moment when the spirits of the Anza party were boosted by the pleasant countryside through which they were passing. On the previous day the colonists had tramped through a ravine so luxuriant and green that they called it La Cañada de Paraíso (Paradise Hollow). The ground was stippled with blackberry brambles, rosemary, and other fragrant herbs. At times Font spotted in the distance large flocks of white geese, and he savored the singing of meadowlarks. "Their song is not a long one," he recorded, "but sweet."[3] He plucked lavender and gathered up the shells of snails like those he had seen in the woods of Spain.

The "floweriness" of the surroundings, as he described it, reminded him of his homeland. Here the travelers encountered fields of wild sunflowers in bloom and ambling grape vines. The only thing missing in the treeless plains was firewood to keep them warm on the cold, damp nights. Font ate the tiny red rose hips he found in the plentiful rose patches, and he drank his fill from the crystalline, fresh-running streams. Perhaps as a consequence, his diarrhea had improved more so than at any time since leaving San Miguel de Horcasitas in Sonora the previous fall. What was more, Font and Anza were on better terms. They rode along side by side at times, talking agreeably with each other. In his diary, Font added in parentheses: "Whole days used to pass without our saying anything to each other except what was strictly necessary."[4]

Before Anza could respond to events in San Diego, he had to get his expedition across the Santa Ana River and on to Mission San Gabriel as soon as possible. Fording the river was a delicate operation. Although it was less than twenty feet wide, the current was so swift that a horse was swept away and drowned after it tried to get a drink at a soft spot along the bank. A bull also was drowned at the ford. It simply was too dangerous for the women and children to attempt to cross on the backs of horses and mules.

When Anza came upon the river at the same location more than a year earlier, the soldiers cut down a large cottonwood tree on the riverbank and used it as a bridge to transport supplies to the other side. This time Anza reinforced the earlier construction so that it could carry more traffic. Sent across the wobbly span first were the women and children, followed by the food and other perishable cargo that could not be allowed to get wet. It's not hard to imagine María Gertrudis Rivas Linares shepherding her three young children across the narrow log catwalk while cradling week-old Salvador in her arms. The crossing was completed without mishap by three o'clock in the afternoon, and Anza rested his train for the night. He would move on upcountry toward San Gabriel early the next morning.

On Tuesday, 2 January 1776, Font said an early Mass and the full expedition was mounted up by a quarter past eight. Camp was established that afternoon under a steady downpour of rain, with sporadic snow, on the banks of El Arroyo de los Alisos (Sycamore Stream). Font gathered a good quantity of tender, lettuce-like greens and took it to Anza's tent, where the two ate it as a salad, adding a healthy dose of vitamins and fiber to their scurvy-prone diet. Thus the thaw in their frosty relationship continued. More than a year earlier, Anza had carved the initials IHS (a Roman Catholic reference to Jesus Christ) in the bark of a large sycamore to mark his passing through the area. Font now took a knife and added to the trunk: "Año 1776. Vino la Expedición de San Francisco" (Year 1776. The San Francisco expedition came here).

Two days later, after crossing a gap called El Puerto de los Osos, so named because Anza had spotted bears there in 1774, the file finally was approaching Mission San Gabriel. At mid-morning Commander Rivera and the padre in charge of the mission, fifty-four-year-old Antonio Paterna, rode out to welcome them. Rivera had stopped at San Gabriel en route to San Diego where, he feared, another Indian rebellion was brewing.

"Our arrival was one of great rejoicing for everyone," Font wrote, as the throng of sojourners descended on the modest station, which consisted of little more than a few adobe brick structures with roofs made of tule bulrushes and little round tule huts for Indian converts.[5] With the snow-covered sierra as a backdrop, the eight escort soldiers of the mission fired their guns in salute and the San Gabriel friars pealed the bells to herald the exodus of settlers, soldiers, cattle, and pack mules bound for northern California. For the colonists, Mission

San Gabriel, primitive though it was, marked the first taste of civilization since setting out across the Sonoran Desert the previous year.

While Rivera and Anza consulted on how to respond to the rebellion in San Diego, Font wandered about inspecting the mission, which several months earlier had been moved three miles to its present location so as to be closer to a reliable source of water. A wide irrigation ditch had been dug to bring a plentiful supply from a spring right through the middle of the compound and on to the surrounding agricultural fields. Font estimated that five hundred Natives, young and old, had joined the mission.

Having subsisted on a meager trail diet for more than two months, Font marveled at the variety of foods now available to him. A herd of fat dairy cows produced delicious milk, along with butter and a variety of cheeses. Pigs and chickens were raised for food, and upon Anza's arrival the mission slaughtered three or four sheep and roasted them for a feast. "The meat was particularly good, and I do not recall ever having eaten richer and finer mutton than this," Font gushed. He also consumed a great deal of wild watercress and celery, along with turnips planted by the padres and large roots that he believed were the same as the parsnips he had eaten in Spain. Father Paterna, an angular, dark-haired, blue-eyed native of Andalusía and a veteran of the Franciscan mission fields, declared that California was like the biblical Promised Land. After the deprivations of the desert, Font heartily agreed.[6]

He next turned his observant eye to the Indians of the mission, describing them as mild-mannered and not very tall, with the women even shorter. They had round faces and snub noses, which made them appear to Font as "a bit ugly."[7] The men went about naked, but the women covered themselves with deerskin skirts and blankets made of otter pelts or hare skins.

The padres' sometimes stern treatment of the Indians was detailed candidly by Font while at San Gabriel, and he was quick to note that the same rules applied at all of the California missions. For starters, the padres did not coerce the Natives into embracing Christianity. Once an Indian chose to become a Christian, however, he had to live by the rigid code enforced by the Spaniards.

Font acknowledged that many Indians decided to become Christians simply because of the meat-laden *posole* (a maize-based stew) and other nutritious foods served at the missions. He declared that these converts were in fact "caught by the mouth." He added, "Since these Indians are used to living like beasts in the fields and mountains," the padres "warn them that if they wish to become Christians they can no longer go to the woods but must live at the mission."[8] The reason for this seemingly unreasonable stricture was that the friars feared the Indians would revert to their pagan practices if they returned to their relatives in the wild. When Indians left the mission without permission and ventured back to their villages and extended families, the Spanish soldiers and faithful Native converts were sent after them. If caught, the fugitives were brought back in chains and chastised severely, sometimes with corporal punishment. A common reason for fleeing was the fear of death after witnessing one's family members perish at the mission from European diseases, syphilis being one of the most prevalent. (In one year alone, nearly a third of the Indian adherents at Mission San Francisco were runaways.)

The French seafarer Jean François de La Pérouse, a battle-hardened officer who had fought Britain's Royal Navy during the American Revolution, visited Monterey and Mission San Carlos a decade after Font's arrival at Mission San Gabriel. Educated in France by the Jesuits, La Pérouse praised the Franciscans' generous spirit toward the Indians. But he was dismayed by the inhumane penalties inflicted on those who disobeyed the Spanish decrees.

La Pérouse found both men and women Natives held in irons and stocks. The "noise of the whip might have struck our ears," he added in his journal, "this punishment also being administered, though with little severity."[9] Compliant Indian leaders, or caciques, selected by the padres usually determined how many lashes they would administer to their fellow tribesmen. Most crimes merited ten to thirty strokes of the whip, but sometimes this punishment was inflicted on the same offender for two or three consecutive days. For very serious violations a *novenario* was imposed. This meant the victim received a beating for nine consecutive days. In one case, an Indian guilty of homicide at Mission San Carlos received seventy-five lashes a day for three days and was imprisoned in chains for a year.[10]

According to La Pérouse, Indian men were whipped in the open, for all to see, as a deterrent to other would-be runaways. The victims "usually ask pardon for their fault, in which case the executioner diminishes the force of his lashes, but the number is always irrevocable," recorded La Pérouse. Indian women, on the other hand, were flogged in enclosed spaces away from public view so that "their cries may not excite a too lively compassion, which might cause the men to revolt."[11] Native women inflicted the punishment on female offenders.

The daily routine of the Natives at Mission San Gabriel was followed in more or less the same way at the other missions. At sunrise the bell was rung and Mass was said, with the Indians required to attend. As part of the morning ritual, the priest recited the catechism, which spelled out the principles of the Catholic faith. This was done in Spanish, even if the priest had learned the Native language. "The

Indians should be taught the *doctrina* [catechism] in Spanish," Font declared, "and the attempt made to have them speak Spanish, since all of the Indian languages are barbarous and very wanting in terms."[12] Spaniards chauvinistically presumed that the metaphysical aspects of Christianity could not be expressed in Indian tongues because they lacked the vocabulary for abstract reasoning. In practice, the Natives merely recited the Spanish by rote, having no idea what the words meant. As one experienced friar declared, "There are no Christians in the world who recite the catechism more often and know it less than these Indians."[13] At the conclusion of Mass, the priest and Indians sang the *Alabado*.

As stipulated by the "Rules and Regulations for Spiritual Direction," a stern directive issued earlier by the Reverend Father Pedro Pérez de Mezquía, superior of the Franciscan College of San Fernando in Mexico City, the Indians were obligated after the liturgical ceremonies to line up for roll call and, when their names were pronounced, to kiss the hand of the priest as a sign of respect for the church and the king.[14] Spaniards themselves routinely kissed the hands of respected men as a gesture of humility and obeisance. Then followed a breakfast of atole (corn gruel), and the Indians were required before eating to make the sign of the cross and give thanks to God for the food. Afterward, the Indians went to work under the austere supervision of the padres. At midday a meal of posole was dished out, followed by another period of work. Font observed that Mission San Diego, the poorest of the early Franciscan settlements, was not able to serve posole to the Indians, which might have helped explain the strife there. At sunset each day, the catechism was recited again and the *Alabado* intoned once more.

The daily work routine for the Indians began with the second ringing of the mission bell about an hour after sunrise and extended until noon. After a two-hour break, the Natives resumed their labors until almost sunset, for a total of about six to eight hours. The work day was shorter in winter than in summer.

Indian men and women were typically employed at the same jobs, from working in the fields to carrying stone to erecting buildings. Women who were in advanced pregnancy or nursing infants were assigned lighter tasks, such as carrying firewood or grinding corn by hand in a metate, a stone mortar. Children were kept busy chasing birds from the vegetable gardens and orchards, pulling weeds, combing wool for the looms, or keeping the livestock from trampling on wet adobe bricks set out to dry in the sun. The only Indians exempted from work were the elderly and frail.

Just before bedtime the unmarried Indian girls of adolescent age and older were locked into a small dormitory to protect them from sexual advances by the soldiers. This practice has been assailed by modern critics as a concentration-camp measure. But the problem of rapes committed against Indian women and girls by unmarried Spanish troopers was very real. Many of the conscripts were low-paid ex-convicts pressed into military service on the frontier. Soldiers were known to slip out at night to prey on women in nearby Indian villages. At Mission San Juan Capistrano the escort soldiers beat Indian men to force them to tell where their women were hiding. Just the previous year, the soon-to-be-martyred Fray Luís Jayme had moved the San Diego mission six miles inland from the presidio, in part to separate the bare-breasted Indian maidens from the Spanish troops. Rapes committed by soldiers at San Diego almost certainly were a contributing factor to the revolt there.

Fearing another imminent outbreak of Native unrest on the coast, Rivera and Anza wasted no time in formulating a plan to relieve the garrison at San Diego and punish the Natives who had sacked the mission two months earlier. They agreed to pool their best mounts and soldiers—seventeen from the Anza expedition and twelve others mustered by Rivera—and march the 104 miles along an old Indian trail, traced more recently by El Camino Real, to the San Diego presidio, a wooden stockade sitting on a bluff overlooking the harbor. Without Rivera having to ask, Anza volunteered to participate in this military foray. In truth there likely was no possibility that this seasoned musketeer could have been kept away from the action.

Anza did not, however, ask Font to join the campaign. This wounded the padre's hypersensitive pride because he had promised Anza before their departure from San Miguel de Horcasitas that he would remain with him wherever he went, regardless of the consequences. In a frank private talk with Anza, Font let his hurt feelings be known, stressing in self-pityingly terms that the commander had every right to free himself of "this useless baggage," as the priest called himself.[15] Staking out the honorable ground, as always, Anza immediately relented, asked for Font's pardon, and said he would be very pleased to have the chaplain with him. Thus with Font, despite his fragile health, vowing anew not to leave Anza's side, the column set out on Sunday, 7 January 1776, and reached the San Diego presidio, posthaste, at ten o'clock on Thursday morning. Now, the gruesome assault on Mission San Diego was cast in sharp relief.

Archeological evidence shows prehistoric habitation of the coastal region surrounding present-day San Diego as far back as ten thousand years ago. But anthropologists believe the Kumeyaay (pronounced Koo-may-YAI) migrated to the area sometime after 1000 A.D. from what is now western Arizona and northern Sonora, Mexico.[16] Composed of a variety of tribes sharing a common linguistic and ethnic heritage, the Kumeyaay occupied a vast territory extending northward from the eastern shore of the Sea of Cortez in present-day Mexico to what is now San Bernardino County in Southern California and southward along the Pacific littoral to Ensenada in Baja California, Mexico. This was the largest and most diverse domain of any Native group in California, encompassing large tracts of the arid Sonoran and Colorado Deserts, the inhospitable mountain ranges to the northwest, and the beneficent coastal plain. Most were hunter-gatherers who moved their villages from place to place in pursuit of the seasonal food supply.[17] But tribes along the Colorado River, the New River, and the Alamo River planted crops that were irrigated by annual floodwaters.

In contrast to the docile tribes farther north, the Kumeyaay resisted the Spanish intrusion from the very start. Within days after Fray Junípero Serra had established Mission San Diego in July 1769, Kumeyaay warriors in small canoes made of tule rushes attempted to pillage the *San Carlos*, the Spanish supply ship anchored in the bay.[18] The soldiers on board repelled the invaders with force.

On 15 August 1769 about twenty Kumeyaay assaulted the sick bay set up in canvas tents on the beach for the scurvy-plagued sailors of the Portolá expedition and even attempted to strip the sick and dying men of their bedsheets and clothing.[19] Then the Natives burned the first mission church, a primitive structure built of wood and thatch. At that moment there were only four armed soldiers to defend the Spanish encampment, and a fierce exchange of arrows and musket volleys ensued. Three Kumeyaay were killed by musket balls. According to Lieutenant Pedro Fages, other Indians who were wounded in the attack were later put to death by the soldiers.[20]

The first Spanish casualty was Serra's servant, twenty-year-old José María Bejarano, who had approached the padre at Loreto in Baja California and offered to be his page for the long journey north. He was struck in the neck by a Kumeyaay arrow. "At the first shot he darted into my hut, spouting so much blood at the mouth and from his temples that I had hardly time to absolve him and help him to meet his end," Serra wrote in a letter to a colleague in Mexico City. "He expired on the ground before me bathed in his own blood. . . . And there I was with the dead man, thinking it most probable I would soon have to follow him, but at the same time praying to God that the victory would be for our Catholic Faith without losing a single soul."[21]

One of Serra's assistants, forty-one-year-old Fray Juan Vizcaíno, an experienced missionary who had arrived in New Spain two decades earlier, was wounded in the right hand, between his middle finger and his ring finger, by a crude arrow made of a sharpened stick without a flint point. The Portolá expedition's surgeon removed the arrow and some wooden splinters from his hand. A blacksmith named Chacón from Guadalajara and a Christianized Indian from Baja California also took arrows. Unnerved by the hostility of the Kumeyaay and with his half-paralyzed hand slow to heal, Vizcaíno sought Serra's permission to return to the safe cloisters of the College of San Fernando in Mexico City.[22] His wish was granted, putting a permanent end to a promising career in the mission fields of California.

In an entry in his journal after arriving at San Diego, Font made reference to Fray Vizcaíno's unfortunate encounter six years earlier with the Kumeyaay Natives and denounced their "evil purposes and wicked hearts." Giving vent to his embittered outlook, Font called the Kumeyaay "poor-bodied, ugly, dirty, disheveled, sooty, stinking, and flat-faced. . . . [T]hey have ever shown themselves as undesirable."[23] This certainly was not the final time that Font disparaged his charges.

Many factors converged to spark the Kumeyaay insurrection in the predawn of 5 November 1775. First off, in April 1773 at least two young Indian girls had been raped by three Spanish soldiers at a nearby settlement known as La Soledad. One of the girls died in the assault.[24] Among the accused was Mateo Ignacio Soto, an original member of the Portolá expedition, who fled to Mexico and disappeared, escaping justice.[25]

Father Jayme himself had documented a number of other sexual assaults by soldiers against Indian women, including an incident in which a Native woman was gang-raped at a corral in her village. In another case reported by Jayme to his superiors, an unmarried Native woman who had been raped by a soldier sought unsuccessfully to abort the resultant pregnancy. She later gave birth to a fair-skinned child and then killed the baby out of a misplaced sense of shame.

Tensions over sexual matters became a volatile undercurrent, given that the Spanish intruders were exclusively male. Some Natives initially mistook the Spaniards' mules to be their wives. They had trouble understanding why the foreigners had no women. Indian wives accompanied their men even into battle. Lieutenant Fages, who served four years as military governor of California, urged the viceroy to expedite the settlement of Spanish wives and children so that the "Indians would soon cease to consider [as they do now] that we are exiles from our own lands who have come here in quest of their women."[26]

Beyond the issue of women, Jayme had written to his superiors complaining that "indolent" Spanish soldiers were allowing the cattle of the settlement to devour the grasslands relied upon by the Indians for seeds, an important food source.[27] The padre sympathized with the Indians' generally suspicious outlook toward the Spaniards. In a letter written 17 October 1772, he stated: "No wonder the Indians here were bad when the mission was first founded. To begin with, they did not know why [the Spaniards] had come, unless they intended to take their lands away from them."[28] Yet another contributing circumstance was an upsurge in Indian baptisms, which meant an increase in the number of Kumeyaay collaborating with the Spaniards. No fewer than sixty Indians had been baptized on a single day a month earlier.[29] Writing not long after the assault, the Franciscan missionary Francisco Palóu concluded that "the motive for killing [Father Jayme] was that he was baptizing so many and that he wished to make an end of heathenism in the neighborhood of San Diego."[30] The transfer of the mission from a site near the bay to one farther inland in the broad valley formed by the San Diego River may also have alarmed the Kumeyaay plotters.

Whatever the causes, the well-orchestrated convulsion of Kumeyaay violence quickly devolved into butchery as hundreds of warriors silently surrounded the mission at 1 A.M. under a full moon. Font heard every gory nugget from Fray Vicente Fuster, the second-in-command at the mission, who narrowly escaped death and composed a dramatic dispatch to Serra, then ensconced at his headquarters at Mission San Carlos near present-day Carmel. Fuster, thirty-three years old, was raised in Alcañiz, a village in Zaragosa Province, Aragón.[31] Light-skinned, with a thin face, dark hair, and a medium build, Father Fuster was a tough-minded man who later confronted Captain Rivera in defense of a Native conspirator involved in the San Diego rampage. But the Indian brutality of that night caused Fuster to develop an abiding antagonism and mistrust toward the Kumeyaay, prompting Serra to transfer him elsewhere nineteen months later.

The assault was carried out with ruthless sway by a surprisingly large force of attackers assembled from forty surrounding villages, including converted Indians from the mission who had turned against their Spanish patrons.[32] Even the padres' Native servant boy was in league with the conspirators. Font termed these Indians "household spies."[33]

At Mission San Diego the centerpiece was a crude church made of brushwood, with a thatched roof, measuring fifty-three feet long and sixteen feet wide.[34] The compound also consisted of an adobe house for the padres, a storehouse, an adobe outbuilding with a flat earthen roof for the forge, a thatched-roof enclosure for the fifty-seven mules and horses, servants quarters made of logs and a thatched roof, thirteen round thatched huts for the Christianized Indians, and a log corral for the fifty-four head of cattle. Most of the mission was as flammable as dry kindling. Wheat had been sown in a nearby field but was doing poorly because of the lack of rain. Ninety-seven Spaniards and Indians lived close to the mission, within sound of the bell, according to an accounting made by Serra earlier in the year. Also belonging to the mission were 104 sheep, 61 goats, 3 donkeys, and 27 pigs.

The mission's inconsequential defenses amounted to four escort soldiers, two blacksmiths, a master carpenter, two padres, and two Spanish youths who were the son and the nephew of the garrison's lieutenant commander. Armed with war clubs, lances, firebrands, rocks, and bows and arrows, the throng of assailants first encircled the Native huts of the compound and warned the inhabitants to stay inside and keep quiet. Then, howling fiercely, they descended on the church from all quadrants, carried off the priests' vestments, ornaments, statues of the Virgin Mary and Saint Joseph, and other religious articles, and set the building ablaze. Built of dried bulrushes, the church flared quickly. Indian women alongside the warriors retreated into the darkness with the loot. Next to be torched were the guardhouse and the adobe structure where Father Jayme kept his quarters, followed by the granary and storehouse, where Fuster slept.

The dozing soldiers were slow to respond to this stealthy incursion. The larger contingent of well-armed Spanish troops at the presidio a few miles away slumbered soundly through the night without hearing the discharge of blunderbusses or seeing the flames leaping above the buildings. This was puzzling, because the presidio's morning musket salute was always audible at the mission. The sentinel on duty that night at the presidio later testified that he thought the firelight he detected in the east was the moon; actually, the moon was in the western sky. Under the Indians' original war plan, their force was divided into two groups, one assigned to attack the mission and the other the presidio, which was fortified with two brass cannons in addition to the troops. The leaders of the second body lost their nerve, because they assumed the presidio soldiers had been forewarned by the flaming buildings at the mission. Instead, the second band of Natives joined in the mission raid.

Once awakened, Fuster dashed into the courtyard amid a hail of lethal projectiles. "I saw on all sides around me so many arrows that you could not possibly count them," he recalled.[35] Even the horses, mules, pigs, and other livestock in their corrals became targets of the Kumeyaay arrows. As the soldiers gathered together behind a shelter and finally began firing their weapons, Fuster went in desperate search of Father Jayme at his house. The structure was engulfed in smoke, the roof blazing. Holding his breath, Fuster rushed into the burning building and felt all over Jayme's bed, only to discover he was not there.

Assisted by the two Spanish boys of the mission, Fuster then retrieved from the burning storehouse a trunk containing fifty pounds of gunpowder in two bags. He gave the incendiary cache to the soldiers, with the injunction to keep it away from the flames, which now raged on all four sides of the enclosed courtyard. After hearing a shot in the blacksmith's workshop, Fuster encountered smithy Felipe Romero, who said he had just killed an Indian with his gun. The mission's other blacksmith, José Arroyo, had tried to fend off the Kumeyaay warriors with a sword, but he was overwhelmed by their arrows. He died of his wounds five days later, after drawing up a will in which he left his saved-up salary from the royal treasury, in a spirit of Christian forgiveness, to the Indians who took his life.

Fuster, the two boys, the blacksmith, and the soldiers then barricaded themselves as best they could in the three-sided, open-roofed cook shelter. Its adobe walls were only about three feet high, but they offered a defensive barrier to crouch behind. "As soon as we reached the cookhouse, our enemies saw us," recorded Fuster, "and with united forces they hurled such a storm of arrows, rocks, adobe [bricks], and firebrands that it seemed they were determined to bury us under them."[36]

Stretched out now on the ground in front of the cookhouse was another Kumeyaay warrior killed by Spanish bullets. For his part, the blacksmith loaded and primed the guns, while the soldiers kept up a steady fire and the Indians plastered the cookhouse with arrows, many of which were now stuck in the walls. One arrow pierced the pillow that Fuster held in front of his face for protection, but he escaped injury.

Meanwhile, he continued to snatch away the firebrands that landed on or near the soldiers' large bags of gunpowder. At one point he even straddled the gunpowder in order to protect it under the skirt of his habit, despite the obvious hazard involved. After a while, the torrent of incoming arrows subsided, but stones and firebrands continued to shower the cookhouse. Fuster felt a painful blow when a rock struck him in the shoulder.

Daybreak brought one last barrage from the attackers. "I could hear numbers of the enemy, who until recently had been my trusted children, giving orders that now they should once and for all make an end of us, and encouraging their own ranks for the final charge," Fuster wrote in his report.[37] Yet, to the astonishment and relief of the survivors, the Indians abruptly withdrew as suddenly as they had arrived, carrying their dead and wounded with them. What, though, was the fate of Father Jayme, who had not been seen or heard during the long night?

Reared on a farm close to the Mallorcan village of Sant Joan, a short distance from Serra's birthplace in Petra, Jayme was the senior padre at Mission San Diego. When he sailed from Spain to the New World in 1770, his embarkation papers described him as somewhat thin and dark-complexioned. At San Diego, he had learned the language of the Kumeyaay and was sufficiently attuned to the indigenous

FIGURE 6. In a massive Native uprising, Father Luís Jayme was bludgeoned and stabbed to death by Kumeyaay warriors at Mission San Diego de Alcalá on the night of 4 November 1775. Detail of a drawing by Alexander Harmer.
Author's collection.

people to know that trouble was in the offing during the fall of 1775. For instance, the unauthorized departure from the mission of a number of converted Indians was a clear sign of smoldering discontent. But Jayme naively refused to believe reports from friendly Natives that an uprising was being planned. With the advantages of hindsight, Font wrote of Jayme: "It is not good to have too much confidence in Indians, since in the end they are unfaithful, ungrateful, and inconsiderate people."[38]

Amid the unfolding chaos of 5 November, Jayme apparently had emerged from his quarters ahead of Fuster and, completely unarmed, had tried to quell the enraged fervor of the Native combatants. Approaching them near a small stream just outside the walls of the mission, he spread his arms and offered the common greeting of the padres to the Indians: *Amar a Diós, hijos* (Love God, my sons).[39] At this, the Indians "fell upon him like a wolf upon a lamb," according to Fray Francisco Palóu's account.[40] When Jayme's naked body was found in the streambed the next morning, his chest was riddled with over twenty arrow punctures, his skull was bashed in by war clubs and stones, and his badly bruised face was disfigured beyond recognition (see figure 6). Only the distinctive shaved tonsure on the crown of his head identified him as a Franciscan. When Jayme's defiled remains were brought to Fuster and placed at his feet, he fainted across the body and had to be revived by the Indian women of the mission.

Upon his arrival two months later, Commander Rivera immediately set about rounding up the ringleaders of the Native revolt and imposing stiff punishments. While Font experienced an outbreak of painful sores on his tongue and elsewhere in his mouth—likely the result of scurvy—Rivera dispatched his troops on multiple patrols into the mountains to capture Indians who were thought to have instigated the attack. This prompted a flurry of smoke signals from the Natives warning of the advancing search parties.

Four Kumeyaay who were brought back to the presidio were given fifty lashes each. Two other prisoners were flogged more severely, with one dying from his wounds and the other gravely injured. On 31 January 1776 Font spotted another prisoner who had been whipped savagely and had come to the padres to see if they could treat his wounds. He recorded that the man's buttocks were ulcerated and "how ill he had become from the blows. . . . The sores on the Indian I saw were black and horrifying."[41]

A principal leader of the insurrection who was locked up at the presidio escaped in February on a day when Rivera had sallied into the field in search of other culprits. The man, called Carlos by the Spaniards, was one of those who had previously received religious instruction from the padres. He therefore was known to Father Fuster, who advised him to seek sanctuary in the makeshift storage hut that was being used to say Mass on presidio hill after the mission had been destroyed. Long-standing Roman Catholic doctrine held that anyone who sought refuge in a church was immune from arrest and could not be seized under any circumstances while in the church.

Upon his return, Rivera challenged the ecclesiastical asylum, on grounds that the place being used as a temporary church was actually a warehouse. He gave the padres a note demanding that Carlos be turned over to him. Otherwise, Rivera wrote, he would arrest the Indian himself. Fuster responded with a note refusing to hand over the offender and stating that Rivera would be excommunicated if he violated the sanctity of the church. To a faithful Catholic such as Rivera, excommunication meant not only that he could never attend Mass or receive the sacraments again, but that he could never enter the gates of heaven.

The matter festered for weeks, with tensions between the military commander and the clergymen mounting ominously. Fuster's rash decision to provide a haven for Carlos was itself a manifestation of the padres' festering unhappiness over

Rivera's brutal punishment of the Native accomplices. Finally, on the afternoon of 26 March 1776, Rivera's men laid siege to the chapel. Still, Fuster refused to budge.

When Rivera pulled his sword from its sheath and approached the church door, Fuster declared: "Don Fernando, see here! If you remove the offender, you will be excommunicated, and I declare this to be so, henceforth." Rivera turned his back on Fuster and marched into the church with his sword drawn in one hand and a lighted candle in the other. As he did so, he waved the back of his hand to the friar and shouted: "All right, Father Vicente, hurl your excommunications, hurl them, but that won't stop me from seizing this rogue."[42]

Rivera then forcibly pulled Carlos from behind the altar where he was hiding and ordered the soldiers to place him in stocks at the guardhouse. For Father Fuster, this was an egregious sacrilege against the church. Thereafter, Commander Rivera was barred from attending Mass or receiving the sacraments. In fact, Fuster publicly turned him away from the church, no doubt a humiliating rebuff for one of the most powerful men in California. All the same, in a letter to the viceroy, Rivera declared: "I have not regarded myself as being excommunicated, given the serious danger that if that culprit should escape he would cause renewed disturbances and harm."[43] Despite the harsh punishments meted out by Rivera, Native violence against encroaching Spanish rule in California was destined only to escalate.

CHAPTER NINE

A Forgotten Soldier of the Cross

> Better than honor and glory, and History's pen,
> Was the thought of duty done and the love of his fellow men.
> —Richard Watson Gilder

On a warm Saturday afternoon the horseshoe bend in the Colorado River, just below its confluence with the Gila River near Yuma, Arizona, is a tranquil spot under serene skies. It is autumn, the benign season of the year both in the surrounding desert, where daytime temperatures have dropped into the mid-80s, and on the river, where the flow has ebbed since its summer peak of Rocky Mountain snowmelt. At a small park on the California side, successive generations of families are picnicking on the green lawn, amid colorful piñatas and balloons fluttering in clusters to celebrate a birthday. Brown-skinned children swim at the edge of the gently coursing river. Gray-haired grandfathers planted in folding chairs on the riverbank fiddle with their fishing poles.

Atop a granite cliff above the waterway gleams Saint Thomas Indian Mission, an alabaster temple on the Fort Yuma Indian Reservation, home of the Quechan people. Built in 1922, the Roman Catholic church marks the spot where the forebears of today's Quechans annihilated the fledgling Spanish pueblo and Franciscan mission of La Purísima Concepción in 1781. In front of the church stands a twelve-foot-tall monument to Francisco Garcés, one of four Franciscans slain in the three-day uprising on the Colorado River. The statue casts Garcés in heroic terms, holding aloft a cross and gazing down beneficently at an Indian kneeling at his feet. But the plaque resolutely reflects the Native view of the massacre 236 years ago: "Colinists [sic] ignored Indian rights, usurped the best lands and destroyed Indian crops. Completely frustrated and disappointed, the Quechans [Yumas] and their allies destroyed Concepción on July 17–19, 1781."

No mention whatsoever is made of Fray Thomas Eixarch, the Forgotten Friar. (In his native language of Valencian, his family name was pronounced "ā-SHARK.") Eixarch, who alternatively spelled his already difficult name as "Eyxarch," followed by a swirling E-shaped rubric, spent a memorable but lonely six months among the Yumas, as the Spaniards called the Quechans, from November 1775 to May 1776. His purpose was to prepare the Natives for Christian conversion and, eventually, to clear the way for the ill-omened Mission La Purísima Concepción. The diary Eixarch kept during his winter on the Colorado offers fascinating insight into the everyday lives of the Indians and one of their principal leaders, Salvador Palma, a linchpin figure in California's mission chronicle. But, in the end, Eixarch vanished into the vapors of history. Both the date and place of his death are a mystery. No known marker designates his grave. His journal is ignored today, as it was in his own day. His contributions to history are overlooked, his ultimate fate in life lost to future generations.

One of the first European explorers to reach the Colorado was the Spaniard Melchior Díaz, who in 1540 named it El Río del Tizón (Firebrand River).[1] Indians living along its shores commonly went about naked even during the coldest days of winter. To stay warm they carried burning sticks, constantly shifting the small torches from one hand to the other and up and down their bodies—a practice that Eixarch himself witnessed nearly two and a half centuries later. Not until the first half of the eighteenth century did the watercourse get its modern name, El Río Colorado (Red River), for the roseate hue of the sediments along its banks.

The Colorado River that Eixarch found when he arrived with the Anza expedition in the fall of 1775 was much more spirited than it is today. In its natural state, before being bridled by the Hoover Dam in 1935, the lower Colorado meandered over an expansive flatland, changing its course frequently from year to year and creating countless sandbars, lagoons, islands, and marshes. More significant, its flow varied tremendously from season to season. In late fall and early winter, the river was a comparatively tame stream, forded without much difficulty. At low ebb the river in Eixarch's day is estimated to have flowed at about 2,500 cubic feet per second. But in late spring and early summer, when runoff from the Rocky Mountain snowpack reached its crest, the flooded plain swelled to eight miles or more in width and the flow accelerated to 100,000 cubic feet per second.[2]

Eixarch was born in 1742 in the town of Liria, about twenty miles northwest of Valencia, Spain.[3] He joined the Franciscan Order of Friars Minor at Valencia at age fifteen, as was typical for boys at the time. At age twenty-seven, now Father Eixarch, he crossed the Atlantic with a contingent of thirty-eight friars bound for the missionary College of Santa Cruz in Querétaro, north of Mexico City. His embarkation papers described him as seven and a half palms tall (five foot, two inches), with black hair, black eyes, and lemon-colored skin.[4] His first assignment was a settlement near San Antonio, Texas, known as San Juan Capistrano. In early 1775 he went to work in the Franciscan fields of the Pimería Alta, the upper land of the Pima Indians, which stretched from Sonora northward into present-day Arizona. The region was marred by unrelenting Apache raids, recurrent floods, and periodic droughts, rendering it one of the poorest corners of New Spain.

Among his first acts was to baptize a baby girl at Mission San José de Tumacácori, on the Santa Cruz River south of Tucson, on 14 March 1775. The pueblo under his ministry consisted of ninety-one Pima and Pápago Indians and twenty-six Spaniards. In a report dated 12 May 1775, Eixarch noted that the Natives at Tumacácori recited the catechism in Spanish, as they were required to do, "although they understand but little, for there is almost no comprehension of the said language (except with some)."[5]

At Tumacácori he came into contact with Father Garcés, who was assigned to nearby Mission San Xavier del Bac, and Captain Juan Bautista de Anza, who was organizing his colonizing expedition to San Francisco in northern California. Garcés, a veteran of the 1774 exploratory venture across the desert to California, was to accompany Anza as far as the Colorado River. Then the plan was for him to embark on his own odyssey of discovery.

It was customary for a friar dispatched to the frontier to be accompanied by another friar as his compañero. After all, the Franciscans did not share in the rowdy lives of the Spanish soldiers, many of whom had unsavory pasts, including time spent in prison. Educated and pious, the fathers held themselves aloof from the grubby world of the military. So, it was important for them to travel in pairs. For this second sojourn with Anza, Garcés requested that Eixarch be his companion. On 21 October 1775, Eixarch joined up with Garcés at the Tubac presidio, about three miles north of Tumacácori, for the advance to the Colorado River with settlers, including expectant mothers and children of all ages, along with soldiers, padres, muleteers, Indian interpreters, and a long parade of pack animals, horses, mules, and cattle.

Eixarch's first entry in his diary was on 4 December 1775, composed in the little hut of bulrushes that Anza's muleteers had built for him and Garcés on the California side of the Colorado River among the Yuma Indians. Soon enough, the thirty-three-year-old Eixarch would be the only white man for miles around (see map 4). The Anza expedition had already moved on toward the California coast and Garcés, with his Native guide Sebastián Tarabal, was to strike out downriver the next day to explore new lands and new tribes. Two leaders of the Yumas, Salvador Palma and his lieutenant Pablo, who commanded villages farther down

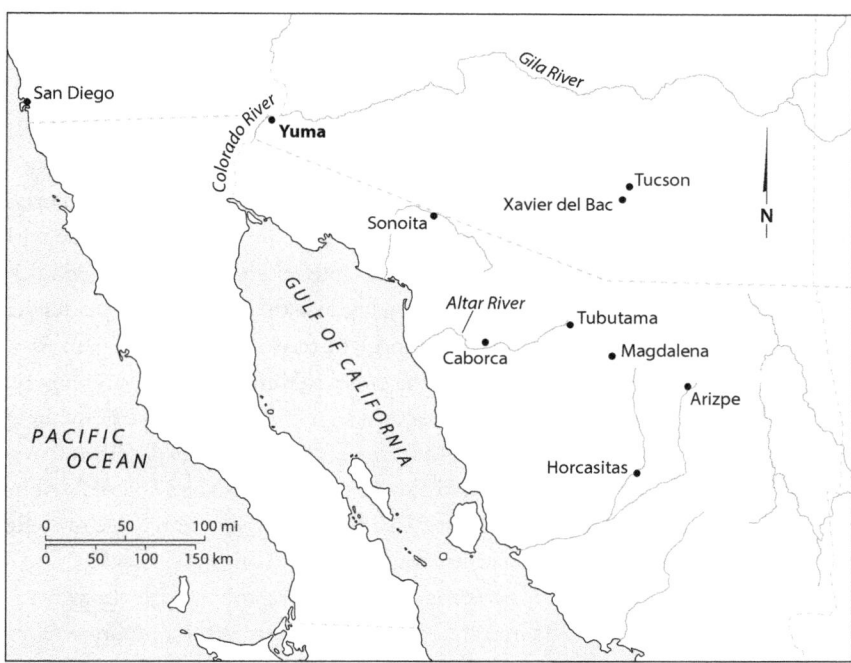

Map 4. New Spain settlements in northern Sonora and southern Arizona. Friar Thomas Eixarch spent a memorable but lonely six months at the Yuma crossing on the Colorado River, isolated from his fellow Franciscan missionaries by hundreds of miles of desert.
Cartography by Bill Nelson. Copyright © 2017 by the University of Oklahoma Press.

the Colorado, immediately brought additional food to Eixarch and pledged they would protect him from anticipated Apache raids. "These two [Indian] captains do not leave me alone during the entire day, and they are so prompt with everything that I request of them that it is a matter to marvel at," Eixarch scrawled in his diary with a quill pen, in a compact legible script. "And so when I get up in the morning they are already at the fire awaiting me, and at night they do not leave me until I retire."[6]

While the Indian women brought him a bounty of beans, maize, squash, and wheat, Eixarch set about fixing up his hut, which had a leaky roof, and cutting willow poles to make an altar on which to say Mass. Two Indians on horseback arrived with a report that the Apaches had attacked the Anza expedition—a disturbing prospect for Eixarch, and one that must have reinforced his crushing sense of isolation. As it turned out, the report was a false rumor spread by the Indians. All the same, Eixarch would be left for a long time in apprehension and uncertainty about the fortunes of the Anza party.

Sitting in a circle with Palma, Pablo, and other Natives around the campfire at night, Eixarch proselytized about the biblical story of creation, the immortality of the soul, the mysteries of the Holy Trinity encompassing a single God, and other aspects of the faith. Before going to bed each night, he recited the rosary with the Indians. This, too, required the Natives to voice their responses in Spanish, which must have been pure gibberish to them because this was their first extended contact with Europeans. Chief Palma was especially receptive to the evangelization, imitating Eixarch in making the sign of the cross, folding his hands, and bowing his head during prayers, beating his breast as a sign of devotion, and showing up at sunrise every morning for Mass and the singing of the *Alabado*. Unlike most of the Natives, Palma even remained on his knees throughout Mass and scolded his brethren if they talked during the service. In a portentous sign of trouble to come, Chief Pablo was indifferent to Eixarch's sermonizing.

The weather turned cold in the second week of December, with the water in pots freezing at night, and Eixarch found that his fingers turned numb when he said Mass on his outdoor altar at the break of day. On some mornings he was out of bed before dawn because it was too cold in his hut to sleep. On 14 December it began to snow heavily, the same storm that was wreaking calamity on the Anza caravan in the high desert. "The old Indians were quite surprised to see the snow," Eixarch recorded, "and some of them, including Palma, said they had never seen such a thing before, and had never known such cold weather" (320).

At this early point in his stay on the river, Eixarch's relationship with Chief Palma had already begun to blossom—with crucial implications for Spain's conquest of California. In contrast to other powerful Yuma men, Palma lived with only one woman, in accordance with the teachings of the padres. His wife had borne him six children—five girls and a boy. Palma's son was fourteen years old, and the chief doted on him. Palma's eldest daughter was married and lived with her husband on the other side of the river. One day she appeared with a child at her breast, presumably Palma's grandchild.

Eixarch tutored Palma on the Catholic catechism and was very pleased that the chief grasped the essentials and was eager to be baptized. For his part, Palma appeared to be mesmerized by the priest and his religious trappings, to the point of spying on Eixarch when he was getting dressed in his silk vestments before saying Mass. The chief also took to kissing Eixarch's hand in greeting each morning.

Aware of the importance of Palma, whose people controlled the river crossing that was the gateway to California, Eixarch encouraged the leader of the Yumas to travel to Mexico City and meet the powerful viceroy Antonio María de Bucareli y Ursúa. In Eixarch's grandiose terms, Bucareli "ruled all the people of the Indies" (323). The friar assured Palma that the viceroy was eager to meet him and would give him many presents that would be even finer than the spiffy attire and cane of office he had recently received from Anza on the viceroy's behalf. Palma needed no prodding. He wanted very much to make the long journey to meet the viceroy, and he wanted to take his son with him. Eixarch may not have realized it at the time, but persuading Palma to meet Bucareli was a critical step forward in Spain's drive to open up an overland route to California.

On 17 December an elderly Yuma man approached Eixarch and asked if he wanted to buy a young Apache boy who had been captured as a slave. The Indian wanted to trade the child, whom Eixarch judged to be only five or six years old, for a horse. Eixarch now confronted the distressing reality that an Indian slave trade flourished on the frontier. Many tribes enslaved the captives they seized in skirmishes with their enemies. The arrival of the Spaniards probably spurred the slave market because they paid handsomely to liberate the Nifora, as the captives were called (322). Nearly all of the hostages were women and children. The bartering of Indian slaves to white people was "altogether contrary to law," Eixarch declared. He added: "I have made this remark because there are many half-breed gentlemen who pride themselves on having Indian captives in practical slavery, ignorant in their pride of the fact that the Indians were born free, and that doubtless they have purer and better blood than their half-breed Spanish lordships themselves" (322).

Despite his condemnation of buying and selling Indian detainees, Eixarch agreed to the transaction on the spot, and the old man left the child with the padre. In the exchange, Eixarch forfeited a young horse with four white feet, the only mount he had for his personal use. It must have seemed a great bargain to the Yuma elder because mounts were valuable and in short supply. Among the Natives, a horse was a coveted status symbol. What became of the boy, Eixarch did not relate in his journal. A child so young would have had to be placed in the care of a woman, and the only women around were Yumas. So, the boy likely was returned to the tribe that captured him.

As the cold weather continued, Eixarch prepared a small plot of land near his hut as a vegetable garden and fenced it in. He planted a peach tree and beans, peas, onions, and cauliflower. He also built a coop to house eight chickens and a rooster given to him by members of the Anza expedition. The Indians were very curious about the hens, which they had never seen before. They brought to Eixarch a kind of waterfowl that he had never seen before. He described it as a "black duck" with webbed feet and a chicken-like body—probably a cormorant from the lower reaches of the Colorado River.

Then came another troubling report from the Indian telegraph that Cucapá warriors downriver had captured Father Garcés, knocked him off his mule, stolen his clothes, the sheepskin mats he slept on, his mount, pack mule, glass beads, tobacco, biscuits, chocolate, and other meager supplies, leaving him naked in the wilderness. Once again it turned out to be a fabrication, but Eixarch was left to worry about the touch-and-go situation in which he himself had been placed, utterly exposed among bellicose tribes. When Chief Palma planned to be away for a few days at an Indian gathering in a distant village, Eixarch expressed concern about being left alone. According to the padre, "this was enough to prevent him from going" (329).

Eixarch, isolated and fidgety, decided at the start of January to travel south to Caborca in Sonora for a few days to make contact with fellow Franciscans there. The trip would traverse more than two hundred miles of barren desert each way. All "of the expanse from Caborca to the mouth of the Colorado River is uninhabited or uninhabitable. . . . [T]here is a total absence of water," recorded the Jesuit missionary Juan Nentvig in 1764.[7] Eixarch set out on a mule with a few provisions of meat, biscuits, and pinole (ground cornmeal). With him was a Yuma guide who was inexperienced with horses. Eixarch not only had to saddle the Native's horse and put the bridle over its head, but he also had to help the guide mount. On the trail the Indian had trouble keeping up with Eixarch, even though the guide was riding a horse and Eixarch a mule.

On the second day, the Indian and his mount abandoned Eixarch altogether. He pressed on alone until he found himself in a dense thicket, with the trail barely discernible. "My fear in having little or no practice in following trails, and the lack of water, which I had not tasted today, caused me to turn back over the same track or trail which I had followed," Eixarch wrote in his diary (331).

Before long he was trotting his mule, going as fast he could back toward the Yuma village where he had started. After spending the night at an encampment of Pima Indians on the edge of the Gila River, Eixarch and his mule forded the Colorado with some difficulty—getting his shoes, leggings, and knee breeches wet in the process—before finally reaching the safety of home. About seven o'clock that same evening, to Eixarch's great delight, Garcés returned from his wanderings downstream.

On 10 January Eixarch witnessed from a distance an exotic fertility ritual performed on Yuma girls when they experienced their first menstruation.[8] In this instance, the girl was buried up to her neck in sand, which had been heated with hot stones. She was attended exclusively by Yuma women, who sang and danced around her for two or three hours a day over a four-day span, during which the girl was not allowed to eat and was permitted to drink water only at sunset. After this the girl's hair was daubed with a mudlike gum for four days and she was given unsalted food to eat, followed by another four days in which her hair was daubed with wet flour. At the end of this ceremonial ordeal, the women scooped up the girl in their arms and tossed her three times in the air, allowing her to fall to the ground the last time.

A Yuma custom that appalled Eixarch was cremation. The common practice was to burn the body of the deceased until it was reduced to ashes, which were placed in a small-mouthed funeral jar.[9] The pottery urn was then hidden among rocks or buried, in the belief that this would prevent the dead from returning. The belongings of the departed also were destroyed, including his jugs, cooking implements, and other possessions, and his dwelling abandoned. According to Eixarch, even the dead person's crops were left to rot in the fields. Because of protests from the Franciscans, the Indians later renounced cremation for those who had converted to Christianity, burying them instead in accordance with the traditions of the church.

Like his fellow missionary Pedro Font, Eixarch was repelled by the personal habits of the Indians along the Colorado River. "These Yumas are very filthy and have no shame whatever," he wrote in his journal. "Most of them go about just as they were born, without the slightest covering. . . . In a word, they are the most immodest people I have ever seen, and the reason is that they do not appreciate and do not know what is so natural in mankind as modesty" (343).

He compared the Yumas unfavorably to the Mojave Apaches, who lived northeast of the Colorado River. When a peaceful delegation of the Mojave Apaches visited Eixarch, they were dressed modestly in deer skins and moccasins, and in Eixarch's estimation were very clean. He also railed against the polygamous ways of the Yuma men, who long had been accustomed to taking numerous wives. The young men, in particular, slept with as many women as they wanted. One of the principal offenders was Chief Pablo, who not only consorted with multiple wives but refused to accept the teachings of the church or to attend Mass or the recitation of the rosary.

Yet another cultural collision occurred when Garcés baptized three adult Yumas and one child who were very ill and near death. For the padres, baptism was required before any soul could enter heaven. But the Indians observed that whenever the padres baptized an ill person he died almost immediately. The Yumas quite naturally blamed the death on the padres' prayers. Although Eixarch and Garcés tried to persuade the Yumas otherwise, it was difficult because, in Eixarch's view, "reason does not enter into their understanding" (345). The friars' case was not helped by the fact that at least one of the four baptized by Garcés, an adult female, died a few days later.

On 17 January a Yuma Native brought to Eixarch a wounded black horse belonging to Father Garcés. The animal had been shot in the stomach with an arrow. Eixarch suspected the culprit was another Yuma tribesman. He also believed the reason for the attack was that the horses, mules, and cattle left among the Yumas by the Anza expedition had destroyed the Indians' winter wheat crop by grazing on it and trampling it. The same problem arose in the spring, because the Yumas planted two wheat crops each year. Eixarch lamented that the Indians should be compensated for their losses, but no restitution was ever offered, which created a festering resentment among the Indians that would only grow as time went on. Much to Garcés's consternation, the wounded horse had a swollen belly where the arrow had struck it. After a Yuma shaman performed a number of rituals, such as blowing on the ground and rubbing handfuls of earth on the horse's underside, the swelling subsided.

By the middle of February the Colorado River began to rise, due to winter rains in the mountains and heavy runoff from the Gila River. When Eixarch heard that a Pima Indian on the east side of the Colorado was to make a trip to Sonora, the padre decided to send with him two letters to the missions at Sonoitac and El Ati in the Altar River Valley. To get his messages across the Colorado, Eixarch enlisted the services of a Yuma woman, who swam across the swollen river pushing along in front of her a tightly woven, waterproof basket containing the letters, and some jerked meat and maize as payment for the Pima courier. "These Yuma Indians are dexterous swimmers," declared Eixarch, "and the women are even better than the men, for they are the ones who cross the river loaded with children, provisions, and other things" (353).

On 14 February 1776 Garcés left Eixarch behind once again and set out on the back of a mule for a six-month journey across the desolate Mojave Desert, over what is now the Tehachapi Range into the broad San Joaquín Valley of California, then eastward to the tribes of northern Arizona and New Mexico, before returning to the Colorado River crossing. With him were two Indian interpreters and his guide, Sebastián Tarabal. Somewhat surprisingly, given Sebastián's long service to the Spaniards, Eixarch condemned him in harsh terms. In his opinion Sebastián was an "evil" man who took advantage of the Spaniards. "This Indian is an unregenerate rogue, without shame, and nothing can be trusted in his hands," Eixarch wrote (257).

Just before Garcés's departure, Chief Palma showed up wearing his gaudy Spanish outfit with the blue cape and gold braid, carrying his royal baton. He donned the fancy clothes whenever he wanted to express his authority and address other Natives. What followed was a long harangue by Palma declaring that all of the surrounding tribes should end their hostilities because the king of the Spaniards wanted only peace.

Garcés embarked on his epic trip even though Palma warned him that the Jalchedún tribesmen upriver had let it be known they intended to kill him and anyone traveling with him. This would not be difficult, because Garcés and his companions were unarmed. As a result of this threat, one of Garcés's Native interpreters backed out of the trip. But the padre was undeterred, as always.

On the night of 26 February two Indian boys roused Eixarch to tell him that twin girls had just been born to a Native woman. This was a rare occurrence among the Indians and cause for celebration. Eixarch rushed to see whether the newborns were healthy or, instead, in need of baptism before dying. He found the infants were doing just fine and the mother was already busy making two cradle boards to wrap them in. The Native custom was to bundle infants tightly in soft rabbit skins, with a little moss as a diaper, and attach them to boards made of willow twigs.[10] This was believed to make their backs grow straight and strong. It also made it easier for mothers to carry their children on their backs or rest them against a tree trunk or even suspend them from a branch as the women worked in the fields.

When the weather turned milder and the river began to flood more rapidly from the winter rains, Eixarch was inundated with hordes of sinister rats, which pillaged his food stocks and undermined the hillside where he had built a new shelter to escape the advancing waters. He helpfully advised in his journal that future missionaries "try to bring some cats if they do not wish to experience the molestation and damage which necessarily will be caused them by such outlandish little beasts" (362).

By the beginning of March Eixarch's sense of extreme seclusion from the civilized world was bearing down upon him. He was much in need of the companionship of his fellow friars and other Spaniards. So, he set his sights again on a trip to the presidio and missions in the Altar Valley of Sonora. The excursion, covering more than four hundred miles round trip, would take seven days in the saddle each way over the difficult route later called El Camino del Diablo. Eixarch's guide this time would be the Yuma leader Pablo, who would guide him through the territory of the friendly Pápago Indians and avert as much as possible the warlike Apaches.

The first challenge was to get across the muddy Colorado River, whose floodwaters were expanding daily from bank to bank. Pablo and a few Yuma elders built a raft of timbers, with a crate-like seat on top. After eating his dinner on 4 March, Eixarch climbed atop the crate and six Yumas swimming alongside steered the raft across the swift-running water. From there the journey southeastward ran through arid terrain where the ground was covered with a foamy salt as white as snow, and the two horses had to be watered from gourds at feeble springs. To spare the steeds from the midday heat and thus the need for more water, Eixarch and Pablo rode much of the way at night under the starlit desert firmament.

During one night ride skirting Apache country, Pablo halted suddenly after hearing a noise in the brush. "I was a little frightened," recorded Eixarch, "especially when we saw three horses nearby, one hobbled and two loose. This fear was well justified, for the barbarian Apaches are in the habit of visiting this region" (367). Unlike other tribesmen, the Apaches wore sandals instead of going barefoot, making their footprints in the sand easily recognizable. In the event, the Apache warriors did not detect Eixarch and Pablo, who continued on their way without mishap.

On 11 March Eixarch reached the Altar Valley and civilization. He suspended writing his journal throughout his stay, which ended on 9 April after the religious festivities of Easter. When he reached the east bank of the Colorado on his return trip, the Yumas once again ferried him across on a raft.

Despite their close association during their five weeks on the road together, Eixarch remained wary of Pablo, declaring: "I do not like him. . . . And from what I have experienced I must say that Pablo has a bad heart, slight love for the fathers, and less for the things of God" (373). It probably did not help that the Spaniards referred to the Indian leader as Pablo Feo (Ugly Pablo). In fact, Pablo had tried unsuccessfully to block the Anza expedition of 1774 from crossing the Colorado River in Yuma territory, as Garcés recounted in his journal. At that time Anza accused Pablo of taking note of the paltry number of soldiers on the expedition and then plotting to kill the Spaniards and steal their horses and materiel. Only after Anza threatened Pablo with the full force of Spanish arms did the chieftain become obsequious, according to Garcés.[11] Within a few years, history would exonerate Eixarch's judgment of Pablo.

On 16 April Eixarch sprinkled holy water on the forehead of a little Indian boy who was very ill. Three days after the baptism, the child died. The incident stoked more Yuma opposition to the Franciscan insistence on baptizing sick children.

Eixarch became alarmed on 25 April when he experienced his first earthquake, and the hill on which his house sat shook mightily. Chief Palma reassured him that temblors occurred every spring due to the river's rising. At first thought, Palma's observation may appear to be a Native superstition. But modern seismologists have discovered that in times past the floodwaters of the Colorado River triggered numerous quakes along the southern San Andreas Fault, and that damming the river in the twentieth century sharply reduced the number of temblors.[12]

Eixarch's musings on his Colorado River stay ended abruptly on 11 May 1776, when he wrote his last entry in his journal: "In the morning the weather was fair and I said Mass. Before noon Father Fray Pedro Font returned with Captain Anza and the soldiers who went from Tubac on the expedition" (381).

By September Father Eixarch had a new assignment at Mission San Antonio de Oquitoa in the Altar Valley. He also served as chaplain at the nearby presidio. After completing his required ten years of missionary service on the frontier, he returned to the Franciscan College of Santa Cruz in Querétaro in 1781. Two years later he joined the Franciscans in Jalisco and lived at a friary named Nuestra Señora de la Asunción.[13] In 1790 he became the superior of a friary at Amacueca, south of Guadalajara. There he disappeared from the pages of history, having sidestepped a smoldering insurrection on the Colorado River.

CHAPTER TEN

Apostolic Pilgrimage

> First recorded white man in this locality. He brought Christianity to the Indian and on Rio Colorado his brave life was crowned with martyrdom.
> —Inscription on statue in Garcés Circle, Bakersfield, California

Beneath a freeway overpass in a gritty barrio of Bakersfield, California, stands a twenty-two-foot-tall limestone likeness of Francisco Garcés. The pioneering padre is shown, saintlike, in a flowing robe, with a knotted cord and a rosary dangling from his waist, a broad-brimmed leather sombrero nestled in the crook of his left arm. The sandal and bare toes of his left foot stick out from under his ankle-length Franciscan habit. An etching on the marble base of the sculpture, created in 1939 as a federal project to put artists to work in the Great Depression, depicts Garcés sitting near a cactus on the trail, reading his breviary, or prayer book. In the background are his pack mule and faithful Indian guide, Sebastián Tarabal, who looks, stereotypically, like the Lone Ranger's sidekick, Tonto, with two feathers protruding from a headband at the back of his head. Green lawn and beds of yellow and gold zinnias surround the statue. Cars and trucks careen helter-skelter around the traffic circle just off Golden State Avenue in the center of old Bakersfield, where for seven decades the towering image of the friar has weathered the advance of time.

Garcés, of course, would not recognize this spot, which he visited on 7 May 1776, the first European to foray into the heart of California's expansive central valley. Nor would he recognize the name. On his exhaustive expedition to find a more direct overland route from Sonora and New Mexico to Monterey in northern California, Garcés called this place San Miguel. Nearly a century later, a prominent American landowner named Thomas Baker fenced off ten acres so that travelers could graze their livestock. The popular references to Baker's field as a stopover stuck, and a city of nearly 350,000 people ultimately emerged.[1]

The eleven months that Garcés spent on the trail, from 21 October 1775 when he left Tubac until 17 September 1776 when he returned to San Xavier del Bac, were an amazing feat of endurance and adversity. He covered more than twenty-five hundred miles on the back of a mule, sometimes in the company of one or two Indian interpreters and sometimes alone because even the Natives refused to trespass on the hostile territory he was intent on crossing. Many times he found himself without food—or, more precariously, without water—in the unrelenting, triple-digit heat of the Mojave Desert. Many times he was given up for dead as he journeyed among warring Indian nations.

He carried out this prolonged odyssey with a bare minimum of supplies—corn gruel for sustenance, a magnifying lens for starting fires with focused sunlight, a sheepskin blanket to sleep on, glass beads and tobacco as gifts for some of the twenty-five thousand Indians he encountered. Most of the time he was at the mercy of unknown tribes to share their meager food with him. Defying the advice of friendly Indians and Spaniards alike, Garcés ventured into unexplored realms with only a compass and a quadrant to guide him. At one point as he traversed especially rough terrain, even his compass failed him. At another, he narrowly escaped with his life after being surrounded by belligerent Natives.

"He lived solely on the bread of providence, without provisioning himself for his long wanderings through barren lands with any food other than the coarse and strange diet of the Indians, and he considered himself fortunate when he could obtain it," wrote Fray Juan Domingo Arricivita, the eighteenth-century chronicler of the missionary activities of the College of Santa Cruz in Querétaro, Mexico. "No bad place or road, however dangerous, rough, bleak or barren, could frighten him or impede his steps. The most appalling dangers were pleasant to him in his endeavor to locate savages and become friendly with them."[2]

In setting out, Garcés was armed with instructions from the king's representative in Mexico City, Viceroy Antonio María Bucareli y Ursúa. Bucareli was casting an eye to the near future when Franciscan missions would be established along the Gila and Colorado Rivers, thereby fortifying the overland route from the center of New Spain to the outposts of Monterey and San Francisco on the coast of northern California. At the moment, Apache raids menaced much of the trail through what is today southern Arizona and northern Sonora. The way to subjugate the Apaches, Bucareli believed, was to develop alliances with tribes who were also victims of the Apaches and to establish a permanent Spanish presence with a string of well-armed presidios and missions.

Bucareli and his junta de guerra, or war council, had decided to strengthen Spain's toehold on northern California by dispatching the pilgrims of a second, colonizing Anza expedition to settle the new mission and pueblo of San Francisco.

Impressed by Garcés's detailed diary of the Anza exploratory expedition in 1774, the viceroy directed him to accompany the second caravan as far as the Colorado River. While awaiting Anza's return to the Colorado after delivering the settlers to San Francisco, Garcés was charged with scouting sites for missions and getting to know the surrounding tribes so as to ascertain, in Bucareli's words, "the spirit and disposition of the Natives toward the [Roman Catholic] catechism and toward vassalage to our sovereign."[3]

Always eager to discover what lay beyond the horizon, Garcés interpreted this mandate as broadly as possible. He promptly abandoned his assigned compañero, Fray Thomas Eixarch, at the Colorado River and never looked back. He continued his travels for five full months after Anza had returned to the Yuma crossing, pressing all the way to what was then New Mexico and the land of the unwelcoming Hopis. In his own thinking, Garcés dreamed of finding a shorter overland route from Santa Fe, the capital of New Mexico, to northern California. The arena was now set for his most trying undertaking ever.

On Tuesday morning, 5 December 1775, Garcés said goodbye to "my well-beloved companion," Father Eixarch, and struck out down the west bank of the Colorado.[4] He took with him a single pack mule, his guide, Sebastián Tarabal, and two Native interpreters. His immediate objective was to follow the river until it entered the Sea of Cortez and to get acquainted with the tribes along its reaches. Before he could make much progress, though, his Yuma interpreters got word from downriver that they would be killed by enemy tribesmen if they continued on. This news reached them as they met up briefly with the Anza party downstream from the Yuma crossing. Sensing the dangers ahead, Father Pedro Font implored Garcés to abort his trip. But Garcés would not be deterred. In the end he persuaded his apprehensive interpreters to stick with him.

Garcés had covered the same ground in 1771, and many of the indigenous people he encountered now remembered him from that trek. In contrast to his previous visit, he found the land much more fertile, with many varieties of cultivated crops flourishing in the river's wide floodplain. "It was astounding to see the abundance of watermelons, corn tortillas, muskmelons, various gruels, and fish that they gave me," he wrote in his journal (174).

This was the land of the Cajuenches, a tribe of three thousands souls who had long been at war with their river neighbors to the north, the Yumas. On his earlier trip Garcés had intervened to establish peace between the two tribes, telling them sternly that it was the wish of both God and the Spanish king that they live in harmony. The newfound prosperity of the Cajuenches was due to their still peaceful relations with the Yumas, who in the past frequently destroyed the Cajuenches' fields at harvest time. This encounter underscored the important role that Garcés played as a peacemaker among rival tribes throughout the Spanish hinterlands. Amicable ties among the diverse Native bands were essential to Spain's conquest of California.

As he pressed on, Garcés periodically paused to make observations of the sun with a quadrant that Font had lent him. This enabled him to record accurately in his journal the latitude—but not the longitude—of the places he visited. Thus he knew his position on a north–south axis but could only guess how far east or west he had traveled.

On 12 December Garcés's mediation skills were challenged again when a Cajuenche man was stabbed in the upper back with a spear by a tribesman from a rival band living close by. A piece of the flint spearhead was lodged near his heart, and the Cajuenche shaman cut open the man's chest to remove the object from the front, inflicting grievous pain on him. The shaman sought to remedy the victim's suffering by running, howling, gyrating, and whirling about.

The Cajuenches then hauled before Garcés the young Jalliquamai warrior who had instigated the attack. They were prepared to kill the Jalliquamai on the spot, but Garcés persuaded them to let him go. As he was returning to his village, his fellow Jalliquamai came out to defend him, and a free-for-all battle erupted against the Cajuenches, with arrows flying about but no serious casualties, save one man who was badly beaten with war clubs. Once the fighting subsided, Garcés did his best to reestablish peace. He also baptized the initial stabbing victim, who died three days later. Seeing the violence, Garcés's interpreters again balked at continuing on. This time they could not be talked into changing their minds. Garcés himself was advised to leave hurriedly because other Indians "might come at night to stab us, or to steal our horses" (180). The renewed peace between the neighboring Cajuenches and Jalliquamai was clearly fragile.

With Sebastián Tarabal and a few Cajuenche guides, Garcés pressed on downriver. On 16 December he came upon one of the many lakes formed by the Colorado River as it made its way to the sea. He called this the Laguna de San Mateo, which now presented a formidable barrier to his progress. Unable to swim, despite the many bodies of water he had crossed in his wanderings, Garcés was entirely dependent on the river Indians, who were strong swimmers. "I crossed in the arms of the Cajuenches who were accompanying me," he wrote in his diary (183). At this point the Cajuenche guides too abandoned Garcés because he was entering the territory of their enemies.

The next day Garcés and Sebastián stopped at an Indian village that the padre had visited four years earlier. The inhabitants, members of the Cucapá tribe, were excited to see him again. He passed out glass beads and tobacco. They kissed the crucifix that he always wore around his neck, fingered the colorful pictures in his prayer book, and passed his compass from hand to hand. They also begged to see his large linen portrait of the Virgin Mary with the Christ child, having heard about it from other Natives to whom Garcés had recently preached.

The padre asked an old woman about the fate of two sick boys he had baptized on his previous journey. The woman began to cry. "Both are dead. Don't you remember? I am the mother of one of them," she said (186). Garcés tried to console the old woman by telling her that her son was in heaven.

On 21 December Garcés finally reached the mouth of the Colorado, where its waters turned salty. He was struck by the dramatic tidal bore, as the rising waters of the Sea of Cortez battled against the opposite flow of the roaring river. "All night I heard the great murmur of waters," he wrote (191), noting that the tide rose and fell more than thirty paces along the sandy shoreline.

As he made his way back upstream he encountered tribesmen who had descended from the mountains to feast on the watermelons, maize, gourds, and other agricultural bounty raised by the river dwellers. "The heathens who come down to the river from the mountains are a distinctly different nation: very poor, very ugly, and in poor health," he recorded, "and they go around in a very filthy state because of the large amount of mescal they eat" (197). Mescal was the large starchy core of the agave plant, which Indians boiled or baked in stone-lined pits. When consumed in large quantities, it caused flatulence and diarrhea.

Garcés was entertained in one nearby village by a ten-year-old Indian girl who, "covering only the absolute minimum" (197), danced and hopped about with a walking stick, throwing her right leg over her left shoulder, then alternating with her left leg over her right shoulder. This brought howls of laughter from the Native men. When Sebastián discovered that a visiting mountain Indian had stolen his short machete, the river Indians vowed to destroy the village of the thief. Only Garcés's intervention prevented the retaliation.

Like many indigenous groups elsewhere, these people had never seen mules before. Some of the Natives mistook the beasts for human beings, believing they were the wives of the Spanish men who, after all, treated their steeds with great affection. Garcés noted that the Indians greeted his mules as if they were human and offered them human food. On successive nights the Indians compassionately removed the mules' hobbles and took them to another village where they offered

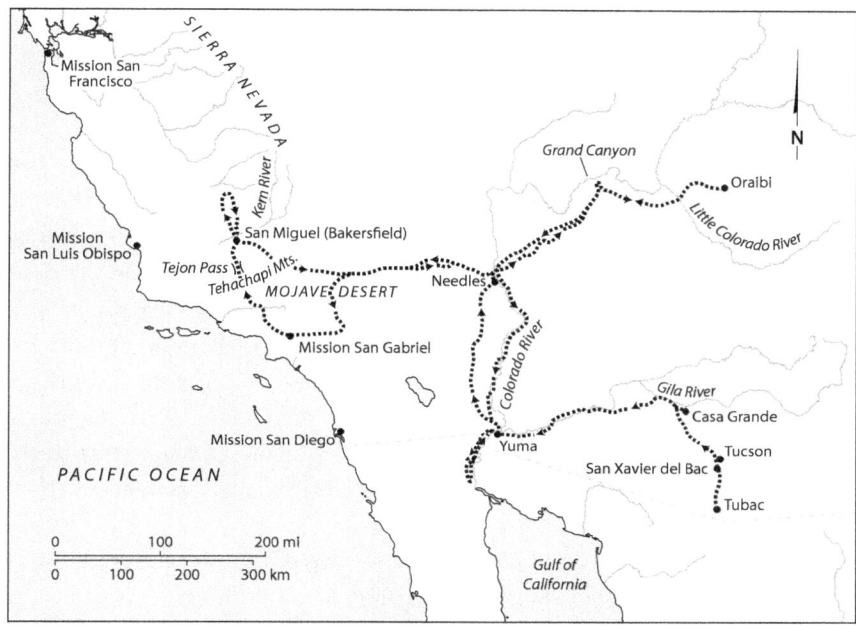

MAP 5. Ever restless, Francisco Garcés covered more than a thousand miles of untrod trails in his solitary wanderings of 1775–1776.
Cartography by Bill Nelson. Copyright © 2017 by the University of Oklahoma Press.

them squash to eat. When a jack mule got stuck in the mud, the Natives lifted him out of the mire in their arms and carried him to the fire to warm him.

On Wednesday 3 January 1776, Garcés reached El Puerto de la Concepción at the Yuma crossing, where Father Eixarch was overjoyed, after a month alone among the Indians, to greet a fellow Spaniard. Garcés remained at the Colorado River with Eixarch for the next six weeks. But he did not stay put for long.

By 14 February 1776 Garcés was on the move again, this time journeying upriver along the California bank to the land of the Jamajabs, also known as the Mojave Indians (see map 5). Accompanying him were Sebastián, two interpreters, and a Jamajab guide. Garcés now headed north-northwest toward the Mojave Desert, a vast stretch of parched terrain that encompassed both the lowest elevation (282 feet below sea level) and hottest spot (summer temperatures routinely above 120 degrees) on the North American continent. The stark beauty of the ruddy landscape was tempered by the scarcity of water and forage for the animals. Over his shoulder to his left, Garcés could spot undulating sand dunes as impassable as the Sahara. On his right was the emerald green ribbon of El Río Colorado coursing through the rocky desert.

A week into his trek, Garcés encountered an assemblage of eighty Jamajabs traveling downriver to meet the Yumas. When he told them of the recently declared peace between the Yumas and the Jalchedunes, the Jamajabs showed him two Jalchedún girls they had taken captive. Garcés pleaded with the Jamajabs to release the slaves. But they refused to do so, until he finally ransomed them in exchange for a bad horse and some trinkets. He sent the girls back downriver to their home among the Jalchedunes, under the guidance of one of his Jalchedún interpreters. With them he sent a strong message that the long-running war between the Jamajabs and the Jalchedunes had come to an end. With this pronouncement, the leader of the Jamajabs made a rousing speech to the girls and the interpreter, endorsing the end of hostilities. Then, as a sign of his commitment, he broke his bow and threw away his arrows.

In the days that followed, Garcés made his way along paths untrod by any Spaniard. He preached to Natives who had never before had contact with a white man. As word of his presence along the river spread, thousands of Natives gathered to meet him, crowding around him so closely that it made him uncomfortable and detaining him for days at a time so that others could come to hear him pray and display his painting of the Virgin and the condemned man. "These people are healthy and robust," he wrote on 29 February. "The women are the most attractive of any along the river. They wear skirts of the same material and design as those of the Yuma women. The men go stark naked; in so cold a land it excites pity. They say they are very hardy, especially in bearing hunger and thirst, and I found this to be so. . . . When giving speeches they give their thighs hard slaps" (230).

By 3 March Garcés and his party reached a point a few miles north of present-day Needles, California, on the Colorado River. His quadrant observation showed he had ascended above thirty-five degrees north latitude. Here he turned southwest across the heart of the Mojave Desert toward central California. His aim was to find a shortcut more or less due west across the desert to Mission San Luis Obispo on the coast.[5] This would provide a straight east–west link between Santa Fe in northern New Mexico and the central coast of California. Garcés knew that Mission San Luis Obispo was situated just north of parallel thirty-five. But his exploration plans were thwarted by the Jamajabs, who steadfastly refused to cross the territory of their enemies. This forced him to redraw his itinerary southward and make a stopover at

Mission San Gabriel east of present-day Los Angeles on his way to explore central California.

Coming to a sierra known today as the Providence Mountains, Garcés encountered four Jamajabs who had traveled across the wasteland all the way from the Pacific coast, where they had traded for coveted shell beads. They carried with them no food, not even bows to hunt with. Garcés was impressed to learn that the Jamajabs of the Mojave Desert could go for four days without food or water. Garcés's admiration for the Natives was uncommon among his fellow Spaniards.

For the next nine days, Garcés learned just how forbidding the desert could be. There was virtually no food to be found, and the weather turned cold and rainy. His Indian interpreters wanted to turn back. When they came at last to a cluster of poor Indian villages on the desert floor, the inhabitants had nothing to eat but roots. Garcés shared with them what little food he had left in exchange for the roots, which he said his Jamajab companions ate "with repugnance" (240). By 12 March the party arrived at a deserted village on what is now the Mojave River, but which Garcés called El Arroyo de los Mártires (Martyrs Stream). Here there were not even roots to eat, and it was believed to be a long distance to the nearest inhabited village. The cold was so severe that one of the Jamajabs deserted the group and headed back toward the Colorado River. To one of the remaining Jamajabs Garcés gave a blanket to keep him warm, and to the other a woolen shirt.

Neither the padre nor his Indian attendants knew how far they were from their next meal. In desperation, Garcés directed that one of the horses be slaughtered for food. The Indians devoured the fresh horse meat with such relish that Garcés had to ration it until they could reach a Native village where food could be procured—whenever that might be. With their other supplies exhausted, Garcés and his men rested for three days to regain their strength on the horse flesh. Even the beast's blood was consumed by the starving nomads.

After resuming their march, Garcés and his three companions rode for two more days without finding food. On 17 March he dispatched Sebastián and one of the Jamajabs on a frantic search for a populated village. While encamped alongside El Arroyo de los Mártires awaiting Sebastián's return, Garcés was greeted by five Jamajabs who were coming back from trading at Mission San Gabriel. The fathers there had given them maize to eat. The Indians playfully imitated the bleating of the mission's calves, which also were fed maize. The next day, Sebastián finally reappeared and Garcés followed him on a thirteen-mile ride to a settlement of forty Beñemé Natives. Here the party feasted on hares, rabbits, and acorn gruel, their hunger relieved at last. Before departing Garcés implored the Beñemés to escort him to the Pacific, but they too refused, on grounds that they did not know the way.

Continuing on a southerly path toward what is now San Bernardino, California, Garcés was extended royal hospitality by the chief of several settlements. White seashells from the coast were the most prized possessions of these desert tribesmen. The chief gave Garcés an impressive strand of shells nearly two yards long. Then the chief's wife sprinkled the padre with acorns and threw away the basket in a sign of respect. Next, the chief's second wife tossed white seashells over Garcés as if they were flower petals. The same ceremony was performed the following day at another village, amid much screeching and dancing, only this time the women tossed acorns and shells over the mules as well. Garcés marveled "that among such rustic people there should be so expressive a show of feeling as their pouring out the shells that are their greatest treasure" (244).

After crossing the summit of the San Bernardino Mountains and catching a glimpse of the blue Pacific to the west, Garcés and his Indian companions rode hard through the day and all through the night under a full moon before reaching Mission San Gabriel on the morning of 24 March 1776. This respite from the trail did not last long.

Despite the pushback he received from the Indians, Garcés was still resolved to reach Mission San Luis Obispo on the central coast and then turn eastward toward the Spanish pueblos of northern New Mexico, which lay at about the same latitude. In this way he would establish a direct overland route linking Santa Fe with San Luis Obispo and Monterey, the capital of California. To carry out this trek, which would cross perilous Indian country along the Santa Barbara Channel, Garcés asked the corporal in charge of Mission San Gabriel for an escort of soldiers and supplies, including fresh mounts. After the corporal rejected his request, Garcés went over his head to the military governor of California, Fernando Rivera y Moncada, who at that moment was at San Diego working to quell the indigenous unrest that had destroyed the mission there five months earlier.

Rivera, who had a strained relationship with the Franciscans throughout California, summarily turned down Garcés's plea. Among other objections, Rivera did not want to encourage the Indians along the Colorado River to develop increased trade with the coastal tribes, as Garcés was promoting. The commander suspected, mistakenly, that Garcés's Native friends on the river, including the Yumas and Jamajabs, had incited the uprising at San Diego. Rivera even wanted to arrest Colorado River tribesmen who showed up on the coast to conduct trade, as they had done for centuries. The truth was that the Kumeyaay at San Diego had urged their brethren on the river to join in the mission massacre, but they got no takers.

In his journal, Garcés spelled out his own passionate arguments against Rivera's shortsighted approach, which relied more on brandishing military force to compel Indian submission than on nurturing mutually beneficial economic relationships. In a classic observation highlighting the ingrained conflict between the Spanish military and the padres, Garcés concluded: "If we preach to the heathen a law of peace and charity, how can we think of sowing discord?" (255).

The padres were united in their stance against Rivera's harsh policies toward the Natives. Recounting this episode in the official chronicle of the College of Santa Cruz, Arricivita also blasted Rivera for his harsh treatment of the Natives. "He must have ignored the frequent orders from the king to the effect that when the savages come to the presidios, they were to be admitted with demonstrations of charity," wrote Arricivita, lamenting "how costly the conduct of this official [Rivera] was."[6]

Rivera's only concession was to grant Garcés one of the worn-out horses left at San Gabriel by the Anza expedition. The friars of the mission gathered for Garcés from their own meager stocks the supplies that Rivera refused him. They also gave generous provisions to his Indian mates. Garcés was determined to continue on to San Luis Obispo, but he prudently accepted the judgment of the mission fathers that it was too risky to follow the shortest route along the Santa Barbara Channel without a military escort. Instead, he decided to strike out to the north through the bosom of central California, an uncharted wilderness that held many surprises.

CHAPTER ELEVEN

Solitary Sojourn in the High Desert

The dead add their strength and counsel to the living.
—Hopi proverb

When Francisco Garcés caught sight of the secluded Hopi pueblo of Oraibi more than two centuries ago, he described it as "tumbledown."[1] The adjective still fits. A hodgepodge of dwellings made of mud bricks and unpainted cinderblocks, with dusty, unpaved streets, Oraibi is home to a few dozen Hopis struggling to maintain a traditional way of life. It has no running water or electricity, except that produced by a few solar panels. Perched on the top of a mile-high mesa and surrounded by hundreds of miles of empty desert, Oraibi is conspicuous for its isolation. The settlement dates back to about 1100 A.D., making it one of the oldest continuously inhabited places in the United States.

The villagers make their living as their ancestors did, raising corn, beans, and melons. It is dry farming, with no irrigation, so the crops are dependent on the scant rain and snowfall of the arid Four Corners region. Not surprisingly, periodic famines have darkened Oraibi's history. The underground kiva on the central plaza remains the focus of religious and cultural life. Its secret ceremonies are dominated by entreaties to the Great Spirit for precipitation to sustain the harvest.

For centuries the reclusive Hopis living here in the far northeastern corner of Arizona have resisted outside intrusions. Today's residents stick to themselves and are wary of strangers. Their insular ways exclude non-Hopis from the daily life of Oraibi, which explains why the U.S. Census Bureau has never obtained an accurate population count. The few visitors who find their way to Oraibi are advised that photography of any kind is prohibited, as is drawing sketches. There are no known photographs showing the town as it looks today, sitting atop the adobe walls and other remains of the old pueblo. Guests are warned not to go near the kiva, whose sacred activities are closely guarded. A fierce detachment from the contemporary world of tablet computers and smart phones is entrenched in Oraibi's ancient DNA.

On 9 April 1776 Francisco Garcés set out from Mission San Gabriel near present-day Los Angeles in the company of Sebastián Tarabal, the two Jamajab Natives who crossed the Mojave Desert with him, plus two Gabrielino Indians from the mission. His aim was to reach Mission San Luis Obispo by traveling north through California's unmapped central plain, thus bypassing the dangerous Indian country along the Santa Barbara Channel. As he skirted the San Gabriel Mountains on his right, traversing the fertile San Fernando Valley, he paused from time to time to record his latitude with the quadrant and to preach at Indian villages. Most of the Natives welcomed him, but as he approached one settlement all of the young women fled and hid. Garcés learned that Spanish soldiers had passed through the area previously and had preyed upon the Indian maidens.

Riding in a northwesterly direction, Garcés was confronted a few days later by the soaring Tehachapi Range, which he named the Sierra de San Marcos. These were the only mountains in California running in an east–west formation, with peaks reaching almost 8,000 feet. Garcés and his party crossed the mountains amid lofty pines and oak trees near what is known today as Tejon Pass, 4,183 feet above sea level. Below him now stretched the boundless flat table of what later would be called the San Joaquín Valley.

As he made his descent from the pass, Garcés came to a settlement where the Indians lived in a large communal lodge made of arched willow branches, with a roof of marsh-grass mats sewn together. The structure had openings to let out the smoke of cooking fires, with a single door at each end guarded at night by sentries. Along the interior were separate sleeping chambers for each family, who gathered around a fire at the entrance to each room before retiring for the night.

These Natives, too, had suffered unfortunate encounters with Spaniards from the coast. When Garcés's two Jamajab interpreters approached the village, one was still wearing the shirt the padre had given him in the cold desert and the other was still wearing the blanket. This prompted the young people of the village to flee into the woods, fearing the Jamajabs were Spaniards. Only after the villagers learned that Garcés had come not from the coast but from the east did they welcome him.

Although they were prone to dancing and shouting and creating a general hubbub, the tribesmen fell silent the moment Garcés began to sing the *Alabado* or to recite the rosary. At his invitation, they kissed the crucifix that he wore around his neck, and they marveled at his compass. They gave him many seashells, trying in vain to trade them for his rosary. At one point as he was praying, the chief's wife poured a basket of edible chia seeds over him as an offering. Other women threw chia seeds into the fire to create bursts of light.

The chief made a very pungent gruel from water and a wild tobacco-like plant. Garcés recoiled at its bitter taste, and one of his Native interpreters vomited so violently after eating it that Garcés feared he would die. In his journal, Garcés made note of the villagers' fine baskets, woven shellwork, and shallow bowls inlaid with mother-of-pearl obtained in trade with the Indians of the Santa Barbara Channel. At bedtime, after visiting convivially with the Native families around their fires in the lodge, Garcés was given a place to sleep inside near the door.

By 27 April Garcés learned from his observation of the sun that he was once again just north of parallel thirty-five, and therefore about due east of Mission San Luis Obispo. Here the locals urged him to venture not a single step farther because he was about to enter the territory of the notoriously bellicose Noche tribe, later known as Yokuts. Sebastián and the two Jamajab interpreters refused to continue on. Garcés spent three futile days trying to change their minds. Eventually, an old man of the Noche tribe who had married a woman from the village where Garcés was staying agreed to accompany him as his guide. Garcés thus instructed Sebastián and the Jamajabs to stay put for four or five days and await his return from his exploratory jaunt northward into the heart of the broad central valley.

When he stopped along a streambed to eat a green herb growing there, Garcés spotted three Noches on higher ground a short distance away. He tried to entice them to come closer by holding out glass beads and tobacco for them, but the Indians kept their distance. After a short while, the Noches came a bit nearer and threw six dead squirrels to Garcés and six more to his old Noche guide, providing them a much needed food supply.

The next day Garcés came upon a rushing river with crystal-clear water making a great noise as it descended from the mountains. He named it El Río de San Felipe, labeled on modern maps as the Kern River. In these parts the Indian women were especially attractive and clean, bathing regularly in the river. They wore deerhide skirts and wraps of animal pelts, and tied their jet-black hair in a topknot on the forehead. Garcés lamented that they were careless about keeping their private parts covered. Perhaps the women were flirting with the bearded stranger, who must have appeared strikingly exotic in his flowing gray habit and broad leather sombrero.

At the next village, a few miles south of present-day Bakersfield, Garcés wanted to cross the river as the Natives instructed him to do. "Difficulties arose when they asked me if I knew how to swim," he wrote in his diary. He told them he couldn't swim and asked them to build a raft to ferry him across. But the Indians didn't know how to build a raft. So, it was decided that four Natives would swim him across, two holding onto his arms and two holding onto his body as he stretched out on his back. The Indians told him to take off all of his clothes, but Garcés insisted on wearing at least his shirt and underwear. With that, Garcés recorded, "I had a fine bath in that beautiful water." His mule had no trouble swimming across the river, and his saddle and robes were taken over in baskets.[2]

Drying out on the opposite bank, he showed his Indian hosts the magnetic needle on his compass. "As they saw that no matter how I kept turning it about, it always pointed to the north, which was the direction I told them I ought to take, they . . . remained looking at one another in wonderment, which is not strange, for when other Indians have seen the compass they have thought it possessed an understanding of its own."[3] Garcés now rode over such rugged ground that his old Noche guide grew tired and left him to forge ahead alone. Continuing on, he found a village where the Indian men grew beards, an unusual sight. One old Indian had a beard so long and white that he reminded Garcés of the religious hermits of Spain.

Here the padre was surprised to see that the girls and even some young women went about completely naked. He also was introduced to the Indian custom of the sweat lodge—an underground cavity covered with sticks and grass. The men lighted a fire in the small enclosure and endured the heat and smoke until their eyes watered and they were dripping with sweat. Then they ran out and jumped into the cold river to bathe. "This is why these people stay clean," Garcés recorded, "but although well formed, they are slender and not hardy enough for travel afoot."[4]

At the next settlement, 150 Natives greeted Garcés with loud cries of "Ba! Ba! Ba!" while slapping their thighs hard with their palms. He passed out his dwindling store of trinkets, and the Indians lined up to kiss the crucifix hanging from his neck. In the middle of this ceremony, an Indian boldly asked Garcés—in Spanish—for paper to roll a cigarette. The man indicated he had been to the coast, which he said was a four-day journey away, and had seen other priests. He also imitated firing a musket and the act of flogging, sure signs that he had been to a mission. Garcés suspected he was a runaway from Mission San Carlos near Monterey.

At this village Garcés asked permission to baptize a sick boy who was near death. When the parents consented, Garcés took the child in his arms with much tenderness, calling him affectionately *muchachito* (dear little boy) and poured a little water over his forehead while reciting the baptismal rite. The Indian who had been to the coast repeated Garcés's Spanish words, leaving no doubt that he was of the missions. In the end, as the Indians danced in circles around a bonfire and sang mournful chants, Garcés placed a little cross on the dying boy's chest and gave his handkerchief to the weeping parents for use as a shroud.

Before long other barefoot Noches arrived from villages to the west and north to hear Garcés preach. They told him of more abuses by Spanish soldiers. According to Garcés's account, two Spanish men, likely deserters from the Monterey presidio, "were very wicked" with the Indian women.[5] Although Garcés did not say so explicitly, it is very likely the Spaniards' crimes were violent rapes. When the pair were captured by Noche warriors, the punishment was grotesque. The Indians cut off their hands and then put them to death by slitting their bodies wide open from the breast downward, slicing them up into small pieces, and scattering the remains.

The visiting Noches pleaded with Garcés to return with them to their villages and visit the large rivers to the north that flowed into the large delta east of San Francisco Bay. He was very tempted to continue his solo explorations, but it had already been four days since he had left Sebastián and the Jamajabs, and he feared they would abandon him if he did not turn back at once.

Returning southward on his mule in the company of an ever-changing retinue of naked Natives on foot, he stopped at a Noche village where he was given dried bear meat to eat. He learned from the Indians that there were large numbers of bears in the surrounding valley, and that the Natives feared the beasts and stayed away from them. In fact, some of Garcés's escorts abruptly jilted him when he entered the bears' domain. The padre also was told about another Spanish deserter who was married to a Noche woman and had a child with her. The man was easily recognizable because he wore clothes and a round medal or locket on his chest.

On 6 May—a full week after he had left Sebastián and the two Jamajabs with a promise to return in four or five days—Garcés encountered four Indians carrying a large quantity of meat wrapped in a gray hide that looked like a mule skin. When the Indians offered Garcés some of the meat, he saw among the chunks what he thought was a mule's head. He could not shake off the dreadful thought that Sebastián had come looking for him and had been murdered by the Noches, who slaughtered his mule. Uneasily, Garcés agreed to go with the Noches to their village, where the Natives staged a celebration with much dancing. They urged him to stay among them, but he resumed his southward march the next morning, still churning with fear over the fate of his friend Sebastián.

On reaching the Indian village where he had been ferried across the San Felipe River the week before, at the site of current Bakersfield, Garcés heard from the Natives about a place five miles downstream where the waterway split into two narrow branches.[6] Here the Indians had built bridges from the trunks of alder trees over which Garcés could cross, albeit somewhat precariously. The river flowed so swiftly through the two channels that Garcés was unable to measure the depth of the water with a nine-foot-long stick because the current bent the stick. The Indians helped Garcés get his mule and baggage across the two rushing streams. His Native helpers also reported that Sebastián and the Jamajab escorts had been at the river a few days earlier in search of him. This only reinforced Garcés's anxieties about Sebastián.

Now growing desperate to find his sidekick, Garcés continued alone in a southeasterly direction through dry lake beds, occasional clumps of trees, and sand hills. The ground was pockmarked with countless holes dug by kangaroo rats. The terrain was so honeycombed by their burrows that the mule and Garcés took a tumble. It was difficult even to walk his normally sure-footed steed without stumbling over the undermined turf. Garcés lost his compass in the fall, but by the time he discovered it was missing he chose not to go back over the dreaded ground and look for it. Stopping for the night at a village of Cuabajai Indians, Garcés feared he would never see Sebastián again. It now had been ten days since they had parted.

Into the Cuabajai village the next day came one of his Jamajab escorts, whom Garcés identified as Luís, the first time in his journal that he called the man by his name. Perhaps it was his sense of profound relief that prompted Garcés to record the Indian's Spanish alias.[7] (In his journal the next day, he cited for the first time the name of the other Jamajab, Ventura.) Luís was carrying a message that Sebastián was still looking for Garcés along the San Felipe River.

By that afternoon Sebastián himself appeared, and Garcés was relieved to find him "safe and sound."[8] Neither Sebastián nor his mounts had been molested by the Noches. To his amusement, Garcés learned later that the animal slaughtered by the Noches was not a mule but an elk.

Once reunited with his three companions, Garcés turned his attention to scouting an overland route from the California coast to the old Spanish capital of Santa Fe, a distance of a thousand miles, almost all of it over desert. (At that very moment, unbeknownst to Garcés, a Spanish expedition led by the Franciscan priests Atanasio Domínguez and Silvestre Vélez de Escalante was preparing to set out from Santa Fe in an unsuccessful search for a direct route to the Pacific. In their explorations, begun at the end of July, the two friars were aware of Garcés's wanderings and believed he was lost in the wilderness. Some Indians encountered by Domínguez and Vélez related stories they had heard about the intrepid padre from San Xavier del Bac.)

Garcés dreamed of the Spanish galleon trade from the Philippines reaching Santa Fe by way of the new port of San Francisco, bearing valuable beeswax for candles, silk fabrics for priests' vestments, chinaware, and pottery. He also envisioned supplies from Spain reaching Santa Fe through the Gulf of Mexico and the Mississippi River. Accordingly, he headed southeast back over the Tehachapi Range and into the withering maw of the Mojave Desert, just as triple-digit temperatures were escalating with the approaching summer solstice.

On 30 May 1776, 103 days after departing Tubac with the Anza expedition, Garcés returned to the land of the Jamajabs on the west bank of the Colorado River in the general vicinity of what is today Needles, California. To celebrate his return, the Jamajabs staged a huge gathering of all of the surrounding tribes from both sides of the Colorado, during which they extolled the newfound peace that Garcés had brokered on his earlier visit. "So great was the crowd, the tumult, and the shouting that these Indians made in this general meeting that on account of it and the excessive heat, I was threatened with illness," Garcés wrote in his diary.[9]

He questioned the Indians closely about how far it was to the land of the Hopis in New Mexico, and what the trip to the east would be like. His ardent plans were potentially spoiled, however, when he found waiting for him two letters, one from Captain Juan Bautista de Anza himself and the other from his erstwhile compañero Fray Thomas Eixarch. Both messages directed Garcés to return without delay to the Yuma crossing, nearly two hundred miles to the south. Anza, who had arrived at the Colorado River on 11 May on his return from Monterey, had expected to find Garcés waiting there for him, as the viceroy's instructions had stipulated. Instead, Eixarch informed Anza that he had heard not a whisper from Garcés since his departure upriver three months before. Pedro Font, who was with Anza, speculated that Garcés may have been killed by the Indians, an entirely reasonable prospect.

Reluctantly, Garcés prepared to head downriver to the Yuma crossing in compliance with Anza's directive. On 31 May, as he was saying his goodbyes and passing out presents, a violent shouting match erupted among some Jamajabs and Hualapais. The two tribes had battled each other in past wars, and Jamajabs whose relatives had been killed by Hualapais threatened to retaliate by killing the visiting Hualapais. In a bid to avert bloodshed, Garcés announced he would escort the terrified Hualapais back to their homeland on the eastern side of the Colorado River. "No one opposed my resolve," Garcés recounted, so his gambit succeeded, even though he feared the vituperative Jamajabs would kill him, too.[10]

Garcés said he made up his mind to go to the land of the Hualapais "on the spur of the moment."[11] That was no doubt true, but it also afforded a convenient excuse for ignoring Anza's order to return to the Yuma crossing. Instead, he would proceed on to the territory of the Hopis. The Hualapai homeland was conveniently on the way.

Garcés no longer had the services of his two Jamajab interpreters, Luís and Ventura, who had returned to their families. Sebastián was now the sole member of his company. But Sebastián refused to follow Garcés any farther, because the

Jamajabs were emphatic that the Hopis would kill them. For generations, Jamajabs and Hopis had been blood enemies. Garcés begged Sebastián to reconsider, but to no avail. Thus the Indian headed downstream to Jalchadún country and Garcés crossed the Colorado, embarking on a dangerous 350-mile journey to the Hopi mesas.

With the heat of June bearing down on him, Garcés rode toward the rising sun along old Indian trails across a high-desert plateau six thousand feet above sea level. Lacking his compass, he navigated by the sun and the stars, sticking to a northeasterly course. The vast plain was furrowed in places with red-rock gorges and punctuated by thickets of junipers and pines. Watering holes were scarce, and Garcés was dependent on the Natives' local knowledge to locate them. Most of the time, an Indian or two, sometimes many more, would escort him to the next village.

He stopped most days at Indian settlements to preach and be fed. He was heavily reliant on the Natives for their hospitality, and they almost never failed him. At one village, an Indian woman went up into the mountains two hours before daybreak to get him drinking water. At another, an Indian who had killed a black-tailed deer cut up the carcass and shared the meat with Garcés and the Indian who was accompanying him. "It is remarkable how these Indians share whatever they get from hunting," Garcés wrote in his diary. "Though the amount may be small they share it with everyone."[12] By the middle of June Garcés observed how the earth had turned a deep red and the land had become a labyrinth of steep canyons carved by the Colorado River and its tributaries. On 17 June 1776, he reached the village of an unmarried Indian who had been serving as his guide. The villagers put on a festive celebration, with much dancing, and fed Garcés mescal, always a staple in dry infertile country. In this hamlet, as in others, Natives who were maimed or blind or infirm asked Garcés to lay hands on them and say prayers for their recovery, which he readily obliged. The Natives also drew in the dirt an elaborate map showing the neighboring Indian nations and the trails to reach them. This was valuable information for Garcés, who surprised the Indians by drawing on their same dirt map his long trek from California to his planned destination among the Hopis.

As he continued on, the terrain became more and more difficult to traverse and it was necessary to descend along narrow trails into the bottoms of deep gorges. On 20 June, his 114th day on the trail, Garcés came to the precipice of a crimson ravine whose steep walls were horrifying to behold, a dizzying plunge of a thousand feet to the bottom. He called this "the New Canfran," after a summit in the Pyrenees Mountains of his native Aragón. The way forward was along a footpath only three handbreadths wide, "with a very high cliff on one side and on the other a hideous abyss," as Garcés described it.[13]

He had to get down from his mule and the Indians from their horses because the narrow trail was not wide enough for the mounts. The animals were led into the canyon by a different, longer route to the east. As frightening as the chasm was, it only got worse when the pathway ended at a rickety ladder made of rough sticks held together by strips of bark. One by one, Garcés and his party climbed down the ladder to the floor of the gorge, where there was a Supai village and cultivated fields of corn. "I have seen no better natural stronghold," Garcés concluded.[14]

This place later became known as Cataract Canyon. In the spring of 1858, the historic surveying expedition led by Lieutenant J. C. Ives came upon the same trail. He reported:

> It seemed as though a mountain goat could scarcely keep its footing upon the slight indentation that appeared like a thread attached to the rocky wall.... Glancing down the side of my mule I found that he was walking within three inches of the brink of a sheer gulf a thousand feet deep; on the other side, nearly touching my knee, was an almost vertical wall rising to an enormous altitude. The sight made my head swim, and I dismounted and got ahead of the mule, a difficult and delicate operation, which I was thankful to have safely performed. A part of the men became so giddy that they were obliged to creep upon their hands and knees, being unable to stand or walk. In some places there was barely room to walk, and a slight deviation in a step would have precipitated one into the frightful abyss."[15]

Passing a few days in the bottomland, Garcés noticed that the Indian women were fond of wearing strips of red cloth obtained in trade from the Hopis. Their complexion was much whiter than that of other Natives, and he theorized their fair skin came from living deep down in the canyon, where they were exposed to little direct sunlight. He also admired how husbands and wives and their older children began working their patches of corn, beans, and greens at daybreak, using digging sticks, hatchets, and grub hoes of Hopi origin. The Indians had a few horses and even some cows that had been branded. They had traded for them with the Hopis, who were known to harbor livestock stolen from the Spaniards in the upper Rio Grande Valley of New Mexico.

Resuming his march across the highlands through pine forests more than seven thousand feet above sea level, Garcés and his escorts reached the western end of the Grand Canyon. He was the first white man to gaze into its magnificent, multicolored depths since the Spanish explorer Francisco Vázquez de Coronado and his men in 1540. Garcés named the great gorge El Puerto de Bucareli, after the viceroy. If the awe-inspiring vista from the south rim of the canyon moved him, he didn't say so in his journal, laconically describing the geologic cleft as "a deep passage . . . steep-sided like a manmade trough, through which the Colorado River enters these lands."[16]

By 28 June Garcés had crossed a plain southeast of the Grand Canyon and reached the deep, ruddy gulch carved by the Little Colorado River, which he named El Río de San Pedro. After dismounting and making his way with great difficulty to the bottom on foot, he found the water was red with silt deposits and undrinkable. At a Yavipai settlement along the riverbank, he encountered his first Hopis, two men who had come to trade with the Yavipais. They were clad almost like Spaniards, wearing leather jackets, tight sleeves, trousers, and boots. One of the Hopis kissed Garcés's hand in a gesture of respect. But when the padre gave the Indian some tobacco and shells, he handed them right back. Garcés called out to the other Hopi, but the man refused to come near. When the Yavipais invited the Hopi to kiss Garcés's crucifix, he shunned it.

This moment should have shaken Garcés's confidence in the reception he would receive when he arrived among the Hopis, whose seven towns were spread out on the top of three remote mesas. Surely he had not forgotten the Jamajabs' warning that the Hopis would put him to death. But, as always, his obstinacy in the face of mortal peril never faltered. Early the next morning the traders departed, carrying advance word to the Hopis that a black-bearded Spaniard was headed their way.

After tarrying at the village for three days, Garcés and eight Yavipai escorts pushed on to the east. Unfurled before them was a striking panorama of soaring red buttes, expansive mesas, and deep chasms chiseled by the unceasing wind and powerful rivers of an earlier geologic epoch. When Coronado entered these badlands in 1540, he called them El Desierto Pintado (The Painted Desert). The arid soil, abundant in iron and manganese, was a vivid red, spawning red dust devils whirling along the desert floor. Composed of stratified layers of easily erodible siltstone, the landscape was studded with striated pigments of burgundy, ocher, tawny, pink, russet, white, and gray.

Approaching the Oraibi pueblo, the first and largest settlement in Hopi country, Garcés met a young Indian who refused the tobacco offered to him. A few miles nearer the pueblo, he spotted two mounted Indians who were well dressed, in the Hopi fashion. When he approached them to shake their hands, they drew away immediately and made gestures for him to go back to where he came from. Unfazed, Garcés pressed on toward Oraibi. But of his eight Yavipai companions, only two continued on with him. They were an old man and a young boy. Following a very narrow path up to the top of the mesa, the trio saw a sheep corral guarded by Hopis, many peach trees in the ravine below, and a cultivated vegetable patch near the spring in front of the decrepit pueblo.

Garcés entered the village on a wide dusty lane littered with discarded corncobs and found himself surrounded by attached, multistory dwellings made of mud bricks. A movable stick ladder provided access to an elevated courtyard ringed by living chambers with wooden doors. Upper levels were reached by still more ladders. Alongside some entry doors there were chicken coops. Higher up, also accessible by ladder, the roof offered a communal plaza connecting the apartments. Large painted earthen jars were visible on the roof.

When Garcés got down from his mule, he saw a bevy of women and children up on the roof, looking down on him. The women were well dressed in sleeveless smocks tied about the waist and accented with multicolored sashes. The older women wore their locks in two braids, and the unmarried ones did up their hair in a large whorl over each ear—a distinctive custom still practiced by Hopis today to signify an unattached female. A woman on the roof told the old Yavipai that he could come up, but that the padre and his belongings were to remain on the ground. The Yavipai turned to Garcés and said: "Stay here by yourself. These people don't like you and they are wicked."[17]

Garcés was not the first Spaniard to visit the Hopi mesas. The tribe's encounters with his predecessors colored their view of him long before he appeared among them. More than two hundred years earlier Coronado dispatched a contingent of troops under Pedro de Tovar to find the Hopi mesas, which he had heard about from the Zuñi tribesmen in the upper Rio Grande Valley to the east. Coronado was searching for the fabled Seven Cities of Gold, a myth created by an imaginative Native for gullible—and greedy—Spaniards. Notorious for his brutal treatment of the Indians, Coronado blundered about the desert for months, scorching a path of annihilation and ruin. Neither the Zuñis nor the Hopis would forget him.

In 1680, the pueblo Indians of Santa Fe organized a massive revolt under the warrior Po'Pay to expel the Spaniards from New Mexico.[18] They succeeded, and in the process killed four hundred Spanish settlers, including twenty-one of the thirty-three priests in New Mexico. The Hopis joined in the pueblo rebellion, the most distant tribe to do so. This event, too, lived on in the Hopis' oral history—even as it does to this day.

The Spaniards eventually reasserted their dominion in New Mexico. But the fiercely independent Hopis retained their autonomy, successfully resisting further

Spanish incursions. In June 1775, the Franciscan adventurer Silvestre Vélez de Escalante visited the Hopis from his mission at Zuñi.[19] With an estimated population of four thousand, Oraibi was the cultural soul of the standoffish Hopi people. Escalante found they wanted no contact with him or any other Spaniard.

It was against this backdrop that Garcés rode into Oraibi on 2 July 1776. After being turned away, Garcés retreated to a secluded spot at the edge of the pueblo and unsaddled his mule. The old Yavipai took it to one of the Hopi corrals. Gathering up a handful of corncobs from the street, Garcés used his magnifying lens to strike a fire and cook a little gruel from his few provisions. His gritty campsite on the periphery of the village was littered with rubbish and human excrement. Throughout the day, men, women, and children came to stare at him. Yet none would get close when he offered them white seashells, even though their faces brightened at the sight of them. In the afternoon the Hopi men returned from their fields, carrying their hatchets, digging sticks, and grub hoes. The six Yavipai escorts who had held back also arrived belatedly, and Garcés could hear them in the houses pleading his case to the Hopis.

At nightfall an elderly man approached Garcés. The padre gave him a present and held out the crucifix for him to kiss, which he did respectfully. Then the man said to him in Spanish: "Dios te lo pague!" (May God reward you!). He turned out to be a Zuñi visitor who had been baptized a Christian. At that particular time, the Zuñis were on good terms with their Franciscan priests. Speaking of the Hopis, the Indian told Garcés: "These are savages who do not wish to be baptized, nor do they believe that you are a priest."[20] The man offered to take Garcés to the land of the Zuñis, in the direction of the sunrise, where the Natives had already heard about "the bearded one"—Garcés—preaching peace. When the padre asked to see the Hopi chief, he learned the leader had gone into hiding.

Asked if he wanted to sleep in the house where the Zuñi was spending the night, Garcés declined because the offer had not been made by the master of the house. Instead, he slept on the ground on his sheepskin mat. After he had lain down, the two youngest Yavipais came to him and scornfully cast back the white seashells he had given them to buy maize with on the trail a few days earlier. The shunned padre could only figure that the Hopis had turned the Yavipais against him. What he did not know was that the Hopi chieftain had sternly warned his people not to provide aid of any kind to the Spaniard. As darkness descended on the mesa and stars appeared in the desert sky, Garcés listened as the Hopis on their rooftops played their flutes and sang.

The next morning at dawn, both Garcés and his mule awoke hungry. The Hopis had refused to provide fodder for the mount, even though it was kept in one of their corrals. The old Yavipai advised Garcés to go to one of the other Hopi pueblos, where they might give him something to eat. He saddled his mule and, with many boys and girls looking on, rode down the steep eastern side of the mesa. "I resigned myself to go on alone," he said, reflecting on his alienation from both the Hopis and some of the Yavipais. As he climbed to the nearest pueblo, about eight miles away on what is now called Second Mesa, he saw two shepherds guarding their flock of sheep and a woman chopping kindling with a hatchet.[21] All three ran away as soon as they saw him.

Discouraged and starving, Garcés decided not to press his fortunes in another truculent Hopi settlement. He turned his mule around and headed back to Oraibi. When he reached the pueblo at nightfall, it appeared the entire settlement was lined up on the rooftops watching him as he returned to his secluded sleeping spot. One of the Yavipais took his hungry mule to the corral.

At first light the next day, Garcés heard singing and dancing in the streets. Hopis with feather ornaments in their hair and dressed in other finery paraded about, banging sticks on shallow wooden basins and playing their flutes. But the ceremony was less a celebration than a war dance. When the sun rose in the sky, a great crowd of Hopis encircled Garcés in a threatening way. Now, for the first time, he really did fear for his life.

The tallest of the Indian men demanded of Garcés: "Why have you come here? Don't stay. Go back to your own land." Garcés motioned to the crowd to sit down, but they declined. Holding his crucifix in his hand, he spoke partly in Spanish, partly in Yuma, and partly in Yavipai, along with sign language, to communicate that Jesus Christ died on the cross and was in heaven. His unruly audience was having none of it. When an old man shouted in Spanish "No, No!" Garcés said, "Fetch me my mule." The outcast padre loaded his belongings, climbed atop the mule, and rode off with a forced smile on his face, surrounded by the villagers until he was well beyond the pueblo (see figure 7).[22]

In a twist of history, the Hopis later regretted their snub of Garcés.[23] Not long after his visit, they began to suffer years of drought, famine, pestilence, and depredations waged against them by the Utes and Navajos. Anza later stated in his journal during a visit to Oraibi in 1780, when he was governor of New Mexico, that the superstitious Hopis blamed their misfortunes on their rejection of Garcés. At the time, the total population of the three Hopi mesas had plummeted to 738 persons, according to Anza's estimate. That was down from an estimated 7,500 during Father Escalante's visit five years earlier. Anza described the Hopis as "in the last stages of extermination." Rain had not fallen on the Hopi mesas for three

Figure 7. When Francisco Garcés reached the Hopi pueblo of Oraibi on 2 July 1776, the wary inhabitants shunned him, refusing him food or shelter. The Hopis had long-held memories of depredations by Spanish conquistadors more than two centuries earlier.
Photo circa 1899, courtesy of Wikimedia Commons.

years. "There is no living water with which to irrigate ten bushes of any plant whatever," Anza wrote. "What they call fields are sand heaps."[24]

The Hopis confided to Anza's Indian escorts that the "calamities came upon them because of the ill-treatment and contempt bestowed by them . . . upon the venerable Apostolic Father Fray Francisco Garcés," Anza recorded. "They declare that not having wished to hear the Gospel preached, which he tried to give them, he prophesied to them that they would not escape the aforesaid miseries which they are experiencing, for which reason they now praise him, which I consider this zealous man of religion has always deserved."[25] In his journal, Garcés made no mention of any such admonition to the Hopis.

After trying to retrace his route from Oraibi to the west and getting lost, Garcés met up with his Yavipai companions, who urged him to expedite his travels. In the distance were dense puffs of smoke indicating the Apaches were gathering for war. When the party camped for the night, the Yavipais shared with Garcés a few tortillas they had brought from Oraibi. But the pancakes were as small as communion wafers and not much thicker. The next day, Garcés finally reached one of the Yavipai villages he had visited previously. Here he ate his first real meal in four days—generous portions of beef and what was likely elk meat.[26]

For the next three weeks, Garcés rode his weary mule back across the high desert, reaching the Colorado River where it forms the northern boundary between present-day Arizona and California. His old friends the Jamajabs greeted him joyfully. They were so excited to see him that they could not stop touching him. Garcés learned they had mourned him for dead because it had been reported that the Hopis had murdered him.

The peace he had negotiated earlier among the river tribes was holding. "I have worked for peace, as my account shows. I can forestall many deaths and the destruction of these nations to whom I owe affection," he concluded, "as well as facilitate the founding of missions and the securing of the desired passage between Monterey and New Mexico."[27]

Among the Jamajabs Garcés learned that his hitherto faithful friend Sebastián Tarabal had not waited for his return, as the friar had instructed him to do. Amid the reports that Garcés had been slain, Sebastián had given away the shells and other supplies left with him. Of his two mules, one had drowned in the river and the other had died. The Jamajabs told Garcés that Sebastián had a bad heart, a judgment the padre must have found hard to accept.

At this point, the singular relationship forged between the Franciscan priest from Aragón and the runaway Cochimí Indian from Baja California came to an abrupt end. The two men had been almost constant companions for more than two years. They had bridged the cavernous cultural divide that separated them. They had eaten, slept, and traveled thousands of miles on the trail together, sharing danger, hunger, thirst, and many other hardships and uncertainties. Through it all, they had stood by each other—except when Sebastián felt his life was in jeopardy and he lacked the unvarnished courage of Garcés to press ahead, anyway.

Sitting together for hours around the campfire under starlit desert skies, Garcés and Sebastián developed an attachment that was rare between any Spaniard and Indian. Although Garcés was about seven years older than Sebastián, both men were restless spirits, driven to see new lands and meet new tribes. El Peregrino

(The Wanderer) was the Spanish nickname Sebastián had earned for himself, but it could just as easily have been applied to Garcés.

Sebastián the pathfinder had provided invaluable service to the Spaniards during their initial thrust into northern California, the Portolá expedition of 1769. He also guided Anza on his 1774 crossing of the desert from Sonora to California, and joined him on the 1775–76 colonizing expedition from Sonora to San Francisco. And he rode alongside Garcés, with some notable exceptions, on his epic sojourn in the southwest desert.

At various times the Indian acted as a guide, an interpreter, even a muleteer, in service to the Spanish crown. Sacagawea, the Shoshone woman who helped guide Meriwether Lewis and William Clark on their 1804–1806 expedition up the Missouri River and on to the Pacific slope, has long held a well-deserved place in American history. No such distinction has ever been extended to Sebastián, even though his legacy of discovery in the Southwest equaled that of Sacagawea. Now, the elusive Sebastián Tarabal simply disappeared. Garcés never saw him again. No other trace of him can be found in the historical record.

Garcés pressed on down the east side of the Colorado River to the land of the Jalchedunes, where he was visited by the two young girls whom he had ransomed from the Jamajabs a few months earlier. They were overjoyed to see him. The older girl brought firewood and cooked him a very pleasing meal. On 14 August he crossed on a raft to the west bank of the river. While spending the night at an Indian village, he was robbed of five of his belongings by Indians from the other side of the river. He sent word to the elders of that tribe and, in their shame, they recovered his stolen possessions. His cloak came back in tatters, but everything was accounted for.

On 27 August he reached the Colorado River crossing at Yuma, where the Indians had given him up for dead. The Natives told him of a Spaniard who drowned trying to swim across the river without the help of the Yumas. Garcés soon arrived among the Pimas along the Gila River, where he had many friends. They chanted in unison: "We are good, we are happy, we know God. . . . We are glad that the old man [Garcés] has come back and that the Apaches have not killed him."[28]

The grueling eleven-month odyssey of the "old man"—Garcés was thirty-eight years old—finally came to an end on 17 September 1776 when he reached his headquarters at Mission San Xavier del Bac in the Sonoran Desert. On his arrival he wrote in his diary that he "gave thanks to God and to my patron saints for having preserved me from every ill."[29] As looming events would prove, Garcés would not always be so fortunate.

CHAPTER TWELVE

Unfinished Quest

> A man in motion always devises an aim for that motion. To be able to go a thousand miles he must imagine that something good awaits him at the end of those thousand miles. One must have the prospect of a promised land.
>
> —Leo Tolstoy

The Royal Presidio Chapel of Monterey is a bustling place on a Sunday afternoon. Worshippers crowd into Mass, leaving no empty pews in the old church, whose cream-colored façade is embellished with tall pilasters, a statue of the Virgin of Guadalupe, and twin cathedral bells. In the courtyard is a weathered wooden statue of Junípero Serra clutching a crucifix with both fists. Parishioners are gathered in the church hall across the street to plan the week's activities. A volunteer docent in the small museum next to the chapel shows off the bug-eaten remnants of an oak trunk under which Sebastián Vizcaíno and his scurvy-stricken crew are said to have knelt in prayer after sailing into Monterey Bay on 16 December 1602. Overlooking the harbor, and close enough to catch a pungent whiff of pelican guano, the Monterey presidio is a serene setting, steeped in California history.

In the horrid winter of 1775–76, this was the longed-for destination of the colonizing expedition under the command of Lieutenant Colonel Juan Bautista de Anza. But it was no showcase. The chapel was nothing more than a shelter of tree branches and bulrushes, surrounded by a crude pole stockade. Although it was the official capital of Spanish California, the isolated garrison was on the edge of starvation due to a scarcity of provisions delivered irregularly by sea.

On 4 January 1776 the settlers of the Anza train had reached the relative haven of Mission San Gabriel near present Los Angeles, 350 miles from their journey's end at Monterey. On their arrival at San Gabriel the travelers were nearly out of food, their clothes tattered and threadbare (especially their underwear) after ninety-eight days in the saddle crossing the desert from Sonora. They almost certainly reeked, since their soap supply had run out weeks earlier. Even though the impoverished mission was in no condition to support the phalanx of visitors for long, Anza lodged them for an indefinite stay while he rushed off with Commander

Fernando Rivera y Moncada and Father Pedro Font to respond to the Indian uprising at Mission San Diego.

While at the San Diego presidio, Font's diarrhea returned intermittently, and he broke out with burning ulcers on the tip of his tongue and throughout his mouth. It was painful to eat or even to speak, and he drooled a great deal. The symptoms betrayed the initial stages of scurvy. Within days his conditioned worsened, with his tongue swollen and inflamed. Ignorant of the cause of scurvy, Font tried various folk remedies, such as gargling a potion of milkweed, alum, and sugar. He also tried a mouthwash of barley, water, and vinegar mixed with rosehips. He finally found some relief when María Antonia Victoria Carrillo, the wife of a presidio soldier, made a powder of ground verdigris (green tarnish scraped from copper pots), which he applied to his mouth sores with a feather each morning and afternoon.[1]

Despite his ill health, Font said Mass regularly in the makeshift chapel set up at the San Diego presidio in a gritty warehouse made of tule rushes after the Natives torched the mission church. On Sunday, 14 January 1776, he sang Mass while accompanying himself on a worn-out spinet, a small upright piano that had been given to the presidio by Father Ángel Somera, founding friar of Mission San Gabriel. Font apparently had left his stringed instrument, the psalterio, at Mission San Gabriel, rueful that he had found very few opportunities to play it on the trail.

He also delighted at seeing for the first time the whooshing spouts and breaches of gray whales in the ocean off San Diego as they made their annual five-thousand-mile migration from the coastal waters of Alaska to the warm lagoons of the Baja Peninsula in Mexico. When a huge dead whale washed ashore, the Kumeyaay Natives swarmed about it, cutting off chunks of flesh and devouring them raw. "Since the whale is usually so fatty, and they themselves are so filthy, in eating it they oil and smear themselves disgustingly with the fat," Font recorded. "They stink so badly that the foul odor they give off is revolting."[2]

After a few weeks in San Diego Anza was mindful of his responsibility to return to Mission San Gabriel and lead his caravan of families upcountry along El Camino Real to Monterey. But Commander Rivera, the top military officer in California, pressured Anza and his troops to stay until the ringleaders of the rebellion were rounded up and punished, which likely would take several more months. Rivera's prickly manner was once again on display.

Complicating matters, Rivera was not at all supportive of establishing the planned settlements at San Francisco, even though they had been ordered by the king. The military governor felt his meager forces were too skimpy already to defend the five existing missions in California. Moreover, he had reconnoitered San Francisco

Bay two years earlier and declared to the viceroy that there were no suitable spots there for a presidio and two missions. As Rivera's subordinate, Anza found himself trapped between his duty to his own expedition and Rivera's contradictory demands on him. Anza wrote privately in his diary: "[F]or me to await the completion of the task in which [Rivera] plans to employ himself . . . I think would be reprehensible conduct on my part."³

Then, at seven o'clock in the morning on Saturday, 3 February, five soldiers on horseback arrived in San Diego bearing a letter from Lieutenant José Joaquín Moraga, whom Anza had left in charge of the settlers bivouacked at Mission San Gabriel. To Anza's great distress, the letter stated that Antonio Paterna, the seasoned Franciscan in charge at San Gabriel, had severely cut back food distribution to the settlers because the mission lacked enough to feed its own people. Even before this action, the settlers had been receiving less than a full daily ration. Now, that amount had been cut in half, barely enough to survive on, and Father Paterna intended to halt the rations entirely in eight days. Amid the shortage of provisions, four Indians had stolen two cows and two hogs and slaughtered them to feed their families. The culprits had been caught and placed in irons.

With Rivera's blessing and the support of the other padres at Mission San Diego, food was drawn down from its warehouse to aid the settlers at San Gabriel. A packtrain set out for Mission San Gabriel the very next morning at ten o'clock after Font said Mass. The provisions consisted chiefly of dried beans and maize infested with worms.

Late the next evening after dinner, with rain falling on a dark night, Font spotted a candle burning in the cramped room he shared with Anza. The two were allotted the same sleeping quarters, an unusual arrangement for a top military officer and a friar, "more by necessity than because of friendship, since there were no other rooms," according to Font.⁴ Candles were in short supply in San Diego, as was almost everything else, and they were to be reserved for saying Mass. When Font went to investigate, he found the cook had lighted the candle and was waiting for Anza to return. From the cook Font learned that Anza had given the order to begin the return march to Mission San Gabriel early the next morning. The commander, once again, had not informed Font of his decision.

Indignant at this perceived slight, Font confronted Anza in front of Rivera and the three San Diego padres in the room where they all ate and spent most of their days. "I told him that I found it difficult that he never told me about his decisions, whereas he told them to the servants with whom he discussed these and other matters," Font related in his diary. Then came a drawn-out harangue against the commander, in which Font poured out his bitterness and hurt feelings, ultimately proclaiming: "I know you, and I am aware that you do not like to take advice from anyone" (203).

Font's diatribe was so studded with vitriol and impertinence that everyone else in the room, including Anza and Rivera, urged him not to continue on with the expedition but to remain instead in San Diego and recover his health. He rejected any such suggestion. "Don't tire yourselves, I have no intention of staying," declared Font, according to his own verbatim account. "If Señor Anza leaves me here with no supplies, then I will have to stay . . . but if Señor Anza will give me some supplies, I will go with [him] wherever he goes and accompany him in all of his hardships and travel, since I can still ride a horse. If I become disabled along the way and am unable to go any further, I am content with him leaving me at any point" (203).

With that, everyone retired awkwardly for the night. One can imagine that Anza and Font exchanged few words as they bunked down together in their small, unlit room. Font later filled several pages in his diary preserving at length the highly personal clash. In pointed contrast, Anza in his journal made no mention of it.

Because of continuing heavy downpours, Anza and his party—including Font—were not able to set out for Mission San Gabriel until 8:45 in the morning on Friday, 9 February 1776. The first obstacle was the San Diego River, which was running four feet deep with a swift current. After fording it on horseback with some difficulty, the travelers pushed northward along the coast. Several small streams had turned into free-flowing rivers. Three more good-sized waterways were crossed before Anza called a halt for the night alongside a stream that earlier had been named Agua Hedionda (Stinking Water).

Once in the saddle, Anza was known for bearing down on the trail at a steady clip throughout the day. He rarely stopped for a midday meal, even when he was shepherding the women and children of the colonizing caravan. For Anza a cup of chocolate in the morning was enough to keep him going until nightfall. With the strains between them still smoldering, Font in his irritating way challenged Anza as they rode side by side on the first day out of San Diego. "Once you are on horseback you don't think of eating anything, or of our doing so, either," said Font, according to the retelling in his diary. "I'm forced to admit I'm a man and I need to eat when I'm hungry. Isn't there anything at hand?" (210).

Overhearing this, Font's servant, probably hungry himself, volunteered that there was some bread and cheese packed for them by the padres in San Diego. Anza declared he was not hungry, but he acquiesced in the lunch break and shared in the food. As Font recounted the story, Anza "had just told me that he had had enough [to eat at breakfast] but right afterward he was hungry enough to eat some cheese!" (10). Thereafter, Anza ordered a servant to have available boiled meat, bread, and cheese for a midday snack, even though he usually insisted that it be eaten while riding.

On the trail over the next three days Font took detailed field notes of the beautiful wildflowers that clothed the countryside. Some of them, such as yellow pansies, reminded him of blossoms he had seen in his youth in the gardens of Catalonia. Others he mistook for tulips, which grew in Catalonia but were not introduced to North America until the next century. He also counted the number of hills over which they rode—125 in all before reaching Mission San Gabriel at 1:30 in the afternoon on Monday, 12 February.

As soon as Anza arrived he learned that a soldier of the mission guard, José Mariano Yépiz, had deserted the night before, joined by an Indian servant and three Indian muleteers from the expedition. They made off with twenty-five of the best saddle animals, along with two muskets, a saddle, and a quantity of beads, tobacco, and chocolate. Lieutenant Moraga and ten soldiers were out searching for them.

Anza's immediate worry was that thoughts of desertion were spreading among the expedition's demoralized soldiers and their families, who had suffered deprivation and boredom at the mission for the last five weeks. He took some encouragement that the soldier who led the conspiracy was not a member of the Anza party and that once before had attempted to flee. But there was no mistaking that Anza's own troops were discontented, and they blamed their commander. Some claimed they had been induced under false pretenses to volunteer, and they were refusing to go on. "They said they had been promised 365 pesos worth of pay and rations," Font noted. "But now they were here without rations, perishing from hunger, with no cows or any of the other things they had been offered when they enlisted" (212).

Adding to their unhappiness, the soldiers were being paid not in silver but in shoddy goods whose prices were inflated. Their wives constantly implored Anza for more food. They had taken to trading their meager belongings to the mission Indians in exchange for something, anything, to eat.

Anza had planned to strike out for Monterey immediately, but now he awaited the return of Lieutenant Moraga and his soldiers, mainly because the men left behind wives and children who needed them as escorts on the trail. Persistent rain showers, buffeting winds, and heavy fog contributed to the doleful mood. Worse still, the monsoons threatened to turn the trail into an impassable mire. Rivers were rising all along the road to Monterey. Anza had intended to reach his destination long before the winter rains set in. He now was many weeks behind schedule.

As gloomy days passed with Moraga still on the hunt for the fugitives, Anza was stricken with stomach distress that caused him to throw up his food every afternoon. The strains of command may have begun to wear on him. Font blamed Anza's chronic vomiting on the poor food and unsanitary conditions of Mission San Gabriel, where the cooks were dirty boys who did everything in an unclean way. Anza and Font ate their meals on a greasy old door that served as a table. "The filth on it could be scraped off with a knife," Font wrote. In an attempt to cheer up the commander, Font played songs on his psalterio for him (213).

After waiting in vain for nine days for Moraga's return, Anza decided to move out without him. The provisions, including the relief shipment from San Diego, were dwindling, and the route to Monterey was likely only to get boggier in the days ahead. He could afford no more delays.

On 21 February, Ash Wednesday, Font said morning Mass and delivered a stern sermon exhorting the settlers to repent for their faults and accept their suffering with patience—a favorite theme of his, even on good days. The train embarked at 11:30 in the morning. Most of the travelers had a dark smudge of ash on their foreheads from the morning's liturgical service. After a march of five and a half hours, Anza ordered that camp be set up for the night. Because of the swampy terrain, the pack train had slipped far behind, and a number of mules loaded heavily with supplies had fallen down.

For the next several days Anza led his caravan to the northwest and followed the coast along the Santa Barbara Channel. The rivers along the way were blanketed with geese, ducks, cranes, and other migrating waterfowl. One day the expedition spotted an enormous herd of antelopes. They "fled like the wind as soon as they sighted us and seemed like a cloud moving over the ground as they vanished from our sight," wrote Font (217). Most of the settlers, coming from the interior of Mexico, had never seen the ocean before. When they first heard the crashing surf in the distance and then rode along its shore, they were awestruck.

One troubling occurrence was that the Indian women in villages along the way fled and hid in their round bulrush huts as soon as they spotted the approaching expedition. Their men stood guard outside. This was a well-trod road, traversed by many unmarried Spanish soldiers in the past. Their violent sexual assaults on Native women were an enduring stain on the crown's colonizing campaign. In his journal Font decried the "unbridled passions" and "stupid acts" committed by the troopers (217).

Among the stupid acts was the stealing of fish and other food from the Natives. The most notorious offender was a Spaniard named Camacho. He was a carrier of venereal disease and infected a number of Indian women.[5] Because of his criminal activity, he was sentenced more than once to time in the stocks at San Diego. He was so well known among the Chumash Indians along the Santa Barbara Channel that they called every soldier Camacho. Font was repeatedly asked by the Natives: "Where is Camacho? Is Camacho coming?" (220).

In his diary Font expressed rare admiration for the industrious Chumash, their handsome appearance, their skill in building oceangoing canoes, and their fishing prowess. But he reverted to form in condemning them as "quite thievish, which is a characteristic of every Indian" (221). After Anza and Font dismounted at an Indian village called La Asumpta, a Native surreptitiously snatched a colorful kerchief from Anza's saddle. The commander did not discover it was missing until after he rode out of the village. He sent a servant armed with a musket back to the village to recover it. At first the villagers claimed to know nothing about it. Only after the servant drew his firearm and threatened to use it did the Indians return the missing cloth.

On another occasion Natives from a nearby village came into Anza's encampment and offered to help clean fish that the settlers had obtained in trade. While the Indians were using their flint knives, the commander pulled out his silver-handled pocketknife in its silver sheath and handed it to one of the Natives for use in cleaning the fish. When no one was looking, the man slipped off with Anza's expensive knife. As soon as he discovered it was missing, Anza sent another Indian to the village with an ultimatum that the knife must be returned or the offender would face punishment—potentially flogging, or worse. A short while later the Indian returned with the knife. He apologized for the man who had taken it, saying he thought it had been given to him. This was an entirely plausible misunderstanding, given that most Natives had no concept of individual ownership of their belongings. In Indian villages, nearly everything was owned in common. All the same, Font concluded that the incident was "proof of every Indian's propensity to theft" (222).

On Saturday, 2 March, as the caravan approached Mission San Luis Obispo, several mules became bogged down in the marshy terrain. In the dry season this was a low, flat plain. But now it had turned into a swamp where many ponds had formed. A number of the settlers tumbled from their mounts as the beasts trudged and stumbled through the mire. In one especially soggy stretch, Anza ordered the packloads removed from the mules and carried on the shoulders of the soldiers. The people slogged through on foot. Many had primped in their best clothes for their arrival at the mission and were distressed by their mud-stained looks.

Anza dispatched a soldier to the mission ahead of the expedition to announce its imminent arrival. The three padres exiled at secluded San Luis Obispo—José

Cavaller, Pablo Joseph Mugártegui, Juan Figuer—staged a colorful welcome when the train arrived at midday. Father Figuer, dressed in his silk vestments and waving a smoking incense burner, led the settlers into the new adobe church as everyone sang the *Te Deum,* the familiar anthem of praise to the Lord. The bells rang out in the church tower and the mission guard fired musket volleys. In his journal Anza wrote that the ceremony "was such as may be imagined with people who spend all the days of their years without seeing any other faces than the twelve or thirteen to which most of these establishments are reduced." Anza was referring solely to European "faces," excluding the numerous Indians at San Luis Obispo.[6]

Not yet four years old, the mission consisted of a half quadrangle of buildings made of logs with thatched roofs, surrounded by a wooden palisade. Only the church was made of adobe. Coming from Apache country, Font was familiar with Indian attacks on missions. In his diary he presciently noted that San Luis Obispo was especially vulnerable to fire because all of the buildings were topped with dry tule rushes. Eight months later, a disaffected Indian attached a burning wick to an arrow and shot it into the church roof, igniting a catastrophic fire.[7] This prompted Mission San Luis Obispo to begin building roofs of inflammable clay tiles. The practice eventually was taken up by all of the California missions.

While at San Luis Obispo Anza asked the Indian artisans to make him a hat, which they wove for him from multihued bulrushes. He also stood as godfather at the baptism of a seven-year-old Native boy, who was christened Carlos Antonio de Anza. Font officiated at the baptism amid more pealing bells and musket salutes. An infestation of biting fleas—Font called it a plague—tormented the travelers during their two-day stay.

Three days later, while Anza rested his train at Mission San Antonio alongside the Santa Lucía Mountains, Lieutenant Moraga and his soldiers finally returned at one o'clock in the afternoon. They had pursued the five deserters almost as far as the Colorado River before apprehending them—with shouts of "Stop, in the name of the King!"—and returning them in irons to Mission San Gabriel, where they were imprisoned in the stockade. It turned out that the desertion was sparked when a corporal of the guard at Mission San Gabriel fell in love with a girl who was with her parents on the Anza expedition. To impress her, the corporal bought some stolen chocolate and brandy from an Indian muleteer, José Ignacio Amarillas, who was entrusted with the provisions. Fearing he would be caught and punished for the missing items, the Indian persuaded the others to join him in fleeing. In his protracted pursuit, Moraga also encountered rebellious Kumeyaay who had participated in the sacking of Mission San Diego and still possessed some of the stolen religious items.

At 4:30 in the afternoon on Sunday, 10 March, after a long day's march in drenching rain, the expedition at last reached the Royal Presidio of Monterey. With it pouring heavily, the settlers were greeted with cannon fire and musket volleys. The trek from Sonora had taken 165 days. By Anza's reckoning, the caravan had logged 823 miles. Three babies had been delivered on the trail. Almost miraculously, the only casualty was Manuela Piñuelas's death in childbirth on the first night out of Tubac.

If the pioneers expected to find comfort in the primitive outpost of Monterey, they were disappointed. There were no sleeping accommodations for them, only a chapel and a few other crude buildings positioned around a small plaza and enclosed by a stockade. Font's downhearted reaction was that "the whole thing amounts to very little" (243). Lieutenant Colonel Anza had to sleep in a warehouse, and Font's bunk was in a dirty little room filled with lime, which was used as a building material. The settlers pitched their tents in the plaza.

The next day Serra, the padre-presidente of the California missions, and four other friars from nearby Mission San Carlos joined Font in singing a solemn High Mass to give thanks for a successful journey. The presidio chapel was packed with nearly every participant in the epic march. Font preached a sermon exhorting the settlers to thank God for their safe arrival, comparing their trek to the exodus of the Israelites from Egypt. He recounted the many hardships of the trail, from the peril of Indian attack to the life-threatening snowstorm in the desert, and he graciously thanked Anza for "the patience, wisdom, and courtesy which he as leader has had in guiding this expedition, and I promise him that God will reward his work" (247).

Tears were streaming down Font's cheeks as he reached his peroration: "I charge all of you, do not forget your obligations as good Christians, and keep in mind what I said to you in a number of addresses along the way, so that you may have patience in the hardships that shall come to you in the future, and by becoming deserving through them, you shall live in God's grace so that when we die we shall come to meet again in Heaven" (247). For the worn-out settlers, Font's exhortations must have seemed tiresome.

Anza now faced the pressing task of identifying suitable sites for an army garrison and two missions on San Francisco Bay, in accordance with the viceroy's orders. As he was at Mission San Carlos making plans for a short surveying expedition, he was stricken suddenly at midday on Wednesday, 13 March, with violent pains in his groin, left thigh, hip, and knee. The pain was so acute that he had trouble breathing and feared he would suffocate. Soon he was overtaken by fever. The medicines applied by the presidio doctor, José Dávila, were of no help. For the next six days, Anza was a prisoner in his bed, unable to stand. The pain and fever continued, draining all of his energy. Not until Wednesday, 20 March, was he able to take a step with the help of others.

Two days later Anza was determined to mount a horse, which he was able to do only with the help of others. Against Doctor Dávila's advice, the commander made the one-hour ride from Mission San Carlos to the Monterey presidio at three o'clock in the afternoon. At his side was Font, who took almost literally his vow to accompany Anza wherever he went. On their arrival, Anza needed help getting down from the saddle.

At 9:30 the next morning, the commander felt strong enough to strike out in wet fog with an exploratory party of twenty men, including Lieutenant Moraga, eleven soldiers, and Font. They carried provisions for twenty days. Their charge was to locate sites for the three settlements and to explore a great river which Father Juan Crespí and others had seen during a reconnoitering foray around San Francisco harbor under the command of Captain Pedro Fages in 1772. Crespí had named the waterway the San Francisco River, after the founding father of his religious order. Left behind in Monterey were the increasingly disgruntled settlers, who now faced another long wait in destitute circumstances, with only tents for shelter, inadequate food, poor drinking water—and still no soap to wash themselves and their clothes.

At the start of Anza's march Font led the train in singing the *Alabado*, as he did every day thereafter. He and Anza were on better terms, perhaps because the chaplain had shown genuine concern when the commander was confined to his bed. When Font proposed to say Mass each morning to sanctify the new territory and pray for the success of the journey, Anza gave his earnest assent.

The small company made swift marches to the northwest and up the western side of San Francisco Bay. On the morning of Wednesday, 27 March, after spotting many bears, Anza reached the tip of the peninsula and the mouth of the harbor, known today as the Golden Gate. It was a clear day, providing a panoramic view of the expansive bay. Wrote Font: "I saw a harbor of harbors, a prodigy of nature" (270).

From a soaring white cliff that formed the southern boundary of the harbor mouth, the party peered down into the ocean and the bay, spotting whale spouts, schools of dolphins, sea lions, and otters. Anza ordered that a wooden cross be built and erected at a high spot on the point, where it could be seen from many miles out to sea. At its base he buried a document detailing his exploration in the name of King Carlos III. Font then blessed the cross.

Just below the point was a wide tableland covered in wild violets. There was plenty of water from nearby streams, ample firewood, and an abundance of pasturage for cattle herds. The site was also at a commanding height, which enhanced its natural defenses. The only thing lacking was tall trees for timber to construct barracks, but not far away were stands of oak, pine, and redwood. Anza designated it an ideal spot for the new San Francisco presidio. Font declared of the setting: "Despite the very good spots and fine country I have seen in the places I have been through, I have seen none that has pleased me so much as this one. I consider that nothing in the world could be finer, were it possible for it to be as well peopled as in Europe, since it has the best advantages for having a most beautiful city established at it" (270).

Always eager to point out the mistakes of others, Font stated repeatedly in his diary that the expedition encountered nothing but dark-skinned, dark-haired Indians along San Francisco Bay. He recorded this to contradict Father Crespí, who in his official report four years earlier asserted that he had seen white Indians with red hair during his reconnoitering survey with Captain Fages. This was not the first time Crespí's ability to judge colors had been called into question. It is entirely possible he was colorblind. But the censorious Font couldn't leave it at that. As soon as he returned to Monterey he took Crespí to task for claiming to have seen white Natives. Crespí responded: "They probably are not white, since you clearly saw them; if that is what I said, then that was how it appeared to me" (282).

The day after choosing the location for the presidio, Anza pressed on to the southeast. About five miles farther on, he passed through a wooded area and came to a robust stream of fine water that appeared to flow year round. Because it was the Friday before Palm Sunday, known to the Spaniards as Viernes de Dolores (Friday of Sorrows), the place was named Arroyo de los Dolores (Stream of Sorrows). Along its banks was a profusion of fragrant yellow chamomile, violets, and herbs. Surrounding it was good soil for planting crops. Lieutenant Moraga sowed a few grains of corn and chickpeas to see how well they would grow. Upstream Font found a small waterfall, which he thought would be a good place for a gristmill. Friendly Indians lived in a small village close to the stream. "I considered this to be a very lovely spot, the best one for establishing one of the two missions," concluded Font (282). On the site emerged Misión San Francisco de Asís, commonly known today as Mission Dolores, in the heart of urban San Francisco.

Later in the afternoon a monstrous brown bear approached the mounted soldiers. It came quite close without showing any sign of fear. The men already had encountered Indians who had been horribly scarred by the bites and scratches of angry bears. They opened fire as the beast stood looking at them. Corporal Robles struck it once in the throat, and others hit it with musket fire as it turned to flee down a hill, across a stream, and into the woods. Leaving a trail of blood, the bear did not get far before it fell dead. The soldiers skinned it, and Anza claimed the pelt as a gift for the viceroy in Mexico City. Then the men butchered the strong-smelling flesh and later consumed the tough meat. Font measured the carcass and found it to be over six feet long and nearly three feet high. From its worn-down fangs and missing tooth, he judged it to be old. "It is a fearsome beast," he wrote in his journal, "ferocious, very large, and corpulent" (285).

The next morning, Saturday, 30 March, Font said Mass and the expedition set out on a southeasterly course to round the southern end of the bay and ride up its eastern flank. Their destination was the San Francisco River, described by Crespí as flowing into the bay at its northeast quadrant. Along the southwest side of the bay the party paused to inspect a giant redwood that grew on the bank of a stream. Using a graphometer lent to him at Mission San Carlos, Font triangulated the tree's height and found it to be 154 feet. The trunk's circumference measured 15 feet, 1.5 inches at the base. Curious Indians gathered and expressed wonderment at Font's use of the strange instrument. The Spaniards named the place Palo Alto (Tall Tree). The behemoth still stands on the east bank of San Francisquito Creek, engulfed by the city of Palo Alto.

For the next five days Anza led his men up the east side of the bay through swarms of tormenting mosquitoes and at least one elk herd until they reached what is now called the Carquinez Strait, where the expansive estuary of the Sacramento River and the San Joaquin River flowed into San Francisco Bay. From there they pressed on to the east in an effort to locate the great river discovered by Crespí and Fages. Even before Anza departed San Diego, Rivera had advised him and Font that there was no such river. He based his conclusion on an earlier exploratory mission he had made through the area. By Thursday, 4 April, Anza and Font both had concluded that Rivera was correct. What Crespí and Fages thought was a massive river was actually what is known today as the Sacramento–San Joaquin River Delta. The eleven-hundred-square-mile marsh, marked by countless shallow channels, sloughs, and low islands, was formed ten thousand years ago by rising ocean levels after the end of the last Ice Age.

Always eager to find fault, Font crowed at length about the error made by Crespí and Fages, and he claimed to be the first in Anza's company who was astute enough to recognize the slipup. Anza was initially willing to give Crespí and Fages the benefit of the doubt, saying to Font: "Father, isn't it enough for the gentlemen to say they have seen the river that they say issues onto the plains here?" Font replied tartly: "Sir, it is not enough, because the river that the gentlemen spoke of is one that they saw very far away from [where we are], and no such river, nor the gap through which they say

FIGURE 8. Mission San Carlos Borromeo, at present-day Carmel, was the headquarters of the California missions, overseen by the strong-willed Junípero Serra. The remains of Serra and his longtime friend Juan Crespí were interred side by side under the main altar. Photo circa 1870. Historic American Buildings Survey, C. W. J. Johnson's Views of California Scenery, Ed Grabhorn's Collection, San Francisco, California.

Courtesy of Library of Congress.

it issues, can be seen from this hill. Here and now we must not judge by guesswork and by what may be, but by what is and what we see. And what we see and have in front of us is not a river but a great deal of pooled water." Font stated in his journal that this conversation put an end to the dispute—in his favor, of course (315).

Before seven o'clock the next morning Anza turned his train back toward Monterey. The route, recommended by Font, was over unexpectedly arduous mountains, which the men dubbed Sierra del Chasco (Joke Range), because of its surprising difficulty. The area was the lair of many bears, whose tracks were seen everywhere. Small bloodsucking ticks now fed on the men. Font plucked fourteen from his body, but still more replaced them. On Monday, 8 April, the expedition returned to Monterey at 10:30 in the morning. News of promising sites for a presidio and settlements on San Francisco Bay boosted the spirits of the settlers.

In the afternoon Anza and Font rode one hour south to Mission San Carlos (see figure 8). Along the way they found some wild strawberries that were just beginning to ripen. The pain in Anza's groin and leg had returned, causing him great suffering. At Monterey he would have had to sleep in his field tent. At the mission he had a room with a bed. But none of the salves applied to the painful parts of his body did any good. Neither Anza nor the presidio surgeon recognized it, but the cause of his abdominal distress was a kidney stone.[8]

Anza now had fulfilled his orders from Viceroy Bucareli. He was ready to go dutifully on to Mexico City to confer with the viceroy, as he had been ordered to do. Font would continue to ride by his side. It would fall to Lieutenant Moraga to lead the remaining 193 settlers to San Francisco and establish Mission Dolores.[9] Fray Francisco Palóu, the founding padre, said the first Mass there under a *ramada*, a crude shelter of tree branches, on 29 June 1776.

At two o'clock in the afternoon on Sunday, 14 April, Anza mounted his horse in the plaza of the Monterey presidio. Assembled before him were the settlers who had followed him for the last six months through misfortune and triumph. Many of the women were sobbing. The affection they felt for their commander was palpable. "They showered me with embraces, best wishes, and praises which I do not merit," Anza recorded in his journal.[10]

There was no such outpouring for Father Font. José Miguel de Silva, the servant Anza had assigned to him at the start of the expedition in October, declared he would no longer serve Font. Instead of returning to Sonora with the chaplain, Silva asked to remain with the settlers in Monterey. In staying, he abandoned a wife in Sinaloa.

On the morning of Anza's departure, Font said Mass as usual in the Monterey chapel. But on this day the settlers ignored the ringing of the church bell and stayed away from the service. Font's diary entry spelled out his chagrin at the settlers' lack of appreciation for him. As Anza led his mounted train from the plaza, the settlers in unison raised their voices to sing the familiar and stirring *Alabado:* "God be praised! Praise be to God!"[11] The departure of Anza and Font closed an important chapter in Spain's colonizing drive in North America. Little did either man know of the violent travails that still lay ahead.

CHAPTER THIRTEEN

Steering through Unexplored Waters

> I am tormented with an everlasting itch for things remote. I love to sail forbidden seas, and land on barbarous coasts.
> —Herman Melville, *Moby Dick*

Hidden away on the secluded northwest corner of Vancouver Island, Nootka Sound is best reached by boat or float plane. Its century-old lighthouse is one of the few still manned along the coast of British Columbia. This is a good thing, because on many days raw, dripping fog swallows up this stretch of coastline. In winter savage storms assault the rocky shore.

Strong tidal currents and heavy ocean swells challenge the salmon-fishing boats that seek refuge in the fjords of Nootka's inner harbor, known as Friendly Cove. Those who come here are mostly anglers, kayakers, and backpackers drawn by the unspoiled landscape and abundant wildlife, including gray whales, sea otters, eagles, cougars, and bears. The few year-round residents tout Nootka Sound's historical roots, the place where Europeans and Pacific Northwest tribesmen had some of their first encounters. To unearth this tale, we turn to the 243-year-old chronicle of Juan Crespí.

In the spring of 1774 Crespí was fifty-three years old and happily settled at Mission San Carlos, the Franciscans' California headquarters on the Carmel River south of Monterey. At his age he was approaching the partial retirement that friars could expect on the northern frontier—not a comfortable rocking chair by the fireside but at least a lessening of the more arduous demands placed on younger clerics.

Yet, Junípero Serra, the padre-presidente of the California missions, had something else in mind for his lifelong companion from their seminary days in Palma de Mallorca. California was buzzing with rumors of a maritime expedition ordered by the viceroy in Mexico City, Antonio María de Bucareli y Ursúa, to take possession of the northwest coast of North America almost as far north as present-day Anchorage, Alaska. Under the command of seasoned navigator Juan Pérez, this would be a passage into the unknown, for no Spaniard had ever ventured into the coastal waters north of Cape Mendocino in northern California. What lay beyond parallel forty-two north was labeled on charts as *mare incognitum*. In an earlier day, superstitious mariners imagined that giant sea serpents infested such unexplored waters in the far reaches of the globe.

To serve as chaplain and diarist of this adventure, Serra selected Fray Pablo Joseph Mugártegui, a thirty-eight-year-old Franciscan from the Basque country of northern Spain. The two had gotten to know each other on a long journey from Mexico City to San Diego, traveling by foot, horse-drawn coach, and sailing ship. Physically fit, with dark brown hair and a large, pockmarked face, Mugártegui appeared well suited to the rigors of a twenty-five-hundred-mile journey at sea.[1] Unexpectedly, though, he fell ill aboard ship before reaching Mission San Diego. The cause of his distress was tertian fever, a common consequence of exposure to malaria, characterized by recurring shaking fits, alternating sweating and chills, shivering, and pain in the bones and joints.

Once on land, Mugártegui made it clear he could not continue on with the ship, the *Santiago*, to Monterey, the jumping-off point for the maritime venture to Alaska. "[C]onsidering how weak he has remained and the horror he has acquired for the bark," Serra explained in a letter to his superiors, "he cannot be induced to continue his expedition, and he begs me to designate someone else."[2] Mugártegui spent the next six months recovering his health in San Diego.

Serra promptly departed San Diego and made his way overland along El Camino Real to Monterey, where he was greeted by Crespí. Serra cannot have been there long before he pressed his best friend into service on very short notice as Mugártegui's replacement. With his advancing years, Crespí was not enthusiastic about the assignment. But given the shortage of friars in California and the imperative to get a competent chaplain/diarist aboard the *Santiago* right away, Serra had little choice but to turn to Crespí.

"[N]otwithstanding that I was much fatigued with so many journeys by land," Crespí wrote, "I made the sacrifice of going on this enterprise, resigning myself to obedience, and expecting through God every success in the voyage."[3] This was classic Crespí, placing obedience above all other virtues and enduring without complaint whatever hardships came his way—attributes that made him a stalwart among Spanish explorers. Besides, Serra was a determined leader whose orders were impossible to refuse.

Apart from his age and the inherent nautical dangers of scurvy and shipwreck, Crespí had other good reasons to be wary of the Pérez expedition. He was chronically afflicted by motion sickness whenever he boarded a ship. It was the one thing "which I never can escape at sea," he wrote in the opening paragraph of his journal, acknowledging there would be times when he would be too seasick to write.[4]

Another drawback was Crespí's unshakeable aversion to cold damp weather. For whatever reasons, this man from the dry, sunny climate of Mallorca suffered inordinately from chilly temperatures. At one point in the spring of 1772 he even sought reassignment to San Diego in order to escape the fog-covered summers at Mission San Carlos. By comparison, the northwest bank of the continent was one of the foggiest, most rain-drenched places on earth. The fog that Crespí was about to encounter was so dank, in fact, that it soaked everyone onboard, and sailors collected the attendant water in buckets as it poured steadily from the sails. On many occasions the fog was so murky that sailors at the stern of the *Santiago* could not see the prow.

One consolation for Crespí was that Serra chose as his traveling companion Fray Tomás de la Peña y Saravia, a thirty-one-year-old Franciscan from Burgos, Spain. Despite the twenty-two-year difference in their ages, Crespí and Peña formed a good working team. The robust younger padre said Mass on deck on days when Crespí was too nauseous to stand on his feet. Of medium stature with an oversized face, Peña also kept a log of his own, recording valuable details of the expedition.

The catalyst for the viceroy's decision to launch the maritime undertaking was renewed fears that the Russians were coming. Seafarers dispatched by the tsarist court in Saint Petersburg were already known to have explored the waters off the Alexander Archipelago in what is today southeastern Alaska. In 1741 a mission under the command of naval Captain Aleksei Chirikov reconnoitered as far south as present-day Prince of Wales Island at the southern tip of Alaska. And as recently as 1768 the Russians conducted an expedition to chart the Aleutian Islands, although the purpose of this foray was kept secret to avoid arousing Spain.[5]

In February 1773 the Spanish minister in Saint Petersburg, the Conde de Lasci, passed along to Madrid an unsubstantiated rumor that the Russians had carried out a two-year voyage of discovery to American shores.[6] The envoy's source was supposedly an official who had access to Tsarina Catherine the Great's secret archives.[7] This stirred alarm among King Carlos III's advisers that the Russians might have established settlements in the vast unmapped North American realm claimed by Spain.

The count's dispatches were forwarded immediately to Mexico City. Acting with remarkable speed, Viceroy Bucareli on 18 July 1773 ordered Captain Pérez to draw up plans for a sea expedition to assert Spain's control of the Pacific coast as far north as the sixtieth parallel, a line crossing the continent through today's Yukon Territory and mainland Alaska. "[A]ny establishment by Russia, or any other foreign power, on the continent ought to be prevented," Bucareli declared flatly.[8] His sense of urgency was spurred by two orders from Spain to dislodge Russian settlers if any were found.[9] Among the Spaniards, so little was known about the northern coastline that, had Pérez blindly sailed northward in the Pacific, he would have struck land before reaching sixty degrees north latitude.

On Christmas Eve 1773, having approved the general plans drawn up by Captain Pérez, the viceroy issued detailed operating instructions for the voyage. The document, composed of no fewer than thirty-two articles, was a vivid display of the top-down management so characteristic of Spanish colonial rule. To begin, Bucareli declared that the true motive for King Carlos III's occupation of the new territories was so that "their numerous Indian inhabitants, attracted to the kind, mellow, and desired vassalage of His Majesty, may receive by means of the spiritual conquest the light of the Gospel which will free them from the darkness of idolatry in which they live, and will show them the road to eternal salvation."[10] As always, Spain's expansionist aims were cloaked in religious righteousness.

Pérez, who bore the title of Alférez Graduado de Fragata (Ensign, frigate grade) was instructed to sail to at least sixty degrees north latitude before turning southward along the coast, "never losing sight of it" and making "the most minute exploration" all the way back to Monterey.[11]

From his desk in Mexico City, the viceroy was not aware that impenetrable summer fog regularly concealed the Pacific Northwest coastline for hundreds of miles, making such detailed reconnaissance impossible. Most important of all, Pérez was directed to find suitable sites for Spanish settlements and to go ashore and take possession of them in the name of the king. This was to be carried out strictly according to the terms of a formulary attached to the instructions. A large wooden cross was to be erected on a pedestal of rocks. A bottle or glass flask containing the testimony of possession signed by Pérez, his two top officers, and the chaplain was to be hidden in the pedestal. "And in order that in the days to come this document may better be preserved and may serve as an authentic testimony," Bucareli directed, "the bottle will be sealed tightly with pitch."[12]

When encountering Indians, Pérez was to ascertain whether they had seen any other sailing ships or had come into contact with other European explorers. To initiate friendly relations with the Natives, Pérez was given four large boxes containing 468 bundles of colorful glass beads to be distributed as gifts. If he found Russian settlements, the captain was to observe them from a safe distance, note their locations, and estimate the number of inhabitants. Under all circumstances, he was to keep secret the objectives of his expedition. Lastly, the viceroy enclosed nautical charts of the far northwest coast published in Saint Petersburg in 1758 and 1773 "concerning the alleged voyages of the Russians."[13]

To carry out the exploration, Bucareli assigned a single vessel, the 225-ton *Santiago*, a frigate armed with six bronze guns and five hundred cannonballs. Launched in 1773, the *Santiago* was the largest ship ever built at the San Blas shipyard—eighty-two feet long at the waterline, with a twenty-six-foot beam. Her timbers were fashioned from the finest hardwoods available at San Blas (see figure 9).

Designed expressly for navigating the Pacific coast, the *Santiago* was in actuality a monstrosity of nautical engineering. On its maiden voyage from San Blas to California, it sprung the crossbeams of two masts and had to put in at San Diego for emergency repairs.[14] While there, its masts were cut down to a shorter height in order to improve its stability.[15] With three masts and a deep draft, the *Santiago* was fine for sailing in the open ocean, even in heavy seas. But it was ill suited to shallow coastal areas where the depth of the water was unknown and strong tidal currents could assert sudden control over a ship's heading.

For Pérez these already challenging circumstances would be compounded by persistent fog, which could conceal rock islets, reefs, sandbars, and other hazards close to the unmarked coastline. In such conditions, uncertainty and the threat of shipwreck were ever present, straining the nerves of captain and crew. Previous maritime expeditions typically included a smaller, more maneuverable vessel to reconnoiter close to shore. But neither Bucareli nor Pérez could anticipate the navigational obstacles the *Santiago* would face in the Pacific Northwest. Thus she would make a solo voyage.

The viceroy ordered that the ship be outfitted with a year's worth of provisions. These included several tons of jerked beef, dried fish, hardtack, and lard, along with ample supplies of rice, beans, lentils, and other staples. For the chaplains' use in saying Mass on board, a barrel of sweet wine was stowed away.

Bucareli assigned a complement of eighty-eight officers and crew, twenty-four more men than the *Santiago* was designed to carry. The extra personnel would be a hedge against losses to scurvy or other vicissitudes. The expedition included, in addition to the captain, a second pilot, a chaplain and his Franciscan companion, a surgeon, a boatswain, a first and second boatswain's mate, a first and second caulker, a first and second steward, fourteen gunners, fourteen helmsmen, twenty seamen, thirty apprentice seamen, six cabin boys, and four cooks.

As stipulated in the roster prepared by the commissary officer and his assistant at San Blas, Captain Pérez's salary was set at seventy pesos per month. His second-in-command, Don Esteban Martínez, received fifty pesos; gunners received twelve

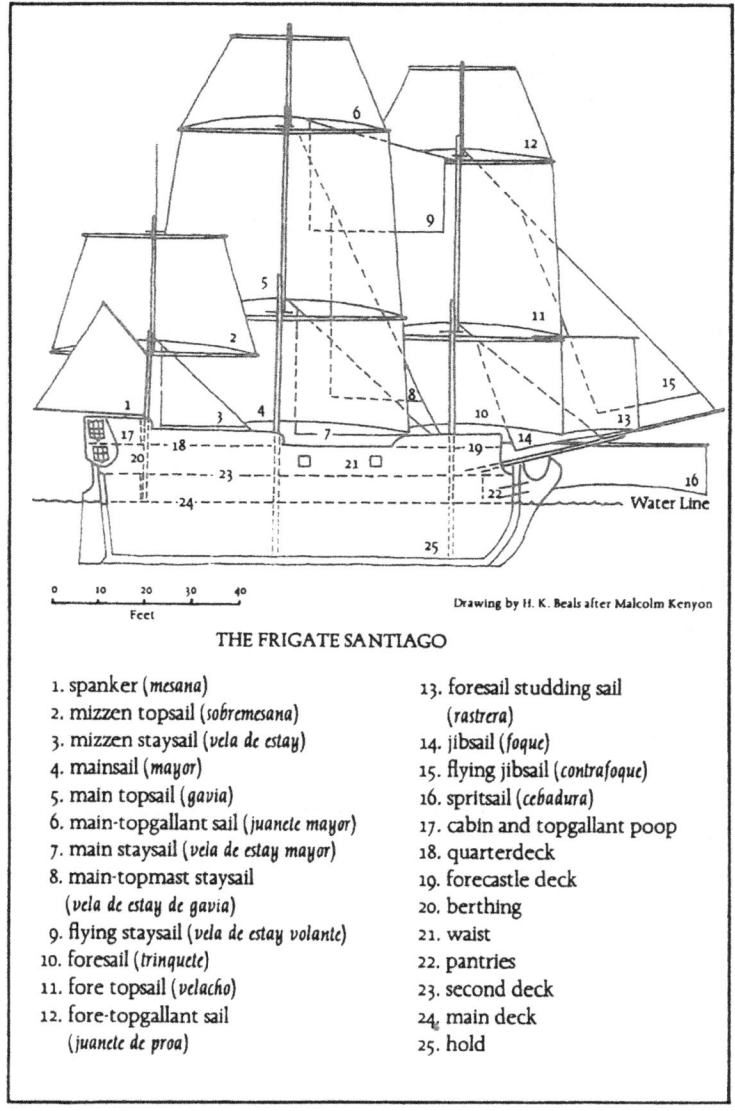

FIGURE 9. The *Santiago* was one of the largest ships built at the San Blas shipyard, but it was not suited to exploring the coastal waters of the Far Northwest, which hampered the voyage of discovery of seasoned navigator Juan Pérez in 1774. Original drawing published in Herbert K. Beals, ed. and trans., *Juan Pérez on the Northwest Coast: Six Documents of His Expedition in 1774* (Portland: Oregon Historical Society, 1989). *Reproduced by permission of the Oregon Historical Society.*

pesos, and seamen ten pesos; the lowest-ranking members of the crew, the cabin boys, were paid six pesos.[16] The two padres, having taken vows of poverty, got no pay.

On Monday, 6 June 1774, the *Santiago* was ready to embark from the port of Monterey. In the late afternoon, Father Serra escorted Crespí and Peña down to the beach where a launch was waiting, gave them a last embrace, and sent them aboard the anchored vessel at sunset. After eating supper, the crew wrestled aboard four young bulls and some pigs, a gift presented to the cabin mess by the commander of the Monterey presidio. Then commenced the laborious process of maneuvering the lumbering *Santiago* out of the roadstead and into the open ocean. A longboat manned with oarsmen initially towed the ship toward the harbor entrance. Then it was warped farther seaward by hauling on a line attached to an anchor dropped near the mouth of the harbor. At nine the next morning the warping anchor was hoisted and the sails unfurled. This was followed by a brief ceremony hoisting the Spanish flag and firing a gun as the *Santiago* set sail into the northwest wind.

Pérez ordered two or three tacks in an attempt to get out of the harbor, but the wind freshened considerably and shifted to a head-on position, forcing the ship back to the anchorage. During the night, the boatswain, Manuel López, fell critically ill with a high fever. Ill omens burdened the expedition even before it left the harbor.

All the next day a driving northwest wind kept the *Santiago* at anchor. Ditto for the next day. On Friday, 10 June, Captain Pérez, his officers, and the two chaplains—still unable to sail—went ashore. A makeshift altar was erected on the beach under a shelter of tree branches, and at Pérez's request, Father Serra sang a special High Mass to Most Holy Mary for the success of the voyage. The spot chosen for the altar was believed to be near the same ancient oak tree where Mass was celebrated in 1602 during Vizcaíno's exploration of the California coast.

Aboard ship in the harbor, boatswain López succumbed about half past four in the afternoon, after making his final confession to Father Peña and receiving the last rites of the church from Father Crespí. The exact cause of his death was not known. His body was rowed ashore and sent to Mission San Carlos for burial.

At dawn the next morning, two longboats towed the *Santiago* from its anchorage. Then a warping anchor was used to drag her toward the outer harbor. Around noon the naval behemoth captured a strong breeze from the north and plowed into the Pacific under full sail with such acceleration that the launch left behind to retrieve the warping anchor could not catch up to her. The armed supply ship *San Antonio*, riding at anchor, fired two cannons in salute, and the *Santiago* responded by firing three cannons.

All afternoon the frigate pitched heavily as the ocean swells broke over her bow. At 6:30 in the evening, the gigantic main topsail split under the force of the wind. It was repaired at once. Five days after starting to depart from the port of Monterey, the *Santiago* was finally underway.

On Sunday, 12 June, at sunrise, Captain Pérez recorded his optimistic outlook in his log: "The weather gives promise of tranquility and being fair, judging by the position of the sun. The wind has been light and variable; the night has been clear and beautiful; the sky mirror-like. It was the same at dawn."[17]

Soon after daybreak, Crespí and Peña said separate Masses on deck. At midmorning, a thick wet fog swallowed up the *Santiago*, obscuring the coastline and the horizon. To pray for a successful expedition, a novena was begun to San Antonio de Padua, a thirteenth-century Franciscan saint, for whom the third of the California missions had been named three years earlier. For nine consecutive days special pleas were offered seeking the Italian saint's beneficent intercession. On most evenings, the two priests also led the crew in reciting the rosary to Our Lady of the Immaculate Conception and singing the *Alabado*.

By midweek the wind and currents were driving the ship to the southwest, the exact opposite heading from that sought by Captain Pérez. A dozen crewmen deemed most capable of handling a musket were placed under the command of Simón Fernández for firearms training. Pérez wanted to be prepared for any contingency, including an armed encounter with Indians or Russians. Indeed, the viceroy had ordered that thirty-six muskets with bayonets be placed on board for just such emergencies. The newly trained sailors certainly would not be marksmen, but at least they could put up a show of force if necessary.

With the ship continuing to lose course by heading southwestward in fog so heavy it felt like rain showers, the captain was stricken with a stomach ailment that kept him up all night on Friday, 17 June. He recovered by noon the next day, but his health was to be a recurring issue for the rest of his days. A week later the *Santiago* was still holding to a southwesterly course under full sail and a full moon veiled by the fog. By now she was just south of present-day Los Angeles, more than three hundred miles southwest of Monterey in the open ocean. At dawn the two padres said Mass on deck, Captain Pérez took communion, and the crew celebrated his forty-ninth birthday.

The next day, Saturday, 25 June, the winds shifted and the helmsman finally was able to steer toward the northwest. From the main topgallant at the tip of the mast to the spanker at the stern, all canvas was unfurled except the small spritsail, which flew from a spar extending from the prow. Pérez's exuberant entry in his log: "We continued the voyage with all sails bent to the wind."[18]

By Tuesday, 28 June, the *Santiago* returned to a latitude about equal to that of Monterey, but she was hundreds of miles out in the Pacific, where the prevailing winds blew from south to north. After twenty-two days of toil, the Pérez expedition was back to where it started, only now it was sailing a northwesterly course, bound for parallel sixty. From here on, the *Santiago* made good progress on a northwesterly track. On 9 July the frigate crossed the forty-fifth parallel, which placed it due west of modern Salem, Oregon. Pérez and his men were now in unfathomed waters, beyond the bounds of the known world.

The sailors spotted birds and sea lions that playfully encircled the ship, creating the erroneous impression that land was nearby. The captain posted a constant lookout in the masthead to scan the sea for reefs or other obstacles, while dense fog and rain showers meant that the *Santiago* sailed blindly much of the time—a potentially dangerous situation even in the vast expanse of the Pacific. With the sun hidden, it often was impossible to make the standard noontime observation to gauge the ship's latitude, prompting more unease among the pilots. In a single day, two barrels of water were filled by collecting the runoff of fog from the sails. The next night apprentice seaman Salvador Antonio, suffering a high fever, made his confession and received last rites in the expectation that he would soon die.

On Monday, 11 July, the *Santiago* was west of the Columbia River, but much too far out to sea for the crew to spot the waterway. A hailstorm struck, and at night freezing rain fell. Crespí noted in his journal that the fog seemed to emit snow rather than mist. At 7:30 in the morning on Thursday, 14 July, a rainbow appeared in the west but was soon obliterated by a hard-driving squall with high winds that forced the sailors to reef, or shorten, the sails. Pérez, worried about his diminishing supply of drinking water, ordered an inventory of the casks. The crew reported there was enough water to last ten weeks at sea.

At this moment, Pérez seems to have experienced a fateful crisis of self-confidence. Navigating alien waters, surrounded by uncertainties and risks and dangers, he became fixated on what he perceived to be a scarcity of freshwater on board. In reality, the expedition would return to Monterey a little more than six weeks later with almost a month's worth of water still in the hold—and without ever having taken on another drop. What was more, the sailors already had demonstrated they could collect considerable amounts of additional freshwater as it poured from the sails. Never mind the obvious question as to why the captain had not stocked more water before departing Monterey. The huge ship certainly had space for it. Having to fret about his water supply only a month into the expedition bordered on negligence.

Taking counsel of his fears, Pérez assembled his officers on 15 July and proposed that, instead of holding a course for sixty degrees north latitude as ordered by the viceroy, the *Santiago* should veer to the northeast in search of land and a place to take on water. After replenishing the casks, the expedition could turn back northward to parallel sixty. There was no dissent among the officers.

When the captain ordered the change of heading, the *Santiago* was northwest of present-day Vancouver Island, just shy of fifty-two degrees north latitude. A thick damp fog was now driven by a fresh south wind, and the ship rolled sharply in the swells. The next day the spouts of whales were seen. In anticipation of making landfall, the carpenters built a fifteen-foot-tall wooden cross. On it were carved the Latin words *Carolus III Hispaniarum rex* (Carlos III, king of the Spains). "We intend to set it up as soon as we go ashore, although we have not yet sighted land," Crespí recorded in his journal.[19]

On the morning of Monday, 18 July, the second-in-command, thirty-one-year-old Don Esteban Martínez, was bled in a crude attempt to alleviate inflammation of his face. He was bled again in the afternoon but found no relief. The next morning the ship's surgeon pulled a tooth from Martínez's swollen mouth, no doubt an excruciating procedure but one that resolved the problem.

Around eleven o'clock in the morning on 18 July, the lookout in the masthead spotted land to the northeast. By two o'clock in the afternoon, snow-covered summits came into view. The mountain peaks were part of what now are known as the Queen Charlotte Islands off the coast of northern British Columbia.

The next morning, with fog and rain severely limiting visibility, Pérez ordered the helmsman to steer away from the coast to avert the threat of shipwreck. For the next two days, the *Santiago* loitered offshore searching for a suitable spot to drop an anchor. To measure the depth of the water near the beach, lead weights fastened to a sounding line were cast over the side. At three o'clock in the afternoon on Wednesday, 20 July, the masthead reported the smoke of many fires rising above an island covered with towering pine trees.

Soon, a large canoe bearing eight men and a boy approached the ship as it sailed slowly northward along the coastline. The Natives were singing as they paddled toward the vessel. One man, whose body was painted, stood up in the canoe, danced about, and spread feathers on the water. These were the Haida Indians. They followed the ship for some distance but did not get close enough to communicate with the Spaniards, who called to them and waved handkerchiefs and biscuits. Eventually, the Natives turned back to shore.

Two hours later the same canoe and another one manned by six Indians drew up to the *Santiago*'s stern, but the occupants would not climb aboard. The Indians were well-built and clad in what looked to Crespí like beaver pelts and sea lion skins. On their heads were pointed hats woven from bulrushes. Some wore beards. Their skin was fair and they had long hair. Captain Pérez gave them strings of beads, and they passed up to him some dried fish that resembled white cod. A sailor traded a large knife for a plaited, conical-shaped rush hat of multiple colors, with a six-inch-wide brim. Another crew member exchanged a knife for a very pretty mat woven of fine palm fronds, decorated with black and white squares. The captain acquired four beautiful blankets woven from the white fur of unknown animals, likely mountain sheep or domesticated dogs.

Around six o'clock in the evening a third canoe carrying seven singing Haida approached the ship, but once again the Natives could not be coaxed to come aboard, even though a rope was lowered to them.[20] They took the rope and were towed along behind the *Santiago* for some distance. But eventually they returned to shore.

The Haidas' oversized wooden dugouts were especially seaworthy, capable of going fifteen miles or more out to sea. Pérez estimated them to be thirty-three-feet long and five-and-a-half-feet wide.[21] They were hewn from a single log and equipped with a wooden keel for stability in the heavy ocean swells. The Indians propelled their vessels swiftly with wooden paddles that were nearly five feet long. Crespí spotted iron implements in the canoes, including axes and harpoons.

Captain Pérez recorded in his journal this first encounter with the Natives. "[W]e took the occasion to examine the character of these people and their things. In the first place, the men were of good stature, well formed, a smiling face, beautiful eyes, and good looking. Their hair was tied up and arranged in the manner of a wig with a tail. Some wore it tied in the back and had beards and mustaches in the manner of the Chinese people."[22] With his extensive naval experience, Pérez was well acquainted with the physical features of the Sangleyes, the Chinese traders in the Philippine Islands.

At daylight the next morning there was drizzle, some fog, and heavy seas. At midday Pérez used his octant to measure the angle of the sun, calculating that the *Santiago* was now at the fifty-fifth parallel. In fact, his observation was a little bit off, even though Pérez called his octant a "marvelous instrument."[23] The expedition was actually at about fifty-four degrees, forty minutes north latitude. This marked the northernmost point reached by the expedition, because Pérez was about to order a turn to the south. The *Santiago* was in waters known today as Dixon Entrance, northwest of Graham Island in the Queen Charlottes. Seventy years later, this line of demarcation became the center of a territorial dispute between Britain and the United States, giving rise to the expansionist political slogan taught to every American school student: "Fifty-Four Forty or Fight!"

Captain Pérez was still looking for an anchorage, but a furious current close to shore gripped the *Santiago*'s hull and pulled it southward. This prompted Pérez to steer some distance offshore into safer water. By now, word of the Spanish presence had spread among the Haidas, who were eager to conduct commerce. At 2:30 in the afternoon a flotilla of twenty-one dugouts carrying some two hundred Indians—men, women, children—swarmed around the *Santiago*. They were singing and casting feathers in the air. Some of the women held infants to their breasts. An old man identified as a chief jingled an instrument that looked like a tambourine. Peña counted twenty-one Natives in one vessel. Another contained a dozen women and no men. There was such pandemonium as the Haidas surrounded the ship that the canoe full of women rammed head-on into a canoe full of men, triggering a boisterous confrontation.

The Natives' boats were laden with items for trade—woven mats; pelts of sea otters, wolves, and bears; hats made of bulrushes, with chin cords to keep them from blowing away; fur caps; beaver-skin quilts with fringes; bunches of feathers arranged in various shapes; woolen blankets a yard-and-a-half square, embroidered with bright figures; decorative wooden trays and wooden spoons. For the Indians' offerings, the sailors traded abalone shells brought from Monterey, articles of old clothing, strands of glass beads, knives, machetes, and swords. The Haidas spurned the Spaniards' colorful ribbons as mere trifles, seeking instead iron items with cutting edges. Some of the Indian men did not hesitate to strip naked after sailors offered to buy their pelt cloaks. Later that night the sailors came to regret such deals when they slept in the cloaks, only to awake scratching the many bites they received from the vermin infesting the Indians' clothing.

An elderly chieftain took a liking to pilot Martínez's red cap.[24] The Spaniard gave it to him and in exchange received an elaborate cape from off the chief's own shoulders. Made of sea otter furs, it was decorated in black and white checkerboards. "It is beautiful for being handmade by people without culture," Martínez penned in his diary. The ambitious young naval officer later sent the robe as a gift to Viceroy Bucareli in Mexico City, where it was duly logged in the "Ynventario de las prendas cambalachadas con los Yndios" (the "inventory of garments swapped with the Indians").[25]

The Native women were fair-skinned, with their black hair falling in braids on their shoulders. Many had blue eyes, and they wore numerous copper bracelets and rings. Their lower lips were pierced, and round painted seashells or wooden disks were inserted in them so that the lip pieces struck their noses when they talked. From a distance, it appeared as though the women's tongues were hanging out. "They are as fair and rosy as any Spanish woman," Peña observed in his diary, "but are rendered ugly by the disk they have in the lip, which hangs to the chin."[26]

Before long, some of the *Santiago*'s crew members climbed down into the canoes, where they danced and frolicked with the Natives. Amid shouts and laughter, the Indians painted the faces of the sailors. Although the Spaniards invited the Indians on board, only two had the courage to accept. In amazement, they were escorted around the frigate. "They entered the cabin and we showed them the image of Our Lady," Crespí wrote, "and after looking at it with much attention they touched it with their hands, no doubt to see if it were real."[27] Before the visitors departed, Pérez gave them bread, cheese, and glass beads.

On Friday, 22 July, strong currents propelled the *Santiago* toward the shore. Once again, Pérez was forced to turn the bow toward the sea to escape the drag of the tidal flow. Once again, the crew lost sight of land.

In light of what he considered to be these dangerous circumstances—and his misplaced obsession with his water supply—Pérez reached a crucial decision. He would abandon entirely the goal of reaching the sixtieth parallel and instead head southward to Monterey. This was a direct violation of the viceroy's explicit orders not to turn back before climbing to sixty degrees north latitude. It was perhaps significant that, in his original plans, Pérez proposed to sail no higher than the fiftieth parallel. Such clear contravention of a viceregal command was rare in New Spain's highly centralized power structure. Pérez was understandably defensive about this rash move, and he sought to justify it in a special note he entered in his log:

> Having reflected on the inconstancy and confusion of the weather, and also the uncertainty of finding a place farther northward where one could anchor and take on water [I realized that] by cutting the daily [water] ration I would scarcely be able to have [enough] for returning. I [therefore] determined not to press on farther, and from this latitude follow the coast to Monterey . . . seeing if I can find a place to put into effect that which was ordered of me . . . because it is impossible to be able to explain all that has befallen [us] due to the bad weather. God grant me good weather.[28]

With contrary winds and hazardous currents keeping the *Santiago* away from the shoreline, Crespí and Peña decided on Saturday, 23 July, to begin a full-scale prayer offensive with two consecutive novenas. The first would be to San Juan Nepomuceno, a fourteenth-century Bohemian martyr, and the second would be to Santa Clara de Asís, one of the first followers of Saint Francis of Assisi. The aim, Peña wrote in his diary, was "to obtain from the Most Holy Majesty, through the intercession of these saints, that bettering of the weather which we need."[29] The crew would offer these extra prayers for eighteen days after reciting the daily rosary.

The next day a rainstorm struck the *Santiago* just as Crespí was getting ready to say Sunday Mass on deck, putting an abrupt halt to the exercise. At eleven o'clock in the evening, the crew watched in wonderment the brilliant, dancing green lights of the aurora borealis. For most of the crew members, this was a unique spectacle. They had never before sailed this far north.

On the morning of Monday, 25 July, Father Peña gave last rites for the second time to the young sailor Salvador Antonio, who had taken another turn for the worse. His age was not stipulated on the ship's roster, but he was young enough that Peña referred to him as a boy. Given that he had been suffering from a high fever, it is unlikely that scurvy was the cause of his distress. Antonio, paid an apprentice's salary of only eight pesos a month, had a wife named María Juliana back home in Mexico, in the town of Guaynamota, about fifty miles inland from San Blas. A little before seven o'clock in the evening, he died. The next morning, amid dark skies and thick fog, his body was brought on deck while Peña said a Mass for his soul. The sea was so heavy that the crew had trouble staying on their feet. As soon as Mass was over, Antonio's remains were consigned to the deep.

At noon the *Santiago* was being driven once again by stiff winds and rough seas toward the rocky coastline. The captain ordered the helmsman to come about and sail away from the shore. The prospect of setting foot on land and planting the cross never looked bleaker.

Four days later, Peña recorded his frustration in his journal: "On the whole coast . . . we have not been able to discover whether there are any harbors, gulfs, bays, rivers, and the like, as well on account of the distance from it which we have kept, as because most of the time it has been cloudy and the horizon and the shoreline have been obscured." The turbulent seaway got even worse. In the evening, Peña wrote, "it was necessary to furl the fore-topsail, so that the topmast might not be carried away, or the foremast itself, by the heavy pitching of the ship. . . . The ship rolled so much that all passed a bad night."[30]

For the next week the ghastly weather persisted, and Captain Pérez kept well out to sea on a southerly track. Most of the time the land remained out of sight. At one point the north wind howled with such ferocity that Pérez ordered all sails furled, leaving bare masts, to keep the frigate from breaking apart.

On the morning of Monday, 8 August, the weather had improved enough that Pérez turned the prow to the northeast in search of land and a spot to drop anchor. At eleven o'clock a heavily forested stretch of land was sighted. This was the northwest corner of today's Vancouver Island, although the crew believed they had reached the mainland.

As the *Santiago* edged toward the shore on light puffs of wind, several casts of lead were taken to gauge the water's depth. A sounding of twenty-four fathoms (144 feet) was entered in the log. At four o'clock in the afternoon, three small canoes bearing nine Indians of the Nootka tribe paddled out toward the ship.[31] With shouts and gestures from a distance, the Natives told the Spaniards to go away. Gradually the Nootkans were coaxed to draw near the ship. Using signs, the crew communicated that they were looking for water. Unimpressed, the Indians returned to shore without offering assistance. At six o'clock, with the *Santiago* about two miles off the beach, another sounding was taken. The water was 150 feet deep, with a good bottom for holding the anchor. For the first time since departing Monterey almost two months earlier, Captain Pérez ordered that the anchor be dropped. Fortuitously, the wind died and the *Santiago* was at rest in what is now known as the outer harbor of Nootka Sound. A party would be sent ashore in the morning. After dark, a number of dugouts surrounded the frigate but kept about a musket-shot away. The occupants cried out in mournful tones until about eleven o'clock at night, when they paddled back to land.

At first light the next day—about four o'clock in the morning—as the crew was getting the launch over the side in order to go ashore, fifteen canoes with about a hundred Indians, both men and women, appeared. Before long a brisk trade was in progress. The Indians sold otter skins, painted bulrush hats, and hemp mats for old clothes, knives, and abalone shells that the sailors had gathered on the beach at Monterey. The abalone shells, with their iridescent mother-of-pearl shine, were especially popular with the Indians.

Two hours after daybreak, the launch was manned and ready to cast off for shore. The small boat was fitted with two masts and sails. Its first assignment was to locate an anchorage with better shelter from the wind.

Without warning, a gale out of the west came up, spurring a strong swell. The ship was driven toward the pounding breakers with such force that its two anchors dragged across the bottom. The sailors in the launch held on as they were buffeted along with the frigate. "It was frightening to see in so short a time the entire sea become angry, stirred up by the blowing wind," Pérez declared.[32] To prevent running aground in the surf, the captain immediately ordered the stream anchor cable cut and all sails unfurled, with the bow turned to the southwest. The longboat was secured with a stout rope and towed erratically from the stern, with the sailors still in it. To make its escape, the *Santiago* barely managed to round a protruding rock ledge and sail into the roiling open water.

Now, the wind was blowing so violently that Pérez ordered all sails furled except the small forestaysail. With great difficulty, the crewmen in the launch were rescued, and the boat was heaved back on board. It was, Crespí wrote in his diary, "only by a miracle [that] we had not lost [the launch] and the sailors who were in it."[33]

Nearly four years later, the British navigator James Cook, in command of *Resolution* and *Discovery* on his celebrated third global voyage, arrived at Nootka Sound believing he was the first European to explore the coast of modern-day British Columbia. During their month-long stay, Cook and his men also engaged in a robust trade with the Indians. One British seaman acquired two silver table spoons from a Native who was wearing them around his neck as an ornament. A first lieutenant aboard the *Discovery*, James Burney, believed the spoons were of Spanish manufacture, an observation that undermined Captain Cook's claim to be the first white man in these waters.[34] "I cannot," wrote Cook in his log, "look upon iron as a mark of the Spaniards having been at this place." He noted that the spoons had no engraving to identify them as Spanish.[35]

In 1789, when the British and Spaniards were haggling over conflicting claims in the Pacific Northwest, the *Santiago*'s Martínez asserted that the Nootka Indians had purloined the spoons from the Spanish frigate fifteen years earlier during the Pérez voyage. None of the firsthand accounts by the expedition's diarists, including Martínez himself, mentioned the spoons. They could just as easily have been traded to the Nootkans by a *Santiago* crew member. At the time of the territorial dispute, Martínez was the controversial commander of a temporary Spanish post at Nootka Sound. In his journal, Captain Cook himself had observed that the Nootkans "were as light fingered as any people we had before met with . . . the instant our backs was [sic] turned."[36]

Martínez's assertions about the spoons' Spanish origin helped to establish that Pérez had in fact reached Nootka Sound ahead of Captain Cook. This was buttressed by Joseph Ingraham, the first mate of the American ship *Columbia*, which visited Nootka Sound in 1788. In a letter written at Martínez's request, Ingraham declared that the Nootkans readily testified to the presence of a Spanish sailing ship forty months before Captain Cook's arrival, "which immediately account'd to me for the two silver spoons Cap Cook found among the Natives."[37]

For the next two days, the *Santiago* sailed southward as Pérez searched vainly for a bay in which to go ashore and take possession in the name of King Carlos III.

Heavy fog and rain repeatedly forced him to steer away from the coastline to avoid foundering in the surf. Morale on board must have ebbed.

On Thursday, 11 August, the weather cleared enough for the crew to spot a high, snow-topped peak many miles inland. The captain named this conspicuous mountain Cerro Nevado de Santa Rosalía (Snowy Hill of Saint Rosalie). Today it is known as Mount Olympus, in Washington state. Pérez turned the bow eastward in the direction of the snowy summit. At dawn the next morning the *Santiago* was drawing close to the coast, but rain and a dark fog descended on the frigate, so that "at four paces we could not see each other," Crespí noted. "The captain, being fearful that we might strike on the shore unexpectedly, ordered the ship put about and the prow turned to the southwest, in order to escape the perils until such time as the weather should clear a little." On this day the frigate rolled so badly in the mountainous swells that neither padre could say Mass. Instead, Crespí wrote, "we conformed to the will of God and offered him our sincere prayers."[38]

Over the course of the next week the *Santiago* continued its steady southward journey, standing out to sea as it slid down the coast past Oregon and Cape Mendocino in northern California. On many days the sails were reefed because of high winds, and the crew had trouble keeping their footing on the pitching deck. At 3:30 in the morning on Tuesday, 16 August, the large main topsail ripped apart in a strong gust. The main topsail yardarm also was damaged and had to be hauled down for repairs.

Most of the time the coastline was hidden in fog, making it impossible to follow the viceroy's instructions to go ashore and plant the cross. The tension onboard was palpable in Crespí's entry for Thursday, 18 August: "Morning broke very dark and foggy, so that at a few steps we could not see each other, a great difficulty in sailing on unknown coasts, for if there should be islands or shoals there would be no one left to tell our story."[39]

Making the situation graver, the crew began to suffer the debilitating effects of scurvy and other ailments. More than twenty men, by Peña's count, were unfit for duty, unable to walk, with painful sores on their legs and in their mouths and throats. Only six or seven healthy sailors were available for each watch. Crespí too was afflicted with symptoms, his mouth so inflamed that he could not say Mass. Stomach distress also hampered him. Other sailors complained of headaches, colds, and aching bones. Weeks of relentless cold and dampness were exacting a toll. "The entire crew is disheartened," Pérez recorded on Friday, 19 August. On the same day Peña wrote: "I believe that if God does not send better weather soon, the greater part of the crew must perish with this disease."[40]

The next afternoon the wind died and the frigate was battered by churning seas. With no breeze in the sails, the ship rolled uncontrollably. Soon the limp sails had to be furled because they were being thrashed to pieces against the rigging by the violent yawing of the ship. The raw weather continued. "This makes all of us very disconsolate," wrote Peña, "for it is seen that the men continue sickening, and we do not know definitely where we are, there having passed three days without the navigating officers being able to observe the sun with accuracy. May it please God to give us that which may seem good to Him."[41]

As the number of sick sailors grew and their conditions worsened, Crespí proposed yet another novena, this time to Our Lady of Talpa, a Mexican saint. In his desperation, he also pledged to sing a High Mass each year on the anniversary of the Blessed Virgin's birth "if she permits us to arrive safely."[42] Crespí's own suffering from scurvy no doubt spurred his devotion to the mother of Jesus Christ.

As soon as it was sunny enough to allow accurate observations of the *Santiago*'s latitude, it became clear that significant southward progress had been made. On Saturday, 27 August, at six o'clock in the morning the frigate was opposite Point Año Nuevo and almost within sight of Monterey. At four in the afternoon, with contrary winds creating problems, Captain Pérez ordered the anchor dropped in fifty-four feet of water in the outer harbor at Monterey, rather far from the regular anchorage. The longboat was launched with a warping anchor, which was used to haul the *Santiago* into the roadstead. Everyone stayed on board until the next morning, when Father Crespí and Father Peña said separate Sunday Masses on deck, no doubt giving thanks for the *Santiago*'s safe return.

In the final entries in their journals, both padres respectfully acknowledged that the voyage had failed to achieve its two key objectives—reaching the sixtieth parallel and taking possession of the northwest corner of the continent for Spain. Pérez had not even managed to chart the coastline, except in the most vague way. The crew's disappointment must have been palpable.

Three days after returning to land, Captain Pérez dispatched by post rider a long letter to Viceroy Bucareli in Mexico City, explaining as best he could why he had not fulfilled his orders. He cited his limited water supply, the weakened condition of his men in the cold and damp, and the omnipresent fog obscuring the coast. He concluded: "Finally, Most Excellent Sir, I have thus endeavored, as the others who have accompanied me, to do as much as has been possible in order to attain success as Your Excellency commanded, remaining regretful for not fulfilling Your Excellency's desire as I might have wished. But as I have already said, whether or not it is the will of God or that such success is reserved for someone else, the fact is that the way is opened and recorded for others who may be worthy of sailing it with better fortune."[43]

This is about the best that can be said for the Pérez expedition. In his own report to the royal court in Madrid, the viceroy repeated the captain's justifications for his failings. "[N]evertheless," wrote Bucareli, "I consider what has been accomplished very useful, as I didn't count on much success in this first exploration; but it will facilitate the success of later ones, and it is persuasive of the fact that in the nineteen degrees [of latitude] higher which we have advanced, there is no danger of foreign establishments."[44]

Historians generally have been forgiving of Pérez, considering the obstacles he faced and his long naval service to his monarch. But contemporary critics were harsher. Serra, as the padre-presidente of the California missions, acknowledged in a letter written three days after the *Santiago*'s return to Monterey: "That I regret the failure, I readily admit. But we must bear it with patience."[45]

Royal naval officer Francisco Antonio Mourelle, a Galician who was a distinguished Pacific explorer himself, pointed out some of the holes in Pérez's explanations of his actions. "The little fruit that resulted from this voyage is immediately apparent from a reading of their diary accounts," Mourelle wrote. The voyage lasted only eleven weeks, he observed, yet "they did not hesitate to call attention to the water shortage they suffered, making it almost the principal cause of their turning back. It is scarcely credible that in leaving Monterey they would fail to bring six months of water, which is the same as was carried on subsequent voyages." Mourelle stressed that the sheltered waters of Nootka Sound were in fact an ideal spot to go ashore, as Captain Cook later showed, and that many other bays and inlets offered the same opportunities. In a scathing summation, Mourelle blamed the expedition's shortcomings squarely on "the insufficiency of the commander [Pérez] and the pilot [Martínez]."[46]

This marked Pérez's last voyage as commanding officer. The next spring, accompanied by the schooner *Sonora*, the *Santiago* was sent on another expedition in northern waters. But this time she was under the command of Lieutenant Bruno Hezeta, and Pérez was assigned the subordinate role of sailing master.

After completing the mission, the *Santiago* departed Monterey bound for San Blas on 1 November 1775, with Pérez onboard. On the second day out of Monterey, Pérez died suddenly of unknown causes at the age of fifty. His body was buried at sea. The news did not reach Monterey until the next year, when full funeral honors were paid to his memory.[47] Despite the maritime setbacks, Spain's campaign to claim the West Coast of North America only accelerated in the years to come.

CHAPTER FOURTEEN

Fatalistic Venture

> The missionaries know perfectly well that at the missions they are only victims ready for the sacrifice ... whether this be on the altar of a hard bed because of the continuous sickness in those lands, or from the merciful thrust of a spear, or from the blows of clubs or arrows.
>
> —Juan Domingo Arricivita, 1787

Tucked into a secluded spot on the Fort Yuma Indian Reservation straddling the lower Colorado River is an inconspicuous stone monument. Surrounded by tall date groves, citrus orchards, and a verdant patchwork of barley and hay, the marker goes unnoticed by pickup trucks as they whisk along a two-lane farm road, kicking up clouds of dust. A few yards away the green waters of the Colorado surge toward the Sea of Cortez, sustaining the rich cropland on the California bank. A bronze plaque identifies this as the site of Mission San Pedro y San Pablo de Bicuñer. Generations of California schoolchildren have studied the twenty-one Franciscan missions strung along the coast, but this inland outpost was forgotten almost as soon as it was founded by Francisco Garcés on 7 January 1781. The truncated history of San Pedro y San Pablo de Bicuñer is one of startling defeat for the Spanish crown and one of tempered remorse for the Yuma, or Quechan, Indians who have dwelled here for centuries.

This lost tale begins on Sunday, 12 May 1776, with Lieutenant Colonel Juan Bautista de Anza and Father Pedro Font bivouacked on the California side of the Colorado River on their return from delivering the caravan of Spanish settlers to populate the new mission and pueblo of San Francisco. Amid the spring snowmelt in the Rocky Mountains, the river is rising and the current is growing stronger. The Yuma Natives are building an oversized raft of wooden poles to ferry Anza, Font, their attendants, and their baggage across the river. The commander is on his way to Mexico City, as ordered, to report on his expedition in person to Viceroy Antonio María de Bucareli y Ursúa.

In the evening, Yuma chief Salvador Palma and two of his subordinates arrived in Anza's camp. For the last two years Palma had been doing everything he could to ingratiate himself with Anza. He very much wanted the Spaniards to establish

211

a mission and town at the strategic ford on the Colorado, smack in the middle of his nation. Anza was keen to do so. Securing the crossing, called El Puerto de la Concepción by the Spaniards, was the key to establishing a crucial overland supply route from Sonora to the struggling missions on the Pacific coast. For his part, Palma saw an alliance with the Spaniards, who were equipped with firearms, valuable horses, and other livestock—and were generous with enticing gifts of glass beads, tobacco, and clothing—as the best defense against his Native enemies. These included not only Apaches but also other quarreling tribes along the river.

Unlike most Indians, Palma attended Mass regularly whenever a priest was around, and he showed his devotion to Christianity by falling to his knees, crossing himself, and beating his breast as he had seen the most ardent padres do. As part of this reciprocal relationship, Anza had bestowed on Palma gifts of fancy clothing and a coveted silver-tipped cane of office, all in the name of the viceroy. These two farsighted men needed each other, but for very different reasons. Spain's occupation of the Pacific coast, and to a lesser extent the fate of the Yuma people, hinged on their singular personal relationship.

On this occasion Palma showed up to implore Anza to take him along to Mexico City, a roundtrip of more than thirty-two hundred miles. Father Thomas Eixarch, who had spent the previous winter among the Yumas, had regaled Palma about the splendors of the capital, the glorious annual pageant to the Virgin of Guadalupe, the vast powers of the Spanish viceroy, and His Excellency's wish to meet the chief and give him presents. Palma wanted to petition Bucareli directly to establish a Spanish settlement on the Colorado and to accept the Yumas as vassals of the king.

After darkness fell Anza convened a gathering of Palma, his two companions, Eixarch, and Font, in a bulrush hut. The commander was at first reluctant to comply with Palma's request, noting that the Yuma leader would be away for a year and that his authority over his people might atrophy during his prolonged absence. Palma assured him that an elderly lieutenant would maintain order. In fact, Palma already had imparted his quiver to the subaltern as a symbolic transfer of Palma's own authority. What was more, Palma asserted, his followers wholeheartedly supported his making the trip.

After conferring with the two padres, Anza agreed to take him along. The chief would be accompanied by a three-man delegation of his choosing—his own brother; the son of Pablo Feo, a rival Yuma leader derisively nicknamed Ugly Paul by the Spaniards, who found him disagreeable; and a tribesman from the neighboring Cajuenches, who were allies of the Yumas downstream on the river. Anza claimed that two hundred Yuma men showed their enthusiasm by volunteering to go along with Palma.

The next morning, Anza began moving his large train of forty men and supplies across the river, which was more than 750 yards wide at a narrows where the current accelerated and dangerous whirlpools formed. Chief Pablo oversaw the crossing, with his tribesmen supplying the essential manpower. The first raft carried heavy equipage and two muleteers. It was guided by twenty-three strong Yuma swimmers who, Anza reported in his journal, "labored very hard against the rapid current to reach the other side."[1] The swimmers then recrossed the river to guide a new load, completing an exhausting roundtrip of more than fifteen hundred yards.

Another raft carrying men crossed at four o'clock in the afternoon as big swirls, floating timbers, and other debris added to the powerful flow. This time the raftsmen were unable to hold their own against the current and were swept far downstream before reaching the eastern bank. "The raft was so battered by the force of the water," Font recorded, "that it had to be taken apart with its grass ropes, poles, and so forth and brought back across to this side, to build it anew."[2] This ended the crossing operation for the day.

On Tuesday, 14 May, the current was even swifter than the day before. The Yuma swimmers, though remarkably athletic, objected to ferrying such a large raft across the stream. Thus the craft was rebuilt as two smaller rafts. Meantime, limited loads were taken across by Yuma women, who pushed along in front of them as they swam baskets made of willows and dried mud. The women were even better swimmers than the men because they were more accustomed to crossing the river with their children and belongings in tow. One of the women, named Francisca by the Spaniards, was the grown daughter of Chief Palma. She painted her body all over with red ochre that did not wear off even after she spent many hours in the water. Throughout the day the women made twelve individual trips across the Colorado and back. The only loss was a consignment of mule shoes. Due to the weight of the iron, the basket took on water and sank before the swimmer could save it. Another female swimmer carried across more than a bushel of beans and asked in payment only two strings of glass beads, a pittance as far as Anza was concerned. Yet the commander paid her only what she asked, while noting in his diary that five strands would have been a fairer fee for her service.

At noon the mounts swam across the river in one large herd without mishap. In the late afternoon the two smaller rafts were completed. The first one was laden with equipment and one Spaniard. Thirty Yuma swimmers hauled it to the other bank. The second was more heavily loaded, with four mule shipments piled high, plus Anza, Font, Eixarch, seven soldiers, and three boys, a total of thirteen people. Forty Indian swimmers, led by Chief Pablo, were at the ready to guide it across.

As soon as the raft left the shore, it began to sink under the weight of the cargo and the swift current. Font was seated on a chest and the water reached up to his calves on the top-heavy, partially submerged craft.

Panic-stricken, a soldier name Angelo leapt into the water, still wearing his clothes and boots. An Indian boy affectionately called Pedrito (Little Peter), who served as Anza's servant, also hurled himself into the river as Font tried to restrain him. With the help of several Indians who jumped at once into the water from the shoreline, the two made it back to land.

The Yuma swimmers wanted to return the sodden raft to the shore but Chief Pablo, who was at the lead steering with much vigor, would not allow it. "He regarded returning as an insult," Font wrote in his diary. Amid much hubbub, more Yuma swimmers came to the aid of the Spaniards, and the raft was steered out into the middle of the stream. Halfway across a soldier fired his musket in the air in celebration, and the tribesmen in the water and on the banks sent up cheers. With its occupants and baggage soaked, the raft reached the other side much lower downriver than the first one.

"At about half past six in the evening we were over our scare," Font wrote. "Certainly these Indians are great swimmers, great friends of Spaniards, and extremely worthy of esteem for their affection and loyalty, since our lives and possessions were at their mercy." Anza in his diary also praised the Yumas for their able assistance: "Nearly everything has been done voluntarily by these Natives, and yet I am able to testify that in all this journey I have not been so overheated or so tired out anywhere else as here in effecting the crossing, and without their help it probably would have taken me twice as long."[3]

At five o'clock in the afternoon of Wednesday, 15 May 1776, Anza led his party back onto the trail. His interim destination was the garrison at San Miguel de Horcasitas in Sonora, where he would bid goodbye to most of his men and proceed on to Mexico City with Chief Palma, his three Native companions, and an Indian interpreter. The party reached Horcasitas safely on Saturday, 1 June, after dodging a band of one hundred agitated Apaches. Since the previous year when the first settlers for San Francisco were being recruited at Horacitas, Anza and Font had traveled three thousand miles together.

Almost immediately upon their arrival, the smoldering tensions between them flared anew. Their odyssey of eight months and three days together, in which they shared many moments of danger and jubilation, was now ended in the place where it began. These two commanding figures no longer needed to get along with each other. Their barely suppressed antagonisms erupted for the last time.

Anza rebuffed Font when he proposed to say a High Mass and deliver a sermon to the people in thanksgiving for their safe return. Font in turn rebuffed Anza when he offered to give him the astronomical quadrant that the padre had used to make observations along the march. Throughout the expedition, Anza had maintained tight control of the instrument, requiring Font to ask permission to use it. When Anza hosted a celebratory dance to entertain the prominent residents of Horcasitas, Font refused to attend, even though Anza sent a messenger with a special invitation. In his final journal entry Font heaped more dirt on Anza's head, then concluded: "I declare and affirm that in everything I say herein I have attempted to tell the truth. . . . I caution, also, that in relating affairs and incidents in which I name persons I do not do this to bring disrepute upon anyone nor to provide any basis for discontent."[4]

On Wednesday, 5 June, Font mounted a mule on his way to the old Jesuit mission of Ures, about fifty miles to the southeast, where he would begin editing his field notes and writing his official report. A few days earlier Anza had made it clear—prematurely, in Font's view—that the friar could leave whenever he wanted, that he was no longer needed. Their relationship had turned sour for keeps, a striking case of what the Spaniards called "amor Apache" (Apache love), which is to say a love between two people who were always fighting with each other. If the two men exchanged any words of farewell upon Font's departure, neither left a record of it. Their paths never converged again.

Anza, Palma, and the three other Natives reached Mexico City in late October after a hard ride of more than twelve hundred miles. On the evening of 26 October, Anza and the Indian delegation presented themselves at the stately, Baroque-style viceregal palace for an audience with Bucareli. It must have been a bizarre tableau, with the four Native men clad in unaccustomed Spanish garb. Appearing before the viceroy in their accustomed nakedness would have been unthinkable. Palma was bedecked in the elaborate attire given to him the previous year by Anza in the viceroy's name: a ruffled Spanish blouse and breeches, a yellow suede jacket with decorations, a blue cape with gold braid, and a black velvet cap studded with imitation jewels. In his hand he clutched his baton, a symbol of his special status among the Spaniards. His Indian companions were "decently clothed," according to Bucareli, in Sonoran-style capes.[5]

His Excellency received the Indians graciously and assured them that, if they embraced Christianity voluntarily, King Carlos III would provide generously for "their temporal and spiritual well-being."[6] This was the first of many official promises that the Yumas would be taken care of if they assented to the absolute authority of the crown. The viceroy emphasized this point by ordering that new suits of clothes

FIGURE 10. As viceroy of New Spain, Antonio María de Bucareli y Ursúa oversaw the crucial early colonization of California from 1771 to 1779. He worked to thwart Russian and English ambitions on the Pacific coast.
Painting dated 1770–1790, artist unknown, courtesy of Wikimedia Commons.

be made for the four tribesmen. Palma was furnished with a glittering uniform that included a coat and breeches made of shiny blue cloth with blue buttons and a scarlet vest trimmed with gold braid. The very next day, Bucareli dispatched a letter to Madrid extolling the idea of establishing a presidio and mission among the Yumas, pledging it would add "to the fold of the Church the considerable number of heathen who live on the two rivers, the Gila and the Colorado."[7]

On 11 November Chief Palma, his brother, and Chief Pablo's son signed the petition to the viceroy requesting a Spanish settlement on the Colorado and vassalage for their people under the monarch. They did so by making three primitive crosses at the bottom of the lengthy document, which was composed by a counselor to the viceroy, Juan Lucas de Lazaga, with heavy input from Anza.[8] Palma signed shakily with his left hand. Anza also signed as witness, followed by his prominent tornado-shaped rubric.

In his testament, Palma asked for baptism for himself, his children, his brothers, his extended relatives, and his three thousand tribal members. He declared that he enjoyed "supreme rule" over the Yumas, a right of primogeniture handed down by his father and grandfathers "from time immemorial."[9] Although tribal leadership actually could shift dramatically from time to time, Palma's statement conformed nicely to the European notion of the divine right of kings. It also served to dispel any worries that Palma did not exercise total control over his tribesmen. Never mind that Garcés, who knew the indigenous people better than any other Spaniard, had warned frequently against relying entirely on Palma, saying he was chief of only one small segment of the Yuma nation.

Unsurprisingly, Anza emerged in a heroic role in the document. Palma gave the commander full credit for persuading him to embrace Catholicism and Spanish rule, stating that he begged Anza "to receive me as a vassal of the king and treat me as such, imposing any commands that he might wish in order to prove my obedience, my sincerity, and my good faith. . . . I know that nothing is more in keeping with the most beneficent spirit of our Catholic Monarch than my conversion to Christianity." Palma even gave up his Yuma name, spelled Olleyquotequiebe by the Spaniards, in order to embrace his Spanish alias.[10]

The chief's obsequiousness was in full keeping with the long-standing protocol of Spain's top-down command structure, leaving no doubt that Palma already was an unflinchingly loyal subject: "I am not so infamous as to have the audacity to fail in the obligation which I contract with God and with the king, with your Excellency, with my Captain Anza, and with all Spaniards. I love them too much to be ungrateful toward them. I know too well the extent of their power to hope to be able to escape from the full punishment which I should deserve for my perfidy."[11]

With such a fulsome declaration, how could anyone question that Palma was the man to do business with? In truth, as events would demonstrate with bitter repercussions, much of Palma's attestation was an act of self-deception by Anza. Juan Domingo Arricivita, official chronicler of the Franciscans' missionary work in New Spain, understated the point when he wrote more than a decade later that "many of the things expressed in the petition were dictated by policy and not by experience."[12] Viceroy Bucareli eagerly accepted Palma's plea and directed that he be given immediate instruction in the Catholic catechism so that he could be baptized as soon as possible. On Thursday, 13 February 1777, a distinguished group assembled in the evening for the baptismal rites in the sanctuary of the magnificent Metropolitan Cathedral of the Assumption of Mary. This imposing structure, still the largest church in the Americas, was dominated by four ornate façades with portals flanked by columns and statues of the saints. The interior was a masterpiece of sixteen gilded chapels, with stunning altarpieces, Baroque paintings, and sculptures. It also featured two of the largest organs in the world. To the untraveled Natives of the Sonoran frontier, it must have been an astonishing sight. For the occasion, the four Indians were decked out in the new Spanish-style suits that the viceroy had ordered for them.

With appropriate solemnity, Don Agustín de Echeverría y Orcolaga performed the baptismal service after acquiring the necessary approvals from the most reverend archbishop of the holy cathedral. His first entry in the sacristy book recorded that he "catechized, anointed with oil, and baptized . . . [the] captain and chief of the Yuma tribe of wild Indians of the banks of the Río Colorado. . . . To this Indian commonly known as Palma, I gave the name of Salvador Carlos Antonio."[13] Anza stood as sponsor and godfather to Palma.

Next to be baptized was the son of Chief Pablo, who was given the Spanish name of Joseph Antonio Marcelo. His sponsor and godfather was Don Ramón Goya. He was followed by Chief Palma's brother, baptized as Ygnacio Joseph, with a man named Don Pedro de Ansa as his sponsor and godfather. The last to have water and oil poured over his forehead was the Cajuenche tribesman, who was given the name Pedro. His sponsor and godfather was Don Juan Lucas Lasaga, a permanent councilor of the city.

While still in Mexico City, Chief Palma received a visit from another high-ranking Spanish official who bore a nobleman's title, Don Teodoro Francisco de Croix, Conde de Croix. A native of Lille, France, Count Croix was the nephew of the former viceroy, Carlos Francisco de Croix, Marqués de Croix. At age forty-seven, Teodoro de Croix had recently been elevated to the newly created post of commandant general of the internal provinces. In this position, created specifically by the king, Croix wielded absolute authority as the supreme ruler on the frontier, independent of even the viceroy. Croix responded very courteously to Palma and pledged on the spot that he would soon order that missionaries and Spanish settlers be sent to the Yuma nation. This must have buoyed Palma, raising his high expectations even higher. But this, too, turned out to be another broken promise, helping to set the stage for a violent backlash against Spanish sovereignty.

A copy of Palma's petition to the viceroy was sent to Carlos III in Madrid, along with a long letter written by Francisco Garcés describing his extended explorations of the previous year and a detailed map of California drawn by Pedro Font. From his ornate hunting lodge at El Pardo, with its frescoed ceiling painted by Gaspar Becerra, the king ordered Croix to grant Palma's requests for a mission and a presidio, as the viceroy had already done. The monarch also sent word to Garcés praising his work. "His Majesty has read with pleasure the information furnished by this friar," wrote José de Gálvez, the king's minister of the Indies, in a letter to Viceroy Bucareli, "and he orders that your excellency thank Father Garcés in the royal name for the zeal and favor that he displays in discovering, treating, and attracting nations so little known."[14]

Palma and his delegation departed Mexico City in early March 1777 and returned to their lands on the Colorado River. In August Commandant General Croix set out on a tour of his vast domain spanning the borderlands from Texas to the Pacific. Among other objectives, he planned to inspect the prospective sites for missions and a presidio in the land of the Yumas and then proceed to Monterey, the capital of Spanish California.

The powerful position held by Croix was created to counter raids by Apaches, Comanches, and other tribes. A soldier since the age of seventeen, Croix was charged not only with strengthening the defenses all along the frontier but also with settling Spaniards in new towns and converting the indigenous people to Christianity. He reported directly to Gálvez, who had returned to Spain to serve as the king's top adviser on all matters related to the New World. When Croix reached the northern territory of Chihuahua, he was taken seriously ill and his tour was suspended indefinitely. This created a dangerous vacuum of leadership. In the past, Anza had exercised a strong hand among the Yumas, but Bucareli had now appointed him governor of Nuevo México and he had departed for Santa Fe. With Croix sidelined, Spain's thrust to the northwest Pacific slope was blunted.

A full year passed without a Spaniard entering Chief Palma's realm to honor the pledges made to him. In March 1778 the Indian leader traveled on horseback to the presidio at Altar in Sonora to inquire why nothing had been done to establish a permanent Spanish presence on the Colorado River. He was told that once Commandant General Croix was able to visit the region, missions and a garrison would be founded. At that moment Croix was still confined to his bed in Chihuahua. When Palma returned to his people, he found they were restless over the unfulfilled promises, and his own credibility was eroding. As Arricivita reported in his Apostolic Chronicle, Palma's tribesmen "began to annoy him, saying that he had been told nothing but lies."[15]

It was not until the end of August 1779, two and a half years after Palma's meeting with the viceroy, that Father Garcés returned to the Colorado River to placate the Yumas and scout sites for missions. He arrived at the peak of the summer heat, having ridden across the scorching Camino del Diablo from the small village of Sonoitac without provisions of his own, counting instead on local Natives to sustain him. Of his twelve escort soldiers, ten turned back because of the scarcity of water.

At the river Garcés learned that the Jalchedunes from upriver had staged attacks against the Yumas, and that Palma and his people were in a surly mood toward the Spaniards. Garcés lacked even glass beads to help assuage their contentious demeanor. "When I reached this nation of the Yumas," Garcés wrote in a letter to Fray Sebastián Flores at the College of Santa Cruz in Querétaro, "I found it moved only by motives of selfishness on account of the talks of Palma, to whom promises were made at Mexico of I do not know what sort. . . . I got the impression that this disposition was very bad and worked by the devil."[16] On 2 October Garcés was joined by another friar, Juan Díaz, a forty-three-year-old Franciscan from Alazar, Spain. He and Garcés had gotten to know each other during Anza's reconnaissance expedition across the Sonoran Desert to the California coast five years earlier. Soon after Díaz's arrival on the river, he and Garcés found themselves surrounded by a mob of Yumas demanding clothing, tobacco, glass beads, and other gifts that they had been led to believe would be given to them upon the Spaniards' arrival. The padres had nothing to give them. In fact, Garcés and Díaz barely had enough to eat. Despite Garcés's repeated pleas, the provisions that were to be sent from Sonora to support two missions and two towns had not yet arrived.

Because of the destructive battles between the Yumas and the Jalchedunes, and because the river that year did not flood the most fertile acreage, food was scarce among the Yuma people. In desperation, a band of Yumas raided the territory of their former allies downstream, the Cajuenches, and stole all of the corn they could carry. This only added to the volatile atmosphere along the Colorado.

In time, a small detachment of twelve soldiers was dispatched to the river. Lieutenant Colonel Anza, in a detailed report to the viceroy in 1776, had outlined what he deemed was essential to establish Spanish settlements among the Yumas. The foremost requirement was an extra large garrison of eighty soldiers. (Garcés had called for two presidios of fifty men each.)[17] Without a strong military presence, Anza argued, no missions or towns should be founded. This advice was ignored by Commandant General Croix, who had recovered his health and was determined to colonize the region on the cheap. He also overlooked Garcés's warnings that some Yuma warriors already were in revolt against Palma's rule.

The few soldiers who reached the river at the end of 1779 were not as eager as the padres to live in impoverished circumstances. They grumbled that they lacked cigars and did not have even flour with which to make tortillas. All the same, the shortage of provisions persisted.

Without consulting the friars in the field, Croix ordered that a new method of conquest be applied to the two towns and two missions on the Colorado. For the first time since the Spanish arrived in the New World, there would be a complete separation between the religious authorities and the military/civil authorities. The missionaries, who in the past were responsible for the general welfare of the Indians, would now be responsible for their spiritual needs only. Natives no longer would be required to live at the missions, and the padres would have to seek them out in their villages. The practical effect of this regulation was to subordinate the material needs of the Indians to those of the Spanish settlers from Sonora who would be brought in to populate the towns. In his recounting, Arricivita decried Croix's scheme as "dictated by a spirit aflame with political notions, adaptable only for towns founded in the heart of Christendom, where a spirit of peace and obedience prevails." The new rules, he declared, would make it extremely difficult for the Franciscans "to quench the fire of hatred for the Spaniards that already burned in (the Indians') breasts."[18] The first mission and pueblo were to be established on a knoll overlooking the Yuma crossing, on the western side of the river in order to gain some protection from Apache attacks, as Garcés had recommended. Named Mission La Purísima Concepción, the site would consist of ten Spanish settlers, six artisans to build structures, and a scant military force of one corporal and nine soldiers. The second mission and pueblo were to be built about ten miles upstream, also on the California bank. This place was to be called Mission San Pedro y San Pablo de Bicuñer and was to be populated by ten settlers, six artisans, a corporal, and eight soldiers. In addition, two padres were assigned to each mission. These fifty-five intruders were to be planted in the midst of three thousand Yuma tribesmen who were showing increasing belligerence toward the Spanish incursion.

Alarmed by the Natives' simmering hostility, Garcés dispatched a soldier to warn the commander of the Altar garrison that, despite Chief Palma's friendly entreaties, many Yumas were no longer receptive to an influx of Spaniards living in their nation. Specifically, he reported that Palma's brother Ygnacio, and the son of Chief Pablo, Joseph, both of whom had been baptized in Mexico City, were now inciting their fellow tribesmen to rise up in revolt. Word already was spreading among the young hotheads of the tribe that the expected Spanish interlopers were all to be massacred. Rumors also were circulating that Ygnacio was plotting to kill his own brother, Palma. In response to this news, the Altar commander, Ensign Pedro Tueros, chose to hasten the departure of the Spanish settlers before the insurrectionist fever spread further.

At this point, a perilous self-delusion began to take hold among senior Spanish officials. Most had never placed a foot on the soil of the Yumas. Commandant General Croix, advised by Garcés that talk of an uprising was in the air, replied: "I am certain that the constant zeal of your Reverence for the spreading of the Gospel and the extension of the King's dominions may be able on this occasion to drive away any ill-feeling that may arise, preserving among the Natives the greatest quiet and content."[19]

The job of recruiting families to settle the new missions was given to Don Santiago de Yslas, ensign of dragoons, a thirty-five-year-old career soldier born in Italy. He drew many of the volunteers from the new pueblo of Tucson and towns such as Tubac farther south in the Sonoran Desert. To minimize the problem of unmarried soldiers molesting Indian women, Yslas selected men with wives and plenty of children. Each family of homesteaders was to be paid ten pesos a month for the first year and given a yoke of oxen, among other inducements. Yslas also would serve as military commander of the river settlements.

On 9 December 1780 Yslas set out from Altar, accompanied by his wife and children, and led the main caravan of settlers to La Concepción on the Colorado River, in the heart of Yuma territory. They arrived on 27 December. Altogether, the party consisted of twenty families of colonists, twelve families of workers, and twenty-one families of soldiers.

In his diary Yslas recorded that the only mishap encountered along the way was a lost horse, which, it turned out, had been stolen and eaten by the Indians.[20] Despite the warning signs of trouble brewing, Yslas was impressed by the greeting orchestrated for him by Palma. "I was received with much applause, pleasure, and rejoicing by the magistrates and Yuma Indians to whom I made known the will of the King," he wrote in a letter to Croix three days later. "After I had given them some advice, they were well satisfied, replying that they would not be found wanting in any respect. At least, I observed in them much goodwill so that all the Indians are very quiet and peaceful and without any sign of disorder."[21]

When the inundation of settlers occurred, they found there were no provisions except those they brought themselves. Yslas put them to work immediately planting beans and squash. Seed corn was scarce due to the poor harvest earlier in the year. Sowing winter crops was critical to the colonists' survival, but the effort was hampered by a lack of oxen to pull plows.

Within a month of his arrival, Yslas began to sense the unrest and mounting threat of violence among the Yumas. He also was aware that, in the event of bloodshed, the nearest detachment of relief soldiers was over two hundred miles away. On 17 January 1781 he asked Commandant General Croix to send ten pairs of shackles and two artillery pieces, "for they would not fail to be of use some day in case there should be an uprising among these Indians."[22] In a stern response, Croix denied the request: "To keep in subjection the Yumas whose submission was voluntary and who have urgently desired and requested and gladly admitted the Spaniards to their country, I do not understand why there is need of the irons or the cannon that you ask for."[23] From his desk in Arizpe, Sonora, four hundred miles away, the commandant general had embraced a very rosy view that obscured the deteriorating reality on the ground.

In the first week of January work was begun on Mission San Pedro y Pablo de Bicuñer.[24] Yslas reported to Croix that at the ceremonial groundbreaking the Indians "looked on and saluted us with shouts, each one by himself crying hurrah for the King." But all was not well. Palma continued to press Yslas for the clothing that he believed the viceroy had promised to provide for the Yumas. He also let it be known that he was ready to pay a visit to the commandant general in a bid to obtain what he felt he was owed. Yslas told Palma bluntly "that the time for giving [clothes] had already passed, and that he should take for an example the industry of the Spaniards, for by this means they would be clothed and in no other way."[25] This emphatic statement that no clothes would be forthcoming must have done great injury to Palma's standing among his tribesmen.

Meantime, Yslas ordered the flogging of an Indian who had wounded a corporal's horse with an arrow. In keeping with Spanish custom, the beating was administered by a Native who had been given the title of *justicia*, or justice, by the Spaniards. In this case, the justicia was Palma himself. Inflicting such harsh punishment on a fellow tribal member in the name of Spanish justice cannot have aggrandized Palma among his people.

In early June Yslas got wind that Chief Palma's brother Ygnacio and another Native were conspiring to murder a soldier, Cayetano Mesa. The ensign commandant had the pair arrested and put in the stocks. With portents of warfare already in the air, this was yet another provocation for the Natives.

Two much larger irritants had been allowed to fester for months. The first was that the colonists appropriated for themselves the best Yuma lands for cultivation, even to the extent of taking over fields cleared by the Indians for their own planting. Both Garcés and the Indians protested to Yslas, but he took no action. Indeed, this deplorable situation was supposed to be no concern of Garcés because he was now confined to addressing the Natives' spiritual needs alone. Even worse, with the scarcity of pasturage the settlers allowed their horses and cows, hundreds of them, to trample and graze on the Indians' crops, including the valuable corn harvest, which was only beginning to make a comeback. At the same time, the 204 head of sheep brought to the river by the Spaniards devoured the wild mesquite seeds and other pod plants that the Yumas relied on for their winter food supply.

Matters turned more tense when the former military governor of California, fifty-six-year-old Captain Fernando Rivera y Moncada, reached the Colorado River in June 1781. He was at the head of a caravan whose aim was to found a pueblo at what is now Los Angeles, California, and two new missions along the Santa Barbara Channel. His train included thirty-seven officers and soldiers and their families, along with nearly a thousand horses and mules. This flood of unexpected Spaniards must have taxed the Yumas' patience as nothing had before. Talk of rebellion grew as the Natives pressed their grievances in vain.

After recuperating for several days at his encampment on the east bank of the river, Rivera sent the main body of settlers on to Mission San Gabriel in California. He remained behind temporarily with seventeen of his men to tend to his herd of worn-out livestock.[26] This included 257 horses, mules, and burros.[27] Their grazing along the riverbank opposite La Concepción only inflamed the Spaniards' predicament. As June drew to a close, Yuma warriors armed with war clubs could be seen brazenly stalking both settlements. The flickering fuse of a much-feared Yuma onslaught was almost at its end.

CHAPTER FIFTEEN

Slaughter on the Colorado River

The sight of blood to crowds begets the thirst of more
As the first wine-cup leads to the long revel.
—Lord Byron

The Yuma crossing on the Colorado River is scarcely noticeable to motorists as they barrel across the high arc of Interstate 8 connecting California and Arizona. Below, the river's flow is obscured by dense wetlands with marsh grasses taller than a man. Before the Colorado was subjugated by the Hoover Dam in 1936, it was defined here by two enormous granite outcroppings, one on each side of the river. This forced a narrowing of the stream as it churned southward, creating the only fordable spot along a thousand miles of free-flowing waterway. Eighty years before the Pilgrims reached the shores of Massachusetts, Spaniards led by the conquistador Hernando de Alarcón explored this stretch of the Colorado and established friendly relations with the Indians. In time, the ford became a peaceful crossroads of cultures—Indian, Spanish, Anglo-American. But in the summer of 1781 a violent tempest was fast approaching.

Francisco Garcés saw the warning signs everywhere. Perhaps the most sinister was that Yuma chief Salvador Palma had abandoned his dwelling close to the new Spanish settlement and had returned to his village across the river. It was clear that Palma, who once had been the most steadfast ally of the Spaniards, was dissociating himself from them.

To bolster the padres' missionary outreach to the Yuma tribesmen, Garcés built a hut in which to say Mass near their cultivated fields about four miles upriver from Mission La Concepción, on the California side of the Yuma crossing. There he learned that a furious, full-scale uprising was being hatched by Yuma warriors on both banks. He now took seriously the circulating rumors that the four Franciscans on the Colorado were to be slain along with the soldiers and other Spanish males. Santiago de Yslas, military commander of the bantam detachment of soldiers assigned to protect the two settlements on the river, believed the rumors were merely scare tactics by young Yuma firebrands. In the words of Franciscan chronicler Juan Domingo Arricivita, Yslas and his men "lived in reckless assurance."[1]

One fact was indisputable to both the Natives and the Spaniards. If the Natives rose in rebellion, their numbers would easily overwhelm the handful of colonists and soldiers newly settled on the river. There could be no effective resistance to the atrocities that were certain to occur if a Yuma rebellion erupted.

Two priests were assigned to each of the missions. Joining Garcés at La Concepción was Juan Antonio Barreneche, a thirty-two-year-old native of Lecaroz in the kingdom of Navarre in northern Spain. While still a boy, Barreneche gave alms to a grateful blind man, a moving encounter that sparked Barreneche's interest in the priesthood. At age nineteen he joined the Franciscan order in Havana, Cuba, and later was assigned to the College of Santa Cruz in Querétaro, Mexico. After sailing from Havana to the port of Tampico, he walked more than five hundred miles carrying nothing but his prayer book to reach Querétaro. Later he and Garcés, who was eleven years older, became close compatriots. Neither complained about the primitive and dangerous conditions on the frontier. Barreneche voluntarily fasted on many days, consuming only bread and water. He also practiced severe bodily mortification, or self-flagellation.[2] Garcés wrote of him: "Father Juan is very much contented. He is of that caliber which conquers many. He is another St. Patrick."[3]

The two ministers assigned to Mission San Pedro y San Pablo ten miles upriver were Juan Díaz, who had initially joined Garcés the previous year, and José Matías Moreno, thirty-seven, a native of Almorza, Spain. Moreno, known for his lively sermons, had long yearned for martyrdom in the cause of saving Indian souls. In a letter to his sister at the time of his departure from Spain, he wrote: "I declare to you that I banish myself from our country, leave my parents, sever myself from my kindred and friends, solely for zeal for the faith, the conversion of souls, and a longing for martyrdom."[4]

The triple-digit heat of July brought only increased strains between the Spaniards and the Yumas, but Yslas minimized the tocsins of trouble. From Commandant General Teodoro de Croix down to the troops on the river, there was an obstinate refusal to believe that the once-welcoming Yumas, especially the compliant Chief Palma, would turn violent. Overlooked was the reality that Palma was now leader of only one small segment of the three-thousand-strong tribe. In the chauvinistic minds of the Spanish authorities, the Indians were too timid to foment war. "If the Yumas continue constant in their docile reduction," Croix naively declared, "it will not be many years before the banks of the Colorado River will be covered with grain fields, fruits, and herds, and settled with faithful vassals of the king."[5]

On Tuesday morning, 17 July, Barreneche said the first Mass at Mission La Concepción. A short time later Garcés stood at the altar saying the second Mass. Attending him as server was Commander Yslas. The only guard on duty at that moment was Corporal Pasqual Baylón. His assignment was to sound the alarm if more bands of young Yuma men brandishing war clubs came marching defiantly through the settlement, as they had done in recent days. In fact, Yslas and Baylón were the only military men at La Concepción. Despite the rumors of a massacre in the making, the other soldiers were off duty in the countryside. As Yslas shifted the heavy bound missal, or book of prayers, to the Gospel side of the altar as part of the ritual of the Mass, the shrieks of hundreds of enraged marauders split the air.

Corporal Baylón was immediately surrounded by warriors before he could fire a shot. They clubbed him in the head and knocked him to the ground. Barreneche forced his way through the gang of howling Yumas in a bid to save Baylón, who was still absorbing blows from the Natives' war clubs. As he lay dying in the dirt, the bloodied corporal reached out and clutched the padre's hand. When the Indians then turned their wrath on Barreneche, he fled to the church, sustaining on the way a savage battering of his own.

As Ensign Yslas ran to his house for his weapons, his wife, María Ana Montijo, gathered up the women and children and sought refuge in the church. Already assembled there were the two Franciscans and most of La Concepción's other residents. This was the moment they all had feared.

Terrified, unarmed, and unable to repel the assault, the settlers argued over who was to blame for the cataclysm. "Let's forget now whose fault it is," said Garcés, "and simply consider it God's punishment for our sins." Doña María, who came from a family of wealthy Sonoran ranchers, recalled that Garcés's "voice was compassionate, though his face was an ashen gray." She also acknowledged in a later letter that "my husband had observed a few armed Indians arriving in the village before he left for church. As commander of the Colorado settlements, he took the precaution of placing Baylón on temporary guard, never dreaming that a full rebellion of the Yuma nation was about to break out."[6]

The prime targets of the warriors were the soldiers of La Concepción. In raids throughout the frontier Indians generally spared the lives of women and children, taking them hostage instead and later ransoming them for lucrative payments from the Spaniards. With mostly women and children holed up in the church, the insurgents roamed the area in search of soldiers. When Commander Yslas was caught in the open, he was engulfed by warriors and coldly pummeled to death as his wife watched from inside the church. Doña María, powerless to do anything for her husband, looked on as the rebels hurled his battered body into the river.

Then they set fire to some of the buildings and torched the books and papers of the padres. Candlesticks and other items sacked from the settlement were thrown into the river. The horses and mules were stolen and distributed among the attackers. Saddles were plundered for their leather, which the Yumas cut into pieces for sandals. The sheep and cattle were herded off. Chief Palma collected as many firearms as he could, amassing an arsenal of fifteen muskets and half a case of pistols.[7] He also helped himself to a glass vinegar cruet and three silver vials containing holy oils.[8] Indians who normally went naked were seen parading about in the sacred vestments of the priests, wearing knee-length silk chasubles as ponchos. At midday, with dead bodies and crushed skulls scattered across the plaza, the brigands took a break from the slaughter.[9]

After dark they resumed the attack, killing anyone found outside the church and setting fire to more structures. Despite the enormous risks to their own lives, Garcés and Barreneche slipped stealthily through the darkness to administer the last rites of the church, hear final confessions, and offer consolation to the wounded and dying.

The day's events at Mission San Pedro y San Pablo were even more grisly. Yuma combatants struck at sunrise. Their assault was so sudden that not a shot was fired in defense. Meeting no resistance, they spared no one. Eighteen soldiers and male settlers were killed.[10] Women and children and at least one soldier, thirty-eight-year-old Joseph Reyes Pacheco, were taken into captivity after being forced to throw into the Colorado the statues and other holy items taken from the church, which was then set on fire. A case of pistols also was heaved into the water.

Although some soldiers escaped, nearly every male encountered by the Yumas perished, including Father Moreno and Father Díaz. Moreno's boyhood wish to become a martyr was fulfilled in gruesome measure. A warrior armed with an ax chopped off his head and made off with it as a souvenir. The padre's decapitated remains, with his crucifix still dangling from the neck, were left to decompose on the ground behind the church. Pacheco begged his captors to allow him to bury the dead, who littered the ground wherever they were slain.[11] The Indians refused. At nightfall a ghostly silence pervaded Mission San Pedro y San Pablo.

When dawn broke the next day, Barreneche offered stoic encouragement to the settlers barricaded in the church at La Concepción. "The devil is on the side of the enemy," he said, "but God is on ours. Let us sing a hymn to Mary, most holy, that she favor us with her help, and let us praise God for sending us these trials."

Barreneche said Mass "as we awaited death at any moment," María Ana Montijo wrote. The padre then occupied himself by pulling arrows and spears out of the walls of the church and climbing onto the roof to observe the movements of the Indians.[12]

On the second day of the rampage, Captain Rivera, his sergeant, and his soldiers encamped on the other side of the Colorado absorbed the warriors' fury. Having watched in the distance the ravages of the day before on the western bank, Rivera's men dug a trench and piled up their baggage around it as a makeshift fortification. Early in the day a large number of insurrectionists swarmed upon the Spaniards. Rivera met them with his troops mounted, firing a volley that killed several. But the Yumas quickly encircled the small contingent of soldiers, pulled them from their horses, and bludgeoned them to death.

A few who escaped back into the trench were overwhelmed and killed, Rivera among them. The lone woman encamped with Rivera, María Manuela Ochoa, the wife of a Spanish deserter, was taken into captivity. Chief Palma took possession of a large cache of Spanish currency carried by Rivera for the new settlements in California. He also kept for himself the commander's leather shield. The hundreds of horses, mules, and burros in Rivera's possession were seized. Many no doubt were butchered for food. In his nearly contemporaneous account of the Franciscans' missionary labors, Juan Domingo Arricivita showed no remorse for Rivera, who frequently was at odds with the padres over the treatment of the Natives: "Thus died this captain who had displayed open contempt for the Indians and whose reckless over-confidence brought him into their hands."[13]

After laying waste to Rivera's camp, the Yumas crossed back over the river at three o'clock in the afternoon to finish off La Concepción. Barreneche saw them coming and declared: "Let each one save himself the best way he can, for whatever we do, we are in danger of perishing at the hands of the enemy." He picked up his breviary and crucifix, and along with Garcés led the settlers out of La Concepción.[14]

They followed a trail of blood left by a wounded man named Pedro Burgues and found him calling out for help on the other side of a shallow lagoon. Barreneche started to wade across the water, with his prayer book and crucifix still in his hands. Unable to swim, he immediately found himself in over his head and thrashing about to keep from drowning. He managed to reach the other side by grasping roots and low-hanging tree branches but lost his breviary and crucifix in the muddy water.

Garcés directed the women and children to stay together and not to resist capture. Drawing on his years of experience living among the Indians, he told the survivors, "The Yumas will not harm you."[15] With that, he removed his habit and cloak, retaining only his tunic. Then he, too, plunged into the lagoon, even though

FIGURE 11. A life-size oil painting by an unknown artist depicts the martyred Francisco Garcés and Juan Barreneche, with the Yuma massacre of July 1781 unfolding in the background. Original at the Museo Regional de Querétaro, Mexico.

he couldn't swim and suffered a fear of the water. Miraculously, he made it to the other bank, where Barreneche heard Burgues's last confession. Then the two padres made their way to the village of a Christianized Indian woman who had shown them kindness in the past. Her husband took them in for the night.

Around ten o'clock the next morning a clutch of Yuma assailants surrounded the hut where Garcés and Barreneche were hiding. Chief Palma, although an active participant in the revolt, had given orders that the padres be found and brought to him unharmed. Even among the Indians there was ambivalence about slaying the Franciscans, the men who had shown the most concern for the Natives' welfare. Inside the hut, Garcés and Barreneche were drinking their morning cup of chocolate.

The rebel leader shouted: "Stop drinking that and come outside. We're going to kill you!"[16]

"We'd like to finish our chocolate first," replied Garcés.

"Just leave it!" the rebel leader demanded.

The two fathers obediently followed the rebel leader outside, where the mob was waiting, spoiling for blood. Among them was a young Indian, Francisco Xavier, who had been raised at the Altar presidio.[17] He had come from a destitute band of Natives who traded their children for horses. He had spent his boyhood as a servant in the house of Captain Bernardo de Urrea, commandant of the presidio, who had been killed by Apaches the previous year. Because of his command of both Spanish and the Yuma language, Xavier had been brought to La Concepción by Garcés as an interpreter. Now, having turned against his Spanish patrons, the renegade was the prime instigator of vengeance.

"If these men are left alive," he shouted, "everything is lost because they are the worst ones!"[18]

No more incitement was needed. The tribesmen rained their war clubs upon the two Franciscans. Both were bludgeoned to death, their last moments spent prostrate on the ground amid "pitiful moans," according to one witness.[19]

The Indian woman who had sheltered Garcés and Barreneche recovered their bodies and buried them, side by side, at a sandy beach near the Colorado River (see figure 11). On top of the graves she placed a cross made of two sticks. The three-day frenzy of brutality had finally come to an end. But the calls for retribution were only just beginning.

CHAPTER SIXTEEN

Retribution on the Colorado

An eye for an eye, and the whole world would be blind.
—Khalil Gibran

The most prominent feature of the sixty-nine-square-mile Fort Yuma Indian Reservation straddling the lower Colorado River is the glitzy, Las Vegas–style Quechan (Yuma) Indian Casino Resort. No longer do the Quechans practice floodplain agriculture as their ancestors did. Today, the river bottom is the site of a flourishing gambling complex. The twelve hundred tribal members' livelihoods emanate from its one thousand slot machines, table games, poker contests (Texas Hold 'Em, Seven Card Stud, Pai Gow), and 166 hotel rooms, augmented by nearby RV parks and convenience stores. Most of the reservation's fertile agricultural lands are leased to corporate farming enterprises. More than two centuries after the massacre at the Yuma crossing, the repository of Quechan tradition appears to be the neighboring cemetery, with its multicolored plastic flowers adorning graves in the desert.

In late summer 1781 word of the Yuma uprising reached the Altar garrison after a wounded soldier taken captive by the Indians, Francisco Xavier Valdés, escaped with a horse, forded the Colorado downstream from Mission La Concepción, and rode bareback 250 miles across El Camino del Diablo during the hottest days of the year.[1] From his headquarters at Arizpe, Commandant General Teodoro de Croix convened a junta de guerra, or war council, on 7 September to plan a punitive expedition against the Yumas. Lieutenant Colonel Pedro Fages, head of the company of Catalonian volunteers who had arrived in California with Gaspar de Portolá twelve years earlier, was given command of the campaign. His second-in-charge was Pedro Tueros, a cavalry captain and commandant of the royal presidio at Altar.

Under Croix's detailed orders, the main body of troops, not counting officers, was to be composed of 170 men—fifty from the Catalonian volunteers, sixty soldiers from the presidios of Altar, Horcasitas, and Buenavista, and sixty friendly Pápago and Pima Indians from the towns and missions of the Sonoran frontier.[2] Named as chaplain was Father Enrique Cenizo. To underscore the urgency of the undertaking, Croix directed that "not a moment's time should be lost in making the necessary preparations for the departure of the expedition, which will take place without delay and without further orders."[3]

Fages's mandate was as ambitious as it was delicate. His first objective was to ransom the scores of Spaniards, mostly women and children, still held by the Yumas. He was well supplied with tobacco, glass beads, yards of cloth, and other trifles favored by the Natives. Freeing the captives was to be achieved without tipping off the Indians that severe punishment awaited the conspirators. Fages also was to recover the remains of Fathers Garcés, Barreneche, Díaz, and Moreno, and send them to Mission Tubutama in northern Sonora for a sacred burial. If possible, he was to retrieve the papers of the slain Captain Rivera in order to determine what happened to the large sum of His Majesty's currency that he was transporting for the two planned missions on the Santa Barbara Channel. Unbeknown to the Spaniards, Chief Palma had taken personal possession of the money and buried it somewhere in the hills.

After all of the hostages were freed, the commander was to round up the Yuma ringleaders and impose the retribution they deserved for their "perfidy"—*perfidia* in Spanish, the strong term used over and over again by Croix and others to describe the Yumas' treachery and breach of trust. The punishment stipulated by Croix was nothing less than torture and execution. At a minimum, these measures were to be inflicted on the three Indians deemed to be the instigators of the rebellion: Chief Palma, his brother Ygnacio, and the turncoat interpreter Francisco Xavier. In a postscript to his instructions, the commandant general added: "Although I say that the ransom of our captives is to be secured at any price, it should be understood that when the said captives have been recovered, all that has been given for them should be taken away from the Indians."[4]

From a strategic standpoint, the primary aim of the punitive expedition was to reopen the needed supply road from Sonora to the missions on the Pacific coast of California. This could be accomplished only if the Yumas were fully subjugated to Spanish rule—and this time, by force. The Fages campaign marked a sharp departure from Spain's long-standing policy of fostering friendly relations with the Natives.

At age thirty-seven Fages was already one of the most experienced military officers on the frontier, having participated in several exploratory expeditions in California as well as campaigns to suppress Apache raids in northern Sonora. He

FIGURE 12. Lieutenant Colonel Pedro Fages, an experienced soldier, led the Spanish punitive expedition against the Yumas in late 1781. A fearless bear hunter, he earned the nickname L'Os, short for El Oso (The Bear). Artist unknown.
Author's collection.

had left his native Catalonia for the New World in 1767 with the Free Company of Volunteers raised in Barcelona, commonly known as Bluecoats. For decades these troops served Spain's colonial empire in elaborate uniforms consisting of a blue coat with yellow collar and cuffs, yellow waistcoat with white buttons, black cravat at the neck, blue breeches, and a black three-cornered hat with the red cockade of the House of Bourbon. Although Fages was sometimes hot tempered—and had lost a notorious clash with Junípero Serra—he was respected by his men and the Natives alike. During the Portolá expeditions of 1769 and 1770, he earned a reputation as a fearless bear hunter (see figure 12).

After Sunday Mass on 16 September 1781 Fages and his troops departed Pitic in central Sonora on a march of more than four hundred miles to the Colorado

River. Along the way they picked up forty Pima Indians who were eager to join in the impending warfare against the Yumas. On Tuesday, 9 October, after passing through an Indian village ravaged by smallpox, Fages reached the Gila River. As his men descended the Gila and drew closer to the territory of the Yumas, he ordered an inspection of arms. All pistols and muskets were unloaded, examined to see that they were in good working order, and then reloaded for battle.

In the afternoon of Thursday, 18 October, the troopers reached the eastern bank of the Colorado. Here they were hailed by Miguel Antonio Romero, a soldier who had been taken prisoner by the Yumas. He was carrying a letter from Palma stating that his people would receive the Spaniards and their Native allies in peace if they approached in peace.

Across the river, a Yuma war party of about five hundred men was assembling. They were brandishing not only war clubs, spears, and bows and arrows but also Spanish firearms seized during the July upheaval. Soon Palma made himself visible on the western bank. He often could be spotted wearing a linen Spanish shirt and carrying the leather shield taken from the slain Captain Rivera. The Yuma leader refused to cross the river to the other side, where Fages and his men were gathered. To strike a conciliatory tone, Fages sent the clothes-minded chief a shirt, a black peaked hat of the Catalonian volunteers festooned with silver braid and a red cockade, and some cigarettes.[5] In return Palma sent across muskmelons, watermelons, squashes, and corn.

Both sides were now ready to engage in the customary ransoming of hostages. Fages readily paid up with blankets, beads, tobacco, leather belts, and yards of cloth. He recorded the results in his diary: "We secured the return of forty-eight captives, including men and women, adults and children." Many of the freed hostages were naked, but they had not been mistreated by the Yumas. While in captivity they were required to weed the Natives' cultivated fields and fetch water and wood.[6]

From their position on the eastern bank, Fages's men found the site where Rivera and his party made their last stand. Their exposed remains had been partially consumed by wild animals, but Rivera's body was identified by a broken shinbone he had suffered years earlier. Fages also recovered some of the commander's papers, most of which the Indians had torn into pieces for rolling cigarettes. The next day, Fages ordered that Rivera's bones be given a decent burial. He also ransomed fourteen more Spaniards, while learning that others were still being held in Yuma villages some distance away.

At dawn on Saturday, 20 October, with Fages still encamped on the eastern side of the river, a war party of six hundred rival Jalchedunes, Pima Gileños, and

Cocomaricopas attacked the Yumas on the western bank, sacking their villages, burning their huts, killing fifteen men, and taking many women and children prisoner. From across the river, Fages watched the assault unfold. Ironically, the Yumas had earlier sought Spanish protection from these very tribesmen.

In the afternoon he ordered twenty-five mounted soldiers under the command of Ensign Manuel Antonio Arbizu to intercept a band of Yuma warriors who had crossed to the eastern bank. The cavalrymen put the Yumas to flight, killing five. One Spaniard was wounded by an arrow. During the day's skirmishes a son of Palma was slain, a brother of Palma was badly wounded, and Palma himself was injured slightly, according to Fages's account. Many more Yumas were killed by the rival Indian warriors.

After the fighting ended, a Native helped a Spanish woman and her baby escape captivity and cross the river to join Fages and the other freed prisoners. On this day the soldiers recovered a silk chasuble, the poncho-like garment worn by the padres during Mass. One of the freed captives also delivered to chaplain Cenizo some small silver vials containing holy oils; another ex-prisoner returned a silver bell and a glass wine container.

At least sixteen Spanish women and several children were still being held by the Yumas. But in light of the day's intense fighting, Fages did not think he could resume ransom negotiations anytime soon. The next morning he called his officers together for a war council. Their unanimous view was that it was time to retreat 130 miles to the Pápago village of Sonoitac in northern Sonora until things settled down. The expedition would return later to the Colorado River to arrange the release of the remaining captives and to punish the Yuma conspirators. In the afternoon of Sunday, 21 October, Fages and his men, accompanied by the ransomed hostages, set out for Sonoitac. After arriving there on Saturday, 27 October, Fages sent the freed Spaniards on to the presidio at Altar. He also requested additional provisions for his troops on their planned return to the Yuma nation. In a report written in his camp at Sonoitac on 29 October, he listed the names of 105 Spaniards who died in the July insurrection.

The return party departed Sonoitac on 23 November and six days later reached the eastern bank of the Colorado upstream from the destroyed Mission San Pedro y San Pablo de Bicuñer. The river was somewhat swollen. After sending out scouting parties to find the best possible ford, Fages crossed the river for the first time, losing two pack mules that were swept away and drowned. He found the once thriving Yuma villages abandoned. But smoke signals arising in the distance told him the Yumas were once again preparing for war.

The next day a peaceful delegation of thirty mounted Yumas appeared. Through them Fages sent word to Chief Palma, who was encamped downriver, to deliver the remaining prisoners for ransom. With the help of Father Cenizo, he rescued a ten-year-old Spanish girl, María Josefa Benítez, in exchange for a blind Indian boy held by the soldiers. A day later seven more Spanish women were released.

In the morning on Tuesday, 4 December, Fages hid three columns of his troops in ambush in an attempt to capture Chief Palma and the two other masterminds of the uprising, the interpreter Francisco Xavier and Ygnacio, the brother of Palma. The three Yuma leaders appeared warily outside Fages's camp, as planned, to ransom the rest of the women and children. The commander succeeded in gaining the release of Juliana Sambrano and her infant, who had been born while in captivity. But the ambush failed when a Yuma drummer sounded the alarm, prompting the Indians to take flight. Renowned as strong swimmers, many hurled themselves into the river to escape as the Catalonian volunteers fired their muskets. When a first-quarter moon arose at ten o'clock that night, Fages and Captain Tueros set out with a small contingent to track down Palma. They returned to camp the next afternoon without finding a trace of the elusive chieftain.

At dawn on Friday, 7 December, Fages, Tueros, and thirty-five soldiers under their command entered the devastated town of San Pedro y San Pablo. They found the decomposing body of Father Juan Díaz, which had lain out in the hot sun for five months. He had been shot to death.[7] His remains were identified by the distinctive tonsure on the skull. For centuries Franciscan clerics had shaved the crowns of their heads as a religious practice. Behind the blackened church the troopers found the headless body of Father José Matías Moreno, which was distinguished by the crucifix hanging from his chest. Fages ordered that the bones of the two friars be gathered up in a leather bag for later shipment to Mission Tubutama.

The skeletal remnants of soldiers and settlers killed as they tried to escape the Yuma attack littered the ground. Many of the bodies had been stripped of their clothing. Fages had them cremated and the ashes placed in two leather pouches. He also retrieved the mission bell from atop the church and loaded it into a hamper for transport back to Sonora.

Meanwhile, a sizable force of mounted Yuma warriors surrounded the Spanish contingent that had been left behind at Fages's main encampment. In a forty-five-minute battle, troops under the command of Sergeant Juan Noriega fired volley after volley of grapeshot to hold off the warriors. Chief Palma appeared on the scene but escaped yet again after a soldier fired three pistol shots at him. In his haste to flee, Palma left behind his horse and the tricornered hat given to him by Fages a week earlier. Fifteen Yumas were killed and the bloodstained ground indicated many more were wounded, according to Fages's entry in his diary.

On Monday, 10 December, Fages and Tueros led their men into La Concepción. Their chief purpose was to find the bodies of Fathers Francisco Garcés and Juan Barreneche. Along the riverbank Captain Tueros spotted a verdant patch of fragrant chamomile. A small cross marked the spot. There the soldiers unearthed the corpses of Garcés and Barreneche, buried side by side in their undergarments and wrapped in coarse shrouds. The remains of both Franciscans were put into a sack and taken back to San Pedro y San Pablo.

The church at Mission San Pedro y San Pablo de Bicuñer had been destroyed by fire, but its walls survived almost intact, as did the high altar. Fages directed that the recovered bones of the four padres be placed on the altar. Lighted candles were placed alongside. Then Father Cenizo led members of the expedition and the rescued captives in reciting the rosary in honor of the martyred Franciscans. Two days later Fages had the bodies placed in a large cigarette crate. The makeshift coffin was wrapped tightly in coarse burlap. The shipment was delivered to the Altar presidio, and the padres were later buried together amid religious solemnity under the left side of the altar at Mission Tubutama.

Fages and his men returned to Sonora without accomplishing their two main objectives. Although most of the captives seized by the Indians were freed, Captain Palma and the two other instigators of the uprising remained at large, and would do so for the rest of their lives. Far more significant, the expedition failed to pacify the Yumas and reopen the vital overland route to the Pacific coast missions. Despite the enormous losses in Spanish blood and treasure in establishing the road over a seven-year span, it was abandoned permanently. This compromised King Carlos III's conquest of California in untold ways. More than a century would pass before another Franciscan would tread among the Natives of the Colorado River.[8]

CHAPTER SEVENTEEN

Final Journey

A man who lives fully is prepared to die at any time.
—Mark Twain

The centuries-old mission of San Diego del Pitiquito faces the sunset atop a small hill dominating the Sonoran farming village of Pitiquito, seventy-five miles south of the U.S.-Mexican border. The surrounding fields yield beans, corn, alfalfa, and feed for the cattle ranches of the Altar River Valley. The whitewashed church, completed in 1780, is a fine example of Franciscan colonial architecture. But the toil that went into building El Templo de San Diego del Pitiquito was supplied by the indigenous laborers of New Spain's northern frontier. Fifty years ago a young girl attending Mass spotted the faint outline of a human skeleton etched on the south wall of the nave. Further investigation uncovered other examples of Pima Indian artwork hidden beneath layers of white paint. The faded drawings were done in ochre and black, depicting religious figures important to the padres. A series of obscured picture frames along both walls of the nave appear to be the original Stations of the Cross.

In the late summer of 1781, Pedro Font was the priest assigned to Pitiquito, along with Fray Joseph Nicolás Mesa. Pitiquito was an auxiliary post of the larger mission at Caborca, six miles to the northwest on the Río de la Concepción. Font recently had received the jarring report that his longtime friend Francisco Garcés had been slain in the three-day Yuma uprising on the Colorado River. This must have stirred Font's recollections of the Indian assault he narrowly survived at Santa María Magdalena five years earlier.

It was not uncommon for Franciscan friars to be beaten to death by Native war clubs, but this news must have distressed Font. He and Garcés had met eighteen years earlier aboard the small Royal Navy frigate *Júpiter* when it crossed the Atlantic with a bevy of young Franciscans bound for the missionary fields of northern Sonora. Although the two had very different temperaments, they were the same age and

239

FIGURE 13. Pedro Font was assigned to El Templo de San Diego del Pitiquito (shown here) in Sonora when he died at the age of forty-three in 1781, just weeks after the slaying of his friend Francisco Garcés. Font went largely unmourned in his day.
Author's collection.

had traversed many dusty miles together in service of church and crown. They had much in common, but fate had reserved one final matter.

Font had served at Pitiquito for the last three years and had helped oversee completion of the lime-mortared brick church, which replaced a smaller chapel-like structure. For years an impoverished station with only primitive structures, Pitiquito had now begun to take on the appearance of a real mission, serving several hundred Native parishioners. On 27 August 1781 Font performed a wedding, after satisfying himself that the couple met the nuptial requirements of the church. He then entered the marriage in the record book in his neat handwriting, followed by his splashy rubric.

But his failing health was becoming apparent. For much of the last two decades he had been sick, suffering chronic diarrhea on the trail and recurring bouts of fever that likely were the result of malaria. "Becoming aggravated by various infirmities, he knew now that his afflictions were a presage of death," wrote the contemporary Franciscan historian Juan Domingo Arricivita. "This he accepted with Christian resignation." In his bed at Pitiquito, the last rites of the church were performed and he received communion (see figure 13).[1]

On 6 September, ten days after conducting the marriage, Font died. He was forty-three—the same age as Garcés at his death less than two months earlier. Following the custom of the time, Font's remains were interred under the altar of the newly built church. The memory of this consequential but acerbic padre soon vanished. Inside San Diego del Pitiquito today, there is no trace that he is buried under the stone floor. Among the Catholic faithful of Pitiquito, his name is forgotten.

At the time of Font's death, Juan Crespí was carrying out his duties at Mission San Carlos, headquarters of the Franciscan outposts in California, at present-day Carmel. He had served there continually for the last seven years, with his longtime companion Junípero Serra, after returning from the onerous maritime expedition under Captain Juan Pérez to the Pacific Northwest. At sixty, he had reached an advanced age for friars on the frontier.

As was the case with both Font and Garcés, Crespí seemed to anticipate his approaching death. Perhaps because the friars had an unshakeable belief in an afterlife to be spent with a beneficent God, declining health was readily seen as a sign that one's demise was at hand. Before it was too late, Crespí wished to visit his friend of more than forty years, Fray Francisco Palóu, who was overseeing Mission Dolores in San Francisco, 125 miles to the north. Although he had explored many thousands of miles of the Pacific coast by land and sea, Crespí had never seen Mission Dolores, founded five years earlier and officially named San Francisco de Asís.

Palóu and Crespí grew up together on the island of Mallorca, where Mallorquín, a variation of Catalán, was their shared first language. From encountering each other as boys, they had been reared together, attended school together, entered the Franciscan order at about the same time (Palóu was two years younger), and braved the Atlantic crossing to devote their lives to rescuing souls in the New World. In their youthful days of seminary study at the Convento de San Francisco in Palma de Mallorca, Crespí, Palóu, Serra, and a small cadre of like-minded padres showed their camaraderie by calling themselves *los condiscípulos* (schoolmates).[2] Palóu, more than anything else, was the link to the life Crespí had left behind three decades earlier and would never see again.

With Serra as his traveling companion, Crespí reached San Francisco on 28 October 1781. During the next fortnight he performed the confirmation rites for sixty-nine new Christians. Perhaps more important, he had time to reminisce with

Palóu and Serra. It must have been a bittersweet moment for the three men. "I had the happiness of seeing my dear fellow disciple," recorded Palóu, "and it seems that he came to bid me farewell until eternity."[3] On 9 November 1781 Crespí and Serra took their leave of Palóu. Their departure filled "my heart with grief, and theirs also," wrote Palóu, "as the pain of saying goodbye was quite as great as the joy with which I had welcomed them."[4]

Not long after his return to Mission San Carlos, Crespí was confined to his bed, suffering chest pains and inflammation of his legs, likely the result of a failing heart. His fellow friars consulted their *Florilegio Medícinal de Todas las Enfermedades,* an anthology of medical advice for times when no doctor was available, as was the case.[5] Crespí did not respond to whatever remedies were attempted. On the last day of 1781, he received the last rites, administered by Father Serra. The next morning around six o'clock he died.

The Requiem Mass was offered by Serra, who had lost his dearest friend, assisted by the two other padres of the mission. In attendance were the commander of the Monterey garrison and all of the soldiers. Also on their knees at the funeral service were the converted Indians who had known Crespí so well. According to Palóu's account their weeping "lamentations eloquently expressed the love which they had for him as their father."[6]

Serra praised Crespí as a model for a new generation of Franciscans, telling Palóu: "Oh! If only the Religious [men] of our [order] . . . were to see what he wrought and the great success he achieved, how many of them would be inspired to come here! Merely reading the journals [of Crespí] would suffice to move no few of them to leave homeland and native province, and take up the voyage to come and labor in this vineyard of the Lord."[7] In his own assessment, Palóu wrote: "God took him away to reward him for all these labors from which he had suffered in so many journeys by sea and land, and I do not doubt he will have great glory in heaven, for they were all directed to these spiritual conquests."[8]

At Serra's direction, Crespí's remains were placed under the altar on the Gospel, or left, side of the church. A little more than two years later, as Serra lay on his own deathbed, surrounded by his compatriots, he paid one more posthumous tribute to his old friend: "[L]ooking straight at me, he said [to Palóu]: I want you to bury me in the church, really close beside Father Fray Juan Crespí."[9] The two remain side by side today in the sanctuary of Mission San Carlos. Crespí's crypt bears the simple title, "Compañero de Serra."

Epilogue

An Imperfect Legacy

> A martyr is not crowned by death only, but also by the purpose
> of the will, for on the latter is reckoned the crown of martyrdom.
> —Saint John Chrysostom

At the order of Lieutenant Colonel Pedro Fages, the unearthed remains of Francisco Garcés and those of the three other Franciscans slain in the Yuma uprising of July 1781 were transported in a wooden cigarette crate wrapped in burlap to the garrison at Altar in northern Sonora, a trip by mule of more than 250 miles. The bodies were then taken to nearby Tubutama, where the mission church was set in a broad lowland surrounded by cultivated fields of wheat, Indian corn, and beans. Pomegranate and peach trees shaded the courtyard. With appropriate solemnity the bones of the padres were interred under the Gospel side of the main altar.

A dozen years later the superior of the College of Santa Cruz in Querétaro petitioned to have the remains shipped there for burial. Getting permission was a bureaucratic ordeal, even though all four men had been sons of the College of Santa Cruz. Finally, on 14 July 1793 Father Francisco Antonio Barbastro, padre-presidente of the Sonoran missions, reported to Querétaro: "I wrote to the Bishop and succeeded in lifting the embargo on the bones of our brothers and got the license to carry them to the college. They will be carried by the muleteer, Felix, who leaves for that city this week from the village of San Miguel de Horacitas with orders to deliver his cargo to the college where he will be paid for the freight hauling."[1] This entailed a journey of more than twelve hundred miles.

On 19 July 1794, the thirteenth anniversary of Garcés's death, the martyred missionaries were given an honorable burial in a crypt under the main altar at the hilltop College of Santa Cruz. Their remains were comingled in a locked box made of juniper and trimmed in iron, measuring thirty inches by sixteen inches.[2] The key was interred with the coffin. When the crypt was opened in the mid-twentieth century, it was found to contain multiple bones and three skulls. The head of

Father José Matías Moreno, which had been hacked off by the Indians at Yuma, was never found.

At the reburial ceremony in Querétaro a sermon was delivered by thirty-two-year-old Father Diego Miguel Bringas de Manzaneda y Encinas, a brilliant and prolific Franciscan writer, described by one of his fellow College of Santa Cruz brothers as "an excellent orator." Quoting a letter written by the apostle Paul to the Philippians, Bringas declared: "Jesus Christ will be glorified in my body, whether through life, or through death, because his spirit gives me life, and to die for him is my greatest interest."[3] He continued: "I remember you, Francisco Garcés . . . but I confess that just the simple sight of your glorious deeds confuses me, surprises me, and makes me feel the hardships of your time in silence and in awe. I hear you tell me: I have worked more than others, continuously fatigued, at every step in the arms of death . . . exposed to the swift currents of the rivers, the insults of thieves, the ferocity of the unconverted, the risks of loneliness, the lack of sleep, afflicted by hunger, tormented by thirst, consumed by fasting, freezing cold, suffering nakedness."[4] Describing Garcés's ascetic life, Bringas noted that he gave away most of his small luxuries to the Indians, that he never used tobacco, that he usually passed up chocolate for breakfast, and that many times on his long wanderings he ate what the impoverished Natives ate—roots, mice, lizards, squirrels—and "in extreme moments of necessity the disgusting meat of a horse."[5] The preacher concluded his sermon with a plea for his listeners to ask the Lord to grant the four Franciscans everlasting life and to place "their souls at rest in the eternal tabernacles of peace."[6]

Although Pedro Font was not the subject of the eulogy, Bringas cited briefly the friar's accomplishments. There is no record of what if anything was said in praise of Font upon his death nearly thirteen years earlier at Pitiquito. Writing a few years before Bringas, Fray Juan Domingo Arricivita, the official historian of the College of Santa Cruz, posthumously lauded Font's perseverance on the trail. "He not only had to endure the many discomforts and hazards . . . but also it was especially hard for him on account of his poor health," wrote Arricivita.[7] For the most part, however, Font was unmourned in his own day.

Lacking Font's prickly character, Juan Crespí was the subject of much affection and praise upon his death in 1782 at Mission San Carlos on the California coast at modern-day Carmel. Father Junípero Serra, the most influential Californian of his day, heaped kind words on Crespí, as did Crespí's lifelong friend, the Franciscan chronicler Francisco Palóu. Even so, the priceless journals kept by Crespí of the seminal Portolá explorations and the maritime expedition to Alaska went largely unnoticed for almost a century after his death. This humble padre who lived his life "with dovelike simplicity," in Palóu's words, was easy to overlook.[8]

The legacy of these three pious frontiersmen is an amalgamation of successes and failures. But their complex record is not reflected in either the overly romanticized view of the missions once taught in California elementary schools or in the overheated charges of genocide leveled against the Franciscans by some contemporary scholars.

Pope Francis's elevation of Serra to sainthood during a papal visit to the United States in 2015 spurred renewed debate over the padres' role in Spain's transitory conquest of the Pacific coast. Examining the Franciscans' conduct through the lens of contemporary standards, some observers have adopted a revisionist view that condemns the friars as the prime agents of Native repression and mass extermination. Within the short span of a generation or so, the academic narrative of Spain's eighteenth-century venture into California shifted profoundly from that of a heroic expansion of European civilization over benighted aborigines to a cruel oppression of unspoiled indigenous peoples. Sloganeering often substituted for scholarship. The term "Indian," which even most Native Americans would regard as neutral, implying no disrespect, was branded by some modern critics as loathsome. "When the Spanish arrived in California and pronounced that Native Americans were savages, ensnared by Satan and requiring instruction in civilization," declared Ramón A. Gutiérrez, professor of ethnic studies at the University of California at San Diego, "they concluded that these people had a history, but one that had to be obliterated. By calling them 'Indians,' the incredible complexity and diversity of Native peoples and cultures in California was erased; henceforth Native Americans would share a subjective legal identity as 'Indians.'"[9]

The California Native American Heritage Commission, established by the legislature in 1976, is funded by the state government and overseen by nine Native American commissioners. The panel's official viewpoint embraces the revisionist perspective:

> The impact of the mission system on the many coastal tribes was devastating. Missionaries required tribes to abandon their aboriginal territories and live in filthy, disease ridden and crowded labor camps. Massive herds [of] introduced stock animals and new seed crops soon crowded out aboriginal game animals and native plants. Feral hogs ate tons of raw acorns, depriving even the non-missionized tribes in the interior of a significant amount of aboriginal protein. Murderous

waves of epidemic diseases swept over the terrified Mission Indian tribes resulting in massive suffering and death for thousands of Native men, women and children. The short life expectancy of mission Indians prompted missionaries to vigorously pursue runaways and coerce interior tribes into supplying more and more laborers for the padres. Missionary activities therefore thoroughly disrupted not only coastal tribes, but their demand for healthy laborers seriously impacted adjacent interior tribes. Finally by 1836 the Mexican Republic forcibly stripped the padres of the power to coerce labor from the Indians and the mission[s] rapidly collapsed. About 100,000 or nearly a third of the aboriginal population of California died as a direct consequence of the missions of California.[10]

Sherburne F. Cook, a mid-twentieth-century pioneer in California ethnohistory, helped spark a broad reexamination of the mission system by bringing forth a wealth of fresh data culled from Spanish colonial records. He provided the first detailed look at how frequently corporal discipline—flogging, confinement in shackles or stocks, imprisonment at hard labor, execution—was imposed by the padres. From 1775 to 1831, there were ninety-four recorded cases of disciplinary action taken against a total of 392 individuals, according to Cook's findings. The offenses ranged from adultery (twenty-five lashes) to stealing livestock (imprisonment, hard labor), and conspiracy with armed resistance (death).[11] The most common crime was "fugitivism," which meant an Indian who had voluntarily joined a mission returned to his village in violation of the padres' strict rules. Whenever possible, deserters were rounded up by Spanish soldiers and returned in chains. The usual punishment was incarceration at hard labor and/or flogging. Based on records compiled by the friars themselves, flogging consisted of up to one hundred lashes for robbery or up to twenty-five lashes a day for nine consecutive days for striking a priest. In practice, the beatings were meted out by Indians who were loyal to the padres.

"Corporal punishment, or flogging, was of course standard practice in the eighteenth century among all white civilizations, particularly when used upon so-called inferior races," Cook noted. "Nevertheless it has been singularly ineffective for . . . the result is usually to inspire [the victim] with an undying, implacable hatred, which in turn communicates itself to all his friends. . . . It was therefore unfortunate that the lash was so quickly resorted to by the Spanish administration and applied with such severity."[12]

Cook's research directly contradicted the claims of Fermín Lasuén, who succeeded Serra as padre-presidente of the California missions. Writing in November 1800 in response to opponents of the Franciscans' practices, Lasuén declared: "The treatment generally accorded the Indians is very gentle. . . . In order to resort to severity (and then only to the minimum extent) it is requisite to have exhausted the ultimate efforts of kindness—in the manner of a gentle and discreet family father with his children. . . . [H]owever grave and serious the misdeed may be, it is never ordered to give anyone more than twenty-five lashes and with an instrument incapable of drawing blood or of causing notable contusions."[13] Font's firsthand account of a Native brutalized by a severe whipping at Mission San Diego (see Chapter 8) also contradicted Lasuén.

Given that the missionaries' overriding objective was to save Indian souls and to assimilate the Natives into Spanish culture, why did they impose corporal punishment on such a scale? Some modern scholars attribute their actions to a calculated campaign of genocide. But in truth the term "genocide," which is the deliberate and systematic extermination of a group, has no meaning if it is applied here. Nor does the word "slavery" fit, even though it is commonly bandied about. No Spaniard on the frontier, least of all the priests, claimed ownership of the indigenous people.

The Franciscan fathers' purpose was to transform the Natives into good Christians and loyal subjects of King Carlos III. The straightforward explanation for their harsh discipline was that they believed it was necessary to acculturate Indians to Spanish ways. The padres did not want to eliminate the Natives but, rather, turn them into Spaniards. Allowing the missionized Indians, called neophytes, to return to their villages was seen as an inevitable regression of the acculturation process. Serra complained that neophytes who retired to their villages for a few days or weeks "came back to us from the gentiles [unbaptized Indians] so changed that we could hardly recognize them."[14]

The Franciscans' "aim was to produce a 'civilized' Christian Native who, like the European peasant, labored for daily bread, received the sacraments, married and produced offspring within the fold of matrimony, prayed daily, went to church on Sunday and festive days, knew his or her place in society, and died a Christian," wrote the modern historian Maria F. Wade. "This was the program of conversion and socialization. It was simple, inflexible, and for most Native Americans, culturally distasteful."[15] The padres' methods were misguided, to be sure, but they were not by any definition genocidal.

The colonial account books showed that between 1769 and 1831, when the Mexican government began to confiscate the missions and their extensive landholdings, thirty-four hundred baptized Indians took flight from the padres.[16] This represented about 4 percent of the total Indian population of the missions. Those who were apprehended were routinely asked why they had absconded. As recorded by Cook, many fled because they had been beaten or because they had not been given enough to eat. Others who had loved ones die at the missions from contagious European diseases said they escaped to avoid the same fate.

One of the most virulent afflictions passed on to the Indians was syphilis, which appeared in California within the first decade of the Spaniards' arrival. Although the cause of this pestilence was not well understood, everyone knew it was spread by sexual contact. The extent to which it rapidly infected the Native population, claiming thousands of lives, underscored not only the rampant sexual abuses of Spanish soldiers but also the robust level of nonmonogamous sexual relations among the Indians.

As governor of California in 1782, Pedro Fages issued an order stating that "the officers and men of these presidios are conducting and behaving themselves in the missions with a vicious license which is very prejudicial on account of the scandalous disorders which they commit with gentile [unbaptized Indians] and Christian women. I adjure you to prevent the continuance of such dangerous behavior."[17] By 1811, one Spanish observer testified, the Natives "are permeated to the marrow of their bones with venereal disease, such that many of the newly born show immediately this, the only patrimony they receive from their parents, and for which reason three-quarters of the infants die in their first or second year, and of the other quarter which survives, most fail to reach their twenty-fifth year."[18]

Sexually transmitted diseases reduced the fertility of Indian women, accelerating the Native population decline. But this was a wholly unintended consequence of sexual relations, at least initially, between infected Spanish soldiers and Indian women, even though much of this was attributable to outright rape. There was no deliberate campaign to introduce syphilis and other European diseases among the Indians to promote their extinction.

Of other diseases such as smallpox and measles that inflicted many deaths, due to the Natives' lack of previous exposure and natural immunity, the Spaniards were clueless as to the causes or cures. The padres regularly lamented the awful death toll during epidemics, but they were powerless to stem the losses. Locking up the unmarried Indian women in confined dormitories at night no doubt promoted the spread of infectious pathogens. But this was done unwittingly by the Franciscans to protect the women and girls from sexual predators.

The traditional view of historians was that the missions at least provided a mostly stable and nutritious diet for Native Americans who often faced malnutrition in the wild. Indeed, the Franciscans were quick to admit that many of their new

Christian adherents joined the missions only because of the food, which usually consisted of three meals a day, including *atole,* a drinkable soup of barley or corn, and a thicker stew, posole, made of grains, peas, and beans, generally fortified with some meat. Cow's milk added protein to the diet. It is important to note that some missions, notably San Diego, fell well short of offering three meals a day on a regular basis. When food was in short supply because of crop failures or other reasons, the Indians were told to return to their villages and forage on their own. Food also was withheld as a disciplinary measure.

The revisionist outlook of some anthropologists today is that the Indians' conventional regimen of ground acorns, mesquite pods, pine nuts, and wild grass seeds, accompanied by the meat of small game such as rabbits and squirrels, was more nutritional and reliable than the products of Spanish agriculture and animal husbandry. Feeding milk to the Indians has come under criticism on grounds that the Natives lacked an enzyme necessary to digest milk after about age five. Under such conditions, milk can promote diarrhea. "The missions could not know about the enzyme problem, which exists for most non-European peoples," asserted Florence Shipek, who studied the Kumeyaay of Southern California extensively, "but they observed the health difference for Indians on their own food supplies but took no action based upon that observation, allowing only occasional trips to the mountains for acorns."[19]

For some modern researchers, the Spaniards' introduction of agriculture and domesticated animals was by itself a form of biological conquest over the Natives. "The colonial invaders of California conquered the land as well as the people, fortified by their cultural traditions and religious beliefs of an innate sovereignty and superiority over all forms of non-Christian life, including the plants, animals, and native people," observed William Preston, a professor of geography at California Polytechnic University, San Luis Obispo.[20] From this extreme perspective, all European encroachment in the New World was pernicious.

One charge that the Franciscans, and all other Spaniards of the frontier, can never escape is that they viewed Native Americans through "Eurocentric" eyes. This criticism is as irrefutable as it is unsurprising. Of course the inheritors of Spanish culture regarded the Indians as primitive. Most Natives along the California coast were hunter-gatherers. They lacked not only such European advances as agriculture, iron implements, and firearms but also the ability to write and read in their own languages or raise livestock. Most of the men went about naked, a Stone Age condition in the minds of Spaniards. For thousands of years Western civilization was rooted in the ideal of material progress from one generation to the next. Other societies, whether European or aboriginal, were judged accordingly.

That Spaniards reflexively saw Indians as uncivilized is hardly an astonishing revelation. The contrast between the underpinnings of European cultures and those of Native cultures could not have been more stark. "I have yet to encounter a tribal tradition in which there is anything remotely resembling the notion of progress," explains contemporary Native American cultural anthropologist Alfonso Ortiz. "It is a distortion, when people who deify a notion like progress, and regard it as inevitable, write about Indian people with the assumption that they too are caught up in and with the notion of progress. . . . [P]erhaps we Indian people who survived with the essences of our cultures intact really want to make contributions first and foremost to the continued survival and perpetuation of these cultures, rather than to something that is called 'civilization,' which is, after all, alien to our traditional cultures, and usually antagonistic to them as well."[21] The noted twentieth-century anthropologist Alfred L. Kroeber, who spent decades studying California tribes, construed it this way: "The Indian was satisfied with his life and his culture, customs and his ways and his ideas. . . . They did not think in terms of progress as such. They thought in terms of achieving a satisfactory method of living."[22]

The California Native American Heritage Commission echoes the contemporary charge that the Franciscans herded the Indians into "labor camps," where their exertions constructing brick and mortar buildings, working the fields, or tending the livestock were "coerced." There can be no doubt that the Natives—men, women, and children—did almost all of the manual labor required to build the missions and make them sustainable, from pounding oak bark for the tannery to cooking the meals and doing the laundry. But typically there were only two padres assigned to remote outposts, and only a few dozen leatherjacket soldiers at the presidios, which often were separated from the missions by many miles. The pair of padres at each mission oversaw the work of several hundred Indians.

Under such conditions, physical compulsion of the Indian laborers by Franciscans was simply not plausible. Other, less harsh methods were surely employed, such as rewarding those who worked with food and withholding it from those who did not. "[N]early everything grown or manufactured in the missions, presidios, and pueblos resulted from the labor of Indians," explained Steven W. Hackel, associate professor of history at the University of California, Riverside. In California, "despite the rapid decline in the Native population, the population of the *gente de razón* (Spaniards and others of European descent) never approached that of the Indians.

In the coastal portion . . . that Spain controlled, scholars estimate that Indians outnumbered the soldiers and settlers 59,700 to 150 in 1770."[23]

In a 1797 report, California governor Diego de Borica stated that the missionized Indians suffered from "the labor which until recently they have performed . . . without regard to their feeble constitutions."[24] During his tenure Borica requested dispatches detailing the working conditions at various missions. As compiled by Sherburne F. Cook, the reports provide a comprehensive account of the Indians' daily routine.

About an hour after sunrise and following a breakfast of communal atole, the Indians were summoned by the ringing of the mission bell to the quadrangle, where work assignments were handed out. (One contemporary observer noted that the thickest part of the atole at the bottom of boiling pots was given to the children who recited their religious lessons best.) Males, females, and youngsters were then given tasks to perform. Generally, only the elderly and women in advanced pregnancy or nursing their newborns were exempted from work entirely. Men and women often engaged in the same heavy labor, such as hauling rocks for building construction or toting sand and cow dung for brick making. "I have seen several Indian women with children at the breast carrying adobes, some pregnant but not in an advanced stage," declared one 1798 report to Governor Borica.[25] Another stated that nursing mothers were allowed to stay at home until they decided on their own to participate in such activities as carrying wood, stoking the cooking fires, or grinding wheat by hand on a *metate,* or stone mortar. Children age nine and older were assigned to pulling weeds in the vegetable garden, chasing birds from the crops, combing wool for the looms and passing the shuttles to the weavers, or guarding the wet bricks and roof tiles laid out to dry in the sun so that animals did not tread on them.

After a midday break of about two hours (as measured by the sundial), during which another meal was served, work resumed for a shorter period in the afternoon. Writing in 1786 of the daily regimen at Mission San Carlos (see figure 14), the Frenchman Jean François de La Pérouse explained, "At noon the bells give notice of the time of dinner. The Indians then quit their work, and send for their allowance [of food] in the same vessel as at breakfast. But this second soup is thicker than the former, and contains a mixture of wheat, maize, peas, and beans. The Indians call it pozole. They return to work from two to four or five o'clock, when they repair to evening prayer, which lasts nearly an hour and is followed by a distribution of atole, the same as at breakfast. These three distributions are sufficient for the subsistence of the greater number of these Indians."[26]

FIGURE 14. The French explorer Jean François de La Pérouse was given a ceremonial welcome at Monterey in 1786. In his journal La Pérouse documented floggings of Indians who disobeyed the Franciscans' strict rules. Copy of an original drawing by Gaspard Duché de Vancy, an artist with La Pérouse.
Courtesy of the Robert B. Honeyman Jr. Collection of Early Californian and Western American Pictorial Material, The Bancroft Library, University of California, Berkeley.

The work day was longer in summer than in winter but averaged six to eight hours a day, five or six days a week, for a total of thirty to forty hours, according to Cook's findings. No work was done on Sunday or religious feast days, which totaled up to ninety-two days a year.[27] "There is no doubt that by modern standards the work was very reasonable both as to hours and nature," Cook concluded. The adult Natives were "not obligated to perform labor which could in any way be injurious physically in either the individual or racial sense. The only possible exceptions were the pregnant women and the children. . . . The purely physical effects of manual labor may therefore be dismissed as a factor effective in the racial disintegration of the mission Indian."[28]

In practice, a handful of Spanish clerics orchestrated nearly every aspect of the day-to-day lives of tens of thousands of Indians who chose to live and work at the twenty-one California missions while at least appearing to learn the Catholic catechism and become good Christians. "Mission Indians—neophytes—constituted the core of the colony. They were the work force upon which all else was built," wrote present-day historian James A. Sandos. "Creating that human base was the task of the Franciscans, who sought to persuade gardeners and hunter-gatherers to abandon coastal plains and forests to become sedentary farmers and pastoralists in a new life. . . . Priests employed the immersion system of conversion by taking complete control of their wards' lives from cradle to grave."[29]

Before rushing to harsh judgments about the Franciscans, one should compare how Native Americans were treated by the American, English, and other European settlers of the eastern half of North America. The leading twentieth-century historian of California, Herbert Eugene Bolton, put it aptly: "[T]he missions were a force which made for the preservation of the Indians, as opposed to their destruction, so characteristic of the Anglo-American frontier. In the English colonies the only good Indians were dead Indians. In the Spanish colonies it was thought worthwhile to improve the natives for this life as well as for the next."[30]

If we face history honestly, and objectively, we must conclude that Pedro Font, Francisco Garcés, and Juan Crespí dedicated their lives to what they perceived to be the betterment of the indigenous people. They cast aside their comfortable lives in Spain and endured tremendous hardships and uncertainties in order to save Native souls from eternal damnation, which was not an abstract possibility in their minds but an absolute certainty. They lived purposeful lives. In the process, these uncommon men scattered on the west coast of North America the spores of European civilization, imperfect though it was. Their aims were entirely humanitarian, as they defined it in their way and in their day. This is where our twenty-first-century assessment of them should begin and end.

Notes

PROLOGUE

Epigraph: Letter to Messrs. Griffin, Martinez, Prince, and other Gentlemen at Santa Fé, 20 July 1883, published in the *Philadelphia Press*, 5 August 1883; original in the Huntington Library, San Marino, California.

1. Pedro Font to Friar Diego Ximénez, very reverend father guardian of the College of Santa Cruz, Querétaro, 30 November 1776, trans. Dan S. Matson, *Ethnohistory* 22.3 (Summer 1975).
2. Ibid.
3. Juan Nentvig, S.J., *Rudo Ensayo: A Description of Sonora and Arizona in 1764*, trans. Alberto Francisco Pradeau and Robert R. Rasmussen (Tucson: University of Arizona Press, 1980), 79.
4. Ibid.
5. Ibid.
6. Ibid., 81.
7. Zephyrin Engelhardt, *The Franciscans in Arizona* (Harbor Springs, Mich.: Holy Childhood Indian School, 1897; repr., Whitefish, Mont.: Kessinger Legacy Reprints, 2007), 183.
8. Font to Ximénez, 18 July 1776, *Ethnohistory* 22.3 (Summer 1975).
9. Derek Hayes, *Historical Atlas of California* (Berkeley: University of California Press, 2007), 42.
10. Francisco Palóu, O.F.M., *Francisco Palóu's Life and Apostolic Labors of the Venerable Father Junípero Serra: Founder of the Franciscan Missions of California*, trans. C. Scott Williams (Pasadena, Calif.: George Wharton James, 1913), 9.
11. John L. Kessell, "The Making of a Martyr: The Young Francisco Garcés," *New Mexico Historical Review* 45 (July 1970): 187.
12. "Apuntes históricos sobre el Colegio de Misioneros de Hebrón de la Esclarecida Orden de S. Francisco," ibid.
13. José M. Bardavio, *California Empieza en Aragón*, pamphlet published by Comisión Aragonesa, 1992.
14. Original baptismal record in parish church of Santa Ana, Morata de Jalón, Zaragoza, Spain, reviewed by the author.

15. Kessell, "The Making of a Martyr," 184.
16. Ibid., 188.
17. Garcés to Viceroy Bucareli, Tubac, 8 March 1773, in Herbert Eugene Bolton, trans., *Anza's California Expeditions*, vol. 5, *Correspondence* (Berkeley: University of California Press, 1930; repr., New York: Russell and Russell, 1966), 68.
18. Romualdo Cartegena to Bucareli, Querétaro, 29 January 1773, in Scott Jarvis Maughan, "Francisco Garcés and New Spain's Northwestern Frontier, 1768–1781" (PhD diss., University of Utah, 1968), 97.
19. Herbert E. Bolton, "The Early Explorations of Father Garcés on the Pacific Slope," in *The Pacific Ocean in History: Papers and Addresses Presented at the Panama-Pacific Historical Congress, Held at San Francisco, Berkeley and Palo Alto, California, July 19–23, 1915*, ed. Henry Morse Stephens and Herbert E. Bolton (New York: Macmillan, 1917).
20. Maynard Geiger, *Franciscan Missionaries in Hispanic California, 1769–1848* (San Marino, Calif.: Huntington Library, 1969), 51.
21. Ibid.
22. Juan Crespí, *A Description of Distant Roads: Original Journals of the First Expedition into California, 1769–1770*, ed. and trans. Alan K. Brown (San Diego, Calif.: San Diego State University Press, 2001), 6.
23. Ibid., 8.
24. Martin P. Harney, *The Jesuits in History: The Society of Jesus through Four Centuries* (New York: American Press, 1941), 292–343.
25. James Culleton, *Indians and Pioneers of Old Monterey* (Fresno, Calif.: Academy of California Church History, 1950), 58. In the first inventory book at Mission San Carlos Borromeo, Crespí described La Sonoreña as "una mula colorada vieja"—an old red mule. Inventory books can be found in the collection at Santa Barbara Mission Archives.
26. Crespí, *A Description of Distant Roads*, 193, 195.
27. Palóu, *Junípero Serra*, 231.
28. Font cited from Crespí, *A Description of Distant Roads*, 62.
29. Herbert Eugene Bolton, trans., *Fray Juan Crespí, Missionary Explorer on the Pacific Coast, 1769–1774* (Berkeley: University of California Press, 1927), xvii.
30. Mark Williams, *The Story of Spain* (Málaga, Spain: Santana Books, 2009), 114.
31. Francis F. Guest, *Hispanic California Revisited* (published by Santa Barbara Mission Archive Library, 1966), 143.
32. Ibid., 144.
33. Engelhardt, *The Franciscans in Arizona*, 180.
34. Report of Bishop Antonio de los Reyes, 6 July 1772, translated by Kieran McCarty, found on the website of Tumacácori National Historic Park, U.S. Park Service, available at https://www.nps.gov/tuma/.
35. Letter to the Apostolic College of San Fernando, 2 February 1820 (Santa Barbara Mission Archives), quoted in Douglas Cutter and Iris Engstrand, "Father President

Mariano Payeras: A View of the California Missions," in *The Human Tradition in California*, ed. Clark Davis and David Igler (Wilmington, Del.: Scholarly Resources, 2002), 24.
36. Steven M. Karr, "Pablo Tac: Native Peoples in Precontact California," in Davis and Igler, *The Human Tradition in California*, 12.
37. Ibid.
38. Lee Motz, Eric W. Witter, and James Rock, "Glass Trade Beads from Two Shasta Sites in Siskiyou County, California," *Journal of California and Great Basin Anthropology* 8 (1986): 116–28.
39. Pablo Tac, "Indian Life and Customs at Mission San Luis Rey: A Record of California Mission Life," in *Ethnology of the Alta California Indians*, ed. Lowell John Bean and Sylvia Brakke Vane (New York: Garland Publishing, 1991), 94.
40. Kevin Starr, *California: A History* (New York: Modern Library Chronicles, 2007), 41–42.

CHAPTER 1

1. Fray Juan Crespí to Fray Francisco Palóu, San Diego, 9 June 1769, in Bolton, *Fray Juan Crespí*, 5.
2. Donald Eugene Smith and Frederick J. Teggart, eds., *Diary of Gaspar de Portolá during the California Expedition of 1769–1770* (Berkeley: University of California, 1909), 39. For the description of the battle gear, see Miguel Costansó, *The Portolá Expedition, 1769–1770: Diary of Miguel Costansó*, trans. Manuel Carpio and Frederick J. Teggart, Publications of the Academy of Pacific Coast History 2, No. 4 (Berkeley: University of California, 1911; repr., n.p.: General Books, 2010), hereafter cited as Costansó, *Diary*. In the time of the padres, a leatherjacket was not only the protective covering but also the man who wore it.
3. Virginia E. Thickens and Margaret Mollins, trans. and eds., "Putting a Lid on California: An Unpublished Diary of the Portolá Expedition by José de Cañizares," *California Historical Society Quarterly* (September 1952): 351.
4. Crespí, *A Description of Distant Roads*, 235.
5. "Instructions issued at Cabo San Lucas, 20 February 1769," trans. Maynard Geiger, *Southern California Quarterly* 47 (1965): 209.
6. Thickens and Mollins, "Putting a Lid on California," 123.
7. See David I. Harvie, *Limeys: The Conquest of Scurvy* (Gloucestershire, England: Sutton Publishing, 2002).
8. "Diary of Sebastian Vizcaíno, 1602–1603" (American Journeys Collection, Document No. AJ-002, Wisconsin Historical Society Digital Library and Archives), 88.
9. Crespí, *A Description of Distant Roads*, 48.
10. Donald C. Cutter, ed., *The California Coast: A Bilingual Edition of Documents from the Sutro Collection* (Norman: University of Oklahoma Press, 1969), 139.

11. *The Portolá Expedition of 1769–1770, Diary of Vicente Vila*, ed. Robert Selden Rose, Publications of the Academy of Pacific Coast History 2, no. 1 (Berkeley: University of California, 1911), 15.
12. Entry for 9 March 1769, ibid., 47.
13. "Pedro Fages and Miguel Costansó: Two Early Letters from San Diego in 1769," ed. and trans. Iris Wilson Engstrand, *Journal of San Diego History* 21 (Spring 1975).
14. Crespí, *A Description of Distant Roads*, 48.
15. Ibid., 44.
16. Harry W. Crosby, *Gateway to Alta California: The Expedition to San Diego, 1769* (El Cajon, Calif.: Sunbelt, 2003), 59.
17. Pedro Fages, *A Historical, Political, and Natural Description of California by Pedro Fages, Soldier of Spain, Dutifully Made for the Viceroy in the Year 1775*, trans. Herbert Ingram Priestly (Berkeley: University of California Press, 1937), 50.
18. Antonine Tibesar, O.F.M., ed. *Writings of Junípero Serra* (Oceanside, Calif.: Academy of American Franciscan History, 1955), 1:134.
19. Crespí, *A Description of Distant Roads*, 187.
20. Ibid.
21. Junípero Serra, *Diary of Fra Junípero Serra, O.F.M., Being an Account of His Journey from Loreto to San Diego, March 28 to June 30, 1769* (North Providence, R.I.: Franciscan Missionaries of Mary, n.d.), 55.
22. Crespí, *A Description of Distant Roads*, 211.
23. Crosby, *Gateway to Alta California*, 55.
24. Thickens and Mollins, "Putting a Lid on California," 350.
25. José de Cañizares, "An Unpublished Diary of the Portolá Expedition by José de Cañizares," trans. and ed. Virginia E. Thickens, *California Historical Society Quarterly* 31.2 (June 1952): 109–24.
26. Crespí to Palóu, San Diego, 9 June 1769, in Bolton, *Fray Juan Crespí*, 5.
27. Gaspar de Portolá to Viceroy Marquis de Croix, San Diego, 4 July 1769, in F. Boneu Companys, *Gaspar de Portolá, Explorer and Founder of California*, trans. Alan K. Brown (Lerda, Spain: Instituto de Estudios Llerdenses, 1983), 397.
28. Crespí to Palóu, San Diego, 22 June 1769, in Bolton, *Fray Juan Crespí*, 14.
29. Crespí, *A Description of Distant Roads*, 251.
30. Portolá to Croix, San Diego, 4 July 1769, in Companys, *Gaspar de Portolá*, 397.
31. Miguel Costansó, *Narrative of the Portolá Expedition of 1769–1770*, trans. and ed. Adolph van Hemert-Engert and Frederick J. Teggart, Publications of the Academy of Pacific Coast History 1, No. 2 (Berkeley: University of California, 1910), 22.
32. Crespí to Fray Juan Andres, guardian of the College of San Fernando, San Diego, 22 June 1769, in Bolton, *Fray Juan Crespí*, 17.
33. Fages, *Natural Description of California*, 11.
34. Crespí to Palóu, 9 June 1769, in Bolton, *Fray Juan Crespí*, 5

35. J. N. Bowen, "The Rose of Castile," *Western Folklore* 6 (July 1947): 204.
36. Serra, *Diary of Fra Junípero Serra*, 42.
37. Crespí to Andres, San Diego, 22 June 1769, in Bolton, *Fray Juan Crespí*, 19.
38. Donald Eugene Smith and Frederick John Teggert, trans., *Diary of the Journey That Don Gaspar de Portolá, Captain of Dragoons in the España Regiment, Governor of the Californias, Made by Land to the Ports of San Diego and Monterey*, Publications of the Academy of Pacific Coast History 1, No. 3 (Berkeley: University of California, 1909; repr., n.p.: Bibliolife, n.d.), 13 (hereafter cited as Smith and Teggart, *Diary of Gaspar de Portolá*).
39. Portolá to Croix, San Diego, 17 April 1770, in Companys, *Gaspar de Portolá*, 397.
40. Companys, *Gaspar de Portolá*, 146; Portolá to Croix, 4 July 1769, ibid., 397.
41. Palóu, *Junípero Serra*, 79.
42. Portolá to Croix, San Diego, 4 July 1769, in Companys, *Gaspar de Portolá*, 397.
43. Susan E. Hough, "Writing on the Wall: Geological Context and Early American Spiritual Beliefs," *U.S. Geological Survey* (Pasadena, Calif.: U.S. Geological Survey, n.d.), 112–13.

CHAPTER 2

1. Geiger, *Franciscan Missionaries*, 109.
2. Crespí, *A Description of Distant Roads*, 295.
3. Ibid.
4. Accounts of the precise number of participants on this leg of the Portolá expedition vary slightly. The figure 67 was compiled by Father Zephyrin Engelhardt, O.F.M., in *The Missions and Missionaries of California, San Francisco or Mission Dolores* (Chicago: Franciscan Herald Press, 1924).
5. Crosby, *Gateway to Alta California*, 168.
6. Ibid., 169.
7. Around 78 A.D., Pliny the Elder, in his *Natural History* (trans. W. H. S. Jones), wrote that mustard "is extremely beneficial for the health. It grows entirely wild, though it is improved by being transplanted: but on the other hand when it has once been sown it is scarcely possible to get the place free of it, as the seed when it falls germinates at once" (Loeb Classical Library, 1956)
8. Crespí, *A Description of Distant Roads*, 305.
9. Smith and Teggart, *Diary of Gaspar de Portolá*, 21.
10. Miguel Costansó, "A Journal of the Overland Voyage Made to the Northwest of California . . . ," trans. Alan K. Brown, in Companys, *Gaspar de Portolá*, 171.
11. Crespí, *A Description of Distant Roads*, 321.
12. Ibid., 341.
13. Fages, *Natural Description of California*, 33.
14. Ibid., 34; Crespí, *A Description of Distant Roads*, 426.

15. Costansó, *Diary*, 53.
16. Ibid., 58; Fages, *Natural Description of California*, 36.
17. Crespí, *A Description of Distant Roads*, 429; Fages, *Natural Description of California*, 39.
18. Crespí, *A Description of Distant Roads*, 469.
19. Costansó, *Diary*, 39.
20. Crespí, *A Description of Distant Roads*, 789n84.
21. Costansó, *Diary*; Crespí, *A Description of Distant Roads*, 509.
22. Crespí, *A Description of Distant Roads*, 509. "Diary of Gaspar de Portolá during the California Expedition of 1769–1770," Read Books Design, 2010, p.43.
23. Crespí, *A Description of Distant Roads*, 790n104.
24. Letter written by Sebastián Vizcaíno from Monterey harbor, 28 December 1602, a copy of which was sent to the viceroy in Mexico City, translated by George Butler Griffin, in *Publications of the Historical Society of Southern California* 2 (1907): 65–68.
25. Crespí, *A Description of Distant Roads*, 541.
26. Crespí to José de Gálvez, San Diego, 9 February 1770, in Bolton, *Fray Juan Crespí*, 42.
27. Gaspar de Portolá, "Report No. 1, First Council of War of the Land-Expedition Which Went in Search of the Port of Monterey. Held on the 4th of October, 1769," in Smith and Teggart, *Diary of Gaspar de Portolá*, 83.
28. Costansó, *Diary*, 57.
29. Hubert Howe Bancroft, *History of California*, vols. 18–24 of *The Works of Hubert Howe Bancroft* (1884–90; facs. ed., Santa Barbara, CA: Wallace Hebard, 1963), 18:155.
30. Crespí, *A Description of Distant Roads*, 541.
31. Fages, *Natural Description of California*, 13.
32. Crespí to Palóu, San Diego, 6 February 1770, in Bolton, *Fray Juan Crespí*, 21.
33. Companys, *Gaspar de Portolá*, 251.
34. Costansó, *Diary*, 62.
35. Ibid., 66.
36. Ibid., 269.
37. Crespí, *A Description of Distant Roads*, 639.
38. Costansó, *Diary*, 66.
39. Crespí, *A Description of Distant Roads*, 671.
40. Crespí to Gálvez, 9 February 1770, in Bolton, *Fray Juan Crespí*, 46.
41. Michael E. Thurman, *The Naval Department of San Blas, New Spain's Bastion for Alta California and Nootka, 1767 to 1798* (Glendale, Calif.: Arthur H. Clark Company, 1967), 81.
42. Juan Bautista de Anza to Bucareli, Terrenate, Sonora, 8 June 1774, in Bolton, *Anza's California Expeditions*, 5:150.
43. Portolá to Croix, San Diego, 4 July 1769, in Companys, *Gaspar de Portolá*, 394.
44. Companys, *Gaspar de Portolá*, 318.

CHAPTER 3

1. The precise location was identified by Alan K. Brown in Crespí, *A Description of Distant Roads*, 797n11.
2. Ibid., 733.
3. Ibid.
4. Entry for 24 August 1770, Smith and Teggart, *Diary of Gaspar de Portolá*, 51.
5. Palóu, *Junípero Serra*, 87.
6. Serra to Palóu, San Diego, 10 February 1770, in Tibesar, *Writings of Junípero Serra*, 1:156.
7. Miguel Costansó, "Diario Histórico de los Viages de Mar, y Tierra, Hechos al Norte de la California de Orden del Excelentíssimo Señor Marques de Croix," Kenneth and Nancy Bechtel Collection, Bancroft Library, University of California, Berkeley.
8. Crespí, *A Description of Distant Roads*, 677.
9. Crespí to Andres, Monterey, 11 June 1770, in Bolton, *Fray Juan Crespí*, 49; Serra to Palóu, "in front of the port of San Diego, April 16, of the year 1770," in Tibesar, *Writings of Junípero Serra*, 1:163.
10. Crespí, *A Description of Distant Roads*, 719.
11. Ibid., 731.
12. Costansó, *Diary*.
13. Crosby, *Gateway to Alta California*, 55.
14. Serra to Palóu, Monterey, 13 June 1770, Tibesar, *Writings of Junípero Serra*, 1:177.
15. Palóu, *Junípero Serra*, 100.

CHAPTER 4

1. Juan Domingo Arricivita, *Apostolic Chronicle of Juan Domingo Arricivita: The Franciscan Mission Frontier in the Eighteenth Century in Arizona, Texas and the Californias*, ed. Vivian C. Fisher, trans. George P. Hammond and Agapito Rey (Berkeley, Calif.: Academy of American Franciscan History, 1996), 1:90. Arricivita (1720–1794) was born near Toluca, Mexico, the son of a storekeeper. After a long career in the frontier mission fields, he was appointed official historian of the Franciscan College of Santa Cruz in 1787.
2. Ibid., 1:91.
3. Garcés to Anza, San Xavier del Bac, 29 July 1768, in Maughan, "Francisco Garcés," 43.
4. Garcés, quoted in Arricivita, *Apostolic Chronicle*, 2:116.
5. Ibid.
6. Arricivita, *Apostolic Chronicle*, 2:155.
7. Crespí cited from Francisco Garcés, *On the Trail of a Spanish Pioneer: The Diary and Itinerary of Francisco Garcés*, trans. and ed. Elliott Coues (New York: Francis P. Harper, 1900), 1:35.

8. Ibid, 44.
9. Ibid., 69.
10. Arricivita, *Apostolic Chronicle*, 2:155.
11. Bucareli to Julián de Arriaga, Mexico City, 27 January 1773, in Bolton, *Anza's California Expeditions*, 5:53.

CHAPTER 5

1. Herbert Eugene Bolton, trans., *Anza's California Expeditions*, vol. 2, *Opening a Land Route to California: Diaries of Anza, Diaz, Garcés, and Palóu* (Berkeley: University of California Press, 1930), 3.
2. *Portraits of Basques in the New World*, ed. Richard W. Etulain and Jeronima Echeverría (Reno: University of Nevada Press, 1999), 51.
3. Bucareli to Arriaga, Mexico City, 26 November 1774, in Bolton, *Anza's California Expeditions*, 5:194.
4. Junípero Serra to the guardian, Franciscan College of San Fernando, San Diego, 31 March 1774, ibid., 5:121.
5. Anza to Bucareli, Tubac, 7 March 1773, ibid., 5:57.
6. Arriaga to Bucareli, El Pardo, 9 March 1774, ibid, 5:107.
7. Serra to the guardian, Franciscan College of San Fernando, San Diego, 31 March 1774, ibid., 5:121.
8. Bolton, *Anza's California Expeditions*, 2:249.
9. Geiger, *Franciscan Missionaries*, 64.
10. Bolton, *Anza's California Expeditions*, 2:13.
11. Juan Díaz, "Diary Kept by Father Fray Juan Díaz, Apostolic Missionary," ibid., 2:261.
12. Francisco Garcés, "Diary of the Expedition which is being made by order of His Excellency the viceroy . . . to open a road . . . to the new establishments of San Diego and Monte Rey," in Bolton, *Anza's California Expeditions*, 2:319.
13. Petition of Salvador Palma to Viceroy Bucareli, made in Mexico City, 11 November 1776, in Bolton, *Anza's California Expeditions*, 5:365. The Indian leader dictated the document with the help of Anza, who put it on paper. Palma and two of his followers then signed it with three rudimentary crosses.
14. "Anza's Complete Diary, 1774," in Bolton, *Anza's California Expeditions*, 2:37.
15. Díaz diary, ibid., 2:266. Díaz reported that the Native was "nine spans and three fingers high"—approximately six feet, three inches.
16. Garcés diary, ibid., 2:322.
17. Ibid., 2:323.
18. "Anza's Complete Diary," ibid., 2:59.
19. Ibid., 2:60.
20. Ibid., 2:63.
21. Ibid., 2:68.

22. Díaz diary, ibid., 2:274.
23. Garcés diary, ibid., 2:334.
24. Ibid., 2:337.
25. Bolton, *Anza's California Expeditions*, 2:78.
26. "Anza's Complete Diary," ibid., 2:80.
27. Díaz diary, ibid., 2:288.
28. Serra to the guardian, College of San Fernando, San Diego, 31 March 1774, Tibesar, *Writings of Junípero Serra*, 2:39.
29. "Anza's Complete Diary," ibid., 2:206; Garcés diary, ibid., 2:347.
30. Bolton, *Anza's California Expeditions*, 5:158.
31. "Anza's Complete Diary," ibid., 2:208.
32. Garcés diary, ibid., 2:369.
33. "Anza's Complete Diary," ibid., 2:230.
34. Garcés story from Arricivita, *Apostolic Chronicle*, 161.
35. Anza, in Bolton, *Anza's California Expeditions*, 2:243.

CHAPTER 6

1. Anza to Bucareli, Mexico City, 17 November 1774, in Bolton, *Anza's California Expeditions*, 5:209.
2. Juan José de Echeveste, memorandum, Mexico City, 5 December 1774, ibid., 5:225.
3. Bucareli to Garcés, Mexico City, 2 January 1775, ibid., 5:269.
4. Pedro Font, *With Anza to California, 1775–1776, the Journal of Pedro Font, O.F.M.*, ed. and trans. Alan K. Brown (Norman, Okla.: Arthur H. Clark, 2011), 75.
5. Ibid., 80.
6. The ages were compiled by Anza historian Donald T. Garate and are available on the Tumacácori National Historic Park website, U.S. Park Service, available at https://www.nps.gov/tuma/.
7. Font, *With Anza*, 89.
8. Ibid., 86.
9. Ibid., 89.
10. Herbert Eugene Bolton, trans., *Anza's California Expeditions*, vol. 3, *The San Francisco Colony: Diaries of Anza, Font, and Eixarch, and Narratives by Palóu and Moraga* (Berkeley: University of California Press, 1930), 14.
11. Font, *With Anza*, 103.
12. Ibid., 104.
13. Anza, in Bolton, *Anza's California Expeditions*, 3:25.
14. Font, *With Anza*, 109.
15. Ibid., 117.
16. Garcés, *On the Trail of a Spanish Pioneer*, 1:150.
17. Font, *With Anza*, 121.

CHAPTER 7

1. Bolton, *Anza's California Expeditions*, 3:46.
2. Anza memorandum, 8 December 1775, at Laguna de Santa Olalla on the Colorado River, ibid., 5:301.
3. Font, *With Anza*, 125.
4. Eixarch from Bolton, *Anza's California Expeditions*, 3:318.
5. Levy cited from Mickey Ellinger, "Native People, the Anza Expedition, and the Settlement of California," *News from Native California* (Fall 2008): 6.
6. Pedro Font, *Font's Complete Diary: A Chronicle of the Founding of San Francisco*, trans. and ed. Herbert Eugene Bolton (Berkeley: University of California Press, 1933), 79.
7. Garcés, *On the Trail of a Spanish Pioneer*, 1:156.
8. Font, *With Anza*, 125; Garcés, *On the Trail of a Spanish Pioneer*, 1:156.
9. Bolton, *Anza's California Expeditions*, 3:47.
10. Font, *With Anza*, 123.
11. This comment was first delivered by Fray Antonio Margil de Jesús, a well-known Franciscan at the missionary College of Santa Cruz in Querétaro, Mexico. Font, *With Anza*, 124.
12. Anza to Bucareli, Laguna de Santa Olalla, 8 December 1775. This is one of seven letters that Anza wrote to Bucareli on this day, in Bolton, *Anza's California Expeditions*, 5:301–13.
13. Font, *With Anza*, 129.
14. Ibid., 135.
15. Ibid.
16. Ibid.
17. Ibid., 136.
18. Garcés, ibid., 136.
19. Ibid., 136.
20. Garcés, *On the Trail of a Spanish Pioneer*, 1:168; Font, *With Anza*, 144.
21. Anza to Bucareli, La Laguna de Santa Olaya, 8 December 1775, in Bolton, *Anza's California Expeditions*, 5:301–13.
22. Ibid.
23. Anza's diary, Bolton, *Anza's California Expeditions*, 3:54.
24. Font, *With Anza*, 147.
25. Anza's diary, in Bolton, *Anza's California Expeditions*, 3:55.
26. M. Steven Shackley, ed., *The Early Ethnography of the Kumeyaay* (Berkeley: Phoebe A. Hearst Museum of Anthropology, 2004), 337.
27. Anza's diary, Bolton, *Anza's California Expeditions*, 3:58.

28. Font, *With Anza*, 154.
29. Ibid.
30. Damany M. Fisher, *Discovering Early California Afro-Latino Presence* (Berkeley, Calif.: Heyday, 2010), 10.
31. Font, *With Anza*, 154.
32. Richard Stoffle et al., *Analyzing 18th Century Lifeways of Anza Expedition Members in Northwestern Sinaloa and Southwestern Sonora Mexico* (Tucson: School of Anthropology, University of Arizona, 2010), 26.
33. Font, *With Anza*, 158; Anza's diary, in Bolton, *Anza's California Expeditions*, 3:67.
34. Juan Bautista de Anza, "Report of the troops recruited in the provinces of the government of Sonora . . . ," in Archivo General de la Nación, Provincias Internas 237, Año 1775, Capitan D. Juan Baptista Ansa [*sic*], Su Corresp de Barios Asumptos, ff. 75, 75v, 76, 76v.
35. Stoffle et al., "Analyzing 18th Century Lifeways," 120.
36. Spanish census of California, 1790.
37. Font, *With Anza*, 161.
38. Ibid.
39. Anza's diary, in Bolton, *Anza's California Expeditions*, 3:70.
40. Ellinger, "Native People," 9.
41. Ibid.
42. Font, *With Anza*, 169.
43. Anza to Rivera, 28 December 1775, in *The Juan Bautista de Anza–Fernando de Rivera y Moncada Letters of 1775–1776: Personalities in Conflict*, comp. Donald T. Garate, Antepasados 12 (San Diego, CA: Los Californianos, 2006), 3.
44. Font, *With Anza*, 167.

CHAPTER 8

Epigraph: Fray Vicente Fuster, San Diego, to Fray Junípero Serra, padre-presidente of the California missions, at Mission San Carlos, Carmel, California, 28 November 1775; in Serra, *Writings*, 2:453.

1. Geiger, *Franciscan Missionaries*, 128.
2. Font, *With Anza*, 175.
3. Ibid., 176.
4. Ibid., 172.
5. Ibid., 178.
6. Ibid.; Geiger, *Franciscan Missionaries*, 183.
7. Font, *With Anza*, 180.
8. Ibid.

9. Jean-François de La Pérouse, *Monterey in 1786: Life in a California Mission: The Journals of Jean-François de la Pérouse*, ed. Malcolm Margolin (Berkeley, Calif.: Heyday Books, 1989), 81.
10. Sherburne F. Cook, *The Conflict between the California Indian and White Civilization* (1947; Berkeley: University of California Press, 1976), 117.
11. La Pérouse, *Life in a California Mission*, 89.
12. Font, *With Anza*, 181.
13. Nentvig, *Rudo Ensayo*, 110.
14. Palóu, *Junípero Serra*, 25.
15. Font, *With Anza*, 182.
16. Shackley, *Early Ethnography*, 34.
17. Ibid., 12–13.
18. Richard L. Carrico, "Sociopolitical Aspects of the 1775 Revolt at Mission San Diego de Alcalá: An Ethnohistorical Approach," *Journal of San Diego History* 43 (Summer 1947).
19. Bancroft, *History of California*, 18:138.
20. Fages, *Natural Description of California*, 9.
21. Junípero Serra to Father Juan Andres, 10 February 1770, in Tibesar, *Writings of Junípero Serra*, 1:151.
22. Geiger, *Franciscan Missionaries*, 121.
23. Font, *With Anza*, 189.
24. Carrico, "Sociopolitical Aspects."
25. Crosby, *Gateway to Alta California*, 168.
26. Fages, *Natural Description of California*, 43.
27. "Letter of Luis Jayme, O.F.M., San Diego, October 17, 1772," trans. Maynard Geiger, *Journal of San Diego History* 17 (Summer 1971).
28. Ibid.
29. Palóu, *Junípero Serra*, 171.
30. Francisco Palóu, *Historical Memoirs of New California*, ed. and trans. Herbert Eugene Bolton (Berkeley: University of California Press, 1926), 4:74.
31. Geiger, *Franciscan Missionaries*, 91.
32. Fuster to Serra, San Diego, 28 November 1775, in Tibesar, *Writings of Junípero Serra*, 2:455.
33. Font, *With Anza*, 190.
34. Tibesar, *Writings of Junípero Serra*, 2:225.
35. Fuster to Serra, San Diego, 28 November 1775, ibid., 2:455.
36. Ibid.
37. Ibid.
38. Font, *With Anza*, 192.

39. Geiger, *Franciscan Missionaries*, 128.
40. Palóu, *Junípero Serra*, 173.
41. Font, *With Anza*, 200.
42. Ibid., 351.
43. Ibid.

CHAPTER 9

Epigraph: Richard Watson Gilder (from 8 February 1844 to 19 November 1909), American poet and editor, Union Civil War veteran, born in Bordentown, New Jersey.

1. Richard Flint and Shirley Cushing Flint, "Melchior Diaz," New Mexico Office of the State Historian, http://newmexicohistory.org/people/melchior-diaz.
2. S. K. Gupta, *Modern Hydrology and Sustainable Water Development* (Oxford: Wiley-Blackwell, 2010), 204.
3. Geiger, *Franciscan Missionaries*, 275. Other sources place Eixarch's birth approximately two years later.
4. John L. Kessell, "Eixarch and the Visitation at Tumacácori, May 12, 1775," *Kiva: Journal of Southwestern Anthropology and History* 30 (February 1965): 77–81.
5. Ibid., 77.
6. "Eixarch's Diary of His Winter on the Colorado, 1775–1776," in Bolton, *Anza's California Expeditions*, 3:311. References to this diary are hereafter given parenthetically in the text.
7. Nentvig, *Rudo Ensayo*, 71.
8. Shackley, *Early Ethnography*, 285.
9. Ibid., 306.
10. Shackley, *Early Ethnography*, 284.
11. "Eixarch's Diary," in Bolton, *Anza's California Expeditions*, 3:373.
12. Hector Becerra, "Scientists Tie Colorado River Flooding to San Andreas Quakes," *Los Angeles Times*, July 6, 2011.
13. Ginny Sphar, "Tomás Eixarch," website of Tumacácori National Historic Park, Arizona, available at https://www.nps.gov/tuma/learn/historyculture/tomas-eixarch.htm.

CHAPTER 10

1. Publication of the Kern County Historical Society, 2008.
2. Arricivita, *Apostolic Chronicle*, 2:176.
3. Bucareli to Garcés, 2 January 1775, in Bolton, *Anza's California Expeditions*, 5:271.
4. Garcés, *On the Trail of a Spanish Pioneer*, 1:163. The story here is taken from this diary, and page references are given parenthetically in the text.
5. Arricivita, *Apostolic Chronicle*, 2:182.
6. Ibid.

CHAPTER 11

1. In his journal, Garcés used the Spanish word *caydas* to describe the entrance to Oraibi. The word, seldom found in modern Spanish dictionaries, refers to something that is collapsing or falling down. Garcés, *On the Trail of a Spanish Pioneer*, 2:362.
2. Garcés, in John Galvin, ed., *A Record of Travels in Arizona and California, 1775–1776* (San Francisco: J. Howell Books, 1965), 48.
3. Ibid., 282.
4. Ibid., 284.
5. This is the 1899 translation in Garcés, *On the Trail of a Spanish Pioneer*, 1:151. Galvin, *A Record of Travels in Arizona and California*, 50, translates the phrase as "behaved badly toward their women."
6. The tall statue of Garcés erected in the Bakersfield traffic circle in 1939 approximates the spot where this Indian settlement was located. Garcés named the village San Miguel.
7. The Spaniards virtually never called the Natives by their given names, instead conferring new Spanish names on them. This was intended to promote Indian assimilation into Spanish culture.
8. Garcés, *On the Trail of a Spanish Pioneer*, 1:302.
9. Ibid., 1:309.
10. Ibid., 1:311.
11. Ibid. 1:312.
12. Ibid., 2:325.
13. Ibid., 2:336.
14. Ibid., 2:337.
15. Lieutenant J. C. Ives, *Report upon the Colorado River of the West: Explored in 1857 and 1858* (Washington, DC: U.S. Government Printing Office, 1861), 105.
16. Garcés, *On the Trail of a Spanish Pioneer*, 2:348.
17. Garcés, in Galvin, *A Record of Travels in Arizona and California*, 70.
18. Po'Pay is the only Native American to be honored in National Statuary Hall in the U.S. Capitol.
19. Maughan, "Francisco Garcés," 171.
20. In his diary, Garcés used the Spanish word *chichimecos*, translated here as "savages." The term *chichimecos* was a slang word originating in Mexico to describe hostile Indians. See Garcés, *On the Trail of a Spanish Pioneer*, 2:365.
21. The Hopi villages were dispersed over First Mesa, Second Mesa, and Third Mesa. The numbers correspond from south to north. Oraibi is on Third Mesa, the northernmost.
22. Garcés, in Galvin, *A Record of Travels in Arizona and California*, 75.
23. Maughan, "Francisco Garcés," 181.
24. Ralph E. Twitchell, "Colonel Juan Bautista de Anza, Governor of New Mexico: Diary of His Expedition to the Moquis in 1780" (paper read before the Historical Society of New Mexico annual meeting, 1918), 36.

25. Ibid.
26. Garcés used the Spanish word *cibola* to describe the meat that was served with the beef (Galvin, *A Record of Travels in Arizona and California*, 78). The Spanish term means "buffalo," but buffalo never ranged as far south as Arizona. The animal most likely was the elk, which still roam Arizona today.
27. Garcés, in Galvin, *A Record of Travels in Arizona and California*, 81.
28. Ibid., 87.
29. Ibid., 88.

CHAPTER 12

1. The woman's name was supplied by Alan K. Brown, in Font, *With Anza*, 203n119.
2. Ibid., 195.
3. Anza quoted from Bolton, *Anza's California Expeditions*, 3:95.
4. Font, *With Anza*, 203. Following Font quotations are from this work and are cited parenthetically in the text.
5. Ibid., 44n80.
6. Bolton, *Anza's California Expeditions*, 3:111.
7. Geiger, *Franciscan Missionaries*, 48.
8. Font, *With Anza*, 330n264.
9. Arricivita, *Apostolic Chronicle*, 1:175.
10. Anza's diary, Bolton, *Anza's California Expeditions*, 3:155.
11. Ibid.

CHAPTER 13

1. Geiger, *Franciscan Missionaries*, 160.
2. Junípero Serra to Father Guardian Francisco Pangua, College of San Fernando, San Diego, 31 March 1774, in Bolton, *Anza's California Expeditions*, 5:121.
3. Juan Crespí, "Diary of the Sea Expedition made by the Frigate Santiago, in Which Went the Father Preachers Fray Juan Crespí and Fray Tomás de la Peña," in Bolton, *Fray Juan Crespí*, 307.
4. Ibid.
5. Herbert K. Beals, ed. and trans., *Juan Pérez on the Northwest Coast* (Portland: Oregon Historical Society Press, 1989), 17.
6. Bancroft, *History of the Northwest Coast*, vol. 27 of *The Works of Hubert Howe Bancroft* (1884–90; facs. ed., Santa Barbara, CA: Wallace Hebberd, 1963), 150.
7. Warren L. Cook, *Flood Tide of Empire: Spain and the Pacific Northwest, 1542–1819* (Yale University Press, 1973), 54.
8. Bucareli to Arriaga, Mexico City, 27 July 1773, quoted in Thurman, *The Naval Department of San Blas*, 121.
9. Bancroft, *Works*, 27:150.

10. Manuel P. Servin, trans., "The Instructions of Viceroy Bucareli to Ensign Juan Pérez," *California Historical Society Quarterly* 40 (September 1961): 239.
11. Ibid.
12. Ibid., 242.
13. Ibid., 234.
14. Thurman, *The Naval Department of San Blas*, 128.
15. Herbert Eugene Bolton, trans., *Anza's California Expeditions*, vol. 1, *An Outpost of Empire* (Berkeley: University of California Press), 192.
16. Roster prepared by Francisco Hijosa and Joseph Faustino Ruíz, at San Blas, 22 January 1774, in Beals, *Juan Pérez*, 151–57.
17. "Continuation of the Diary kept by acting ensign, frigate grade, Don Juan Pérez," ibid., 58.
18. Ibid., 66.
19. Crespí, "Diary of the Sea Expedition," 320.
20. The sequence of visits by Haida canoes is based on Peña's diary. Crespí offered a somewhat different account. See Cutter, *The California Coast*, 159.
21. Beals, *Juan Pérez*, 241.
22. Ibid., 75.
23. Ibid., 81.
24. Cook, *Flood Tide of Empire*, 61.
25. "Ynventario de las prendas cambalachadas con los Yndios," ibid.
26. Tomás de la Peña, "Diary of Fray Tomás de la Peña, Kept During the Voyage of the Santiago—dated 28th August, 1774," in Cutter, *The California Coast*, 161.
27. Crespí, "Diary of the Sea Expedition," 332.
28. Beals, *Juan Pérez*, 81.
29. Peña diary, in Cutter, *The California Coast*, 163.
30. Ibid., 169.
31. Peña recorded that three canoes approached the ship (ibid., 179). Crespí counted only two (ibid., 255). Pérez stated in his log that three canoes came near the ship, but that a number of others were in the vicinity (Beals, *Juan Pérez*, 89).
32. Beals, *Juan Pérez*, 89.
33. Crespí, "Diary of the Sea Expedition," 351.
34. Beals, *Juan Pérez*, 236.
35. James Cook, *James Cook: The Journals* (Cambridge: Published for the Hakluyt Society at the University Press; London: Penguin Classics, abridged ed., 1999), 540.
36. Ibid.
37. Extract from Joseph Ingraham to Esteban José Martínez, in Beals, *Juan Pérez*, 216.
38. Crespí, "Diary of the Sea Expedition," 353.
39. Ibid., 354.
40. Peña diary, in Cutter, *The California Coast*, 193.

41. Ibid., 195.
42. Crespí, "Diary of the Sea Expedition," 362.
43. Juan Pérez to Viceroy Bucareli, Monterey, 31 August 1774, in Beals, *Juan Pérez*, 55.
44. Bucareli to Arriaga, Mexico City, 26 November 1774, in Bolton, *Anza's California Expeditions*, 5:194.
45. Serra to Father Guardian Francisco Pangua, College of San Fernando, Monterey, 31 August 1774, in Tibesar, *Writings of Junípero Serra*, 2:39.
46. Francisco Mourelle, "Voyage from Puerto de S. Blas to Monterey and the Northern Coast of California by Ensign, Frigate Grade, D. Juan Pérez," dated 15 February 1791, in Beals, *Juan Pérez*, 103.
47. Bancroft, *History of California*, 1:244.

CHAPTER 14

Epigraph: Arricivita, *Apostolic Chronicle*, 2:201.
1. Bolton, *Anza's California Expeditions*, 3:179.
2. Font, *With Anza*, 383.
3. Bolton, *Anza's California Expeditions*, 3:181.
4. Font, *With Anza*, 406.
5. Bucareli to Gálvez, Mexico City, 26 November 1776, in Bolton, *Anza's California Expeditions*, 5:395.
6. Arricivita, *Apostolic Chronicle*, 2:202.
7. Bucareli to Gálvez, Mexico City, 27 October 1776, in Bolton, *Anza's California Expeditions*, 5:363.
8. Vladimir Guerrero, "Lost in the Translation/Chief Palma of the Quechan," *Southern California Quarterly* 92 (Winter 2010–2011): 336. Guerrero provides a detailed account of how the petition was drafted.
9. "Instancia del Capitán de la Nación Yuma Salvador Palma sobre que se establesan Misiones en su territorio . . . ," written at Mexico City, 11 November 1776, in Bolton, *Anza's California Expeditions*, 5:365.
10. Ibid. 5:373.
11. Ibid., 5:374.
12. Arricivita, *Apostolic Chronicle*, 2:203.
13. Elizabeth Ellinwood Roberts, "The Spanish Missions at Yuma: A Translation of the Original Documents with Introduction and Notes" (master's thesis, University of California, Berkeley, 1920).
14. Gálvez to Bucareli, Madrid, 3 May 1777, in Arricivita, *Apostolic Chronicle*, 2:205.
15. Arricivita, *Apostolic Chronicle*, 2:207.
16. Garcés, ibid., 2:208.
17. Report compiled by Garcés at Tubutama, 3 January 1777, in Galvin, *A Record of Travels in Arizona and California*, 93.

18. Arricivita, *Apostolic Chronicle*, 2:211.
19. Croix to Garcés, Arispe, 28 January 1781.
20. "Diary Kept by the Ensign Commandant of the New Settlements of the Río Colorado . . . ," in Roberts, "Spanish Missions at Yuma," n.p.
21. Santiago de Yslas to Croix, La Concepción, 30 December 1780, ibid.
22. Yslas to Croix, La Concepción, 17 January 1781, ibid.
23. Croix to Yslas, Arispe, 22 February 1781, ibid.
24. Yslas to Croix, La Concepción, 17 January 1781, ibid.
25. Ibid.
26. "List of the Soldiers and Recruits who Remained Behind at the Río Colorado with Captain Don Fernando de Rivera y Moncada and who were Killed by the Heathen Indians that Inhabit that Region," ibid., n.p.
27. "Statement of the Number and Kinds of Animals which were with Captain Don Fernando de Moncada on the Río Colorado," ibid., n.p.

CHAPTER 15

1. Arricivita, *Apostolic Chronicle*, 2:220.
2. Geiger, *Franciscan Missionaries*, 29.
3. Engelhardt, *The Franciscans in Arizona*, 163.
4. Ibid., 167.
5. Croix, general report, 1781, in John L. Kessell, *Friars, Soldiers, and Reformers* (Tucson: University of Arizona Press, 1976), 122.
6. "María Ana Montijo to Father Francisco Antonio Barbastro, Altar, 21 December 1785," trans. and ed. Kieran McCarty, *Journal of Arizona History* 16.3 (Autumn 1975): 221–25.
7. Eyewitness account of Pedro Solares, in Roberts, "Spanish Missions at Yuma."
8. Eyewitness account of Juan Joseph Miranda, ibid., 157.
9. Eyewitness account of Ensign Don Cayetano Limón, ibid., 114.
10. Maughan, "Francisco Garcés," 248.
11. Eyewitness account of Joseph Reyes Pacheco, in Roberts, "Spanish Missions at Yuma."
12. "María Ana Montijo to Father Francisco Antonio Barbastro, Altar, 21 December 1785."
13. Arricivita, *Apostolic Chronicle*, 2:223.
14. Ibid.
15. "María Ana Montijo to Father Francisco Antonio Barbastro, Altar, 21 December 1785."
16. Ibid. Montijo relied on a firsthand account told to her by Gertrudis Cantud, wife of the man whom Barreneche and Garcés assisted on the bank of the lagoon.
17. The interpreter's name was supplied in a sworn account by a captive soldier, twenty-two-year-old Pedro Solares, translated by Roberts, in "The Spanish Missions at Yuma."

18. Arricivita, *Apostolic Chronicle*, 2:224.
19. "María Ana Montijo to Father Francisco Antonio Barbastro, Altar, 21 December 1785," quoting Gertrudis Cantud.

CHAPTER 16

1. Arricivita, *Apostolic Chronicle*, 2:225.
2. "*Expediente* drawn up for the investigation of the outrage committed by the Yuma Indians upon the establishments of the Río Colorado," signed by Croix at Arizpe, 9 September 1781, in Roberts, "The Spanish Missions at Yuma."
3. Croix to Don Jácobo Ugarte y Loyola, military governor of Sonora, Arizpe, 10 September 1781, ibid., 94.
4. Croix to Don Jácobo Ugarte y Loyola, Arizpe, 16 September 1781, ibid., 106.
5. Pedro Fages, *The Colorado River Campaign, 1781–1782: Diary of Pedro Fages*, ed. and trans. Herbert Ingram Priestly (Berkeley: University of California Press, 1913), 21.
6. Eyewitness account of Joseph Reyes Pacheco, in Roberts, "The Spanish Missions at Yuma."
7. Eyewitness account of Joseph Urrea, in Roberts, "The Spanish Missions at Yuma."
8. Engelhardt, *The Franciscans in Arizona*, 152.

CHAPTER 17

1. Arricivita, *Apostolic Chronicle*, 2:283. The exact day of Font's death is in dispute. Some historians believe it occurred after 8 September 1781.
2. Crespí, *A Description of Distant Roads*, 4.
3. Palóu, *Historical Memoirs*, 4:194.
4. Palóu, *Junípero Serra*, 230.
5. Geiger, *Franciscan Missionaries*, 54.
6. Palóu, *Junípero Serra*, 232.
7. Crespí, *A Description of Distant Roads*, 3.
8. Palóu, *Historical Memoirs*, 4:195.
9. Crespí, *A Description of Distant Roads*, 4.

EPILOGUE

1. Letter written at Aconchi, in "The Martyrdom and Interment of Padre Francisco Garcés," by Clarence Cullimore (Bakersfield: Kern County Historical Society, 1954), 6.
2. Letter written in Mexico City by Manuel Touissaint, director of National Monuments of Mexico, 13 August 1953, ibid., 7.
3. Diego Miguel Bringas de Manzaneda y Encinas, *Friar Bringas Reports to the King: Methods of Indoctrination on the Frontier of New Spain, 1796–97*, trans. and ed. Daniel S. Matson and Bernard L. Fontana (Tucson: University of Arizona Press, 1977), 2.

4. Diego Miguel Bringas de Manzaneda y Encinas, "Sermón que en las solemnes honras celebradas en obsequio de los vv. pp. predicadores apostólicos Fr. Francisco Tomás Hermenegildo Garcés, Fr. Juan Marcelo Diaz," trans. by the author from original document published in Madrid by D. Fermin Villalpando, 1819 (photocopy; Madrid: Sabin Americana Print Editions), 52.
5. Ibid., 74.
6. Ibid., 94.
7. Arricivita, *Apostolic Chronicle*, 2:283.
8. Palóu, *Junípero Serra*, 53.
9. Ramón A. Gutiérrez, "Contested Eden: An Introduction," in *Contested Eden: California before the Gold Rush*, ed. Ramón A. Gutiérrez and Richard J. Orsi (Berkeley: University of California Press, 1998), 4–5.
10. "California Indian History," California Native American Heritage Commission, https://www.nahc.ca.gov.
11. Cook, *California Indian and White Civilization*, 116, table 5.
12. Ibid., 122.
13. "*Representación*," Mission San Carlos, 12 November 1800 (Santa Barbara Mission Archives, 2.199–211).
14. Serra to Bucareli, Mexico City, 21 May 1773, in Tibesar, *Writings of Junípero Serra*, 1:353.
15. Maria F. Wade, *Missions, Missionaries, and Native Americans: Long-Term Processes and Daily Practices* (Gainesville: University Press of Florida, 2008), 208.
16. Cook, *California Indian and White Civilization*, 59.
17. Ibid., 25.
18. Ibid., 26.
19. Florence Connolly Shipek, "Saints or Oppressors: The Franciscan Missionaries of California," in *The Missions of California, A Legacy of Genocide*, ed. Rupert Costo and Jeannette Henry Costo (San Francisco: Indian Historian Press, 1987), 30.
20. William Preston, "Serpent in the Garden: Environmental Change in Colonial California" in Gutiérrez and Orsi, *Contested Eden*, 288.
21. Alfonso Ortiz, "Breaking Barriers: Perspectives in the Writing of Indian History," ed. David L. Beaulieu (Chicago: Newberry Library Center for the History of the American Indian, Occasional Papers Series no. 1, 1974), 40.
22. A. L. Kroeber, Brief before the Indian Claims Commission, findings of fact (1955), in *The Missions of California: A Legacy Of Genocide*, ed. Rupert Costo and Jeannette Henry Costo (San Francisco: Indian Historian Press, 1987), 23.
23. Steven W. Hackel, "Land, Labor, and Production: The Colonial Economy of Spanish and Mexican California," in Gutiérrez and Orsi, *Contested Eden*, 122.
24. Borica quoted in Cook, *California Indian and White Civilization*, 91.
25. Ibid., 92.

26. La Pérouse, *Life in a California Mission*, 87–88.
27. Cook quoted from Hackel, "Land, Labor, and Production," 122.
28. Cook, *California Indian and White Civilization*, 94–95.
29. James A. Sandos, *Converting California: Indians and Franciscans in the Missions* (New Haven, Conn.: Yale University Press, 2004), 8.
30. Herbert Eugene Bolton, "The Mission as a Frontier Institution in the Spanish-American Colonies," *American Historical Review* 23.1 (October 1917): 642–80.

Index

References to illustrations appear in italics.

Acapulco, 24, 25, 28
acorns, 160; as food, 57, 122, 159, 245, 249
agriculture, 128, 132, 156, 249, 253;
  Cajuenche, 154, 155; Havasupai, 170;
  Hopi, 162; La Concepcíon, 222; Mission
  San Diego, 134; Yuma, 148, 211, 223–24,
  232. *See also* corn (maize); wheat
Alarcón, Hernando de, 225
Alaska, 16, 17, 91, 179, 192, 193, 244–45;
  Apache emigration, 77; Russians and,
  25, 194
alcohol, 102, 120–21, 122. *See also* brandy;
  wine
Altar presidio, 79, 80, 92, 219, 221–22, 231;
  Yuma uprising aftermath, 232, 236, 238,
  243
Altar River Valley, 81, 148, 149, 150, 151,
  239
Álvarez, Fernando, 30
American Revolution, 7, 129
Andres, Juan, 34, 38
Ansa, Pedro de, 218
antelopes, 44, 46, 49, 183
Antonio, Salvador, 200, 205
Anza, Juan Bautista de, 61, 72, 74, 75,
  211–15, 217, 218, 220; directive to
  Garcés, 168; expedition of 1774, 76–95;
  expedition of 1775–76, 7, 96–128, *101*,
  109, 131, 142–45, 153–54, 178–91; Font
  on, 111–12; on Indians, 83, 119–20;
  Mexico City trip (1776), 211–15, 217, 218;
  military career, 77; visit to Oraibi, 174–75
Apache people, 97, 99, 100, 176, 214;
  Eixarch and, 149, 150; Pima relations,
  102; raids, 70, 76–77, 98, 142, 233; Santa
  María Magdalena and Sáric attacks, 3–6,
  20; San Xavier del Bac attacks, 69, 70,
  97; slaves, 145; Tubac attacks, 76, 77, 88;
  Yuma relations, 75, 143, 212, 219, 221
arachnids. *See* fleas, ticks, etc.; scorpions
Arballo, María Feliciano, 118–19
Arbizu, Manuel Antonio, 236
Arriaga, Julián de, 79
Arricivita, Juan Domingo, 70, 72, 217, 219,
  221, 226, 261n1; on Font's demise, 240,
  244; on Garcés, 74, 153; on Rivera, 161,
  229
Arroyo, José, 136
artifacts, beached, 59, 61
atole, 130, 249, 251

Bakersfield, Calif., 152, 166
baptism, Christian, 17, 18, 42, 71, 72, 114,
  134, 185; death of children following, 19,
  147–48, 150; by Eixarch, 97, 142, 150;
  by Font, 104, 122, 185; by Garcés, 71,
  72, 147, 148, 155, 156, 165; Palma's, 79,
  144, 217, 218; Portolá expedition (1769),
  41–42
Barbastro, Francisco Antonio, 243
Barreneche, Juan Antonio, 226–31, *230*,
  233, 238
beached artifacts. *See* artifacts, beached
beads, 21, 212, 213, 220; Anza expedition
  (1774), 84, 85, 87, 89; Anza expedition
  (1775–76), 103, 108, 112, 113, 114, 182;
  Garcés, 146, 153, 156, 164; Pérez expedition (1774), 195, 202, 203, 204; Portolá

beads *(continued)*
    expedition (1776), 35–36, 38, 44, 47–48, 50, 55, 60; as ransom payment, 233, 235; shell, 159
bears, 50–51, 60, 65, 90, 127, 166, 187, 188–89, 191; brown, 188–89; Fages and, 50, 234; pelts, 189, 203
Bejarano, José María, 131
Beñemé people, 159–60
Benítez, María Josefa, 237
Benno, Juan Evangelista, 27
birth of children. *See* childbirth
Bluecoats. *See* Catalonian Volunteers (Bluecoats)
Bolton, Herbert E., 14, 17, 253
Borica, Diego de, 251
brandy, 36, 98, 102, 109, 120, 185
Bringas de Manzaneda y Encinas, Diego Miguel, 244
Britain, 26, 28, 203; explorers, 207. *See also* England
Bucareli y Ursúa, Antonio María de, 61, 78, 97, 99, 145, *216*; Anza expedition (1774), 92, 94; Anza expedition (1775–76), 111, 115, 153–54; bear pelt gift, 189; commendation of Garcés, 75; as namesake, 171; Palma and, 212, 215–18; Pérez expedition (1774), 192, 194–96, 203, 209–10
buffalo, 54, 77, 269n26
Burgues, Pedro, 229, 230

Caborca, Sonora, 74, 81, 110, 146, 239; maps, *143*
Cabrera Bueno, José González, 42, 51, 56, 66
Cajuenche people, 85, 86, 112–13, 154–55, 212, 220
California Native American Heritage Commission. *See* Native American Heritage Commission (California)
Callegari, Antonio, 31
Calvo, José, 9
Camino del Diablo. *See* El Camino del Diablo
Camino Real. *See* El Camino Real

candles, 108, 110, 167, 180
Cañizares, José de, 23, 35, 36
cannons, 36–37, 40, 68, 135, 186, 196, 198, 223
canoes, 48, 132, 184, 201–2, 206
canyons, 169–71
capital punishment, 132
Carlos III, king of Spain, 8, 17, 19–20, 25, 26, 79, 195, 215; expulsion of Jesuits, 15–16, 26, 69; land claims, 39, 67, 201; Masses honoring, 91; namesake, 122; Palma and, 219; praise of Garcés, 12, 219
Carmel Mission. *See* Mission San Carlos Borromeo de Monterey (Mission Carmel)
Carrillo, Guillermo, 125–26
Carrillo, María Antonia Victoria, 179
Cartagena, Romualdo, 12
cartography, 7–8
Castro, Juan José de, 9
Catalán language, 14, 241
Catalonian Volunteers (Bluecoats), 234
Cavaller, José, 184–85
Cedros Island, 29
cemeteries, Chumash, 48–49
Cenizo, Enrique, 233, 236, 237, 238
childbirth, 96–97, 104–5, 112, 115, 120, 121–22, 149, 186
Chirikov, Aleksei, 194
chocolate, 91, 104; as breakfast drink, 36, 113, 115, 181, 231, 244; provisions, 36, 60, 63, 78, 98, 108, 146; stolen, 146, 182, 185
Christian baptism. *See* baptism, Christian
Christianized Indians. *See* Indians
Christian missionizing of Indians, 15, 18, 129–30, 247; Anza expedition (1774), 87; Anza expedition (1775–76), 99, 113, 114, 142, 144; as conquest, 17–18, 195; Garcés, 72, 114–15, 156, 158, 163, 174; "gentle yoke," 40; "outreach," 8, 225; Portolá expedition (1769), 41–42, 46; resistance to, 18–19, 132, 162, 172–75
Chumash people, 48–50, 64, 184
church-state separation, 221
Clement XIII, Pope, 16

clothing: Anza expedition (1775–76), 98, 123, 178; coveted/stolen by Indians, 35, 38, 110, 132, 220, 223, 237; gifts of, 94, 110, 111–12, 212; Palma's royal outfit, 110, 111–12, 149, 212; soiled, 110; traded, 203; underwear, 98, 123, 178; uniforms, 216, 234
Cochimí people, 43, 79
Cocomaricopa people, 236
Cocopa people. *See* Cucapá people
Cojats. *See* Cajuenche people
College of San Fernando (Mexico City), 14, 34, 38, 130
College of Santa Cruz (Querétaro, Mexico), 8, 12, 15, 141, 151, 220, 226; Arricivita chronicle, 153, 161; reburial of missionaries, 243–44
colonists. *See* settlers
Colorado River: Cataract Canyon, 170; El Puerto de la Concepción, 157, 211–14, 225; flooding, 73, 93–94, 150–51; Garcés and, 13, 71–72, 73, 84, 155, 158; Grand Canyon, 170–71; naming, 141. *See also* river fording
Columbia (U.S. ship), 207
Columbus, Christopher, 21
Concepción. *See* Mission La Purísima de Concepción
Cook, James, 207, 210
Cook, Sherburne F., 246, 248, 251, 252
corn (maize), 156, 159, 170, 173, 188; grinding, 130; Hopis, 162; livestock feed, 116, 159; mush (gruel), 33, 78, 98, 153; Spaniards' supplies, 63, 91; spoiled, worm-infested, etc., 9, 180; theft of, 220; tortillas, 91, 154; Yumas, 73, 105, 110, 143, 148, 222, 224, 235. See also *atole*; pinole; posole
Coronado, Francisco Vázquez de, 171–72
corporal punishment, 165, 184, 223, 246, 247, 248; of Kumeyaay uprising ringleaders, 138; of runaway Indians, 79, 102, 129, 246
Costansó, Miguel, 29, 37, 43, 48, 52, 53, 59; on earthquake, 46; on Chumash music, 49, 50; Portolá expedition (1770), 66, 67; on Santa Lucía Mountains, 51
Coyote Canyon, 108
Cozinero, Juan 4
cradle boards, 51, 149
Crespí, Juan, 6–7, 14–17, 22, 187, 189, 244–45, 253; baptisms, 41–42; on bears, 50; on Indians, 38; last years, 241–42; Monterey, 62; Pérez expedition (1774), 192–209; Portolá expedition (1769), 22–23, 26, 27, 31–60; Portolá expedition (1770), 62–68; on Santa Lucía Mountains, 51–52; suffers cold, 16–17, 51, 59, 194; on "white Indians," 188
Croix, Carlos Francisco de Croix, marquis de, 68, 218
Croix, Teodoro Francisco de, 218–23, 226, 232–33
Cruzado, Antonio, 38
Cucapá people, 146, 156

Dávila, José, 186–87
death penalty. *See* capital punishment
deserters and runaways, Native, 79, 129, 165, 182, 185, 246, 247–48; Anza expedition (1774), 89; Anza expedition (1775–76), 101–2; Portolá expedition (1769), 34, 58, 65; in Santa Maria Magdalena attack, 4
deserters and runaways, Spanish, 166, 182, 185
Díaz, Juan, 220, 226; Anza expedition (1774), 80–83, 86–88, 91, 92, 94, 220; Yuma uprising (1781), 228, 233, 237
Díaz, Melchior, 141
diet. *See* food, Spaniards'; food, Native
Discovery (ship), 207
disease. *See* illness and disease
Domínguez, Atanasio, 167
drinking (alcohol). *See* alcohol
drinking water: at missions, 128; overland expeditions, 82, 88, 112, 116–17, 126; Pérez expedition (1774), 200–201, 204, 209, 210; Portolá expedition (1769), 28, 29, 33; Portolá expedition (1770), 64. *See also* wells
dwellings, Native. *See under* Indians

earthquakes, 46, 65, 123, 150–51
Echeverria y Orcolaga, Agustín, 218
Echeveste, Juan José de, 98
Eixarch, Thomas, 140–51, 154, 157, 168, 212, 213; Anza expedition (1775–76), 97, 99, 102, 104, 108–11, 114, 142
El Camino del Diablo, 13, 74, 81, 149, 220, 232
El Camino Real, 44, 88, 93, 131, 179, 193
elk, 54, 167, 176, 189
El Peregrino. *See* Tarabal, Sebastián
England, 8, 17, 26, 97; American colonies, 253
Escalante, Silvestre Vélez de, 167, 173, 174
Estorace, Jorge, 31, 61
excommunication, 138–39
execution. *See* capital punishment
expedition provisioning. *See* provisioning of expeditions

Fages, Pedro, 16, 49, 132, 133, 187, 188, *234*, 243; on bears, 50; on Chumash music, 50; on Indians, 38, 49, 55; Portolá expedition (1769), 29, 37–38, 42–43, 49–51, 53; Portolá expedition (1770), 62, 65, 66; retributive campaign against Yumas, 232–38
Farallon Islands, 56, 57
Felipe III, king of Spain, 24
Felíz, José Vicente, 96–97
Felíz, Manuela Piñuelas, 96
Fernández, Simón, 199
Figuer, Juan, 185
fish and fishing, 38, 46, 60, 154, 184, 196, 202; Chumash people and, 48, 49, 184
fleas, ticks, etc., 56, 185, 191, 203
flogging. *See* corporal punishment
flora, 38, 44, 47, 123, 126, 259n7; pines, 52, 53, 66; redwoods, 55; wildflowers, 16, 123, 126, 182, 187, 188; Yuha Desert, 76. *See also* mesquite
Flores, Sebastián, 220
fog: Anza expedition (1775–76), 112, 120, 122, 182, 187; Crespí aversion to, 16, 55, 194; Pérez expedition (1774), 192, 194, 195, 196, 199–202, 205, 208, 209; Portolá expedition (1769), 51, 55
Font, Pedro, 3–9, 17, 61, 151, 168, 211, 253; Anza expedition (1775–76), 7, 97–106, 108, 110–22, 125–31, 179–91; Arricivita on, 240, 244; on corporal punishment, 138, 247; on Crespí, 17; on Garcés, 12–13; Garcés relations, 154, 155; on Indian languages, 130; on Indians, 6, 12, 105, 113, 114, 119, 128, 133; on Indian "propensity to theft," 103, 113, 184; Kumeyaay uprising (1775), 125, 134, 137; last years, 239–40; mapmaking, 219; Mexico City trip, 212–15; scurvy, 138, 179; Sebastián Tarabal and, 43
food, Native, 18, 156, 159, 249; acorns, 57, 122, 159, 249; beans, 113; bear meat, 166; mescal, 32–33, 156, 169; Garcés and, 72, 73, 114, 159, 166, 169, 244; mesquite pods, 73, 224, 249; "nasty and dirty," 12; roots, 117, 159, 244; sage gruel, 46, 57; seeds, 46, 52, 57, 73, 117, 133, 163, 224, 249; Spanish destruction of, 19, 224; traded, 38, 46, 60, 114; venison, 60; whale, 179; worms, 81; Yumas, 73, 105, 110, 114, 143. *See also* fish and fishing
food, Spaniards': acorns, 57; Anza expedition (1775–76), 98, 108–10, 113, 114, 128, 181–82, 183; antiscorbutic, 55, 127; bear meat, 60, 65, 166, 189; berries, 55, 191; goose, 58, 59; greens, 127, 128; horse meat, 159; Mission San Diego, 128, 130; mule meat, 56, 58, 59–60; Pérez expedition (1774), 196; Portolá expedition (1769), 31, 32–33, 36, 38, 46, 57; rats attracted to, 149; rationing, 60, 61; rose hips, 126; shipboard, 31, 196; shortages, 31, 54–58, 60, 61, 77, 91–92, 220, 221; tainted, spoiled, etc., 91–92, 180; theft of, 146, 183, 220; trade, 21, 38, 55–56, 60; withholding of, 249, 250. *See also* chocolate; corn (maize); hunting; wheat
fording rivers. *See* river fording
Fort Yuma Indian Reservation, 140, 211, 232

France, 26, 129, 218
Francisco Xavier (Yuma interpreter), 231, 233, 237
Francis of Assisi, Saint, 10, 15, 47, 53, 205
fugitives. *See* deserters and runaways, Native; deserters and runaways, Spanish
fur trade, 17, 25
Fuster, Vicente, 134–39

Gálvez, José de, 16, 24, 26, 35, 63, 67, 68, 219; letters to, 53, 60
Garcés, Francisco, 6–10, 12–14, 17, 43, 152–77, 217, 253; Anza expedition (1774), 76, 78, 80–94, 150; Anza expedition (1775–76), 97, 99, 100, 106, 108, 109, 111, 116; Eixarch and, 142, 146–49; on Indians, 83, 156, 158, 165; letter to Carlos III, 219; Mission San Pedro y San Pablo, 211; monuments, 140, 152, 268n6; reburial, 243–44; royal commendation, 219; Yuma uprising (1781), 227, 229–31, *230*, 233, 238, 239, 243; Yuma uprising run-up, 220–25
gardens and gardening, 130, 145, 251, 253
geese, 58, 59, 90, 126, 183
"genocide" (word), 247
ghost ships, 24
gift-giving, Native, 49, 51, 72
gift-giving, Spanish, 153, 195, 212, 220; Anza expedition (1774), 84, 87, 89; Anza expedition (1775–76), 103, 114; to Bucareli, 189, 203; to Palma, 94, 110, 111–12, 145, 212; Pérez expedition (1774), 204; Portolá expedition (1769), 24, 35–36, 55; resistance to, 171; to Yumas, 114
Gila River, 70, 83, 84, 93, 102, 146, 148, 177, 235; maps, *109, 143, 157*
Golden Gate, 56, 57, 187
Gómez, Francisco, 41–42, 44, 46, 47, 53, 55, 64
Goya, Ramón, 218
Grand Canyon, 170–71
Great Britain. *See* Britain; England
Grijalva, Juan Pablo, 104

Guadalupe, Virgin of. *See* Virgin of Guadalupe
Guest, Francis F., 18
Guevavi Mission, 70
Gutiérrez, Ramón A., 245

Hackel, Steven W., 250–51
Haida people, 201–2, 203
Halyikwamai people, 155
Havasupai people, 170
"heathen" (label), 4, 18, 23, 24, 25, 35; Bucareli use, 216; Crespí use, 46, 66; Garcés use, 156, 161
Hezeta, Bruno, 210
historical markers, 14, 76, 108, 125, 127. *See also* monuments
HMS *Discovery*, 207
Hopi people, 94, 103, 154, 162, 168–76
Horcasitas, Sonora. *See* San Miguel de Horcasitas, Sonora
Hualapai people, 168
hunger, 14, 74, 77, 159–60; Anza expedition (1775–76), 182; Portolá expedition (1769), 22, 34, 36, 57; Yumas, 158. *See also* starvation
hunting, 44, 46; bears, 50, 51, 60, 65; buffalo, 77; geese, 58, 59; hares, 117; as Indian lifeway, 18, 19, 132, 169, 249, 253; use of horses in, 32, 46, 56, 60, 65

illness and disease: Anza, 186–87, 191; Anza expedition (1775–76), 103, 104, 108, 111, 118, 183; Font, 99–100, 103, 105, 116, 240; Crespí, 242; Croix, 219; Garcés, 70, 72; Pérez expedition, 193, 198, 199, 200, 201, 205, 208, 209; Portolá expedition (1769), 56, 57. *See also* Indians; scurvy; sexually transmitted diseases; smallpox
Ímuris, 3, 20
Indians, 18–24, 245–53; Anza expedition (1774), 77–94; Anza expedition (1775–76), 101–3, 105, 106, 108–20, 122, 123, 185; Anza on, 83, 119–20; Arricivita on, 70; assimilation, 19, 247, 268n7; burning of grass, 52; canoes, 48, 132,

Indians *(continued)*
184, 201–2, 206; cemeteries, 48–49, 55; childbirth, 51; Columbus relations, 21; Crespí on, 38; dress (traditional), 47, 49, 82, 110, 113–14, 128, 147, 164, 202, 203; dress (European), 94, 110, 171, 215–16; dwellings, 37, 46, 163; Eixarch on, 147, 148; Fages on, 38, 49, 55; fertility rites, 146–47; flatulence, 113, 156; Font on, 6, 12, 103, 105, 113, 114, 119, 128, 130, 133, 184; funerary customs, 49, 147; Garcés on, 83, 156, 158, 165; Garcés relations, 12–13, 72–75, 81–90, 111, 114–15, 153–77, 244; generosity and sharing, 73, 169; hairstyles, 49, 84, 103, 114, 147, 164, 172, 202; hare hunting, 117; "hostile," 3, 42, 72; hunting as lifeway, 18, 19, 132, 169, 249, 253; illness and disease, 19, 20–21, 71, 245–46, 248; infant care, 51, 149; infantilization, 43; Juan Díaz on, 81; languages, 130; Martínez on, 203; Mission Tilaco, 15; music, 47, 49, 50, 73, 105, 173, 174; nakedness, 37, 47, 49, 71, 82, 113, 119, 128, 147, 158, 165; Nentvig on, 6; Pérez expedition (1774), 195, 199, 201–2, 203, 206, 207; polygamy, 47, 114, 144, 147; population figures, 20–21; Portolá expedition (1769), 22–24, 35, 37, 38, 40, 46–51, 54–55, 61, 132; Portolá expedition (1770), 63–67; raids, 3–6, 19–20, 61, 76–77, 88, 93, 220; rebellions, 20, 21, 81, 125–26, 131, 133–39, *137*, 160, 172, 211–24; San Xavier del Bac, 69; self-decoration and ornament, 37–38, 46, 49, 74, 103, 114, 204; as servants, 134, 182, 231; sexual favors, 35, 37, 73, 114; skin color, 188, 204; slaves and slavery, 145, 158; Spaniards' execution of, 132; as Spaniards' laborers, "helpers," etc., 15, 43, 61, 65, 130, 239, 250–52; Spaniards' rape of, 130–31, 133, 163, 166, 183; Spaniards' renaming of, 4, 27, 34, 42, 74, 79, 218, 268n7; Spanish captives, 235; sweat lodge, 165; swimming, 13, 88, 94, 105–6, 148, 155, 164, 213–14, 237; taken to Rome, 21; tattoos, 16; trade of children, 145, 231; trade with Indians, 74, 94, 103, 159, 160, 164, 170, 171, 207; trade with Spaniards, 21, 38, 44, 46, 114, 202, 203, 206; wars, 55, 174. *See also* Christian missionizing of Indians; deserters and runaways, Native; food, Native; languages, Native; shamans; two-spirit people
"infidel" (label), 18, 70
Ingraham, Joseph, 207
Isla Cerros. *See* Cedros Island
Ives, J. C., 170

Jalchedún people, 94, 111, 149, 158, 177, 220, 235
Jalliquamai people, 155
Jamajab people, 157, 158, 159, 160, 163, 168–69, 176
Jayme, Luís, 125, 131, 133–38
Jesuits, 4, 6, 20, 27, 31, 43, 69, 70; expulsion by Carlos III, 15–16, 26, 69; Pious Fund of the Californias, 99; Ures mission, 215
Joseph, Saint, 47, 55, 63, 64, 135
Júpiter (frigate), 8–9, 239

Kern River, 164; map, *157*
King Carlos III. *See* Carlos III, king of Spain
King Philip III of Spain, 24
Kino, Eusebio Francisco, 20, 69
Kroeber, Alfred L., 250
Kumeyaay people, 74, 89, 185; beached whale, use of, 179; identity and homeland, 131–32; Portolá expedition (1769), 22–24, 37, 38, 40, 61, 132; uprising of 1775, 125–26, 131, 133–39, *137*, 160

La Brea Tar Pits, 47
La Concepción. *See* Mission La Purísima de Concepción
language, sign. *See* sign language
language, Spanish. *See* Spanish language
languages, Native, 12, 71, 114, 129–30 136, 174, 231
La Pérouse, Jean François de, 129, 251, *252*

La Purísima de Cadegomó. *See* Mission La Purísima de Cadegomó
Lasúen, Fermín, 91, 246–47
Lazaga, Juan Lucas de, 217, 218
Levy, Barbara, 110
Linares, Ignacio, 105, 120
Linares, María Gertrudis Rivas, 120, 121, 122, 123, 127
Linares, Salvador Ignacio, 107, 108, 122
Linck, Wenceslaus, 27, 32
López, Juan Francisco, 119
López, Manuel, 198
Loreto, Baja California, 16, 43, 64, 92, 132
Los Angeles, 47, 224
Luiseño people, 21

malaria, 103, 104, 105, 111, 193, 240
Mallorca, 14, 17, 28, 125, 136, 241; map, *11*
measuring tools, 7, 32, 52, 99, 189, 202, 215; Garcés use, 153, 155, 158, 163
mapmaking, 7–8
Maricopa people, 236
Mariposa people, 164–67
maritime voyages. *See* ocean voyages
Martínez, Andrés Antonio, 9
Martínez, Esteban, 196, 201, 203, 207, 210
Medina, Augustín, 28
Mesa, Joseph Nicolás, 239
mescal, 32–33, 34, 156, 169
mesquite, 15, 76, 94; as forage, 81; pods as human food, 73, 224, 249; as water indicator, 89
Mexico City, 12, 19, 68, 77, 78; Anza, 191, 215, 216, 217; couriers to, 80, 92, 115, 209; expedition outfitting in, 98; Palma, 145, 212–19; Serra, 65, 93. *See also* Bucareli y Ursúa, Antonio María de; College of San Fernando (Mexico City)
milk, 128, 249
Mission Carmel. *See* Mission San Carlos Borromeo de Monterey (Mission Carmel)
Mission Dolores. *See* Mission San Francisco de Asís (Mission Dolores)
Mission Guevavi, 70

Mission La Purísima de Cadegomó, 26, 31, 34
Mission La Purísima de Concepción, 140, 141, 221, 222, 224; Yuma uprising (1781), 227–31, 238
Mission San Antonio de Oquitoa (Sonora), 151
Mission San Antonio de Padua (California), 185, 199; map, *109*
Mission San Borja, 34
Mission San Carlos Borromeo de Monterey (Mission Carmel), 26, 61, 68, 93, 165, 186–87, 189, *190*; Crespí, 14, 192, 194, 241, 242; Serra interment, 14, 242
Mission San Diego de Alcalá, 39–40, 60–64, 68, 74, 194; Kumeyaay uprising (1775), 125–26, 131, 133–39, *137*, 160
Mission San Diego del Pitiquito, 239–41, *240*
Mission San Fernando. *See* San Fernando de Velicatá
Mission San Francisco de Asís (Mission Dolores), 188, 191, 241–42
Mission San Francisco del Valle de Tilaco, 14–15, 38
Mission San Gabriel, 38, 90–91, 111, 123, 126–28, 159–61, 178, 224; burials, 97; founding friar, 179
Mission San Ignacio, 20, 34, 43, 65
Mission San José de los Pimas, 99
Mission San Juan Capistrano, 131, 142
Mission San Luis Obispo, 158, 160, 161, 163, 164, 184–85; maps *109, 157*
Mission San Pedro y San Pablo de Bicuñer, 211, 221, 223, 226; Yuma uprising (1781), 228, 229, 237, 238
Mission Santa Gertrudis, 34, 43, 44, 79
Mission San Xavier del Bac, 69–75, *71*, 142, 177
Mission Soledad, 20
Mission Tilaco. *See* Mission San Francisco del Valle de Tilaco
Mission Tubutama, 233, 237, 238, 243; map, *143*
Mission Tumacácori, 99, 142

"Mojave Apaches" (Yavapai), 147
Mojave Desert, 148, 153, 157–59, 167–68
Mojave people. *See* Jamajab people
Monterey and Monterey Bay, 24–26, 40, 62, 66–68, *67*, 75, 78; Anza expedition (1774), 92–93; misidentification, 52–53; naming, 52; presidio, 166, 178, 186. *See also* Mission San Carlos Borromeo de Monterey (Mission Carmel); Portolá, Gaspar de
Montijo, María Ana, 227–28, 229
monuments, 125, 140, 152, 211
Moqui people. *See* Hopi people
Moraga, José Joaquín, 180, 182, 183, 185, 187, 188, 191
Moreno, José Matías, 226, 228, 233, 237, 243–44
Mount Olympus, 208
Mourelle, Antonio, 210
Mugártegui, Pablo Joseph, 185, 193
music, 87; Christian, 7, 102, 112, 179, 183; Native, 47, 49, 50, 173, 174
mussels, 38, 58, 66, 116
mustard, 44, 259n7

naming of places, 8, 52, 141; Anza expedition (1774), 82, 85, 86, 90, 127; Anza expedition (1775–76), 102, 119, 120, 126, 188, 189; after Carlos III, 90, 122; by Coronado, 171; by Crespí, 187; by Garcés, 86, 155, 159, 163, 164, 169, 171; Pérez expedition (1774), 208; Portolá expedition (1769), 46, 47, 51, 55, 56, 58; San Diego Bay, 25; after Sebastián Tarabal, 90, 119
Native American Heritage Commission (California), 245–46, 250
Native Americans. *See* Indians
Navajo people, 174
Nentvig, Juan, 6, 146
New Mexico, 48, 174, 219; Garcés, 94, 148, 152, 154; Hopis, 103. *See also* Santa Fe
Noche people, 164–67
Nootka people, 206, 207
Nootka Sound, 192, 207, 210

ocean voyages, 8–9, 16, 27–31, 78; Pérez expedition (1774), 192–210
Ochoa, María Manuela, 229
Olleyquotequiebe. *See* Palma, Salvador
Oraibi, 162, 171–76, *175*
Ortega, José Francisco, 43, 54, 56
Ortiz, Alfonso, 250
Osuna, Ana María de, 104, 105
Our Lady of Guadalupe. *See* Virgin of Guadalupe
outfitting of expeditions. *See* provisioning of expeditions
ownership. *See* private property

Pablo (El Capitán Feo), 82, 87, 142–44, 147, 149–50, 212–14; son (Joseph), 212, 216, 218, 221
Palma, Salvador, 74, 75, 211–12; Anza expedition (1774), 79, 80, 82, 83, 85, 87, 88, 92, 94; Anza expedition (1775–76), 105, 108, 110, 113, 115; brother (Ygnacio), 218, 221–22, 223, 233, 237; daughter, 213; Eixarch and, 141, 142–43; Mexico City trip, 212–19; Yuma uprising (1781), 225, 226, 228, 229, 230–31, 233; Yuma uprising aftermath, 233, 235, 236, 237–38; Yuma uprising run-up, 221–23
Palóu, Francisco, 8, 40, 63, 64, 68, 241–42; on Crespí, 17; Crespí relations, 36, 241–42, 244; on Jayme's death, 134, 137; Mission Dolores, 191, 241
Pame people, 15, 38
Papágo (Tohono O'odham) people, 69, 70, 72, 73, 81, 82, 142, 149; in retributive campaign against Yumas, 232–33; Sonoitac, 236
Parrón, Fernando, 30, 39, 61, 64
Paterna, Antonio, 127, 128, 180
Payeras, Mariano, 20
peace offerings and signs, 55, 66
Peña y Saravia, Tomás de, 194, 198, 199, 203, 204, 205, 208, 209
Pérez, Juan, 28, 31, 61, 64, 91; death, 210; expedition of 1774, 192–210
Pérez de Mezquía, Pedro, 130

Philippines, 24, 28, 202
Philip III, king of Spain, 24
Piato people, 4, 6, 20
Piipaash people, 236
Pima people, 20, 101–2, 142, 146, 148, 232–33, 235
pinole, 70, 108, 146
Piñuelas Felíz, Manuela, 96–97
Pitiquito Mission. *See* Mission San Diego del Pitiquito
place naming. *See* naming of places
plants. *See* flora
Point of Pines, 58, 59, 62, 66
Pope Clement XIII, 16
Portolá, Gaspar de: expedition of 1769, 16, 22–61, 65, 79, 132–33; expedition of 1770, 62–68
posole, 128, 130, 249, 251
Prat, Pedro, 29, 31, 39
Preston, William, 249
private property, 19, 184. *See also* theft
provisioning of expeditions, 80–81, 98, 196
psalterios, 7, 102, 112, 179, 183
Pueblo Oraibi. *See* Oraibi
Pueblo Revolt of 1680, 172
punishment, capital. *See* capital punishment
punishment, corporal. *See* corporal punishment
punishment of Indians. *See under* Indians
punishment of Spaniards, 166, 185

Quechan people. *See* Yuma people
Queen Charlotte Islands, 16, 201, 203
Quiquima people, 72, 87

Ramos, Antonio, 20
ransom, 158, 177, 227, 233, 235, 236, 237
rape, 130–31, 133, 163, 166, 183, 248
rats, 76, 149, 167
Reconquest, 8, 18
redwoods, 55
Reyes, Manuel, 30
Reyes Pacheco, Joseph, 228
ribbons, 35, 203
Rivera y Moncada, Fernando, 224; Anza expedition (1775–76), 123, 125–26, 127, 131, 179–81; Fuster and, 134, 138–39; Kumeyaay uprising (1775), 138, 160, 179; Portolá expedition, 23, 26–27, 32, 34–36, 39, 43, 51, 52; resupply expedition, 63; Yuma uprising (1781), 229, 233, 235
river fording, 177; Anza expedition (1775–76), 181; Carmel, 66; Colorado, 72, 105–6, 141, 146, 148, 149–50, 155, 225, 236; Colorado (Anza expedition, 1774), 73, 75, 83, 84, 85, 87–88, 93–94; Colorado (Yuma crossing), 79, 93–94, 105, 177, 211, 213–14, 229, 236; by Fages, 236; by Garcés, 13, 73, 75, 84, 85, 87–88, 155, 164–65, 166–67, 177; Gila, 83–84, 93, 105; Kern, 164–65; raft use, 13, 73, 85, 88, 93–94, 149–50, 164, 177, 211, 213–14; San Diego, 181; San Felipe, 166–67; Santa Ana, 90, 126–27; tree bridges, 90, 127, 166
robbery, 146, 177
Rodríguez Cabrillo, Juan, 21, 52
Romero, Felipe, 136
Romero, Miguel Antonio, 235
roses, 16, 38, 44, 123, 126
Ruelas, Francisca, 105
runaways. *See* deserters and runaways, Native; deserters and runaways, Spanish
Russians, 17, 25–26, 78, 97, 194–96, 199

Sacagawea, 43, 177
Saint Francis. *See* Francis of Assisi, Saint
Saint Joseph. *See* Joseph, Saint
Saint Thomas Yuma Indian Mission, 140
Sambrano, Juliana, 237
San Antonio (ship), 28, 31, 36–37, 39, 63, 64, 66, 68
San Antonio de Oquitoa (Sonora), 151
San Antonio de Padua (California). *See* Mission San Antonio de Padua (California)
San Blas, 61, 78, 92; Gálvez, 26; *San Antonio*, 39, 63, 64; *San Carlos*, 28, 69; *San José*, 31, 59, 61; *Santiago*, 196, 210; shipbuilding, 28, 196
San Borja Mission. *See* Mission San Borja

San Carlos (ship), 28–31, 36–37, 39, 43, 61, 64, 69, 132
San Carlos Mission. *See* Mission San Carlos Borromeo de Monterey (Mission Carmel)
Sánchez, Manuel, 31
San Diego, 22, 24–31, 34, 36–44, 57–66, 160; map, *45*; presidio, 91, 131, 179, 184; Serra, 34, 39; Vizcaíno location of, 54. *See also* Mission San Diego de Alcalá
San Diego del Pitiquito. *See* Mission San Diego del Pitiquito
San Diego River, 37, 125, 134, 181
Sandos, James A., 253
San Fernando College. *See* College of San Fernando (Mexico City)
San Fernando de Velicatá, 32, *33*, 63
San Francisco, 16, 56–57, 167; Anza expedition (1775–76), 96, 97, 101, 179–80, 187–91
San Francisco de Asís (Mission Dolores). *See* Mission San Francisco de Asís (Mission Dolores)
San Francisco del Valle de Tilaco. *See* Mission San Francisco del Valle de Tilaco
San Francisco River, 187, 189
San Gabriel Mission. *See* Mission San Gabriel
San Ignacio, Sonora, 5, 6, 20. *See also* Mission San Ignacio
San José (ship), 31, 39, 40, 54, 56, 57; disappearance, 61, 78
San José de los Pimas, 99
San Juan Capistrano Mission. *See* Mission San Juan Capistrano
San Luis Obispo, 50, map, *45*. *See also* Mission San Luis Obispo
San Miguel de Horcasitas, Sonora, 99, 214–15, 232, 243; maps, *109*, *143*
San Pedro y San Pablo de Bicuñer. *See* Mission San Pedro y San Pablo de Bicuñer
Santa Ana River, 46, 90, 125, 126–27
Santa Cruz College. *See* College of Santa Cruz (Querétaro, Mexico)
Santa Cruz River, 69, 76, 96, 142; map, *109*

Santa Fe, 94, 154, 158, 160, 167, 172, 219
Santa Gertrudis Mission. *See* Mission Santa Gertrudis
Santa Lucía Mountains, 51–52, 59, 65
Santa María Magdalena, Sonora, 3–6, 20, 239
Santa Rosa de las Lajas, 76, 79, *90*, 116
Santiago (ship), 16, 91, 193–210, *197*
San Xavier del Bac. *See* Mission San Xavier del Bac
Saubel, Katherine Siva, 122
scorpions, 44, 96, 108
scurvy, 78; antiscorbutic foods, 55, 127; Font, 138, 179; recovery from, 55–56, 58; Pérez expedition (1774), 208, 209; Portolá expedition (1769), 24–25, 30–31, 37, 39, 52–56, 61, 132; Portolá expedition (1770), 66
sea lions, 62, 187, 200
sea otters, 25, 187, 192; pelts and skins, 49, 203
seashells. *See* shells
sea voyages. *See* ocean voyages
Seri people, 4, 20, 77
Serra, Junípero, 8, 14, 22, 72, 80, 186; Anza expedition (1774), 91, 93; Crespí relations, 14, 241–42, 244; death and interment, 14, 242; Fages relations, 234; Fuster relations, 134; Pérez expedition (1774), 192, 193, 198, 210; Portolá expedition (1769), 26, 27, 34, 36, 39–40, 61, 79; Portolá expedition (1770) 63, 66–68, *67*; sainthood, 245; statues, 178
servants, 109, 132, 214; Anza expedition (1774), 80; Anza expedition (1775–76), 100, 101, 104, 180, 181, 182, 184, 191; Indians as, 134, 182, 231; Portolá expedition (1769), 27
settlers, 96–97, 100, 178, 180; Mission La Concepción, 221 222; Mission San Pedro y San Pablo, 221, 222; outfitting of, 98; Yuma uprising (1781), 227, 228. *See also* women settlers
sexual assault. *See* rape
sexual favors, wife-sharing, etc., 35, 37, 73, 114

sexually transmitted diseases, 20, 183, 248
shackles, 223, 246
shamans, 46, 148, 155
shells, 160, 163, 171, 173, 176; abalone, 203, 206; fishhooks from, 48; inland, 116; as ornament, 37–38, 49, 74, 204; tools from, 49
shelters; 98; Eixarch, 108, 142, 143, 144; Garcés-built, 225; lack of, 55; Mission San Diego, 134; Mission San Gabriel, 127; Monterey, 186, 191; Portolá expedition (1769), 32, 37. *See also under* Indians; tents
Shipek, Florence, 249
ships. *See names of individual ships*
Shoshone people, 43, 177
sign language, 48, 56, 57, 174
Silva, José Miguel de, 104, 191
slaves and slavery, 145
smallpox, 20, 21, 71, 72, 235, 248
soap, 98, 108, 123, 178, 187
soldiers, Catalonian. *See* Catalonian Volunteers (Bluecoats)
Soledad Mission, 20
Somera, Ángel, 179
Sonoitac, Sonora, 148, 220, 236
Sonora (ship), 210
Spain, 8–10, 14–18, 79, 234; map, *11*. *See also* Carlos III, king of Spain; Mallorca
Spanish deserters and runaways. *See* deserters and runaways, Spanish
Spanish language, 109, 129–30, 142, 144, 174, 231
spoons, 203, 207
Starr, Kevin, 21
starvation, 22, 34, 36, 40, 57, 178
stocks (punishment), 129, 139, 184, 223, 246
Supai people, 170
sweat lodge, 165

Tac, Pablo, 21
Tarabal, Sebastián, 43–44, 79–80, 119, 176–77; Anza expedition (1774), 80, 81, 85, 89–90, 91; Anza expedition (1775–76), 101, 109, 114, 119; disappearance, 176–77; Eixarch on, 148; Garcés

and, 142, 148, 152, 154–57, 159, 163, 164, 166, 167, 176–77; monuments, 152; Palma and, 79; Portolá expedition, 43–44, 79
tar pits, 47, 48
Tehachapi Mountains, 148, 163, 167; map, *157*
tents, 32, 36, 44, 56, 81, 132; Anza expedition (1775–76), 96, 98–101, 103, 104, 110, 111, 117, 119; Monterey, 187, 191
tertian fever, 103, 193
theft, 156; Anza expedition (1774), 85; Anza expedition (1775–76), 118; "every Indian's propensity," 19, 38, 83, 103, 113, 184; of food, 183, 220; of livestock, 73, 76, 87, 118, 170, 180, 182, 222, 246; punishment for, 246; by Spaniards, 60, 183, 185; Yuma uprising (1781), 228. *See also* robbery
ticks and fleas. *See* fleas, ticks, etc.
Tilaco Mission. *See* Mission San Francisco del Valle de Tilaco
tobacco: as gift, 5, 35, 84, 85, 87, 89, 114, 153, 156, 212; Crespí, 32; provisions, 36, 80, 108, 233; in ransom, 235; refusal of, 164, 171; theft of, 146, 182; in trade, 46; Yuma demands for, 220
Tohono O'odham people. *See* Papágo (Tohono O'odham) people
tools, measuring. *See* measuring tools
toponyms. *See* naming of places
Tovar, Pedro de, 172
trade, fur. *See* fur trade
trade, transpacific, 24, 28, 167
trade, Native. *See under* Indians
Tubac: Anza, 72, 80, 93, 99; Apache raids, 76, 77, 88; Eixarch, 142; Font and Garcés, 100; maps, *109*, *157*; Palma, 79; soldiers, 105, 120, 222
Tubutama Mission. *See* Mission Tubutama
Tucson, 69, *71*, 94, 101, 222; maps, *143*, *157*
Tueros, Pedro, 222, 232, 237, 238
Tumacácori Mission. *See* Mission Tumacácori
two-spirit people, 49, 114

Urrea, Bernardo de, 231
Ursúa, Antonio María Bucareli y. *See* Bucareli y Ursúa, Antonio María de
Ute people, 174

Valdés, Francisco Xavier, 232
Valdés, Juan Bautista, 80, 92
Valenzuela, Augustín, 119
Vancouver Island, 192, 201, 206
Vanyume people, 159–60
Velicatá. *See* San Fernando de Velicatá
venereal diseases. *See* sexually transmitted diseases
Ventura, Calif., 68
vermin. *See* fleas, ticks, etc.; rats
Viceroy Bucareli. *See* Bucareli y Ursúa, Antonio María de
Vila, Vicente, 28–31, 39, 61
Virgin of Guadalupe, 99, 100, 117, 178, 212
Vizcaíno, Juan, 39, 131–32
Vizcaíno, Sebastián, 24, 37, 48; Farallon Islands, 56; Monterey, 25, 42, 53, 54, 59, 66, 67, 178, 198; Point of Pines, 66; Punta Año Nuevo, 52; San Diego, 25, 38; Santa Lucía Mountains, 51

Wade, Maria F., 247
water, drinking. *See* drinking water
weather: cold, 16, 141, 144, 159, 194; cold (Anza expedition, 1775–76), 104, 105, 111, 112, 116–18; cold (Pérez expedition), 200, 208; cold (Portolá expedition, 1769), 51, 55, 59; drought, 174–75; hail, 200; heat, 13, 71, 77, 150, 153, 169, 220, 226; rain, 108, 182, 184, 194, 201, 205, 208; snow, 107, 112, 116, 117, 127, 144, 186; storms, 9, 58, 107, 108, 116, 117, 200, 205; wind, 110, 200, 206. *See also* fog
wells, 32, 80, 82, 86, 88, 89, 116–17; Yuha Desert, 76, 79, *90*, 116
whales, 179, 192, 201
wheat, 5, 88, 134, 243, 251; Yumas, 105, 110, 143, 148
Williams, Mark, 18
wine, 36, 98, 109, 110, 196
women and girls, rape of. *See* rape
women settlers, 96–97, 98, 100, 102–5, 118–19, 123; childbirth and miscarriages, 7, 96–97, 104–5, 115, 121–22, 186

Yavapai people, 171–76
Yokuts people, 164–67
Yslas, Santiago de, 222–23, 225–28
Yuha Desert, 76, *90*
Yuma people, 19, 79, 82–83, 105, 106, 110; Cajuenche relations, 154–55; captives, 145; dress, 113–14; Eixarch relations, 108, 140–51; Fort Yuma Reservation, 140; Garcés relations, 72–75, 106, 108; Jalchedún relations, 158; Kumeyaay uprising and, 160
Yuma uprising (1781), 225–31, 243–44; retributive campaign, 232–38; run-up, 211–24

Zúñiga, Francisco Sánchez, 6
Zúñiga y Acevedo, Gaspar de, 52
Zuñi people, 172, 173

www.ingramcontent.com/pod-product-compliance
Lightning Source LLC
Chambersburg PA
CBHW020745160426
43192CB00006B/255